STRONG HELPERS' TEACHINGS

The Value of Indigenous Knowledges in
the Helping Professions

SECOND EDITION

Cyndy Baskin

Canadian Scholars' Press
Toronto

Strong Helpers' Teachings: The Value of Indigenous Knowledges in the Helping Professsions, Second Edition
By Cyndy Baskin

First published in 2016 by
Canadian Scholars' Press Inc.
425 Adelaide Street West, Suite 200
Toronto, Ontario
M5V 3C1

www.cspi.org

Library and Archives Canada Cataloguing in Publication

Baskin, Cyndy, 1957-, author
Strong helpers' teachings : the value of Indigenous knowledges
in the helping professions / Cyndy Baskin. -- Second edition.

Includes bibliographical references.
Issued in print and electronic formats.
ISBN 978-1-55130-942-2 (paperback).--ISBN 978-1-55130-943-9
(pdf).--ISBN 978-1-55130-944-6 (epub)

1. Social service. 2. Counseling. 3. Social values. 4. Native
peoples--Canada--Social life and customs. I. Title.

HV40.B38 2016   361.3'208997071   C2016-902332-X   C2016-902333-8

Text design by Aldo Fierro
Cover design by Em Dash Design
Cover image: Shutterstock/SibsUK

Printed and bound in Canada by Webcom

MIX
Paper from
responsible sources
FSC FSC® C004071
www.fsc.org

Canada

Table of Contents

Author Biography

Cyndy Baskin, Ph.D., is of Mi'kmaq and Celtic descent. Originally from New Brunswick, she has been living in Toronto for many years. Her clan is the fish and her spirit name translates as something like "The Woman Who Passes on the Teachings." She is currently an Associate Professor in the School of Social Work at Ryerson University in Toronto, Ontario. Her teaching and research interests centre on working with Indigenous communities, especially on how Indigenous worldviews can inform education, spirituality, decolonizing research methodologies, violence prevention, and justice for missing and murdered Indigenous women and their families. Cyndy is the author of three books and numerous journal articles and book chapters.

Cyndy is the Chair of Ryerson University's Aboriginal Education Council and the Academic Coordinator of the Certificate in Indigenous Knowledges and Experiences, which is housed in the Chang School of Continuing Education. She also sits on several boards of directors and advisory committees in the social services field.

Prior to joining Ryerson, Cyndy worked as a helper/social worker for many years within Indigenous agencies in Toronto and assisted many First Nations communities with setting up culture-based programs, the latter of which she continues to do today. She is also a consultant in the area of Indigenous programming within various components of both Indigenous and mainstream social services.

Cyndy enjoys spending time with her son and her friends, watching movies, reading, travelling, and listening to music. She is inspired by many strong Indigenous women, her spirituality, and the learners who engage with her in their efforts to make the world a better place for all.

Acknowledgements

First, *chi meegwetch* (a big thank you) to my son, Minadoo Makwa Baskin, for bringing joy into my world and for giving me a strong reason to do the work that I do. Thank you, my boy, for all those afternoons, evenings, and sometimes late into the nights when we perched ourselves beside each other, me working away on the first edition of this book on my computer and you playing video games on your 360—your patience was a gift of understanding. And I got to learn a little bit about video games even though I still suck at playing them. During the writing of the second edition, you grew into a young man that I could not possibly be more proud of. How I enjoy our exciting talks about history, racism, identity, and the future for Indigenous youth, and listening to our favourite hip-hop artist, Kendrick Lamar. I love you best, Makwa.

Next, *we'lalin* (thank you) to all the people who shared their stories with me for both editions of this book. Your generosity of time, knowledge, and insight makes this book important.

A special thank you to the latest "academic warrior" to join the crew, Danielle Sinclair, for your research, literature reviews, interviews, and very interesting conversations during the writing of the second edition—I would never have been able to do it without you. My thanks also goes to the Vice-Provost's Aboriginal Education Council at Ryerson University, which assisted with funding so I could hire an amazing research assistant. Not only did you help me, but you provided outstanding opportunities for an Indigenous learner to build on her knowledge and skills.

Chapter 17 is dedicated to Grandmother Jo-Ann Kakekayash (May 11, 1937–February 20, 2014), who taught me and so many others about Indigenous research.

Chapter Three is for Terra. Thank you for being a part of our lives and for leaving us teachings that make all of us better people.

Chapter One

STARTING AT
THE BEGINNING

MI'KMAQ WELCOME

The following is an excerpt from a speech by Daniel N. Paul to the Nova Scotia Tourist Association, November 16, 2003:

Welcome my friends, I hope you have a pleasant visit!

I'll start my discourse about Mi'kmaq welcome by relating how it came to be that my people always welcomed visitors to the land of the Mi'kmaq with open arms—a practice dating back into infinity. In fact, in pre-Columbian days, they often entertained visitors and traders arriving from other First Nations located across Turtle Island.

Such hospitality resulted from the early indoctrination of children with the worthy social values of a people-friendly civilization, which our ancestors had developed with great wisdom over the ages.

One of the most important of these values, taught to the young by the Elders, was that the Great Spirit created all people equal—which prevented the development in their minds of biases against people who were different. Thus, intolerance was not a vice harboured in the hearts of the Mi'kmaq.

In view of this, it should come as no surprise to anyone that during 1604 my ancestors welcomed strange looking visitors to their land. When Champlain landed on our shores, in spite of their white skins, bearded faces, strange clothing and behaviour, they were warmly welcomed by the Mi'kmaq. The most important among the Mi'kmaq Peoples' values, which made hospitality to strangers a must, was personal honour. It was an individual's most valued personal asset. To fail to keep one's word, or to be disrespectful of others, was punishable by being ostracized by peers. A fate considered worse than death.

Therefore, children were taught to be generous and non-confrontational with each another, or with strangers. This is how Bernard Gilbert Hoffman, a history researcher, described it: "The behaviour pattern required of any Mi'kmaq was such as to virtually eliminate any overt and direct forms of aggression. The ideal man was one who was restrained and dignified in all his actions, who maintained a stolid exterior under all circumstances, who deprived himself of his possessions to take care of the poor, aged, sick, or the less fortunate, who was generous and hospitable to strangers …"

Our ancestors had no notion of greed. All shared alike…. The absence of [greed] made it easy for the Mi'kmaq to give gifts of precious possessions to visiting friends and strangers. Such was a fundamental part of Mi'kmaq life….

This is the type of welcome that [Maritimers] must endeavor to bring to the fore again. Visitors must be treated with consideration and respect. They must never be viewed as passers through, who will never return, and whose money can be taken without giving them excellent value in exchange.

When they come, treat them like beloved visiting members of the family circle, give them quality value for their money. This will cause them to return and encourage others to come visit. Warm feelings of satisfaction instilled in visitors by caring hosts is what a healthy tourist industry is built from.

Such a universal new approach is a must. I say this because I've often seen in recent years, like most of you probably have, the quality of the offerings of the [Atlantic] provinces' hospitality industry to guests diminish in favour of a better profit line…. It's wise to remember: The best way to make and keep a new friend, is to lavish on him or her the very best you can offer!

In closing, I strongly urge you to try the Mi'kmaq way. It's tried, tested and proven. If you need proof of the veracity of this declaration about the effectiveness of Mi'kmaq hospitality look around you—we have close to a million visitors abiding in this part of Mi'kmaq land, who show no sign of preparing to leave!

INTRODUCTION

Warm greetings! Welcome to *Strong Helpers' Teachings*! This book aims to encourage students, faculty, and practitioners in the helping professions, as well as anyone who has an interest in decolonization and healing the world, to learn and understand fundamental aspects of Indigenous world-views that can be applied to all peoples. However, it discourages attempts at teaching and taking up specific cultural practices that are not one's own. A way to gain from Indigenous knowledges—while not attempting to practice cultural specifics without the proper protocols, training, and respect—is to strive to embody Indigenous values that underpin and inform cultural practices. Indigenous worldviews can be learned and acted upon, whereas even though one may be aware of cultural practices, it does not mean that they should be taken up. I warmly invite readers to see that cultural practices need to remain in the hands and control of Indigenous Peoples, but that there is much to be gained by welcoming Indigenous worldviews into one's life and work.

This introductory chapter will provide a background and a context to Indigenous approaches to helping that I believe can be valuable to all peoples of the world. But first it will provide some basic information about the history of colonization and its current impacts on Indigenous Peoples; the historical role of social work with Indigenous Peoples; and my concerns about the current appropriation of Indigenous cultural and spiritual practices. Although I tend to focus on social work, as that is my discipline, all of the knowledge throughout these chapters is applicable to all of the helping professions. For example, the first edition of this book has been used as a resource in nursing, midwifery, psychology, and education, as well as social work in postsecondary education both nationally and internationally.

WHO ARE INDIGENOUS PEOPLES?

Indigenous Peoples are the original inhabitants of what the Haudenosaunee Nations call Turtle Island or what is also referred to as North America. According to the Canadian Constitution, there are three groups of Indigenous Peoples—Indians, Métis, and Inuit. There is much diversity amongst us as seen by languages, cultures, spirituality, political systems, and geographical territories. However, there is a foundational basis within Indigenous worldviews, values, and beliefs. This, along with a history of colonization, ties us together. For the purposes of this book, the term Indigenous Peoples will be used to include all three groups mentioned above as well as those global peoples who are the original inhabitants of their territories. However, other terms, such as Aboriginal and Native, are used by quoted authors and interviewees throughout the book.

In 2011, 1,400,685 people identified as being Indigenous, which represents 4.3 percent of the total Canadian population. The number of Indigenous people is steadily increasing: in the 2006 Census, 3.8 percent of the population identified; in 2001, 3.3 percent did; and in 1996, 2.8 percent identified (Statistics Canada, 2011). This means that the Indigenous population increased by 232,385 people, or 20.1 percent, between 2006 and 2011, compared with 5.2 percent for the non-Indigenous population (Statistics Canada, 2011). The largest numbers of Indigenous people live in Ontario, Manitoba, Saskatchewan, Alberta, and British Columbia and make up the largest population in Nunavut and the Northwest Territories (Statistics Canada, 2011).

In addition, the Indigenous population is young. Children aged 14 and under make up 28 percent of the total Indigenous population and 7 percent of all children in Canada. Non-Indigenous children aged 14 and under represent 16.5 percent of the total non-Indigenous population (Statistics Canada, 2011). Indigenous youth aged 15 to 24 represent 18.2 percent of the total Indigenous population and 5.9 percent of all youth in Canada. Non-Indigenous youth account for 12.9 percent of the total non-Indigenous population (Statistics Canada, 2011). Of the 637,660 First Nations people who reported being "registered Indians" according to the Indian Act, nearly half (49.3 percent) live in a First Nation community (Statistics Canada, 2011). Cities with the largest populations of First Nations people *with registered Indian status* are Winnipeg (25,970), Edmonton (18,210), and Vancouver (15,080) (Statistics Canada, 2011). Those with the largest populations of First Nations people *without registered Indian status* are Toronto (14,505), where they represent 0.3 percent of the total population; Vancouver (13,635 or 0.6 percent); Montréal (10,540 or 0.3 percent); and Ottawa–Gatineau (6,495 or 0.7 percent) (Statistics Canada, 2011).

It is important to keep in mind, however, that these numbers come from the first release of data from the National Household Survey (NHS). Roughly 4.5 million households across Canada were selected for the NHS, representing about one-third of all households (Statistics Canada, 2011). In order for Indigenous Peoples to be included in the survey, they would have had to be selected and then participate and, typically, many do not and so are often under-represented in statistics such as these. To illustrate, research in the city of Toronto over the past several years indicates that approximately 60,000 Indigenous people live there, but this includes status, non-status, Inuit, and Métis, whereas the NHS includes only First Nations people without registered Indian status (Toronto Aboriginal Support Services Council [TASSC], 2014).

In addition, even Statistics Canada (2008) has differing statistics. According to the 2006 Census, 54 percent of the Indigenous population lived in urban centres and the median age of the Indigenous population was 27 years, compared with 40 years for non-Indigenous people. Children and youth aged 24 and under made up almost one-half (48 percent) of all Indigenous people, compared with 31 percent of the non-Indigenous population.

We have all grown up learning in school that Christopher Columbus called the people of the land he came upon in 1492 "Indians" because he thought he had found a route to the Indies or India. However, some scholars and historians believe that Columbus was not trying to find India when he set sail because there was no such country with this name (M. Switzer, personal communication, April 1, 2015; Wolfe, n.d.). In fact, the term "India" was not used until the British presence in the 17th century (Wolfe, n.d.). If this is the case, and there was no country, land, or people named India prior to 1492, what was Columbus referring to? He landed in what is now known as the Caribbean islands and soon described the original people there as having "no vices among them ... no thieves or liars ... and they give freely of all that they have" and, therefore, "are truly as the children of God" (Wolfe, n.d.). Hence, the term "las niñias de la endeo" (feminine) and "los niños de la endeo" (masculine), which translates as something like "the children of God" or "people of God" (M. Switzer, personal communication, April 1, 2015; Wolfe, n.d.). Over time, the term became "Indio" and later "Indian."

This is quite a significant statement to make as it presents Indigenous Peoples in a very different light. It certainly fits the traditional values that Indigenous Peoples across the world have built their societies on and that many continue to practice today. If accurate, though, why not teach this meaning and history rather than the usual one? I would say since the colonizers slaughtered almost all of the Indigenous Peoples of the Caribbean and then moved on to other areas and stole land and resources from Indigenous Peoples, it would be, perhaps, less easy to behave this way if those peoples were referred to as "children of God" instead of savages and heathens.

OVERVIEW OF THE HISTORY OF COLONIZATION

In order to understand the current struggles of Indigenous Peoples today, one needs to have an understanding of the history and treatment of Indigenous

Peoples since the time of contact with those who came from European countries. I take the position that the near destruction of a land-based way of living, economic and social deprivation, substance misuse, the intergenerational cycle of violence, the breakdown of healthy family life, and the loss of traditional values for many Indigenous people today are the direct result of colonization and ongoing systemic oppression. This is the history that has been deliberately left out of the Canadian consciousness and, of course, negated by former Prime Minister Stephen Harper who, in 2009, made the statement that Canada has no history of colonization. Read the following and decide for yourself:

> Colonialism involves one society seeking to conquer another and then rule over it. Colonialism in Canada took the form of settler colonialism. Settler colonialism took place where European settlers settled permanently on Indigenous lands, aggressively seized those lands from Indigenous peoples and eventually greatly outnumbered the Indigenous population.... As capitalism developed, it spread a new way of organizing how goods and services were produced which focused on profit at all costs. The needs of humans and of the natural world with its land, air and water, were given little to no consideration under this new system. In a short amount of time Europe's appetite for the natural resources found in the lands it would colonize grew enormously.... The main goal of settler colonialism was not to take advantage of the labour of Indigenous peoples. Instead, it was to displace Indigenous peoples from their lands, break and bury the cultures that grew out of relationships with those lands, and, ultimately, eliminate Indigenous societies so that settlers could establish themselves. Canadian colonial capitalism would not survive without access to Indigenous peoples' lands. This was true in 1867 when Canada was founded, and it is still true today. (Woroniak & Camfield, 2013, paras. 1–3)

European peoples came to this continent with a worldview based on Christianity and capitalism. Thus, the process of colonization grew in large part out of a belief that humankind was to "fill the earth and subdue it, rule over the fish in the sea, the birds of heaven, and every living thing that moves upon the earth" (Hamilton & Sinclair, 1991, p. 21). This worldview was in direct contrast to the interconnected, holistic one of the original peoples of this land.

Historical events of systemic violence toward Indigenous Peoples, as summed up succinctly and accurately by Adams over 15 years ago, include:

- the brutality perpetrated upon Indigenous Peoples by the French and English in securing pelts during the fur trade;
- abuse against Indigenous Peoples during the period of their slavery (early 1600s to 1833) in New France;
- the use of women for the purpose of breeding as the direct result of a law passed in 1770 that sought to address the shortage of English and Scottish labourers;
- the extermination of the entire Beothuck Nation on the East Coast of Canada;
- the wars waged against the original peoples of the Plains as a result of the British government's desire to "settle" the West;
- the hanging of seven Indigenous men, including Louis Riel, in 1885 in Western Canada; and
- the banning of political activity in Indigenous communities from the 1800s to the 1960s, which served to eliminate any challenges to colonial rule. (Adams, 1999)

The Indian Act of 1876 was the vehicle by which the goal of assimilating Indigenous Peoples was to be implemented and it governed every facet of Indigenous life. This act, along with the creation of the reserve system, imposed a White, capitalist, patriarchal governance structure on Indigenous communities. Through the Indian Act, the Canadian government sought to make Indigenous Peoples into imitation Europeans, to eradicate Indigenous values through education and religion, and to establish new economic and political systems and new concepts of property. An oppressive, bureaucratic system of government has been imposed upon Indigenous Peoples at the cost of many of our traditional governing practices and spiritual beliefs. A colonizing government, through the Indian Act, promoted hierarchical, male-dominated political, economic, and social structures that led to the disintegration of traditional tribal structures that were clan-oriented and based on the concepts of extended family and collectivity. This act, which continues to control the lives of Indigenous Peoples today, created the reserve system, outlawed many spiritual practices, eliminated an egalitarian economic system, and ignored our inherent right to self-government. This, in turn, has created great social confusion within Indigenous communities and provided the environment in which the profound social and economic problems have taken root.

Specific practices of assimilation were the outlawing of traditional Indigenous ceremonies, the enforced training of men to become farmers and women to become domestics, and a systematic indoctrination of Christian theory and practice through the residential school system. The establishment of residential schools was rationalized by the assertion that these institutions would make Indigenous children competitive with their White counterparts, moral, industrious, and self-sufficient. These schools equated Euro-Canadian socio-economic standards and materialism with success, progress, and civilization. The schools taught Indigenous children to aspire to be like Euro-Canadians rather than who they were, and yet Euro-Canadians never accepted them as equals in Canadian society.

The residential school system is an example of Canada's shameful and paternalistic "Indian" policies used over a long period (Dion Stout & Kipling, 2003). These institutions disrupted and even destroyed many traditional ways of life for Indigenous Peoples during the time of their existence and for subsequent generations. These schools removed children at an early age from their homes and communities, and then forced them to reside within one of the institutions, where their languages and cultures were forbidden. In recent years, many Indigenous Peoples have disclosed their experiences in these schools, which include painful stories of sexual and physical abuse from the authorities that operated the schools and the death of many children at the hands of these same authorities (Aboriginal Healing Foundation [AHF], 2009; Annett & Lawless, 2007; Dion Stout & Kipling, 2003; Truth and Reconciliation Commission of Canada [TRC], 2015).

Residential schooling is a direct cause of the many struggles in Indigenous communities because, in addition to the widespread abuse of the children who attended these institutions, it led to the decline of parenting skills as children were denied their appropriate parental role models. This removal of Indigenous children from their parents, extended families, and communities continued with the child welfare system, which consistently placed children in White families and communities. Hence, generations of

Indigenous children did not learn about the central role of family in their cultures (Bombay, Matheson, & Anisman, 2009). The experiences of the residential school system were detrimental to the development of Indigenous Peoples, as was the "sixties scoop" that followed when most of the residential schools were phased out in the 1960s (Royal Commission on Aboriginal Peoples [RCAP], 1996; TRC, 2015). The "sixties scoop" is the term used to describe the practice that emerged in the 1960s whereby large numbers of Indigenous children were removed from their families and placed in White homes, where many were treated in the same way as those who attended the residential schools (Blackstock, 2009; Sinclair, 2009; Sinclair, 2010). The subsequent generations of the survivors of both the schools and the child welfare system continue to have poor overall health status, commonly referred to by Indigenous Peoples as intergenerational effects. Ongoing effects of colonization produced various effects that include poverty, high unemployment rates, lack of education, inadequate or lack of affordable housing, family violence, dependency on social services, and substance misuse (Shah, 2004). In view of this, many Indigenous Peoples experience severe social and health inequalities as compared to other Canadians (Campaign 2000, 2005). In addition, in 2013, over half of all Indigenous children throughout Canada were identified as poor and, in comparison to non-Indigenous people, Indigenous people's income tends to be below the Canadian average (Hildebrandt, 2013). In 2006, the median income for Indigenous people was 30 percent lower than the median income for the rest of Canada ($18,962 vs. $27,097) (Sawchuck, 2011). The ongoing oppression of Indigenous Peoples has been summarized in just a few words by former finance minister Ralph Goodale, who declared during the 2005 federal budget release that "for too long in too many ways, Canada's Indigenous Peoples as first citizens—have been last in terms of opportunity for this country" (Fontaine, 2005).

It is also important to note that since jurisdiction over "Indians" and land resources for "Indians" is assigned exclusively to the federal government, urban Indigenous people's organizations and social services agencies are severely underfunded (RCAP, 1996). Generally, the federal government has a fiscal responsibility for "status Indians" living on reserves, and all other Indigenous people living off-reserve are the responsibility of the provinces. This leaves the increasing population of urban Indigenous people dependent on municipal services and programming for survival.

In the effort to manage its fiscal position, the federal government has also limited the growth of expenditures related to a number of existing Indigenous programs by capping them (RCAP, 1996). In fact, there has been a 2 percent funding cap since 1996, which obviously has not kept up with inflation or the increase in the Indigenous population across the country (Assembly of First Nations [AFN], 2014). The federal government has also cut funding for some services including those under health care, such as the Diabetes Prevention Program and the Prescription Drug Program, and has generally been reluctant to implement new programs, which has resulted in increasing pressure on the provinces to assume responsibility for some essential services (AFN, 2005, 2014). Thus, Indigenous people perpetually find themselves caught between this jurisdictional volleying back and forth of responsibility by the provincial and federal governments, which tends to leave them without services.

Everyone who lives in Canada today—both Indigenous Peoples and Canadians—has inherited the Indian Act. Today's citizens did not write the Indian Act or send Indigenous children to residential schools, but we all need to deal with the injustice that has arisen because of these policies. We did not create the Industrial Revolution either, but nevertheless, we have to deal with the effects of it today, which include global warming and climate change. All peoples who live in Canada today are also all treaty peoples because these treaties do not only address Indigenous Peoples and communities, but rather, they address relationships between Indigenous peoples and Canadians. Despite the fact that Indigenous Peoples did not make things how they are in the world today, we are all in this together and everyone in Canada is here to stay. This reality means that we all need to work together to create positive change for the future.

THE ROLE OF SOCIAL WORK IN COLONIZATION

Social work educator and activist Akua Benjamin (2007) notes that the profession of social work has a long history of social justice–oriented activities, forms of resistance, and organizing against oppressive forces. She, like most social work academics, credits Jane Addams with the early formation of the profession in the 1890s, which centred on activism that began a long period of social action and reform. Then came a time when social work began to seek recognition from other helping professions, such as psychiatry and psychology, and moved into a period of what has been referred to as "scientific philanthropy" whereby the role of the social worker was to rationally and scientifically help the client deal with whatever problems she or he had. Fortunately, as Benjamin (2007) writes, later on, during the 1960s, "social work again expressed methods of resistance, advocacy and transformation through social movements such as the feminist movement, civil rights movement and peace movement" (p. 199). Generous with her praise, Benjamin (2007) goes on to write,

> With the early settlement house movement, as well as these later phases, social work has a wonderful history of resistance and transformation. We need to thank these pioneers for their vision, their voices and their legacy. They provide examples of social work using radical strategy and tactics to address the major problems of society. These radical social workers were some of the main catalysts for change, laying the foundations of our current anti-oppressive approaches to social work and social transformation. (p. 199)

Is this view true of the profession of social work with *all* populations? Benjamin (2007) addresses this question as well in her work, stating, "However, let us not forget that while social movements were mobilizing in North America, whole populations were being decimated and systematically marginalized. Populations such as First Nations peoples faced genocide during Jane Adams's [*sic*] era and again with the continuation of the residential schools" (p. 199). In fact, Indigenous Peoples were facing genocide long before Jane Addams began to form the profession of social work, and residential schools began operating in 1874, while Addams was practising, with the last one not to close until 1996 (Truth and Reconciliation Commission of Canada [TRC], n.d.). Furthermore, during the 1960s when social movements were flourishing, Indigenous children across North America were being removed from their families and communities by the thousands, not through residential schools but through social work's most significant area—child welfare (Bennett, Blackstock, & De La Ronde, 2005; Crichlow, 2002; Hart & Rowe, 2014; Sinclair, 2009). Social workers were the people removing these children. Clearly, when it came to the feminist, civil rights, and peace movements, Indigenous Peoples were not only excluded, they were still being targeted for assimilation and cultural genocide.

Cree social work practitioner and academic Michael Hart (2002) takes up the topic of colonization by implicating social work as part of the continuing problem. He emphasizes that social work is not meant to challenge the colonial system since it hides behind its colonial altruism. Typically, social work with Indigenous Peoples implements cultural sensitivity models as a way to account for difference. Such practices and guidelines are insufficient as they divert attention from the current impacts of colonization upon Indigenous Peoples while individualizing their struggles.

Lakota social work scholar Hilary Weaver (2000) also implicates social workers in the colonization process as they have too often been an extension of it. She clearly and passionately provides a personal and political example of this implication by stating, "I have frequently heard Native people share stories from their childhoods of social workers who came and took them away or took away their relatives, in the midst of tears, screams, and much bewilderment. I cannot recollect ever hearing a story of a social worker who came in during a time of need and used advocacy or activism skills to make a positive difference" (p. 14). In 2014, in *Social Issues in Contemporary Native America*, Weaver and other social work educators and activists, including Andrea Tamburro, Paul Tamburro, Robert Prue, Diane McEachern, and Cindy Blackstock, continued to emphasize in their work how the profession of social work continues to, at times, create more harm than good for Indigenous families and communities.

FEARS OF APPROPRIATION

I have one fear about Indigenizing social work and other helping professions. This concern has to do with responsibility and appropriation. I have the responsibility to teach Indigenous ways of knowing and helping within the context of helping/social work, and I am accountable to students, communities, the Elders, and Traditional Teachers who have passed on their knowledge to me, and to the Creator for how this is done. I also have the responsibility to safeguard against the appropriation of Indigenous knowledges by students, colleagues, and educational institutions, as explained by George J. Sefa Dei (2000):

> As we seek to integrate these knowledges into the conventional school systems, we must guard against appropriation and misappropriation. This is a contemporary challenge for educators. The process of validating Indigenous knowledges must not lead to Indigenous peoples losing control and ownership of knowledge. (p. 47)

Indigenous teachings have so much to offer the world, but we need to figure out how to share their meanings and purposes without our practices being appropriated. It is disturbing to see that one can go on the Internet, find a "shaman," and pay them to participate in a "sweat lodge ceremony." In fact, some Traditional Teachers I know welcomed a non-Indigenous person into their lodge a few times and this person went off, without the Traditional Teachers' knowledge, and conducted these ceremonies with unsuspecting people for money. I also see countless posters in New Age shops and non-Indigenous healing centres advertising "women's full moon ceremonies," weekend retreats about finding one's "clan and animal guides," classes on how to become a "shaman," receiving a "spirit name"—all led by non-Indigenous people who charge money. It disturbs me that some people believe it is all right to appropriate our practices while taking advantage of those who do not have the proper information to make informed decisions about their participation.

Jacqui Lavalley is an Anishnawbe Elder originally from Shawanaga First Nation, who worked for 23 years as a Traditional Cultural Teacher at First Nations School of Toronto. She conducts ceremonies and shares teachings with many people throughout Toronto, as Elder on Campus with the Indigenous Education Network at the Ontario Institute for Studies in Education (OISE) at the University of Toronto and working with our brothers and sisters living on the streets through Native Men's Residence of Toronto. Jacqui also has a Master's of Environmental Studies. She succinctly states her position about how disrespectful and unethical appropriation is:

> Throughout Western history, Indigenous peoples have always been considered as being of no account. Many times over the course of any given day we are aware of the abuses of stealing and taking away our sacred languages and spiritualities. With respect to the value we place on all of creation, we believe that you cannot use indiscriminately our sacredness or our traditional practices. (J. Lavalley, personal communication, June 22, 2009)

Ruth Koleszar-Green, a Mohawk woman who recently acquired her Ph.D., is a tenure-track faculty member in the School of Social Work at York University. She addressed the appropriation of Indigenous spirituality in an interview we did together. She spoke about this topic from the lens of a student:

In my classroom experiences, students wanted to know about Aboriginal spirituality. They wanted to know about ceremonies or traditions they had read about in a book and they expected me to explain these. They wanted to take part in ceremonies and thought that I could teach them how to do so. They wanted to use our sacred medicines like sweetgrass and sage as though it was incense. Damage was done to my spirit in the classroom by professors practicing Aboriginal spirituality. It was damaging as they didn't know what they were doing. They put students sitting in a circle without explaining why. When asked, they said it's just a way to set up a room; that it's not anything to do with spirituality or Aboriginal peoples; that sitting in a circle is a way for everyone to have eye contact. This isn't what a circle is all about. Aboriginal peoples are seen with disrespect, yet some of our practices can be appropriated to use whenever wanted, such as sitting in a circle. (R. Koleszar-Green, personal communication, November 26, 2008)

Appropriation is not only hurtful, it is also dangerous. Some non-Indigenous people include versions of our ceremonies and rituals, such as the sweat lodge, and use of medicines and sacred objects as part of their work with others (Matheson, 1996). Such helpers appear to believe that because they have participated in smudging or a spiritual ceremony, they are authorized to imitate what they experienced in their own work with people. But consider what Lou Matheson (1996) has to say about this:

In current American society, it is unacceptable and usually illegal for people to perform surgery or provide legal representation without proper credentials. There are set standards for mental health practitioners and academic degrees for theologians. It is nearly unheard of for a person to publicly practice that for which he or she is not prepared. The road to shamanistic practice is made of knowledge. This knowledge is accumulated through years (sometimes as many as 10 or 15 years) of direct, sometimes life-threatening experiences with the earth, the elements, and the spirit world. These experiences are guided by centuries of shamans learning to understand the universe and our relation to it as kept by generations before. The shaman's gift is power, earned through years of extreme sacrifice and self-discipline. His or her "diploma" is the understanding of how to use instruments, and plants, and songs, and communication with spirits for the power to heal. These tribal specific practices have become integrated into the shaman's culture, but the concept is the same in nearly every Indian group. (p. 51)

When I refer to the appropriation of Indigenous spirituality as dangerous, I am not exaggerating. Consider the example of James A. Ray, the non-Indigenous president of a multimillion-dollar company in California, who was viewed as a New Age self-help guru and promised his followers a path of "harmonic wealth in all areas of life" (Archibold, 2010). Ray, who had been organizing retreats for seven years at the Angel Valley Spiritual Retreat Centre near Sedona, Arizona, conducted a "sweat lodge ceremony," which he referred to as a "warrior ceremony," in October 2009 (Archibold, 2010; Katz, 2009). The "sweat lodge" was part of a five-day spiritual retreat that is reported to have cost participants thousands of dollars to attend (Archibold, 2010). Apparently, the participants fasted for 36 hours prior to the ceremony and between 55 to 65 of them were packed into a 415-square-foot "sweat lodge" for a period of over two hours (Katz, 2009). Three people died and a further 18 people were hospitalized following this "ceremony" (Archibold, 2010; Katz, 2009). Ray was charged with three counts of manslaughter for the deaths of the "sweat lodge" attendees (Archibold, 2010) and was convicted by a jury on all three counts of negligent homicide (Ortega, 2011). These are the devastating consequences that can happen when those who do not know what they are doing dabble in spiritual undertakings that they have not been diligently trained to conduct. The sad deaths of these three people teach us all how cautious we need to be when we enter into the spiritual realm through ceremonies and other practices, and about with whom we enter.

How do non-Indigenous students, faculty, and practitioners in the helping professions take up Indigenous ways of helping then? The answer lies in concentrating on Indigenous worldviews rather than on cultures and spiritual practices. A worldview is a foundation that guides how one sees the environment/land, people, communities, challenges, causes of problems, and possible solutions. It provides principles, values, and ethics for research, teaching, and practice. The position of this book is that much of Indigenous worldviews—such as a holistic approach, connection to the land, a focus on the family and community rather than the individual, healing instead of punishment, and the inclusion of spirituality—can be considered universal for many peoples of the world. Cultures, on the other hand, grow out of worldviews. Cultures are expressed through languages, ceremonies, governance, clan systems, and yes, food. Complex, ever-evolving, and adapting to environments and circumstances, cultures make little sense out of context and, unless one lives that culture, can be easily misunderstood.

Worldviews and knowledges can be learned as they are general. Cultures cannot be learned unless one is immersed in the particular culture by, for example, living and working for a substantial amount of time in an Indigenous community or working for an Indigenous agency where specific practices are taught and one participates in them. This view is, of course, applicable to all peoples of the world. For example, there are African worldviews and African-centred approaches to helping. However, there is no single African culture. How can there be—Africa is a continent! Rather, there are many African cultures, which differ from one territory to another.

Here is an example of a difference between a worldview and a culture: within Indigenous worldviews, a holistic approach means, in part, looking at a person as having four aspects—spiritual, physical, emotional, and psychological—that impact on each other and need to be addressed in the healing process. *All* people are believed to have these aspects. However, there are specific ways in which the healing of these aspects will occur according to each particular culture of each particular Indigenous Nation. The idea is not to attempt to learn the healing practices specific to every culture of every Nation, which is not possible anyway. Rather, the suggestion is to consider the belief that people have four aspects that need to be taken into account in healing. What practices to implement in this process will depend on the service user and the helper.

Jennifer Ajandi, Ph.D., currently teaches as a part-time instructor in the School of Social Work at Ryerson University and in the Centre for Women's Studies and in Sociology at Brock University. Jennifer is an active community member in advocating for the well-being of women and children and, in 2014, became a trustee of the District School Board of

Niagara for the St. Catharines and Niagara-on-the-Lake Public School Board. She is not Indigenous. In an interview for this book, she spoke briefly about how she views appropriation:

> There is a line between valuing Aboriginal knowledges and appropriating them. I would say that it's a never ending journey to learn where the balance lies between these. I do a lot of reflection through journaling and questioning which usually helps me know what is appropriate through what feels right to me. Some people view Aboriginal peoples' spirituality as exotic which is clearly in part where appropriation comes from. There are some things that I would never do such as conduct a smudge or a sacred circle in the classroom as these would clearly be appropriation. What I do is focus on anti-colonial theory and acknowledging Aboriginal perspectives as equivalent to all other perspectives which I see as appropriate and helpful to my teaching. (J. Ajandi, personal communication, December 8, 2008)

Liz Arger is a non-Indigenous psychotherapist and visual artist with many years of experience in a helping profession with Indigenous Peoples, including with the Centre for Addiction and Mental Health (CAMH) Aboriginal Services and in a private practice in Toronto. When I asked Liz to talk about what is and is not appropriation of Indigenous ways of helping, she told me,

> If a non-Aboriginal social work practitioner has an Aboriginal mentor to teach them and they are learning by living the particular teachings, then this is not appropriating. However, such a helper needs to keep in mind at all times that this learning is not about one's ego nor is the helper to romanticize the situation. Such fortunate helpers need to honour the generosity of Aboriginal people, especially Elders, who welcome them, appreciate their diversity and share their teachings—all of which helps to expand the understandings of the helper and which can be transmitted to how they work with people. It's amaz-

ing how some Aboriginal people share a little of what they know with others considering the history of colonization, appropriation and lack of acknowledgement of what has come from Aboriginal worldviews and cultures and how this has shaped and influenced Canada. Learners must always be sure to name where, from whom and in what context knowledge comes from as not doing so is appropriation. They also need to be respectful of what they do not know about Aboriginal people and their worldviews. This sets them up as ongoing students who are open to learning. I think those students and practitioners who connect with others on a spiritual level will likely be open to many tools for helping. They are the ones who will see how Aboriginal knowledges can inform their practice and help them to take care of themselves. (L. Arger, personal communication, April 3, 2009)

There is literature that supports what Jennifer and Liz communicate about appropriation. Both Indigenous and non-Indigenous writers caution that misunderstandings can occur when non-Indigenous peoples attempt to interpret or conduct Indigenous spiritual practices without a true understanding of the meaning or power of these practices (Garrett, Brubaker, Torres-Rivera, West-Olatunji, & Cornwill, 2008). When writing about group counselling, for example, these authors emphasize that the choice to include Indigenous healing methods "should be based on the intent to use a technique that provides healing for group participants in very universal ways" (Garrett et al., 2008, p. 190). They also address what must not be done by non-Indigenous practitioners taking up Indigenous practices. They state that this "should not be based on the intent to represent themselves as 'healers' in a Native tradition, to conduct Native ceremonies, or to make Indians out of group participants. Thus, intention is the key to respectful implementation" (Garrett et al., 2008, p. 190).

In the winter of 2009, I taught a graduate course in the School of Social Work at Ryerson, Indigenous Knowledges in Social Work. The students came from diverse backgrounds: a few were Indigenous, while others identified as South Asian, Caribbean, and mixed blood; they differed in ages and sexual orientations; some were parents while others were working in the field of social work while they attended school. At the end of the course, I invited the students to participate in a sharing circle with me for the first edition of this book. Most of them responded with excitement at this request. The following is a discussion they had about appropriation:

> *Eddy:* Conscious awareness will help to make sure that one does not appropriate Indigenous knowledges.

> *Nathalie:* Yep, in order not to appropriate, we need to know our own identities. And everyone needs to look at how knowledge is claimed to be known and be accountable for this.

> *Julia:* There are some Indigenous Peoples who will say no one else should be picking up our teachings. It is a form of resistance to be strict about sharing; we need to honour our teachings and hold them close. Some of us are afraid to share much with non-Indigenous peoples as they know that the teachings can be taken and used inappropriately. I am talking about how teachings have been misconstrued, for instance, by taking a teaching and only using a piece of it to suit one's interest. Here's an example: recently at my placement, a well-intended colleague had a medicine mask from our society and was attempting to respect it and use it as a way of protecting himself/herself. However, this is seen as inappropriate because when one receives a mask, there is a ceremony about taking care of it and it must be continued to be taken care of forever through ceremonies. This person purchased a book written by a non-Native person who observed our teachings. S/he believed because it was written in a book, a mask could be used by anyone. Of course, I shared my teachings about this and now it is up to him/her to do what s/he wishes.
>
> There are times when it is appropriate to share knowledge. Sometimes we need to advocate for the clientele we are working with or explain or educate other helpers about ceremonies or teachings which involve a person's well-being. For example, if a client belongs to a bear society and

has dreams or visions of bears while awake, this may seem as a delusion or hallucination to the worker, especially if the dream or vision is directing the person toward some form of action. If this is not discussed, the worker may be focused on a mental health diagnosis. We would want to engage the worker in exploring a spiritual possibility for this behaviour first and then see what happens. (Eddy, Nathalie, & Julia, personal communication, April 6, 2009)

WHO IS THIS BOOK FOR?

It is my hope that this book will be taken up by both Indigenous and non-Indigenous students, practitioners, and faculty across the globe in areas of the human services disciplines. For some who are Indigenous, the content of the book may confirm and reinforce what they already know. For others, perhaps it will offer new ideas, possibilities, and insights that can be implemented into their practice and lives. For others still, the content, or some of it, may not have been heard before. One area of diversity amongst Indigenous Peoples is being on a continuum in terms of knowing about and practising our knowledges and worldviews. At one end of the continuum are those who have a deep understanding of our knowledges and live the practices every day. At the other end are those who never had the opportunity to learn about their worldviews due to the effects of colonization, such as growing up in White adoptive homes where their knowledges were not appreciated. Then, of course, there is a range of understanding and experiences between these two positions.

This book is also written for non-Indigenous peoples in the helping professions for several reasons. The first is that, especially for today's social work students, Indigenous Peoples and their concerns and perspectives must be central to any discussion about the discipline. This stance is significant because the descendants of the original peoples of this land need to be recognized, the descendants of the settler population can be assisted in acknowledging and appreciating whose land they are on, and the profession of social work would gain more respect by taking responsibility for its role in the past and ongoing oppression of Indigenous Peoples and including our knowledges as a legitimate theory in the area of helping.

Another reason why this book is for non-Indigenous students and practitioners is because of its encouragement to those who are not White to consider that they may have much in common with us in terms of worldviews, such as how we view Elders, the family, and the community. If this book speaks to you in such a way, perhaps it will offer pathways to collaboration with Indigenous Peoples and to the recognition of your knowledges within the profession of social work.

Third, since many social work and health policies and practices are clearly not helping the vast majority of service users, why do we continue to repeat what is not working? Why not open ourselves up to other ways of helping? This is particularly significant for practitioners who work in urban centres where the populations are diverse in terms of worldviews and, of course, cultures. There is no doubt that we all have something to teach one another. If we want to have the finest helping approaches possible, does it not make sense to bring the best of the entire world's knowledges together?

Lastly, for faculty and other instructors of social work, this book may be useful as a teaching resource that does not problematize Indigenous Peoples. This is a shift for students' learning as it provides an opportunity for them to see Indigenous Peoples as strong and active contributors to ways of helping, rather than as constant victims and mere recipients of social services. In addition, Indigenous faculty are expected to inform themselves about and then teach social work theories that do not arise from our knowledges and about many populations other than our own. It follows, then, that non-Indigenous faculty be expected to learn and then teach something about Indigenous theories of helping and both the historical and contemporary challenges facing Indigenous Peoples to ensure equity within the discipline. This book, which includes the voices of many Indigenous helpers, could offer a comfortable beginning point for such teaching.

WHAT THIS BOOK IS AND IS NOT ABOUT

This book will focus on a general application of some aspects of Indigenous worldviews and how these can be implemented with all peoples involved in the helping professions within contemporary practice environments. It privileges Indigenous knowledges as having relevance for all. It offers a foundation of values and ethical principles that can be applied in social work practice with individuals, families, and communities. Centring Indigenous knowledges will be viewed as one area that can be a part of decolonization in Canada and elsewhere.

As this book is written by an Indigenous scholar and social worker, its standpoint does not come from an observer of Indigenous worldviews and helping practices, but rather from someone who is immersed in and connected to these experiences. The book privileges and, therefore, places to the forefront the scholarship of Indigenous academics and social workers with an experiential orientation, which is different from work written *about* Indigenous Peoples. The approach to the book is consistent with Indigenous, critical, postmodern, and post-colonial approaches, although the latter three theories may be challenged at times.

What this book will not focus on is the history of colonization and its current impacts although these will inevitably come up now and again. It will not focus on legislative, jurisdictional, and social welfare contexts or their analysis. Of course, these "bigger picture" issues are crucial in the teaching and learning of social work and in fact need to be emphasized in all areas of education at every level. However, I and many other Indigenous scholars and community members have written extensively on this topic (Adams, 1999; Baskin, 2003, 2006; Coleman, 2013; Crichlow, 2002; Montgomery, 2013; Younging, Dewar, & DeGagné, 2009), but few have emphasized the value of our worldviews for the betterment of all humanity and what this could look like in the helping professions.

INDIGENOUS APPROACHES CAN ENRICH THE HELPING PROFESSIONS

Indigenous Peoples have been living according to a holistic approach, which includes spirituality, since the beginning of Creation. It is only recently that some Western methods are making space for incorporating these practices, as a result of their having been "proven" to be helpful in maintaining good holistic health. In addition, it is clear that the problems of the world are not being solved merely by professional expertise. There is an obvious interest in self and spiritual development, evidenced by the fact that books on this topic were the fastest-growing reading materials in non-fiction in both North America and Europe more than a decade ago (Jayanti, 1999). This interest has continued to grow as, according to a national survey conducted by the Higher Education Research Institute at UCLA in 2004, 80 percent of students have an interest in spirituality (Intervarsity, 2005). There is also fascinating information on the growth of the spiritual tours industry. According to Radigan (2007), one travel company called Globus in Littleton, Colorado, which has a religious travel division, saw a 650 percent increase in the first three years of business. Furthermore, the market for spiritual and religious travel has grown into an $18-billion industry worldwide (Radigan, 2007). Clearly, many people of the world are seeking to incorporate spirituality into their lives. Indigenous Peoples are leaders in including spirituality in our everyday lives and within helping processes. We have so much to offer in assisting in the healing of all humankind.

Most importantly, perhaps, is the concept of incorporating spirituality as power and knowledge throughout everyday life. In social work discourse, reminding service users of their inner power and knowledge is called "prevention." Incorporating a belief in spirituality as power involves reflexive knowledge that is less preoccupied with outcome and more concerned with process. Spirituality encourages helpers not to construct an understanding of the service user's reality through knowledge derived only empirically, as this may block other ways of knowing. Alternative means to knowledge and power acquisition, such as those that arise from emotion and intuition, can be explored in social work discourse. Intuition in particular allows the helper to have "direct, immediate knowledge of something without relying on the conscious use of reason or sense perception" (Percesepe, 1991, as cited in Damianakis, 2001, p. 5). With respect to spirituality, intuition is usually rooted in the collective unconscious. In its most valuable application, a helper's offering of intuitive insights, or "hunches," with service users can affect those who experience them in integrative, powerful, and meaningful ways. To make this even more powerful, however, practitioners can assist service users in learning how to access and implement their own intuitions and other spiritual gifts. In addition, social work practitioners can help with service users' positive identity formation through a relationship with the collective unconscious that they share with other people.

No helping profession can be whole without including the spiritual dimension. If practitioners ignore it, then they are not fully responding to the needs of people who access services. Ideally, social work practice includes a focus on the strengths of service users. Spirituality is the most powerful source of strength because everyone who chooses to go on in this world operates on some form of faith. A spiritual value or belief can be a powerful resource in a person's life that can be used in problem-solving, in coping, and in trauma recovery. I advocate that spirituality be implemented within all aspects of social work. We must not relegate spirituality to only concerns about death and dying for it is just as much about life and living!

Spirituality within Indigenous worldviews also includes one's connection to the land. Throughout history, the place of learning has most often been within the community and on the land for Indigenous Peoples. Watkins (2001) explains Indigenous Peoples' relationship to the land as "not one of ownership per se, for we are owned more by the land, tied to it by obligations and responsibilities established by our ancestors in times far back, and we pass those obligations on to our children and grandchildren" (p. 41).

I see these elements of Indigenous worldviews as valuable to *all* peoples. If we see a person's concerns as inevitable life problems that everyone encounters from time to time, then we will see them as manifestations of an ongoing collective struggle instead of seeing them as individual deficits. This speaks to the impacts of colonization and other forms of oppression in society and moves away from judgement, pathologizing, and blaming those who are struggling. Involving natural helpers could be valuable for all practitioners as well, in that collaborating with these helpers is about community organizing and building on capacities, which leads to self-determination.

CONCLUSION

The messages in this introduction—the importance of understanding the current impacts of colonization for both Indigenous and non-Indigenous peoples; how current social work theories can work with Indigenous approaches to helping; and how these approaches have much to offer social work education, practice, and research—will all be explored in greater detail in the rest of this book. The next 17 chapters will discuss self-reflexivity and self-care, social work theories as seen through an Indigenous lens, centring *all* helping approaches, values, an emphasis on a holistic approach, the significance of community, spirituality, justice that can be healing, caring for families and children, global connections, research, pedagogy, the gifts of Two-Spirit people, and being an ally. The final chapter wonders "what if?" All of these topics will be viewed through a lens of how Indigenous approaches to helping can enrich the world for all peoples.

Throughout the book, readers will note that I capitalize "Elder" and "Traditional Teacher." This is fairly common amongst Indigenous writers and it signifies the respect that is given to those who carry the traditional teachings and ceremonies and are able to pass them on to others. Thus, there are "Elders" and there are "elders," the latter being older people known as seniors for instance, who do not focus their time and energy on teaching, helping, and healing. Elder, then, is a title and is capitalized in the same way as Doctor. This is basically the same for "Traditional Teacher," as this too is a title signifying that a person can pass on some teachings, but is still learning, gaining experience, and growing into an Elder.

Another significant naming also occurs in this book with regards to the authors that I quote. I intentionally state the Indigenous Nation of the authors, as I want readers to know that the information is coming from specific Indigenous people who identify with particular Nations. I view this as important because all of us need to know who is writing what we are reading—are they first voice, are they members of communities they are referring to, do they have experiences related to these communities? This is something like insider–outsider researchers, which will be covered in the chapter on research. At times, I refer to non-Indigenous writers as non-Indigenous, allies, White, Black, and so on, as I also believe it is important to know that the views and experiences are coming from writers who have a different voice and lens, and are coming from a place of supporting Indigenous Peoples while working toward decolonization. I make these distinctions in my teaching as well and emphasize the importance of scholars' identities when students are learning from them.

Finally, just before proceeding with the next chapter, I would like to emphasize a fact that is rarely noted regarding Indigenous Peoples. Despite the tremendous horrors of colonization and its ongoing implications for Indigenous Peoples today, including the fact that our rates of youth suicide, incarceration, and addictions are higher than that of the non-Indigenous population, the majority of us are not in prison, addicted to alcohol and drugs, or violent. Rupert Ross (2008), a non-Indigenous Assistant Crown Attorney in northwestern Ontario, is one of the few writers who raises the possibilities about this fact:

> The logical question, then, involves asking where such families found the vision, strength and psychological wherewithal to maintain their health through decades living in this psychological war zone. If we can identify what has kept them healthy, we might then be closer to identifying what is needed to return health to others as well. (p. 12)

Shall we begin the journey then?

REFERENCES

Aboriginal Healing Foundation (AHF). (2009). *Residential schools and HIV/AIDS among Aboriginal people in Canada.* Retrieved from http://www.ahf.ca/downloads/hivaids.pdf.

Adams, H. (1999). *A tortured people: The politics of colonization.* Penticton: Theytus.

Annett, K.D., & Lawless, L. (Producers). (2007). Unrepentant [DVD]. Available from: http://topdocumentaryfilms.com/unrepentant-kevin-annett-canadas-genocide/.

Archibold, R.C. (2010, February 3). Guru indicted in 3 deaths at Arizona sweat lodge. *New York Times*. Retrieved from http://nytimes.com.

Assembly of First Nations (AFN). (2005). Lack of federal funding threatens vital diabetes prevention program. *First Nations Health Bulletin*, Winter-Spring.

Assembly of First Nations (AFN). (2014). Assembly of First Nations responds to federal fiscal update, calls for urgent investments in First Nations families and communities. Retrieved from http://www.afn.ca/index.php/en/news-media/latest-news/assembly-of-first-nations-responds-to-federal-fiscal-update-calls-for-.

Baskin, C. (2003). Structural social work as seen from an Aboriginal perspective. In W. Shera (Ed.), *Emerging perspectives on anti-oppressive practice* (pp. 65–79). Toronto: Canadian Scholars' Press Inc.

Baskin, C. (2006). Aboriginal world views as challenges and possibilities in social work education. *Critical Social Work, 7*(2). Retrieved from http://www.critical-socialwork.com.

Benjamin, A. (2007). Doing anti-oppressive social work: The importance of resistance, history and strategy. In D. Baines (Ed.), *Doing anti-oppressive practice: Building transformative politicized social work* (pp. 196–204). Halifax: Fernwood Publishing.

Bennett, M., Blackstock, C., & De La Ronde, R. (2005). *A literature review and annotated bibliography on aspects of Indigenous child welfare in Canada* (2nd ed.). Ottawa: First Nations Child and Family Caring Society of Canada. Retrieved from https://fncaringsociety.com/sites/default/files/docs/AboriginalCWLitReview_2ndEd.pdf.

Blackstock, C. (2009). Why addressing the over-representation of First Nations children in care requires new theoretical approaches based on First Nations ontology. *First Peoples Child & Family Review, 3*(1), 65–82. Retrieved from http://www.socialworker.com/jswve/content/view/135/69/.

Blackstock, C. (2014). Mosquito advocacy: Change promotion strategies for small groups with big ideas. In H.N. Weaver (Ed.), *Social issues in contemporary Native America* (pp. 219–232). Burlington: Ashgate.

Bombay, A., Matheson, K., & Anisman, H. (2009). The intergenerational effects of Indian residential schools: Implications for the concept of historical trauma. *Journal of Social Work Values and Ethics, 6*(3), 1–18.

Campaign 2000. (2005). *Decision time for Canada: Let's make poverty history: 2005 Report card on child poverty in Canada*. Retrieved from http://www.campaign2000.ca/reportCards/national/2005EngNationalReportCard.pdf.

Coleman, J. (2013) Writing over the maple leaf: Reworking the colonial Native archetype in contemporary Canadian-Native literature. *Bridges: An*

Undergraduate Journal of Contemporary Connections, l(1). Retrieved from http:// scholars.wlu.ca/bridges_contemporary_connections/vol1/iss1/3.

Crichlow, W. (2002). Western colonization as disease: Native adoption and cultural genocide. *Critical Social Work, 3*(1). Retrieved from http://www.uwindsor. ca/criticalsocialwork.

Damianakis, T. (2001). Postmodernism, spirituality, and the creative writing process: Implications for social work practice. *Families in Society, 82*(1), 23–34. doi: 10.1606/1044-3894.218

Dei, G.J.S. (2000). Rethinking the role of Indigenous knowledges in the academy. *International Journal of Inclusive Education, 4*(2), 111–132. doi: 10.1080/136031100284849

Dion Stout, M., & Kipling, G. (2003). Indigenous people, resilience and the residential school legacy. Ottawa: Aboriginal Healing Foundation.

Fontaine, P. (2005, February 23). Federal budget fails to offer solutions to First Nations poverty crisis. *Assembly of First Nations News Release*. Retrieved from http://www.afn.ca.

Garrett, M.T., Brubaker, M., Torres-Rivera, E., West-Olatunji, C., & Cornwill, W.L. (2008). The medicine of coming to center: Use of the Native American centering technique—Ayeli—to promote wellness and healing in group work. *Journal for Specialists in Group Work, 33*(2), 179–198. doi: 10.1080/01933920801977322

Hamilton, A.C., & Sinclair, C.M. (1991). *Report of the Indigenous justice inquiry of Manitoba*. Winnipeg: Government of Manitoba.

Hart, M.A., (2002). *Seeking mino-pimatisiwin: An Aboriginal approach to helping*. Halifax: Fernwood Publishing.

Hart, M.A., & Rowe, G. (2014). Legally entrenched oppressions: The undercurrent of First Nation peoples' experiences with Canada's social welfare policies. In H.N. Weaver (Ed.), *Social issues in contemporary Native America* (pp. 23–41). Burlington: Ashgate.

Hildebrandt, A. (2013). Half of First Nations children live in poverty. *CBC News*. Retrieved from http://www.cbc.ca/news/canada/half-of-first-nations-children-live-in-poverty-1.1324232.

Intervarsity. (2005). Spiritual interest high among college students. Retrieved from http://www.intervarsity.org/news/spiritual-interest-high-among-college-students.

Jayanti, S. (1999). Valuing the future: Education for spiritual development. In *Experiencing the difference: The role of experiential learning in youth development. Conference report: The Brathay Youth Conference* (pp. 43–50). Ambleside, England.

Katz, N. (2009, October 12). Sweat lodge death investigation turns to self-help guru James Arthur Ray. *CBS News.* Retrieved from http://www.cbsnews.com/news/ sweat-lodge-death-investigation-turns-to-self-help-guru-james-arthur-ray/.

Matheson, L. (1996). Valuing spirituality among Native American populations. *Counselling and Values, 41*(1), 51–59.

McEachern, D. (2014). Reflecting out of the box: Locating place and practice in the decolonization of social work. In H.N. Weaver (Ed.), *Social issues in contemporary Native America* (pp. 77–92). Burlington: Ashgate.

Montgomery, N. (2013). Dear Rex: Colonialism exists, and you're it. *Cultivating Alternatives.* Retrieved from http://cultivatingalternatives.com/2013/10/20/ dear-rex-colonialism-exists-and-youre-it/.

Ortega, B. (2011). Sweat-lodge case: Ray guilty on 3 counts of negligent homicide. *The Arizona Republic.* Retrieved from http://www.azcentral.com/news/ articles/2011/06/22/20110622sweat-lodge-case-james-ray-verdict-arizona. html#ixzz3duEVon6V.

Paul, D.N. (2003, November 16). *A speech to the Nova Scotia Tourist Association.* Retrieved from http://www.danielnpaul.com/Mi'kmaqCulture.html.

Prue, R. (2014). A standpoint view of the social work profession and Indigenous peoples in the United States: From the profession's origins through its first century. In H.N. Weaver (Ed.), *Social issues in contemporary Native America* (pp. 59–76). Burlington: Ashgate.

Radigan, M. (2007, February). Companies see increased interest in spiritual tours. *Religion News Service.* Retrieved from http://www.beliefnet.com.

Ross, R. (2008). Colonization, complex PTSD and Aboriginal healing: Exploring diagnoses and strategies for recovery. Adult Custody Division Health Care Conference. British Columbia Ministry of Public Safety and Solicitor General, Vancouver.

Royal Commission on Aboriginal Peoples (RCAP). (1996). *Perspectives and realities: The search for belonging, perspectives of youth.* Ottawa: Indian and Northern Affairs Canada.

Sawchuck, J. (2011). Social conditions of Aboriginal people. *The Canadian Encyclopedia.* Retrieved from http://www.thecanadianencyclopedia.ca/en/ article/native-people-social-conditions/#h3_jump_2.

Shah, C. (2004). Indigenous health. In D. Raphael (Ed.), *Social determinants of health: Canadian perspectives* (pp. 267–280). Toronto: Canadian Scholars' Press Inc.

Sinclair, R. (2009). Identity or racism? Aboriginal transracial adoption. In R. Sinclair, M.A. Hart, & G. Bruyere (Eds.), *Wicihitowin: Aboriginal social work in Canada* (pp. 89–113). Winnipeg: Fernwood Publishing.

Sinclair, R. (2010). The sixties scoop: Implications for social workers and social work education. *Critical Social Work, 11*(1). Retrieved from http://www1. uwindsor.ca/criticalsocialwork/introduction-to-special-indigenous-edition.

Statistics Canada. (2008). *Aboriginal peoples in Canada in 2006: Inuit, Métis, and First Nations, 2006 Census.* Catalogue no. 97-558-XIE. Ottawa: Minister of Industry. Retrieved from www12.statcan.ca/census-recensement/2006/as-sa/97-558/pdf/97-558-XIE2006001.pdf.

Statistics Canada. (2011). *National Household Survey: Aboriginal peoples in Canada: First Nations people, Métis and Inuit.* Retrieved from http://www12. statcan.gc.ca/nhs-enm/2011/as-sa/99-011-x/99-011-x2011001-eng.cfm.

Tamburro, A., & Tamburro, P. (2014). Social services and Indigenous peoples of North America: Pre-colonial to contemporary times. In H.N. Weaver (Ed.), *Social issues in contemporary Native America* (pp. 45–58). Burlington: Ashgate.

Toronto Aboriginal Support Services Council (TASSC). (2014). *Toronto Aboriginal research project report.* Retrieved from http://www.tassc.ca/tarp-report.html.

Truth and Reconciliation Commission of Canada (TRC). (2015). *It's time for reconciliation.* Retrieved from http://www.trc.ca/websites/trcinstitution/index.php?p=3.

Truth and Reconciliation Commission of Canada (TRC). (n.d.) *Residential school locations.* Retrieved from http://www.trc.ca/websites/trcinstitution/index.php?p=12.

Watkins, J. (2001). Place-meant. *American Indian Quarterly, 25*(1), 41–45. doi: 10.1353/aiq.2001.0014

Weaver, H.N. (2000). Activism and American Indian issues: Opportunities and roles for social workers. *Journal of Progressive Human Services, 11*(1), 3–22. doi: 10.1300/J059v11n01_02

Weaver, H.N. (2014). Sovereignty, dependency, and the spaces in between: An examination of United States social policy and Native Americans. In H.N. Weaver (Ed.), *Social issues in contemporary Native America* (pp. 7–22). Burlington: Ashgate.

Wolfe, D.M. (n.d.). *Lies teachers tell us about Columbus.* Hot Springs Reservation: Manataka American Indian Council. Retrieved from http://www.manataka. org/page1735.html.

Woroniak, M., & Camfield, D. (2013). First Nations rights: Confronting colonialism in Canada. *Global Research: A Centre for Research on Globalization.* Retrieved from http://www.globalresearch.ca/first-nations-rights-confronting-colonialism-in-canada/5321197.

Younging, G., Dewar, J., & DeGagné, M. (Eds.). (2009). *Response, responsibility, and renewal: Canada's truth and reconciliation journey.* Ottawa: Aboriginal Healing Foundation. Retrieved from http://www.ahf.ca/downloads/trc2.pdf%20.

Chapter Two

THE SELF IS ALWAYS FIRST IN THE CIRCLE

INTRODUCTION

There is an understanding within Indigenous worldviews that individuals locate themselves within their collective identity, which includes the values by which they live. This location of the self is somewhat like the concept of self-reflexivity within critical forms of social work theory and practice. I believe that the ability to engage in an ongoing exploration of our subjectivity in relation to how we teach and practise our disciplines ought to include self-care. However, helpers are not solely responsible for taking care of themselves. The agencies, organizations, and institutions that employ helpers also need to take responsibility for their well-being. In order to be effective in their work and healthy in mind, body, spirit, and heart, social workers need strong institutional support from the places that employ them. Help for the helpers is one of the areas that is much emphasized within Indigenous worldviews and can be of value to all who work in the helping professions.

LET'S BEGIN WITH ME

For all Indigenous Peoples that I come into contact with, there is always an understanding about how we identify ourselves. We introduce ourselves geographically, politically, and genealogically. This is the first step in introducing and positioning myself.

My name is E'pit Ta'n wen Elasga'latl Gegina'matimgewei in the Mi'kmaq language, which is my Nation, and On-koo-khag-kno kwe in Anishinaabemowin, which honours the territory I now live in. My name roughly translates into the English language as the woman who makes links or who links things, such as our teachings and people together. I am a woman who makes links or who passes on our teachings, spirituality, understandings, and insights. I have come to see myself as "The Woman Who Passes on the Teachings," for that seems to be exactly what I do. I am a teacher. According to Mi'kmaq teachings,

> We each have a spirit name from the moment our spirit first comes into existence, and the name follows us from life to life, and back into the spirit world afterwards. For this reason, we are not "given" a spirit name by someone, we can only be reminded of the name we already carry. It is possible, however, that a person's spirit name will be added to, depending on the roles and experiences that are given to that person. If you ask for your name, be prepared to accept it as it is given to you, even if it is not

something you may have hoped for. Remember, this name
has been yours for much longer than you might think,
and its importance reflects into many levels of existence.
(Muin'iskw [Jean] & Crowfeather [Dan], 2014)

My Nations are Mi'kmaq and Celtic. I believe my name also connects
to the fact that I am of mixed heritage. I see myself as a link between
Indigenous and non-Indigenous peoples in a similar way to how Métis
people are viewed as a bridge between these two peoples. I do not practise
Celtic teachings, but I am proud of this ancestry and see many similarities
between its teachings and Mi'kmaq ones. I come from very small communities in northern New Brunswick. In the Mi'kmaq language, I come
from Wejkwapeniaq, which means "the coming of the Dawn." I am part
of the Lnu'k (the people) of Mi'kma'kik (homeland territory), who are
the keepers of the eastern door (Muin'iskw [Jean] & Crowfeather [Dan],
2014). I say "communities" because I come from more than one; there's my
mother's home community, my father's home community, the town where
I was born, and another hamlet where we had our house. I lived in all of
these places and they are all home to me.

In Mi'kmaq tradition, our clan is a way of determining our family
lineage. Clans are identified by animals, fish, and birds. We each inherit
our clan from our mothers. In Mi'kmaq tradition, a person's clan is very
important as all members of one's clan are your relatives. My clan is the
salmon. My clans also tells something about me, for those who are a part of
the fish clans are said to be the intellectuals, philosophers, mediators, and
those who help others when they are struggling.

I have lived in Toronto for most of my life now and, while here, I proud-
ly follow the teachings of the Anishnawbe Nation, in whose territory I live.
These instructions were given to me by the Elders and Traditional Teachers
who became my guides and mentors when I first came to Toronto. I was
warmly welcomed into these Teachers' lodges and ceremonies, but explicitly told that while I was in their territory, I was to follow their specific teachings and practices. They added that when I was back home in Mi'kmaq
territory, I would then follow my own ways. I am greatly privileged to carry
the teachings of two Nations, which came about through the generosity
and acceptance of the Anishnawbe who took me under their wing.

Actually, it has been remarkably easy for me to transition between Mi'kmaq
and Anishnawbe teachings and practices because they are so much alike. We

both refer to the sun as our Grandfather and the earth as our Mother; we each have seven clans and practice similar ceremonies, such as the pipe ceremony; we both use sweetgrass as a purifier. This is absolute proof that we are indeed connected and that there truly is an Indigenous worldview. However, in my experience, all Nations are connected through Indigenous worldviews.

I have four university degrees—one in English, two in social work, and one in sociology and equity studies in education. Although now separated, I was married (traditionally and civilly), with one biological son, two stepchildren (one who has passed on to the spirit world), a woman who I will always see as my daughter-in-law (even though she is no longer with my stepson), and, as I write this, five grandsons (two of whom are the biological children of my stepson). I am committed to my family and to my community.

I was doing social work long before I got any academic degrees. I have worked for Indigenous communities—mostly in Toronto—for the past 30 years in community development, child welfare, family violence interventions, culture-based program development, healing initiatives, and training of other service providers. All of this work has taken place in Indigenous agencies and in communities striving to implement culture-based and community-controlled approaches. Most of what I learned that was valuable to me as a social worker came not from school, but from other Indigenous helpers, from service users, and from experiences.

Two things led me to become an educator. First was the failure on the part of my social work education to provide me with either theories or practice skills that enhanced or even related to the work I was doing in Indigenous communities. Second, I came to believe that I must have something of value to share with others after all those years of social work practice. I am determined to make change within the system by making education more inclusive, especially for Indigenous students. Despite my critique of social work, I am honoured to be a part of a profession that grew out of the values of love, justice, community, and mutual responsibility. Each of these values encompasses my own spirituality. I believe that spirituality is the connection to all that is in existence. It comes from within and from outside the self. It is meant to assist us as individuals, families, and communities. Spirituality is also about resistance, and it connects us to the work of social change which, I believe, must be the major focus of social work. As an educator, I strive to follow in the footsteps of renowned Mi'kmaq educators such as Dr. Marie Battiste from the Potlotek First Nation in Cape Breton, Nova Scotia, who is a much-respected educator, researcher, leader, author, and role model. She has made so many Mi'kmaq people proud of who they are and is transforming education from an Indigenous lens. Another role model is Dr. Pamela Palmater, whose family originates from Ugip'ganjig or Eel River Bar in northern New Brunswick, which is one of my home communities; who is a lawyer, educator, and tireless activist; who I believe will be the first woman to lead the Assembly of First Nations. As you can see, I am part of a group of strong Mi'kmaq women. I have privilege in this society. I am able-bodied, in good physical health, heterosexual, light-skinned, highly educated, a university professor of the middle class. I am oppressed because dominant society assigns me multiple marginalized identities as an Indigenous woman with (dis)abilities such as clinical depression and an anxiety disorder. Some of my family members and I have also been the clients of social workers. Subsequently, part of locating myself is to state what Craig Womack of the Creek-Cherokee Nations (1997) does when he writes, "I'm not simply writing *about* Indians; I'm telling my family's story, and my story, which is at once Indian and poor and southern and white and a combination of all these things" (p. 48).

This brings me to some thoughts on being an insider/outsider person. I am, of course, an insider as I am an Indigenous person who is involved in many capacities with Indigenous communities. Yet, at the same time, I am an outsider because of the privileges that I have. Hence, I am an insider with many privileges, which make me an outsider. I am a combination of the two. I do not view myself as one who moves from one to the other and back again as some of my Indigenous colleagues do, meaning that they compartmentalize their identities depending on whether they are engaged in professional or personal activities. Rather, I am a complete, holistic package, such that, regardless of whether I am writing a paper or attending a sweat lodge ceremony, my privileges are with me.

I am quite conscious of the fact that I am viewed as a role model in Toronto's Indigenous community and in my home communities as well. I am also a helper to the Elders that teach me. Therefore, I am closely watched. Thus, how I conduct myself both professionally and personally lives with me (and likely with my family) forevermore. It is personal as well as political for us insiders. Of course, having been a social worker for several years in Indigenous communities, I am used to this. Interestingly enough, this has benefited me in a way because it has always kept me on my toes. Accountability is important for all of us.

Māori scholar Linda Tuhiwai Smith (2012) has good advice about being and staying accountable or keeping on one's toes. She writes about being an insider conducting research:

> The role of an "official insider voice" is also problematic. The comment "she or he lives in it therefore they know" certainly validates experiences, but for a researcher to assume that their own experience is all that is required is arrogant. One of the difficult risks insider researchers take is to "test" their own taken-for-granted views about their community. It is a risk because it can unsettle beliefs, values, relationships and the knowledge of different histories. (p. 140)

The politics of representation is, of course, a contentious issue, so I will make my position as an educator, practitioner, and researcher explicit. This is in part why I am sometimes writing this book in the first person. The other major reason for this is that I intend to write from a place constructed from the values and principles of Indigenous traditions for gathering and passing on knowledge. These values privilege and respect a first-person voice. Hence, for me, there is a political project that connects to the intellectual agenda.

Until attending the Ontario Institute for Studies in Education (OISE) at the University of Toronto (2001–2005) to get my doctorate, I never had teachers who were not White, readings that were not written by White authors, and fellow students who were not White. I was always the only one who was "different." Being at school was painful. I was an isolated, persecuted, sad student. And yet, I learned how to read and write in these places, and this became my escape from the hurt. No matter what was done to me, it could not stifle my desire to learn. The harder schooling became for me, the more I delved into my studies. The more I heard that I would not make it to university, the more I grew determined to do exactly that. Great damage was done to me; some of it has been repaired, while some of the damage will never be repaired. It is a part of who I am. There were many times when I fell down, dropped out, and changed direction, but education is clearly my calling, and it has become a powerful symbol for me.

My story is, of course, a familiar one for many Indigenous Peoples across the globe. Education, like social work, has more often than not been our enemy, a major arm of colonialism. For me, this is a lived reality. Being in the academy and becoming an educator, then, is one of my most powerful acts of resistance and anti-colonial activity.

SELF-REFLEXIVITY

It has always struck me as odd, especially from an anti-oppressive perspective which has a strong focus on issues of power, that practitioners expect service users to reveal incredibly personal information about themselves usually right from the initial contact. These encounters occur without the helpers revealing anything about themselves other than a name, job description, and credentials. Without any relationship-building, service users are expected to share their stories of, for example, childhood sexual abuse, pain, or reasons for drug misuse. Service users are supposed to trust such intimacies to this stranger sitting across the room, asking questions, filling out forms—someone who most likely has no idea what it is like to not have a place to live or to feel so utterly desperate that they must go through this humiliating experience in order to receive help. Should a service user refuse to answer some of the service provider's questions, they take the risk of being viewed as "uncooperative," "resistant," or "not ready for help," which means that services may be denied. How many of us would feel comfortable walking into a stranger's office and disclosing that we are being physically abused by a partner or that we do not have enough food to feed our children today?

This power imbalance between practitioner and service user is what I think of first when the notion of self-reflexivity comes to mind. However, despite the fact that social work education today refers to reflexivity as good practice, in that students and workers are encouraged to constructively critique their role and participation within their day-to-day activities, I do not see relationships included in this writing. Many social work authors (Baines, 2007; de Montigny, 2005; Miehls & Moffatt, 2000) write about self-reflexivity. As Baines (2007) explains, reflexivity is a helpful process for our practice because without it "we lose an invaluable source of information when we fail to use our own insights, frustrations, disappointments and successes as entry points into improving theory and practice" (p. 22).

It is also just as important to consider how one's social location impacts upon service users and the work that we are trying to do with them. Yet how are we ever going to know what the impact is if we do not acknowledge and share aspects about ourselves that are relevant to the helping process? When a young mother comes to a social worker, does she not have the right to know if this worker is a mother? Does an African-Canadian man need to know if the worker has experienced racism? Would it matter if the service provider grew up in Toronto or in rural

India? Does the worker have any idea what it is like to live on the streets or spend time in jail? Has the worker ever lost a loved one to suicide or gang violence? Is it significant if the service provider grew up in an upper-middle-class family and has never gone without the basics of survival, such as food, or other material things? Chances are questions such as these are going through a service user's mind as they sit in the social worker's office, answering all sorts of questions, but not being able to ask the social worker questions that might help build a stronger relationship.

When it comes to building a good helping relationship with a service user, it is the responsibility of helpers to look at what aspects of their subjective positions will impact upon service users and the specific situation each person is in. Thus, what is it about the helper that may act as a challenge or as a route to connection with the service user? Is it age, race, class, sexual orientation, gender, skin colour, or religion or spirituality? Is it whether or not one is a parent, student, or experienced in a helping profession? Is it the protocols the worker must follow, the amount of time allotted to a service user, the level of transparency, knowledge of resources, or willingness to bend rules?

In my work as a social work practitioner, educator, and researcher, I share information about myself, such as that in the first section of this chapter, with service users, students, and participants. I invite them to ask questions about me, adding that if they ask something I do not want to share, I will tell them, "That's none of your business!" People appreciate the humour! Relationship-building is one aspect of Indigenous approaches to helping that can be applied to all helping professions, taking into consideration the safety and comfort level of the worker and the policies of the agency. It is important to "walk your talk" should you strive to truly be an anti-oppressive social worker who is open to many ways of seeing the world and helping.

One of my dear friends and mentors, Charlene Avalos, who is currently the Supervisor of the Healing Team at Native Child and Family Services of Toronto (NCFST), worked as a social work practitioner in two First Nations communities in British Columbia during the 1980s. She has been at NCFST since it opened in 1989. Charlene is not Indigenous. In talking about self-reflexivity, she shared this with me:

> It seems that when self-reflection is discussed within dominant social work, it's confined to what is known as "professionalism" meaning that, for example, what triggers us

when we work with people, like in pushing our buttons or what makes us angry, and therefore leads to us not acting professionally. In Indigenous approaches though, self-reflection is part of one's life long journey to knowing oneself on the physical, emotional, psychological and spiritual realms. It's also about our own personal healing as taught to me by [Anishnawbe] Elder Vera Martin, who always said "You can't take anyone any further than you yourself have gone." (C. Avalos, personal communication, December 20, 2008)

Charlene's thoughts about self-reflexivity, which she refers to as self-reflection, are echoed by many Indigenous social workers. For example, two Indigenous social work scholars, Jacquie Green of the Haisla Nation and Robina Thomas of the Coast Salish Nation (2007), conducted a research project with Indigenous social workers in the area of child welfare. They offer an example of how workers emphasized the importance of knowing oneself:

One worker talked about always having to remember where she was from and why she was doing this work. It was the personal commitment to her community that kept her strong and wanting to do social work, but also remembering that she was, at the same time, a social worker and a First Nations person. She always had to remember the historical issues that have impacted our people while at the same time remember our traditional ways. (p. 37)

Here are some of the above worker's suggestions to others, which fall within the process of self-reflexivity even though they do not call it this:

I would recommend that they really try to deal with their own issues first before going out there. I mean things are still going to happen that will trigger things for them, that will happen to everybody no matter how much you work out your own stuff.

Why do you want to get into this line of work? How do you define success?

You have to know yourself, who you are, work with yourself, be comfortable with your own self and always, always take care of yourself. Be balanced at all times.... You are never too old to learn.

[It's important to] do a lot of things to develop yourself cognitively, spiritually, and all kinds of ways. (p. 18)

I will finish this section on self-reflexivity with a few words from Buddhist nun Pema Chodron (2000), who gets the message across with both insight and humour:

In all kinds of situations, we can find out what is true simply by studying ourselves in every nook and cranny, in every black hole and bright spot, whether it's murky, creepy, grisly, splendid, spooky, frightening, joyful, inspiring, peaceful, or wrathful. We can just look at the whole thing. (p. 74)

HELP FOR THE HELPERS/SELF-CARE

Social workers do a lot of caring about and helping others, whether they are doing one-on-one counselling or working with whole communities or presenting research findings to social policy developers. But who takes care of us? My own observations and conversations with many social workers over the years unfortunately indicate that the answer to this question is often "no one." This reality includes social workers not taking care of themselves as well. We tend to be a busy group, working extra hours that we do not get paid for, digging for resources for service users that sometimes are not there, taking our files home so we can get our case notes completed, doing many tasks that are not included in our job descriptions, seeing service user after service user without a break, and eating lunch at our desks as we make return telephone calls. Sound familiar?

Certainly there are many reasons for social work "burnout," but I believe that not being cared for by our workplaces and not taking care of ourselves is a major reason for it. Much of the work we do entails listening to sad stories, witnessing people's pain and trauma, being frustrated because we live in a wealthy country and yet so many people face poverty, and carrying feelings of helplessness when we cannot achieve social justice goals fast enough. The feelings of sadness, fear, and anger that social workers and other helpers experience on a daily basis do not simply disappear at the end of the work day. Rather, these emotions are stored within our bodies, minds, and spirits, and if these emotions are not released, over time, they make us sick. This sickness may come in the form of physical ailments such as headaches, or psychological struggles such as depression, or spiritual illness such as hopelessness. These impacts are not left at the office, but rather travel with us wherever we go, thus leaking into our home lives and personal relationships.

My observations are backed up by other social work researchers. For example, in a recent research project, researchers found that 88.9 percent of social workers deal directly with service users' trauma; of these workers, 70.2 percent experienced at least one symptom of secondary traumatic stress such as disturbing dreams; avoidance of people, places, and things; emotional numbing or hypervigilance; and 15.2 percent met the criteria for a diagnosis of post-traumatic stress disorder (PTSD), which meant that they experienced six of the designated symptoms occasionally, often, or very often (Bride, 2007). Other research indicates that the costs of not dealing with secondary traumatic stress can lead to short- and long-term emotional and physical disorders, strains on interpersonal relationships, substance misuse, and burnout for all helpers (Baskin, 2009; Bride, 2007; Land, 2015).

There is another layer to trauma that helpers may face—their own. It is not uncommon for those of us who have suffered past trauma to enter into a helping profession. This is understandable, but has the trauma been dealt with? The question is, should this past trauma resurface, are workers supported? Charlene Avalos notes that "mainstream social work does not address the fact that workers may be carrying unhealed trauma. In fact, I do not know anyone who has not suffered some form of trauma in their life. Yet due to this lack of support, many social workers feel embarrassed to disclose past trauma" (C. Avalos, personal communication, December 20, 2008).

The expectation that helpers have not experienced trauma themselves and are somehow experts on the impacts of these experiences does not fit. Such a spiritual schism of one person being damaged and the other not is unrealistic and can only promote unequal relationships in helping. The message is clear—social work needs to take care of its own!

Within Indigenous worldviews, a holistic approach to helping applies to everyone, including those doing the helping. Within Indigenous helping frameworks, we often refer to this notion as "help for the helpers." This means that it is in our best interests and in the interests of our loved ones and those we help that we take care of ourselves in order to be the best we can be. Since we are impacted on all levels—physically, psychologically, emotionally, and spiritually—by the work we do, we need to ensure that we are taking care of all aspects of the self. Help for the helpers or self-care is another area that does not appear to be much taken up as a topic in education or supported by many workplaces, which is, I believe, irresponsible on the part of educators and managers. This lack of self-care may be one reason why some helpers leave the field prematurely (Baskin, 2009, forthcoming; Bride, 2007; Land, 2015).

What does self-care look like? In many Indigenous traditions, self-care involves taking care of all four aspects of a person, but there is no specific prescription for individual self-care. For Indigenous Peoples, help for the helpers includes the kinds of cultural and spiritual activities that we offer to service users, including ceremonies such as the sweat lodge, fasting, praying, and smudging. Other ways of taking care of the self are:

- Quieting the self through meditation, deep breathing, or being with nature
- Exercise like yoga, baseball, martial arts, or weight training
- Relaxation such as warm, sea salt, or bubble baths
- Distractions via movies, reading, and video games
- Having fun
- Rest
- Being with people other than those in your profession
- Rewards for all the hard work one does
- Setting limits as to what you can and cannot do
- Not being overly responsible, including learning how to say "no" or "I'll think about it and get back to you" and then saying "no"
- Pencilling self-care in our appointment journals and treating this as just as important as all the other appointments

The research project conducted by Green and Thomas (2007) found that

> Workers strongly believed that helpers must have a self-care plan. This plan must include identifying who your support people are. Other questions that must be con-

templated included, "what role does the agency that you work within play in self-care?" [In addition], each worker talked about how important laughter and fun is when the work that they do is so intense. (p. 21)

Workers had the following to say about how support from one another and from the agencies they are employed by is an important component of self-care:

> The support and the relationships that we have with one another are very strong and I don't think that I could do this work without it. Especially from a management level … I never lack for support from them for direction, for advice, for compassion, for whatever. They really take care of our needs—personal, professional, whatever. We take the time that we need to sit with each other or listen to each other. (Green & Thomas, 2007, p. 21)

Each of us needs to come up with our own list of self-care activities and regularly implement them simply because we need and want to be well and healthy for ourselves and our loved ones. We also need to be well for those we are attempting to help. Indigenous teachings tell us that we need to be as healthy as possible in all four aspects of ourselves if we are to truly be of help to others. I have heard this expressed in several ways, such as "you need to make sure your own house is in order before you try to help someone else put theirs in order." In other words, it is difficult and inappropriate to be in the work of helping if you are not helping yourself. In fact, research indicates that when helpers are not able to attend to the impacts of secondary traumatic stress, their abilities to help those who seek their services may be impaired (Baskin, 2009, forthcoming; Bride, 2007; Land, 2015).

PROTECTION FROM ISOLATION

Connected to help for the helpers or self-care in the work of practitioners is the suggestion of protecting oneself from isolation. Help for the helpers is certainly not only the responsibility of individuals, however. Rather, it is also a collective and political endeavour whereby all involved—educators, researchers, practitioners, managers, supervisors, and members of boards of directors—need to take up the work of caring for those on the front lines.

Both education and the professional associations of each particular occupation need to be concerned with working environments and working conditions for practitioners. They, along with researchers and practitioners, need to work together to create and then evaluate the ways in which workers are cared for within their agencies and organizations. Managers need to be carefully assessing their agencies on an ongoing basis for situations that can contribute to the distress of their front-line practitioners. Supportive supervision, which looks to how practitioners are feeling, addresses any concerns they may have about a service user's situation, and makes room for self-care, is a must. Helpers need to be encouraged to ask for help before they are overwhelmed, and supervisors and managers need to welcome their calls for assistance. If all of these collective efforts do not occur, then it will not matter how much time researchers put into methods of improving services for service users and how much educators teach on how to best deliver such services. None of these efforts will matter if workers are not cared for and supported (Siebert, 2004).

Within Indigenous worldviews, being part of a collective is much more powerful, educational, and safer than being on one's own. There is only so much that an individual can do, but when groups come together for a common purpose, a great deal more can be accomplished. Everyone needs allies, alliances, and to be with like-minded people for support, problem-solving, and activism. The following suggestions, based on Indigenous worldviews and values, can be useful to all social workers as they consider the importance of being a part of a group:

- Use of humour
- Learning lasts forever
- Storytelling
- Sharing of food
- Circle work

I have heard from relatives and old people from various Indigenous Nations all my life that laughter is good medicine. I could not agree more. An experienced Cherokee healer and medicine man, Harvey Walks With Hawks Doyle (n.d.), writes:

> According to Elders of the Native Nations emotions that
> have the most bearing on humans are respect, compassion,

love, generosity, courage, modesty, and humor. I am sure some of you wonder why humor is so important to us and is common among us. It is a traditional teaching in many speeches. Humor comes from having a flexible mind. When we find humor in our life it is full of surprises. Usually a surprise that has humor in it will make you laugh and feel better. Laughter takes us away from bad events or bad areas in life. Sometimes we can look back on bad events in our life and get a laugh from it. Humor is healing; also reminds us that all people are similar and imperfect and also equally capable of making mistakes and tripping on our own shoe laces. Another thing about humor is that it helps people soften the impact and soften pain. It also makes the person relax and find comfortable solutions to the problem. Humor was a survival for Native Americans. It has helped our Brothers and Sisters survive the horror of colonialism.... Humor is also a powerful teaching tool when used the proper way. Teachers can tell their history and stories in a humorous way that is not easy to offend others. After all you can't truly laugh and be angry at the same time.

This is healthy advice for all helpers as it is an excellent way to relieve stress, distract us from the seriousness of our work, bring us together, and have fun.

Learning, or education, does not end once one completes a bachelor or a master's degree or a Ph.D. There is only so much learning that can take place in a classroom, no matter how exemplary the professor is at teaching or how relevant the reading materials are. Rather, as emphasized within Indigenous worldviews, education is a lifelong journey that requires patience, introspection, and making mistakes and learning from them. Furthermore, learning comes in many ways other than through the mind. It comes through all four aspects of self. This means that we can learn through spiritual experiences, such as dreams and meditation. This could also mean moving through feelings of loss and coming out the other end being okay. Helpers learn through professional development training, attending conferences with diverse professionals, reading, talking with one another, paying attention to their bodies and emotions, raising children, looking up resources, and so on.

More than likely though, helpers learn the most from those who come to their agencies for services. Who else can teach us so intimately what it is like to live below the poverty line, to try to get off and stay off of crack cocaine, to live with the scars of a childhood full of abuse, or to struggle with living on their own after being thrown out of their home at the age of 16 after disclosing that they are Two-Spirit? Service users also teach professionals how to be resourceful, resistant, and resilient—traits that we too need to do good work. Much of our learning comes through the stories that service users share with us. As Métis educator Mary Anne Lanigan eloquently wrote 17 years ago:

> Storytelling is the oldest form of the arts. It is the basis of all other arts—drama, art, dance and music. It has been and is an important part of every culture. It is necessary for the revitalization of First Nations cultures and can be a starting point for moving away from assimilationist to liberationist education. Stories provide the intergenerational communication of essential ideas. Stories have many layers of meaning, giving the listener the responsibility to listen, reflect and then interpret the message. Stories incorporate several possible explanations for phenomena, allowing listeners to creatively expand their thinking processes so that each problem they encounter in life can be viewed from a variety of angles before a solution is reached. All people, young and old, love stories. (1998, p. 113)

Getting together with other helpers—whether this be in supervision sessions or on the way home after work with a co-worker—to talk about one's experiences and concerns with the doing of helping is indeed revitalizing, liberating, and offers new angles to situations in which we may be stuck. Telling our stories affirms our thoughts and emotions. Listening to someone else's story shows respect and a desire to be helpful. We gain ideas and suggestions from others that we may not have considered before. We acquire a fresh outlook on a situation. Telling and listening is a reciprocal process. Today, one helper needs the other's take on an issue; tomorrow it will be the other way around. In addition, all peoples of the world have been telling their stories in one form or another since the beginning of time. It's in our blood.

Like telling stories, the sharing of food is another communal activity that all peoples participate in. Many people, including Indigenous Peoples around the world, view food as not only sustenance, but also as a way to holistically nurture the self and others. Having lunch dates with co-workers or those in other agencies, gathering for potluck suppers at each others' houses, and going out to dinner occasionally breaks isolation while offering opportunities to tell our stories, relax, and enjoy one another's company and cooking.

Lastly, in this section, I will write a little about circle work as a way for helpers to connect and stay more connected. Of course, circles are important for sharing, telling stories, resolving conflicts, teaching, and so on, and are a much-implemented method within most Indigenous Nations. The circle is significant and symbolic in that it represents everything in the natural world around us—the seasons, the shape of the planets, stars, sun, and moon. The circle also represents the cycle of life, which has no beginning and end since human beings come from the spirit world and return to the spirit world. The circle is also important because, within the circle, everyone is equal. There is no "head" of a circle. Everyone in a circle is able to look at every person there rather than look at someone's back.

Cree educator and author Michael Hart (2002) writes,

> Sharing circles are both helping techniques and processes, which set the stage for people's ongoing healing, growth and self-development. The general purpose of circles is to create a safe environment for people to share their views and experiences with one another. They have several goals, including the initiation of the healing process, promotion of understanding, joining with others and growth. (p. 61)

There are a wide variety of activities and protocols that are a part of sharing circles depending on what particular Nation the participants belong to or the circle facilitator belongs to. I do not support the implementation of any of these activities or protocols in a circle without Indigenous Peoples in it. Even if there is an Indigenous person in the circle, this certainly does not mean that they will want to bring their specific cultural practices into the circle to share with non-Indigenous peoples. This is the individual's decision and will be based on their comfort with sharing these practices, their teachings about doing so, and the attitudes and behaviours of the others who are in the circle.

When helpers come together in a circle, I suggest that they decide as a collective how the circle will be run. Clearly, Indigenous Peoples do not own the circle as it shows up as a significant symbol in many parts of the world, nor are we the only ones who are spiritual. Helpers can come up with their own particular activities and protocols to be used each time they have their gatherings. Alternatively, they can take turns bringing in activities from their own cultural and spiritual teachings to guide the circle process.

TURNING ANGER INTO ACTIVIST POWER

Social work is doing and taking action. Social workers do not wait passively to be told what to do. Rather, they interact with people, communities, policy makers, and politicians. The work ranges from one-on-one counselling to community development to organizing social movements. The profession is wide open, in that social workers are visible in many diverse areas and agencies, from hospitals to grassroots initiatives, and from government to youth shelters. There is continuous room for social change within all of these positions and places, and social change is most definitely the business of social work. However, involving oneself in social justice issues is not only about protesting at Queen's Park or Parliament Hill. Activism expresses itself in many ways. Examples of activism include: advocacy for adequate housing for one person or a whole community, writing letters to politicians to support raising the living wage, conducting research that leads to policy changes in eligibility for subsidized daycare, and organizing the workers of an agency to become unionized so their working conditions can be improved. Activism is more than marching with placards on major urban streets.

What are the feelings that motivate you to engage in social action? For me, feelings such as fear and sadness about the conditions of the world tend to immobilize me. Anger, on the other hand, energizes and pushes me to take action. When a particular situation stirs up anger in me, I know that there is something wrong with that situation, and I am motivated to speak up about it and join in some sort of action to try to change it. Used constructively, anger is a powerful force that can greatly help to achieve positive change. We were born with the emotion of anger and ought not to push it down or be afraid to feel it. We can also assist service users to see anger as a motivator, rather than have it come out in destructive ways that hurt themselves and others, or hold onto it until it makes them sick.

Non-Indigenous peoples can learn a great deal from Indigenous Peoples about activism. Indigenous Peoples have always resisted colonization and its ongoing impacts in many ways, despite our meagre resources, low numbers, and our powerful opponent, the state. Throughout history, Indigenous activists have rallied their people, such as Métis leader Louis Riel, who led a movement of resistance in Western Canada in 1885 and is seen as the father of Manitoba; and Lakota warrior Crazy Horse, who resisted the American army and protected the sacred Black Hills territory in South Dakota for ten years up to his death in 1877 (Matthiessen, 1980; Stanley, 1963). In more recent times, there has been the late Anishnawbe-Cree politician Elijah Harper, who was a member of the Manitoba Legislative Assembly. Harper was frustrated with the exclusion of Indigenous issues in the 1990 Meech Lake Accord talks on the status of Quebec, and refused to waive a request for a two-day waiting period to start the debate, which led to other events that squashed the accord (CBC, 1990). Then there is Leonard Peltier, another Lakota from South Dakota, who was part of a resistance against massive energy developments on treaty lands and who supported sovereignty for Indigenous Peoples; he has been imprisoned since 1977 (Matthiessen, 1980). Further, activism has also led to several mandated, Indigenous-controlled child welfare agencies; successful land reclamation; and inroads into education, health, and justice.

The Indigenous activists that I am personally the most proud of are women. In particular, I am drawn to Jeanette Corbiere-Lavell and Sandra Lovelace-Nicholas. Corbiere-Lavell is an Anishnawbe woman from Ontario who challenged the discriminatory provisions of the Indian Act, which dispossessed Indigenous women of their status when they married non-Indigenous men or Indigenous men without Indian Status. She became involved in this work in 1971 and took the issue all the way to the Supreme Court. Corbiere-Lavell continued her fight as one of the founding members of the Native Women's Association of Canada. In 2006, she and her daughter, D. Memee Lavell-Harvard, edited a book titled *"Until Our Hearts Are on the Ground": Indigenous Mothering, Oppression, Resistance and Rebirth*, which includes Corbiere-Lavell's journey as well as other stories of Indigenous women's resistance. Sandra Lovelace-Nicholas followed in the footsteps of Jeanette Corbiere-Lavell. Lovelace-Nicholas, a Maliseet woman from New Brunswick, was instrumental in bringing the case of discrimination in the Indian Act before the United Nations Human Rights Commission and lobbying for the 1985 legislation that reinstated the rights of First Nations women and children. Lovelace-Nicholas was a member of the Senate representing the province of New Brunswick as a member of the Liberal Party of Canada from 2005 to 2014. Appointed by Paul Martin, she was the first Indigenous woman to be a member of the Senate. In 2014, Liberal Party leader Justin Trudeau removed all senators from the Liberal Senate caucus, stating that they will sit as independents with no formal ties to the Liberal party (Cudmore, 2014). And, of course, when Trudeau became Canada's prime minister in 2015, he did so. He also appointed Justice Murray Sinclair, one of the leaders of the Truth and Reconciliation Commission, to the Senate.

The changes to Canadian legislation—the Indian Act—came about because of the efforts of Indigenous women during the 1970s and 1980s. Indigenous women are, according to every measurement scale, the most marginalized population in the country (CBC, 2006; Guccairda, Celasun, & Stewart, 2004; Health Canada First Nations and Inuit Health Branch, 2003; Leschies, Chiodo, Whitehead, & Hurley, 2006; Raphael, 2007). In fact, Sandra Lovelace-Nicholas was homeless during the time of her activism that challenged and brought about changes to the Indian Act in 1985. Twenty-five years later, in 2010, another woman, Sharon McIvor, challenged and brought about further changes to the act. Imagine what a large group of organized practitioners with various privileges and resources could accomplish if they were to try. What if such a group of practitioners were to ask Indigenous women activists for guidance on how to achieve such incredible change with so few resources to work with? It seems obvious how much could be learned from such women.

Spirituality (which will be discussed at length in a later chapter) has a major place within activism, as each of us has a responsibility to use our spirituality in creating a better world. I explain my existence in terms of how I value my own life, the lives of others, and honour my connections within my community and the world. This connection and its emphasis on spirituality was succinctly explained by Kurt Alan Ver Beek (2000), who wrote over 15 years ago that "a sick child, dying livestock, or the question of whether to participate in risky social action are spiritual as well as physical problems, requiring both prayer and action" (p. 33). Ver Beek's description of Lenca "pilgrims" marching on a day of protest, "singing religious songs ... and blowing on their conch shells—all traditional means of calling villagers to worship" (p. 33) reminds me of my own community's spiritual and holistic approach to social action. When Indigenous Peoples engage in social justice activities, our Elders, prayers, medicines, songs, sacred fire, and the drum are always present as sanctions of the spiritual importance of the activities. They are also present as ways to support those who are participating in the activities of social movements. The drum, in particular, is a universal tool used in many ways and in many circumstances, including activism. The drum is said to represent the heartbeat of Mother Earth. It is the first thing a fetus hears when in a mother's womb. Babies and small children typically fall asleep when they listen to the drum as they are reminded of this. Drums are alive because they are made with living materials—wood and animal hides.

There are different teachings around the origin of various types of drums. For some Nations, the hand drum is believed to have been given to a childless woman during a full moon. She was told that the drum represented Grandmother Moon, and that she must care for it as though it was her child. The Lakota Nation teaches that the big drum was given to a girl who snuck into an enemy village, as a way of bringing peace to fighting Nations (Dragonfly Consulting Services Canada, 2012). Similarly, Maurice Switzer of Mississauga, Mohawk, and Jewish descent and the Director of Communications for the Union of Ontario Indians, as well as the editor of *Anishinabek News*, teaches that the large drum was given to a woman who then passed it on to the men. The direction given was that the men were to get rid of their weapons and pick up drumsticks instead (M. Switzer, personal communication, April 1, 2015).

According to many Indigenous Nations,

> both women and men play the hand drum and the water drum. However, the big drum, which is referred to as the grandmother or grandfather drum is typically not played by women. This is because the big drum is said to have been brought to humankind by a woman, to help men stay connected to the earth. As such, women stand around the big drum as the men play, singing if they wish, but always watching to make sure that the men are treating the drum with care and respect. This is a position of power. (Dragonfly Consulting Services Canada, 2012)

Once again, I encourage all those within the helping professions to consider how their own particular spirituality can be connected to social movements, social justice, and change, and to take guidance from Indigenous Peoples in how to do this.

CONCLUSION

This chapter has attempted to offer encouragement to *all* helpers who believe and engage in forms of activism as one of the paths to social justice and change. The chapter attempted to show how Indigenous approaches to social justice have made incredible inroads and positive changes in legislation despite great obstacles. Clearly, there is a need and an interest in creating bridges between Indigenous approaches to activism, which include methods that lead to structural change, and other ways of engaging in social movements. Indigenous approaches to helping and working toward social and political change have always lived on the periphery of the centre of all that is seen as "Canadian." An open mind will tell us clearly that a multiplicity within the centre can only bring about more options, creativity, and fresh outlooks that help us understand particular situations and make positive changes for the collective good, which includes all the people who live in this country. When European peoples first landed on Turtle Island, they obviously had to rely on the Indigenous Peoples to ensure their survival. What better way to now give thanks than to engage in activism led by Indigenous Peoples that will lead to Indigenous worldviews being equal to mainstream thought and action?

In addition, helpers may want to consider Indigenous ways of helping in the areas of more egalitarian relationships with service users, what power imbalances look like on a micro level, and self-care as an essential aspect for those who do the helping. It may be that these Indigenous teachings can assist social helpers to further incorporate anti-oppressive work on a more practice-oriented basis.

REFERENCES

Baines, D. (2007). Anti-oppressive social work practice: Fighting for space, fighting for change. In D. Baines (Ed.), *Doing anti-oppressive practice: Building transformative politicized social work* (pp. 1–30). Halifax: Fernwood Publishing.

Baskin, C. (2009). Evolution and revolution: Healing approaches with Aboriginal adults. In R. Sinclair, M.A. Hart, & G. Bruyere (Eds.), *Wicihitowin: Aboriginal social work in Canada* (pp. 133–152). Winnipeg: Fernwood Publishing.

Baskin, C. (forthcoming). Evolution and revolution: Healing approaches with Aboriginal adults. In R. Sinclair, M. Hart, & G. Bruyere (Eds.), *Wicihitowin: Aboriginal social work in Canada* (2nd ed.). Halifax: Fernwood Publishing.

Bride, B.E. (2007). Prevalence of secondary traumatic stress among social workers. *Social Work, 52*(1), 63–70. Retrieved from http://www.ingentaconnect.com.

CBC. (1990, June 12). A vote of protest. *CBC Digital Archives*. Retrieved from http://archives.cbc.ca.

CBC. (2006, May 22). UN Committee again condemns Canada's treatment of people living in poverty. *CBC News*. Retrieved from http://www.cbc.ca.

Chodron, P. (2000). *When things fall apart: Heart advice for difficult times*. Boston: Shambhala Publications.

Cudmore, J. (2014, January 29). Justin Trudeau removes senators from Liberal caucus. *CBC News*. Retrieved from http://www.cbc.ca/news/politics/justin-trudeau-removes-senators-from-liberal-caucus-1.2515273.

de Montigny, G. (2005). A reflexive materialist alternative. In S. Hick, J. Fook, & R. Pozzuto (Eds.), *Social work: A critical turn* (pp. 121–136). Toronto: Thompson Education.

Doyle, H. (n.d.). *Medicine for the people*. Retrieved from http://www.manataka.org/page2210.html.

Dragonfly Consulting Services Canada. (2012). *Aboriginal worldviews: Drum*. Retrieved from http://dragonflycanada.ca/resources/aboriginal-worldviews/.

Green, J., & Thomas, R. (2007). Learning through our children, healing for our children: Best practices in First Nations communities. In L. Dominelli (Ed.), *Revitalizing communities in a globalizing world* (pp. 175–192). Farnham, UK: Ashgate.

Guccairda, E., Celasun, N., & Stewart, D.E. (2004). Single-mother families in Canada. *Canadian Journal of Public Health, 95*(1), 70–74. Retrieved from http://journal.cpha.ca.

Hart, M.A. (2002). *Seeking mino-pimatisiwin: An Aboriginal approach to helping*. Halifax: Fernwood Publishing.

Health Canada First Nations and Inuit Health Branch. (2003). *A statistical profile on the health of First Nations in Canada*. Ottawa: Author. Retrieved from http://www.hc-sc.gc.ca.

Land, H. (2015). *Spirituality, religion, and faith in psychotherapy: Evidence-based expressive methods for mind, brain, and body*. Chicago: Lyceum Books.

Lanigan. M.A. (1998). Indigenous pedagogy: Storytelling. In L.A. Stiffarm (Ed.), *As we see ... Indigenous pedagogy* (pp. 103–120). Saskatoon: University Extension Press.

Lavell-Harvard, D.M., & Corbiere-Lavell, J. (Eds.). (2006). *"Until our hearts are on the ground": Aboriginal mothering, oppression, resistance and rebirth*. Toronto: Demeter Press.

Leschies, A.W., Chiodo, D., Whitehead, P.C., & Hurley, D. (2006). The association of poverty with child welfare service and child and family clinical outcomes. *Community, Work and Family, 9*(1), 29–46. doi: 10.1080/13668800500420988

Matthiessen, P. (1980). *In the spirit of Crazy Horse*. New York: Penguin Books.

Miehls, D., & Moffatt, K. (2000). Constructing social work identity based on the reflexive self. *British Journal of Social Work, 30*(3), 339–348. doi: 10.1093/bjsw/30.3.339

Muin'iskw (Jean) & Crowfeather (Dan). (2014). *Mi'kmaq spirit.* Retrieved from http://www.muiniskw.org/index.htm.

Raphael, D. (2007). *Poverty and policy in Canada: Implications for health and quality of life.* Toronto: Canadian Scholars' Press Inc.

Siebert, D.C. (2004). Depression in North Carolina social workers: Implications for practice and research. *Social Work Research, 28*(1), 30–40. Retrieved from http://find.galegroup.com.

Smith, L.T. (2012). *Decolonizing methodologies: Research and Indigenous peoples* (2nd ed.). London: Zed Books.

Stanley, G.F.G. (1963). *Louis Riel.* Toronto: Ryerson Press.

Ver Beek, K.A. (2000). Spirituality: A development taboo. *Development in Practice, 10*(1), 31–43. Retrieved from http://www.jstor.org.

Womack, C. (1997). Howling at the moon: The queer but true story of my life as a Hank Williams song. In W.S. Penn (Ed.), *As we are now: Mixblood essays on race and identity* (pp. 28–49). Los Angeles: University of California Press.

When Bad Things Happen to Those Who Do the Helping

INTRODUCTION

It seems to be a given that when one is well-educated and working in a helping profession that their life runs smoothly, they can handle any amount of stress, and the people around them, especially their children, are healthy and well. These are the people who have arrived and their lives are now easy. They do not fall off the pedestal and nothing bad happens to them. Of course, this is not true and when something bad happens to one of us, we feel the eyes of judgement on us and maybe hear some whispers, although rarely does someone criticize us to our faces.

Chapter Three will look at what happens when a helper experiences a traumatic event and will suggest ways in which those around them who are also helpers can offer support, rather than judgement or callousness. This chapter is deeply personal, so I am asking readers to please cradle this story in their cupped hands.

TERRA (PART ONE)

On May 14, 2013, which just happened to be my birthday, my stepdaughter deliberately walked in front of a freight train and was killed. As I write this, my stepson has been in prison for over two years. They came into my life as young children and, although they did not call me "mom," because I insisted that they had a mom who was their biological mother, they saw me as their mother. How did the children of an educated helper and educator fall into such despair? I still do not have the answer, even though I have been searching for it for the past few years. I have, however, found information that sheds some light on what may have happened to my stepchildren that has very little to do with me or their father. I am going to include some of this here, as it helped me to understand better and will hopefully be helpful to someone who reads this who has had similar experiences.

Gabor Maté (2008) is the most significant author who has helped me to understand what happened to my stepdaughter. Much of Maté's (2008) work focuses on hardcore users of drugs and alcohol living in Vancouver's Downtown Eastside or what he refers to as "Vancouver's drug ghetto" (p. 3). Although my stepdaughter did not use drugs, she was a binge drinker who sometimes lived on the streets and, at times, hung out with a group of chronic alcoholics who were almost always homeless. The people in Maté's (2008) book, *In the Realm of Hungry Ghosts: Close Encounters with Addiction*, are deeply wounded people who have suffered with the impacts of childhood abandonment, all forms of abuse, poverty, and structural marginalization. For the most part, their stories are not those of my stepdaughter.

SUICIDE IS NOT A PRIVATE ACT

In mainstream helping professions, such as social work and psychology, suicide is typically viewed as a personal choice. However, many Indigenous Peoples view suicide as a social dilemma that is tied to family and community and connected to collective suffering. Thus, it is "a public expression of collective pain" and an "outcome of rampant social disorder initiated by European colonization" (Wexler & Gone, 2012, p. 802). Suicide has a ripple effect with parents making up a high percentage of suicide survivors (Bennett et al., 2015, Jones & Meier, 2011). Parents are not meant to live longer than their children and mourning the loss of a child to suicide is usually harder than losing them to natural causes. It is one of the most traumatic and painful losses that any person can experience and it comes with intense feelings of guilt and self-blame, which are heightened by stigmatization and isolation (Cvinar, 2005; Jones & Meier, 2011; Jordan, 2001).

Not surprisingly, the literature on the experiences of helpers who face traumatic events is sparse. This could be because those who help are busy enough helping others. Or it could be that the fear of stigma keeps us from writing about these experiences. What literature is available on this topic focuses on the general population who face the stigma of a family member who died by suicide (Jones & Meier, 2011; Jordan, 2001). For the most part, the few articles I could find on the well-being of helpers who experience adversity discusses how they implement spirituality to help them make sense of their experiences (Graham & Shier, 2011; Graham & Shier, 2014). Mindfulness is sometimes linked to spirituality, which covers both responses to past experiences while interpreting one's experiences in the moment (Graham & Shier, 2011; Shier & Graham, 2013). I greatly appreciate such writings about spirituality in the lives of helpers, but they do not speak of serious events like the suicide of a child nor do they take up stigmatization.

An article by Brown (2006), a professor of social work at the University of Houston who conducts research on the shame and vulnerability of women and how they develop resiliency in relation to it, is helpful in that it discusses the socio-cultural expectations particularly placed on women, especially mothers. Based on research about how women experience shame, Brown (2006) notes that participants

> most often experienced shame as a web of layered, conflicting and competing expectations that are, at the core, products of rigid socio-cultural expectations. The socio-cultural expectations are narrow interpretations of who women are "supposed to be," based on their identity … and/or their role (e.g., mother, employee, partner, group member). These socio-cultural expectations are often imposed. (p. 46)

Certainly, this is what seemed to be my experience in terms of other people's expectations of me as a social worker, educator, and mother, regarding what should and should not happen in my family.

Another finding from this research that somewhat speaks to my experience is that the participants reported that they felt shame the most when they were vulnerable and feeling as though they were open to attack (Brown, 2006). Although these findings are not about Indigenous women, it certainly applies to us. It is the "kick a person when they are down" or "crabs in the bucket" scenario, when one crab tries to get out of the bucket and the rest pull that crab back down. In other words, they cannot be proud, appreciative, and supportive of such a person because they have not been able to do what such a person has done or are insecure in some way. Another way of explaining this is to consider the very real impacts of internalized colonization where marginalized groups, such as Indigenous Peoples, hurt those of the same group because they can, but are not able to do the same to those who are the cause of all the pain. There are two ways, however, in which the experiences of the women in Brown's research differ from mine. First, none of them lost a family member through suicide, and second, I did not feel shame about what happened. What I felt was hurt and disappointment in how some members of my community responded to me.

THOSE YOU THINK WILL UNDERSTAND

Graham and Shier (2011), who conduct research and write about the subjective well-being of social work practitioners, have found that in some cases when service users experience horrific trauma and have little hope, the helpers may fall into self-blame as well. They may feel that they did not help enough and, at a time when they need the most support, their work environment is not helpful in supporting them to work through the harm done to their subjective well-being. One of their research participants shared,

> I think that trauma experienced in the workplace is not acknowledged enough. I worked in the Child Welfare system in two different provinces, and it almost killed me. It was not the trauma that was experienced in the one or two situations that most of us will experience in our career that will be life changing, but what the system's response to that was. Whether it was like, "What's the big deal? Carry on" or creating some sort of pathology around it. (Graham & Shier, 2014, p. 105)

This helper's experiences reflect my own regarding the expectations placed on me, as even some of my social work colleagues expressed startling behaviours during the year following Terra's death. Two incidents in particular are engraved in my heart. The first was a time when I was in a colleague's office, discussing some tensions between us. At one point, this person made a reference to Terra being my stepdaughter rather than my daughter, implying that I, therefore, should not be so upset. I began to cry after hearing this and this person's response to my tears was to ask if it was okay for them to keep talking while I cried. The second incident was a group of us chatting before the start of a meeting. As strange as it sounds, myself and another person in the room had a passenger train delay the day before because someone had been hit on the tracks and was killed. This person stated they were worried about me and asked if I was okay. At that point, another colleague wanted to know what had happened. The first briefly explained and then the second led a discussion about the protocols surrounding what happens when a person walks in front of a train or jumps in the subway. Let me remind you that all of the people I am referring to are social workers and social work educators who are my colleagues.

THE JOURNALISTS

Brown (2006) also makes reference to the huge impact that the media has on society's expectations of women. Unfortunately, I had a negative experience, not so much with the mainstream media but with the Indigenous media. Assumptions were made and inaccurate statements published on a couple of occasions without any input from Terra's family. About a year and a half after her passing, I challenged representatives of this media within a public forum. I had not planned to, but the subject arose and I knew if I did not speak up, it would eat at me for a long time to come. The representatives explained that they wrote about Terra because there was a concern that the police had not done a thorough investigation on her death. Concern by who? We, her family, did not have any such concerns. These journalists said they had made attempts to contact her father. They had not. They quoted a non-Indigenous outreach worker who had apparently worked with Terra, but who we had never heard of, nor had the Indigenous service providers who knew Terra well. To the journalists' credit, after their presentation, they apologized if they presented the information about our girl in a way that was hurtful to me and offered to meet with me to write a piece about Terra from her family's perspective. I find it interesting, however, that they said this only to me and not the entire audience. I have not taken them up on the invitation.

The press, both Indigenous and mainstream, also alluded to the possibility of Terra having been murdered, thereby placing her with the 1,200 missing and murdered Indigenous women and girls across Canada. They noted that Terra was a witness in a murder trial, that she had been receiving death threats, and that the police had put her up in a hotel for, apparently, only two nights. The press and many members of the Indigenous community of Toronto, including those who knew her and those who did not, implied that the police did not protect her and she was concerned about being seen as a "rat." All of these things were true. Perhaps this frightening situation influenced Terra's decision the night of May 14, 2013. Terra's name came up again in the Indigenous press in December 2014 when the accused's trial took place with the charge being reduced from second-degree murder to manslaughter. He received a two-year sentence. The deceased's family believes that this would have turned out differently if Terra had been alive to testify at the trial. Maybe it would have, but my point in writing this is that Terra's death was difficult enough without adding speculation to it. It concerns me that sensationalism continues to be the hook in the news, and I am both saddened and disappointed that Indigenous journalism falls into this. My daughter was not murdered. She was not missing. She completed suicide. How do I know this? Her spirit told me through a gifted Elder who called her to speak to me.

Needless to say, Indigenous Peoples have a long history of not being treated well, or even accurately, by mainstream media. Two decades ago, the Royal Commission on Aboriginal Peoples (1996) reported that, "In the eyes of most Canadians, largely because of the treatment of [Indigenous Peoples in Canada's media], First Nations and Aboriginal Peoples are seen as either noble environmentalists, pitiful victims or angry warriors." Anishnawbe CBC reporter Duncan McCue (2014) has stated, "an elder once told me the only way an Indian would make it on the news is if he or she were one of the 4 D's: Drumming, Dancing, Drunk or Dead." I am never surprised by mainstream media's stereotypical and inaccurate portrayals of Indigenous Peoples and communities. Critiquing mainstream media's misrepresentations of Indigenous Peoples is an important endeavour that is finally being brought to light.

One of the ways in which Indigenous Peoples are pushing back is by creating our own forms of media as well as working within mainstream ones. I have always believed that doing so is a political endeavour to bring Indigenous voices, stories, and perspectives into journalism for all Canadians to hear. After all, simply being Indigenous means you are a political being. I picture this as being parallel to my own work of bringing Indigenous voices, stories, and perspectives into the helping professions. I freely admit that I have a bias here, believing that, as Indigenous Peoples, we have a responsibility to do this work for our own communities, our children, and all those waiting to be born. Thus, when I heard the Indigenous journalists at the speaking event talk about being unbiased, neutral, and just reporting the facts of the stories they write about, I grew confused and distressed. I heard one of the speakers relate how they were writing a story about an Indigenous community, and one of the members who had a stake in the story and was interviewed made the comment to the journalist that they were happy that an Indigenous spin would be put on the story since an Indigenous journalist was writing it. The journalist, however, made certain the community member understood that this was not the case and they would be writing only about the facts.

It just so happened that, a few months after this event, I was a speaker at a conference about Indigenous-based community research. An Anishnawbe journalist who is a veteran in this profession also spoke at this conference. During the discussion after his talk, I raised my concern about Indigenous journalists who believe their job is to communicate the facts without an Indigenous spin on a story and asked for his opinion. This journalist acknowledged that there are indeed Indigenous journalists who follow this mainstream approach to delivering stories, and diplomatically stated that this was "unfortunate."

There are plenty of critiques written by Indigenous Peoples about mainstream media's depiction of us and rightly so. I could not, however, find anything written by Indigenous Peoples critiquing Indigenous media or journalism. I sincerely hope that my critiques are seen for what I mean them to be, as they are coming from a place of confusion, disappointment, and hurt. Not being in their moccasins, I do not know the challenges they face, but I am sure they have many painful stories regarding the work they do. Perhaps sometime in the future, a dialogue amongst us can take place in a search for understanding one another and the professions we have chosen to work in.

TERRA (PART TWO)

Although as a young Indigenous woman, Terra certainly faced systemic oppression and the impacts of colonization, she was never a part of the child welfare system, did not grow up in poverty, and had the consistent involvement of one parent as well as extended family who were not substance misusers. The only fact I am aware of that may have been some connection to Gabor Maté's (2008) interviewees is that her biological mother left her when she was a baby and their contact after that was sporadic. Her father always had custody of her and her brother, and his family stepped in to care for them as well.

Maté (2008) writes a lot about the development in an infant's brain and the importance of attachment, particularly with one's mother. Could the absence of Terra's mother and the stress of her father as a single parent have had such an impact on her? According to Maté (2008),

> Happy, attuned emotional interactions with parents stimulate a release of natural opioids in an infant's brain. This endorphin surge promotes the attachment relationship and the further development of the child's opioid and dopamine circuity. On the other hand, stress reduces the numbers of both opiate and dopamine receptors. Healthy growth of these crucial systems responsible for such essential drives as love, connection, pain relief, pleasure, incentive and motivation—depends, therefore, on the quality of the attachment relationships. (pp. 188–189)

There is no judgement in Maté's (2008) observations and conclusions, which is one of the reasons why I find his work so fascinating. He goes on to write,

In a very real sense, the parents' brain programs the infants', and this is why stressed parents will often rear children whose stress apparatus also runs in high gear, no matter how much they love their child and no matter that they strive to do their best. (p. 186)

As I read and reread Maté's (2008) book, I saw my stepdaughter in descriptions such as engaging in activities that provide short-term relief, little concern for long-term consequences, loss of control, mood swings, self-hate, abusive intimate relationships, low motivation, and defeatism.

Terra came into my life when she was eight years old, and her father, brother, she, and I moved in together a few years later. One summer, she lived with her mother in northern Ontario and, a while after returning, stated she wanted to live with her. After a lot of agonizing over whether or not she would be okay with her mother, her father and I agreed. I always maintained that Terra should have contact with her mother and half-brothers in northern Ontario and, if she wanted to live with them, we should allow it. This was how I approached my work with families, so why would I not practise it in my own situation?

As a teenager, she returned to us, but she had changed during the few years she was away. Then began several years of her coming and going—sometimes she lived with us, other times in a transition house; sometimes renting a room in a house, living with a boyfriend, or living on the streets; and, at the same time, making impulsive choices and decisions that were not in her best interests. I know this sounds like a hardcore drinker and, likely, Terra was in the last part of her life and, of course, she was intoxicated when she made the impulse decision to step onto those railroad tracks. I will never completely understand all of her behaviours, but I am thankful that there are people, such as Gabor Maté, who share their work with the world that does not blame those who live and die this way nor the families who both love and struggle with them.

I need to add here that her father and I were far from being perfect parents. We both worked a lot and were raising a young son who got most of our attention. There were arguments with Terra and her older brother. We were social drinkers and once Terra was old enough to legally drink, we allowed her and her friends to have a few beers in our home. I think part of her leaving our home was because she was drinking more and more and we would not allow this. There were times when we were furious with her, did not speak to her, pushed her away, and were relieved when she was not with us.

Addiction can cover many areas, however, so even if Terra was not addicted to alcohol, perhaps she was addicted to a way of life. My Wisdom Master Maticintin (2014), of HUMUH Clear Mind Buddhism, writes that

> A person who habitually follows what is familiar to them—"This is the way I am. This is the way I live"—is frozen into a manner of living. We have blinded ourselves by our senses continuously enjoying this business of familiarity and the comfort it gives us. This hunger for familiarity can constitute an addiction. (p. 17)

We do indeed gravitate to what is familiar to us, which helps to explain the reasons behind why abused women stay with their abusive partners and those who have been sexually abused as children sometimes grow up to do the same to others. I find this especially interesting because both the Wisdom Master and Gabor Maté use the words "hunger" and "addiction." What is familiar to us, no matter how destructive it may be, is easier for us to live with because we know it. Changing these behaviours means moving into the unknown, which is frightening, so it is best to stay with what we know. I believe this has relevance to my stepdaughter because, no matter how settled she became at times, it never lasted and suddenly she would be gone again. She could not fit into, or perhaps conform to, what most of us see as a "normal" life. It was never her intention to hurt those who love her, but we certainly did allow ourselves to be hurt.

Also of significance were the number of service providers, most who were Indigenous and a few who were not, that reached out to Terra again and again. This was also the case with her brother. However, nothing stuck for long with either of them. To all of you who tried so hard to help, *we'lalin* for your efforts.

VIEWS ON SUICIDE

It is extremely difficult to predict who may commit suicide since we cannot hear from those who have completed it to ask them why. However, we can hear from those who tried but survived to find out how they view themselves and others around them, what led to the decision to try suicide, and what can help them to be happier people. Unfortunately, due to the stigma attached to suicide, survivors may be reluctant to talk about it. Hence, there is still little research on preventing suicide amongst Indigenous youth (Bennett et al., 2015; Middlebrook, LeMaster, Beals, Novins, & Manson, 2001; Storck, Beal, Bacon, & Olsen, 2009). Furthermore, assessment and treatment programs for trauma and substance misuse, especially for Indigenous youth, are also in the beginning stages of development (Bennett et al., 2015; Gone & Alcantara, 2007; Storck et al., 2009).

Research on youth suicide needs to also look at what Indigenous Peoples and communities are currently talking about in this area. Many Elders teach that suicide is a response to youth's "loss" of cultural identity and pride and confusion about what they believe (Bodnar, 2014). I continue to be flabbergasted at the choice of the word "loss." Once again, we did not "lose" our cultures, identities, and pride—they were stolen from us. Even more problematic, however, is that an Elder interviewed by Bodnar (2014) "explains to youth that according to traditional teachings, people who die by suicide are not released from their pain, but live in the in-between land of the living and the dead, and continue to suffer" (p. 293). So many questions immediately come to mind after reading this. Whose "traditional teachings"? Does this not sound like the Catholic Church's teaching on "limbo"? And, most importantly, how is this of help to Indigenous youth who have tried suicide or are contemplating it? Is it intended to scare them into staying alive or make them feel guilty? What about all of us who have experienced the suicide of a loved one—is this supposed to help us? Is this not another form of stigma placed on us by those who are charged with helping us?

To be brutally honest, I prefer Gabor Maté's (2008) words to those of the Elder above. Maté (2008) does not pretend to have the answers, but his humility and humanity are expressed in the following:

> Spiritual teachings of all traditions enjoin us to see the divine in each other. "Namaste," the Sanskrit holy greeting, means "The divine in me salutes the divine in you." The divine? It's so hard for us even to see the human. What have I to offer this young Native woman whose three decades of life bear the compressed torment of generations? An antidepressant capsule each morning, to be dispensed with her methadone, and half an hour of my time once or twice a month? (p. 55)

COMMUNITY SUPPORT

In communal cultures, people tend to come together over the death of a member in practical ways. True community spirit is reflected in hosting guests who come from away to attend the funeral ceremony, digging graves, making the coffin, preparing the body, and feeding people. School is often cancelled and stores are closed as a sign of respect so members can attend the services. These actions remind individual members of their roles as community members. An Indigenous participant in Graham and Shier's (2014) research spoke of how funerals provide a public space where people can grieve while receiving support. She stated, "When [someone dies], the whole community gets together and has fund raising and raises money for the family and cooks for the family, (and gives) donations" (p. 802). In some situations, the support is more prominent in the case of suicide. As one youth explained, "[T]hey [the family and community] get more respect [if a member died of suicide].… [E]verybody [is] always nice to them, giv[ing] them comfort" (p. 802). Another youth agreed, saying, "If somebody killed their self [compared to when] somebody died accidentally, the person who killed their self, that family probably gets more … one-on-one attention" (p. 802).

The authors explain this special attention as being connected to cultural erosion and how suicide can be a time of community grieving. They write, "as many indigenous people have reflected, a suicide allows the whole community to come together to mourn for the deceased and his or her family, but also affords an opportunity to acknowledge other losses, including culture loss" (Graham & Shier, 2014, p. 802). My family certainly experienced much of this when we held Terra's memorial ceremony. A community centre offered space for the ceremony; a social services agency cooked the food for the feast; many community members took time off work to attend the services and bring needed medicines; members of Terra's family from northern Ontario flew to Toronto to be a part of the memorial, and friends and other family members made the drive in to be there. The majority of the organizing was taken up by community members and social services providers who knew Terra, so that her immediate family did not have to be concerned about all of the many tasks that were required. A few Elders participated with smudging, prayers, and remarks about Terra and her family, offering support to us in many ways. Her friends offered wonderful stories about their experiences with her and hugged and cried with us. A sacred fire was kept going for many hours by some of the community's young men.

Experiences such as ours also showed up in Graham and Shier's (2014) research when a young man explained,

> Everybody around here kind of, kind of knows their role when something like that happens like the elders and the friends, they know who to talk to and who to comfort. It's kind of like a crisis response team, everybody has their role. Some people comfort the family, others take care of family chores so they don't have to worry while they are thinking about the suicide. (p. 802)

My heartfelt thanks goes to each and every person who attended the ceremony and helped us with it. During this time, we felt cared about and supported because the Indigenous community of Toronto came together to share the social suffering of Terra's death while connecting it to historical and structural roots that are reflected in the massive number of deaths of young Indigenous women by murder, suicide, and violence.

WHAT HELPS

Both Graham and Shier (2014) and Jones and Meier (2011) have conducted research on what is helpful for those in the helping professions, the former regarding general well-being and the latter specifically for parents of children who have died of suicide. Graham and Shier (2014) write about a helper whose adult child's addictions greatly concerned her, but how she was able to "turn it over to a Higher Power and let him [respondent's child] go" (p. 761). She came to the realization that when the researcher "talked about the [parent-child] relationship—I was trying to be his Higher Power" (p. 761). Other respondents talked about the importance of routine practices in their lives, which were as simple as eating a leisurely breakfast or more structured activities such as participating in yoga and meditating. For some, positive interactions with their children were significant to their general well-being in their workplace: "I have pictures of my kids and special events. Some are very calm, and some are very fun ... so if I at one point am not as positive as I would like to be, I look at that and I reground myself" (p. 762). I believe this is especially important to those of us who have lost children to suicide as a way to remind us of the gifts we have in our children who are still with us.

These researchers also found that seeking help for situations that they could not work through on their own and mentorship in their workplaces

were of value to the well-being of the participants. According to one, pro-
cessing concerns as they arose—in other words, being in the moment—
included

> either writing them out or talking them out—like chal-
> lenges and barriers ... [I try to] face them and work
> through them as best I can. If I can't, then I reach out
> and get support from somebody who can help me when I
> am struggling. (Graham & Shier, 2014, p. 763)

People to reach out to can include friends and mentors made in the workplace, particularly if the need for support focuses on situations regarding
service users, stressful conditions within the agency, or if one is concerned
about how their personal situations are interfering with their interactions
with service users. Often, it is only the people who work in one's field that
can understand what one is going through.

For some research participants, their subjective well-being involved
their relationships with friends. It has been shown that friendships, in
terms of social networks, can have a positive import on a person's physical
and psychological health (McLeod et al., 2008, as cited in Graham &
Shier, 2014). However, those who participated in Graham and Shier's
(2014) research provided further information on how friendships affect
their overall subjective well-being. For example, some talked about the
positive influence of lifelong friendships: "We are really blessed that way.
We have had friends for years and years—like growing up—and they're
still a big part of my life" (p. 765). This is likely due to the history and
longevity of long friendships as they are usually the friends who know you
best. However, having friends, who are not a part of one's immediate or
extended family, for any length of time is also of help. It is sometimes the
case that a person prefers to speak with a friend about concerns rather than
a family member as confiding in the latter may feel uncomfortable or one
does not wish to worry one's family. There was also some discussion with
research participants about their approach to friendships as indicated by
this blunt response from one:

> I don't want to waste my time on friendships and rela-
> tionships that aren't purpose-filled and aren't going to be
> healthy for me. So let's move forward, and let's make our

time together quality time and learn from each other and support each other. (Graham & Shier, 2014, p. 765)

A sense of belonging and identity in terms of culture was also influential on participants' well-being. As one participant explained:

I've been involved in the French community for almost 20 years, and because of my involvement in the [identifies cultural organization] at different levels, and being involved in the school community as a worker and as a volunteer, I'm quite close to the kids and the families and want to help out somehow and strengthen our community. (Graham & Shier, 2014, p. 767)

Another respondent added:

I like feeling connected to my culture and traditions. It's very important to me … I love attending functions that have to do with our culture and our traditions, and I love listening to the music, and I love being around people that are part of my culture. (Graham & Shier, 2014, p. 767)

Finally, a response that I feel the most connected to is the following:

I guess the only thing I can think of is honesty. Looking in the mirror and not ripping yourself apart, but more daring to look in the mirror and just saying, "Ok, who am I and am I walking a good path?" (Graham & Shier, 2014, p. 762)

It is important to keep in mind that help and support for those who do the helping can come in a variety of creative ways, including through the use of technology. One such example is the e-support community called Parents of Suicide (POS), which has been in operation for the past 15 years. According to researchers Jones and Meier (2011), this online support community has lasted so long because of "(1) its adaptive capacity, especially in regards to technology and (2) the empowering of members to become leaders and organizers" (p. 116). POS has a Website, chat rooms, social network pages, and memorials for children who have completed suicide. For those who live in isolated First Nations communities and rural areas, those who have caregiver roles that keep them at home, or those living with physical (dis)abilities, it may be extremely difficult to access services in the usual ways. Thus, the use of the Internet is becoming less costly and public spaces such as schools, libraries, and community centres typically have computers available to community members regardless of where they are located.

Jones and Meier (2011) suggest that POS has been effective in establishing an informal team of leaders who have empowered themselves and the community of parents at large. They explain this process in the following way:

> As members "listen" to others and their acute loss is validated, they in turn discover their capacity to reach out and help others. Through listening and learning from others, members have been able to see that they and their family are not alone. Through the stories of others and educational resources within POS, many individuals over time come to understand their child's death in ways that go beyond their own failings as parents. The ultimate outcome of empowerment is taking action. For some this has occurred through volunteering and working within the POS community. For others it has involved educating the public about suicide and advocating for increased mental health services and research for the prevention of suicide. Members marginalized by their own or society's reactions to their children's suicides have learned how to reclaim a sense of control over their lives. (2011, p. 116)

Empowerment, through assisting others who have also lost children to suicide and educating the public about the topic, is incredibly healing. This is what has made such a positive impact on both Terra's father and myself. He attended programming at Bereaved Parents of Ontario, later on took the training to become a peer support facilitator, and now facilitates both one-on-one sessions and groups for parents who have lost their children to suicide. His volunteerism is so important to others because he can speak to their intense feelings, such as guilt; acknowledge what they are experiencing; and offer ideas about what can help in the moment. He also supports me in my efforts at educating both Indigenous and non-Indigenous communities about violence toward Indigenous women through his creative and respectful fundraising for events such as the Sisters in Spirit Vigil, which is hosted by Native Women's Resource Centre of Toronto each October.

PREVENTION THROUGH RELATIONSHIPS

If suffering parents can be helped by those who have had similar experiences, what does this say about relationships in connection to the prevention of suicide? If you recall, earlier in this chapter, I wrote about suicide as it connects to societal/community origins and significance rather than only to psychological origins and significance. This position is reflected in a young Indigenous man's comments on his own suicide attempt:

> Well if they have problems and then they try to turn away from it, the problems will just keep following them because it's part of them, too, until someone else that wasn't part of it tries to help them out and get the story straight and end the problem. (Glaser, 2009, as cited in Wexler & Gone, 2012, pp. 802–803)

What stands out here are the two words "someone else," which the authors explain as "someone who has relationships with the key people, but is not directly involved in the interpersonal issue" who are in the best position to assist in preventing suicide (Wexler & Gone, 2012, p. 803). And the best people to assist suicidal Indigenous youth are their peers as they "are the most likely to have trusting relationships with each other and can thus begin to create relational solutions in the context of age-based status hierarchies" (Wexler & Gone, 2012, p. 803). As the following example shows, a peer or friend might talk to the suicidal person's boyfriend or girlfriend to help them work through their differences:

> Interviewer: Your friend attempted suicide? And what was going on? What happened?
> Clara: When her and her boyfriend broke up.
> Interviewer: Yeah, and what happened to her?
> Clara: We talked to her and made it better.
> Interviewer: Cause she was talking about killing herself?
> Clara: Um-huh.

Interviewer: And what did you guys do?

Clara: Talked to her, talked to him.

Interviewer: Talked to the boyfriend?

Clara: Um-hum.

Interviewer: And then what happened?

Clara: They got back together and she got good.

Interviewer: So they did get back together?

Clara: Um-hum.

Interviewer: Oh, okay. What do you think would have happened if they didn't get back together?

Clara: Maybe she would kill herself. (Wexler, 2005, as cited in Wexler & Gone, 2012, p. 803)

In this case, relational intervention was critical in preventing the suicide of the youth through trusted caring actions on the part of friends. In Indigenous communities, suicidal ideation and attempts of youth let their peers know they need them to engage with them in a relational way, thereby offering them opportunities to address what is happening. Thus, suicidal acts can rebuild important relationships so that youth can be supported to change the dynamics of their interpersonal interactions. Certainly, it is often the case that youth will speak with their peers, rather than family members, about suicidal thoughts. As Wexler and Gone (2012) emphasize, "these responses can foster community efficacy, belongingness, and family cohesion, all of which have been associated with positive behavioral health indicators and reduced suicide rates" (p. 803). However, what then is the role for family and other community members in such situations? Perhaps it is to teach youth how to help their peers, give them some tools that are known to be helpful, support them, and ensure they take care of themselves. I would say too that we must not put pressure on young people to address such serious concerns on their own.

CONCLUSION

I am going to close this chapter with more information from Brown (2010, 2012). Her positive messages about shame and vulnerability are:

- Vulnerablity is not weakness;
- To be vulnerable is to be courageous;
- Vulnerability is emotional risk and uncertainty;
- Shame is the swampland of the soul;

- We cannot have a conversation about race without shame;
- We cannot talk about race without talking about privileges and when people talk about privilege, they get paralyzed by shame;
- Empathy is the antidote for shame; and
- Vulnerability is the birthplace of creativity, innovation, and change.

How true this is. How many creative people imagine important pieces of work when they are most deeply troubled? And having empathy is a human response, is it not? Then again, perhaps it isn't, and so the lack of it is one of the reasons why our planet is in such turmoil. It seems such a simple thing, especially for those of us in the helping professions.

REFERENCES

Bennett, K., Rhodes, A.E., Duda, S., Cheung, A.H., Manassis, K., Links, P., ... Szatmari, P. (2015). A youth suicide prevention plan for Canada: A systematic review of reviews. *Canadian Journal of Psychiatry, 60*(6), 245–257.

Bodnar, A. (2014). Perspectives on Aboriginal suicide: Movement toward healing. In P. Menzies & L. Lavallée (Eds.), *Journey to healing: Aboriginal people with addiction and mental health issues* (pp. 285–299). Toronto: CAMH.

Brown, B. (2006). Shame resilience theory: A grounded theory study on women and shame. *Families in Society: The Journal of Contemporary Social Services, 87*(1), 43–52.

Brown, B. (2010, June). The power of vulnerability. TED Talk. Retrieved from http://www.ted.com/talks/brene_brown_on_vulnerability.

Brown, B. (2012, March). Listening to shame. TED Talk. Retrieved from http://www.ted.com/talks/brene_brown_listening_to_shame#t-946310.

Cvinar, J.G. (2005). Do suicide survivors suffer social stigma?: A review of the literature. *Perspectives on Psychiatric Care, 41*(1), 14–21.

Gone, J.P., & Alcantara, C. (2007). Identifying effective mental health interventions for American Indians and Alaska Natives: A review of the literature. *Cultural Diversity and Ethnic Minority Psychology, 13*(4), 356–363. doi: 10.1037/1099-9809.13.4.356

Graham, J.R., & Shier, M.L. (2011). Making sense of their world: Aspects of spirituality and subjective well-being of practicing social workers. *Journal of Religion & Spirituality in Social Work: Social Thought, 30*, 253–271. doi: 10.1080/15426432.2011.587386

Graham, J.R., & Shier, M.L. (2014). Profession and workplace expectations of social workers: Implications for social worker subjective well-being. *Journal of Social Work Practice: Psychotherapeutic Approaches in Health, Welfare and the Community, 28*(1), 95–110. doi: 10.1080/02650533.2013.810613

Jones, A., & Meier, A. (2011). Growing www.parentsofsuicide: A case study of an online support community. *Social Work with Groups, 34,* 101–120. doi: 10.1080/01609513.2010.543049

Jordan, J.R. (2001). Is suicide bereavement different? A reassessment of the literature. *Suicide and Life-Threatening Behavior, 31*(1), 91–102.

Maté, G. (2008). *In the realm of hungry ghosts: Close encounters with addiction.* Toronto: Alfred A. Knopf.

Maticintin. (2014). *The lit passageway.* Oroville, WA: Dharmavidya Publishing.

McCue, D. (2014, January 29). What it takes for Aboriginal peoples to make the news. *CBC News.* Retrieved from http://cbc.ca/news/aboriginal/what-it-takes-for-aboriginal-people-to-make-the-news-1.2514466.

Middlebrook, D., LeMaster, P., Beals, J., Novins, D., & Manson, S. (2001). Suicide prevention in American Indian and Alaska Native communities: A critical review of programs. *Suicide and Life-Threatening Behavior, 31,* 132–149.

Royal Commission on Aboriginal Peoples. (1996). Arts and heritage. In *Report of the Royal Commission on Aboriginal Peoples. Volume 3: Gathering strength.* Ottawa: Author. Retrieved from http://www.collectionscanada.gc.ca/webarchives/20071211060706/http://www.ainc-inac.gc.ca/ch/rcap/sg/si60_e.html#3.2.

Shier, M.L., & Graham, J.R. (2013). Organizations and social worker well-being: The intra-organizational context of practice and its impact on a practitioner's subjective well-being. *Journal of Health and Human Services Administration, 36*(1), 61–105.

Storck, M., Beal, B., Bacon, J.G., & Olsen, P. (2009). Behavioral and mental health challenges for Indigenous youth: Research and clinical perspectives for primary care. *Pediatric Clinics of North America, 56,* 1461–1479. doi: 10.1016/j.pcl.2009.09.015

Wexler, L.M., & Gone, J.P. (2012). Culturally responsive suicide prevention in Indigenous communities: Unexamined assumptions and new possibilities. *American Journal of Public Health, 102*(5), 800–806. doi: 10.2105/AJPH.2011.300432

Chapter Four

CURRENT THEORIES AND MODELS OF SOCIAL WORK AS SEEN THROUGH AN INDIGENOUS LENS

INTRODUCTION

Although Indigenous approaches to helping/social work stand on their own as theories and practice, there are some connections between these approaches and anti-oppressive, structural, postmodernist, and post-colonial theories and frameworks of social work. Both an anti-oppressive framework and structural theory include the history of Indigenous Peoples in their critique of power while postmodern theories acknowledge that there are many ways, including Indigenous ways, of seeing the world. Post-colonial theory goes further and focuses on Indigenous knowledges. Indigenous approaches to helping arise out of Indigenous worldviews, which emphasize introspection, connectedness, reciprocity, and spirituality. These four concepts are intertwined and will be explained in this chapter.

ANTI-OPPRESSIVE AND STRUCTURAL SOCIAL WORK THEORIES

An anti-oppression social work framework and practice contends that present-day society is characterized by many social divisions, such as class, race, gender, age, and ability, which personify and produce inequality, discrimination, and marginalization. Society is characterized by differences that are used to exclude certain populations since relationships among us are created through the use of power on individual, interpersonal, and institutional levels.

According to social work scholar Bob Mullaly (2002), who writes extensively on anti-oppression frameworks and structural social work theory,

> oppression—not individual deficiency or social disorganization—is the major cause of, and explanation for, social problems. This, of course, necessitates an anti-oppressive form of social work practice to deal with these problems in any meaningful way. Such a practice requires an understanding of the nature of oppression, its dynamics, the social and political functions it carries out in the interests of the dominant groups, its effects on oppressed persons, and the ways that oppressed people cope with and/or resist their oppression. (p. 15)

Mullaly (2002) also links the anti-oppression framework and practice with anti-racism and anti-colonialism. He writes,

The "personal is political" analysis forces the social worker beyond carrying out mere psychological manipulations, which in effect pathologize people. This type of analysis has relevance and utility for understanding all forms and sources of oppression in our society. It can be used to understand better the nature and extent of racism in our society and how it contributes to the oppression of visible minority groups. It can be used to understand better the nature of colonialism and how it contributes to the oppression of Indigenous persons in our society. (p. 180)

Similarly, structural social work understands social problems as originating from a particular liberal or neo-conservative societal context. Structural social work theory focuses on the structures in society, such as education, employment, and justice, which create barriers for specific populations based on oppressions such as racism, capitalism, and sexism. Thus, instead of blaming individual people or groups for the social conditions they live with, structural social work examines the structures that create barriers to accessing resources, services, and social goods. Like the anti-oppression framework, it emphasizes consciousness raising, advocating with and on behalf of service users, incorporating a historical analysis, and recognizing internalized oppression.

Such an emphasis is necessary in order to uncover the roots of the oppression of Indigenous Peoples and begin to dismantle the institutions that continue to perpetrate the ongoing effects of colonization. Brittany Martell (2013), the Education and Community Engagement Coordinator at the First Nations Child and Family Caring Society of Canada, uses a well-known parable in the world of social work to explain how structural social work theory works within the area of Indigenous child welfare:

Structural interventions are programs/services targeted to reducing the impact of structural risks. The parable of the river is a helpful story to illustrate the importance of structural interventions. There once was a village on the edge of a river where life was good. One day a villager noticed a child floating down the river and they jumped in to save them. The next day there were two children, and the villager called for help and jumped in to save them as well. But eventually there were so many children floating down the river that the whole village became involved in rescuing the children. They had a watch tower and rescue shifts that went all day and all night. Until one day when one villager said, "But where are all these children coming from? Let us organize a team and go up river." So half of the villagers stayed to rescue children from the water, and the other half went to find the cause of the problem upstream. By not addressing the structural risk factors upstream in child protection, it means that more children will continue to get caught in the river current, who may or may not be rescued by the villagers downstream (Blackstock, Cross, George, Brown, & Formsma, 2006; Lundy, 2004). The lack of specific recognition of structural risks in child welfare legislation makes it challenging to incorporate structural interventions in practice in the context of child safety; however, it is important that child welfare workers are able to differentiate between family risk and structural risk, and respond meaningfully to both. (Blackstock et al., 2006)

However, although both anti-oppressive and structural social work include a historical analysis in their understanding of the detrimental impacts of colonization on Indigenous Peoples, they lack any discussion of worldviews that might include values that could guide helping approaches. This is problematic from an Indigenous perspective as a majority of Indigenous social work scholars stress the significance of worldviews in community social work practice. Thus, from an Indigenous perspective, anti-oppressive and structural social work approaches are not very different in this regard from more conventional social work theories. Furthermore, these approaches are grounded in Western worldviews, thereby limiting them in working with Indigenous Peoples and communities.

In addition, despite the commonalities between anti-oppression and structural social work, these theories tend not to emphasize that the marginalization of Indigenous Peoples is different from other oppressed groups. As community development worker and educator Anne Bishop (2015) asserts, many people add the struggles of Indigenous Peoples in with those of other marginalized populations, which denies the unique history, current circumstances, and relationship that only Indigenous Peoples have with the federal government. In Canada, the struggles of Indigenous Peoples differ from those of other populations because the oppression of Indigenous peoples is the result of colonization. *All* Canadians, and in particular the privileged sector of society, benefit from the stolen land of Indigenous Peoples, the exploitation of resources, and the violation of treaties. In fact, Indigenous Peoples across the world face similar situations.

POSTMODERNISM

Postmodernism, which was first used in architectural criticism and then became a theory that rejected Enlightenment-era, Eurocentric thought that promoted one knowable reality, has been taken up by a growing number of academics in the social sciences. At the core of postmodern theory is the thinking that reality is socially constructed through language, maintained through narrative, and carries no essential truths. Reality is multiple and fluid, as well as historically specific. There is no way to be certain of social reality. All one can do is interpret reality based on one's own values, culture, biases, and so on. Thus, in their analysis, postmodern theorists do not make normative statements about social reality or when visioning social justice claims (Moosa-Mitha, 2005).

As in both anti-oppressive and structural social work theory, the subject of power is also taken up by postmodern theorists. According to Michel Foucault (1965, 1980a, 1980b, 1985), language is an instrument of power and those who have the most power in society are the ones who have the most ability to participate in the discourses that shape society. Societal discourses determine what knowledge is viewed as true or right, so those who control the discourses also control the accepted knowledge. Again, like the first two theories, postmodernism asks the critical question of *whose* languages, knowledges, and voices are being privileged and heard. Yet, within postmodernism, power is also seen as something that moves about within a society rather than something that is always held by a particular group. This contradicts an understanding that it is the state and powerful corporations, which support the state, that hold the most power, which is then imposed on others (Strega, 2005).

Postmodern theorists also reject what might be called "identity politics." Identity politics tend to support the idea that only women can speak about women's experiences, only Black people can talk about Black people, and only Indigenous Peoples can tell the stories about Indigenous Peoples. This means that individual and group identity may be reduced to one identity characteristic, aspect, or label. Identity politics also shape who is allowed to speak on behalf of a particular community, what moral position can be taken, and what is allowed to be spoken. Postmodernist theory recognizes that identity politics may be reductionist or limiting.

Even though I agree with many aspects of postmodernist theory, there are some areas that I find difficult to accept. I agree that language has power and there are multiple ways of interpreting social reality. I also believe that postmodern theories have much to offer and can challenge other social work theories. However, I disagree that there are no essential truths and there is no right or wrong. Tell that to the Indigenous survivors of the residential school system! For Indigenous Peoples, organizing under a common identity is the backbone of political action that has helped bring about much-needed social and political change. It continues to be very important for Indigenous Peoples to be able to assert our truths. Organizing under a common identity has been important for many other populations as well, such as women of colour, gay men, and people with (dis)abilities.

This notion of no truth or many truths connects to the idea of identity politics as well. As will be seen throughout this book, identity is a crucial concept for Indigenous Peoples and communities throughout the world. Connecting with others in terms of a common identity as Indigenous Peoples emphasizes our unique place in this territory or country. This connection speaks to a specific and shared colonial oppression. This connection has also led to massive healing and reclamation initiatives across the country and has mobilized Indigenous Peoples to fight for critical social change and Indigenous collective rights. It is not possible to be an Indigenous person without being political. Politics is interwoven into our day-to-day existence and it revolves around shared worldviews, a shared history, and our inherent rights.

A postmodern view that says that there is no ultimate holder of power, such as the state and/or corporations, and says that there are no determining factors related to power such as race, class or gender, may be misleading. A more fluid view of power should not ignore the stories, experiences, and concerns of those who have faced and continue to face the terribly real effects of structural inequalities that shape our current society.

Of course, there are different forms of power and lenses from which to view power. A structural analysis of power is relevant because it focuses on the relationship between Indigenous Peoples and the state.

However, such an analysis cannot be allowed to limit the power of Indigenous knowledges and peoples themselves. The great strength of many Indigenous people, both past and present, is expressed through the ability of Indigenous Peoples to survive and, at times, thrive, sometimes against all odds. Such strength can, at times, poke holes in this idea of fixed structural oppression. In Canada, this strength was evident when Indigenous Peoples mobilized in the so-called Oka crisis of 1990 and was reinforced by the creation of the northern territory of Nunavut in 1999, the responses to the 2008 state apology for the horrors of the residential school era, and the Truth and Reconciliation Commission's work and recommendations on moving forward with Indigenous–Canadian relationships (CUPE, 2009; First Nations Drum, 2000; Truth and Reconciliation Commission [TRC], 2015).

The fact that some of our languages, spirituality, and teachings in areas such as medicine and science continue to survive today speaks to the strength of global Indigenous knowledges. There is also power in Indigenous ways of helping for they too continue to exist in adapted ways. Our ceremonies heal. Our customary laws restore. Our emphasis on the collective is inclusive. Furthermore, as this book asserts, the power of these knowledges is greater when we come to appreciate that these knowledges have value for *all peoples* of the world.

Finally, many of the tenets that postmodern theorists advocate are still familiar. Many ways of knowing? Alternative worldviews? I agree with Strega (2005), who writes:

> Although Hekman believes that post-structural, Foucauldian "analysis also suggests the possibility of the creation of a discourse that does not constitute itself as inferior" (1990, p. 21), it seems that such a discourse cannot, however, be created by those who *are* "inferior": women and other marginalized people—or perhaps it is that we cannot be credited with the creation of such a discourse. Feminists and other holders of subjugated knowledge such as Indigenous scholars and critical race theorists have for some time been delineating "ways of knowing," and of researching that challenge Enlightenment epistemologies and methodologies. Thus it is difficult to believe Hekman's contention that "postmodernism involves a crisis of

cultural authority" (1990, p. 13) when the poststructural-
ist challenge to authority resides primarily in the hands of
white, privileged men. (p. 212)

POST-COLONIAL THEORY

Post-colonial, or anti-colonial, theory grew out of literary criticism and was
developed by writers from countries which had been colonized (Bhabha,
1994; Deloria Jr., 1969; Fanon, 1963, 1967; Said, 1978, 1993; Spivak,
1999). The term "post-colonial" was originally intended to replace the term
"third world," but has been expanded to include non-Western critiques
originating in the West that are presented as credible knowledges.

According to Appiah (1992), the hyphen in post-colonial writing is a
marker that separates post-colonial theory from poststructural and postmodern theories. However, this hyphen can be misleading, "particularly
if it suggests that post-colonialism refers to a situation in a society 'after
colonialism,' an assumption which remains tediously persistent despite
constant rebuttals by post-colonialists" (Ashcroft, 2001, pp. 20–21). On
the contrary, "post-colonial discourse is the discourse of the colonized,
which begins with colonization and does not stop when the colonizers go
home" (Ashcroft, 2001, p. 23). Thus, the post-colonial dialogue examines
Eurocentric Western thinking and colonization from the worldview of
peoples who have been colonized. This dialogue can provide language and
concepts that may help explain the experiences of peoples who have been,
and/or continue to be, colonized.

Post-colonial theorists discuss how colonization has affected Indigenous
Peoples as well as the particular relationships that exist among colonized
peoples and between colonized peoples and colonizing peoples. Post-colonial
theory does not provide specific answers about how the helping professions
should function within Indigenous communities. However, post-colonial
writers in diverse countries such as India, Guyana, Australia, Kenya, and
the United States have examined issues of colonization, exploitation, resistance, and transformation and have suggested some important questions.
The answers to some of these questions may come from Indigenous Peoples
and communities and from other groups as well. In partnership, Indigenous
Peoples and other groups can work together to help inform the helping professions and work toward a process of decolonization.

Post-colonial theory also provides a message that Indigenous Peoples in
Canada are not alone in their struggles to decolonize. Post-colonial writers

around the world look at patterns among colonized peoples and provide information about decolonization strategies that have been attempted in other places. Post-colonial theory can help create space and credibility in the academy and help bring the knowledges of Indigenous writers from the margins to the centre. By examining patterns of colonization and decolonization in other countries, Indigenous Peoples in Canada can gain insights and strategies in their efforts to decolonize this country. Of course, the social context from country to country varies. However, the patterns of colonization and the themes of decolonization, such as remembering Indigenous histories and languages and the need for self-determination and control over economics and education, are similar. The universal need to make space in social work education, research, and practice for worldviews other than only a Western one, is something Indigenous Peoples have in common. This need makes post-colonial theory useful for all helping professions.

When it comes to the discourses of power, post-colonial theory not only critiques the notion of power, but also focuses on resistance. This resistance takes the form of a post-colonial analysis, which is explained by Shawnee Piqua scholar Andrea Tamburro (2013):

> A post-colonial approach includes the worldviews and cosmovisions of the Indigenous peoples who have been and continue to be affected by colonization. The term post-colonial is not intended to describe a period of time after colonization, since colonization continues today. Post-colonial resistance and discourse began at the beginning of colonization; there has always been resistance by Indigenous peoples, which continues today (Ashcroft, 2001). The Indigenous peoples in the Americas and Canada have survived and resisted colonization, as have many Indigenous peoples around Mother Earth. (p. 4)

Tamburro (2013) quotes Mi'kmaq educator Marie Battiste, who wrote,

> Postcolonial is not a time after colonialism, but rather for me represents more an aspiration, a hope, not yet achieved. It constructs a strategy that responds to the experience of colonization and imperialism ... it is about rethinking

the conceptual, institutional, cultural, legal and other boundaries that are taken for granted and assumed universal, but act as barriers to many including Aboriginal people, women, visible minorities, and others. (p. 4)

CULTURAL COMPETENCY MODELS

In attempting to address "issues of diversity," many helping professions have attempted to create service providers who are culturally competent or cross-culturally sensitive to people who are not like them. Over the past three decades, the cultural competency model has directed helpers to become more aware of, and sensitive to, the specific norms, practices, and behaviours of "cultural" and "ethnic" groups (Hines, Garcia-Preto, McGoldrick, Almeida, & Weltman, 1999; Ontario Federation of Indigenous Friendship Centres [OFIFC], n.d.). Developing heightened sensitivity to these norms, practices, and behaviours is seen to be beneficial to the relationship between the service provider and the service user. Services may then be offered within the framework of a particular culture. The cultural competency model was the popular means of addressing "difference" in many helping professions during the 1980s and 1990s and continues to be taught, written about, and practised in some areas of the profession. In fact, some Indigenous organizations and agencies support the cultural competency model. For example, the Ontario Federation of Indigenous Friendship Centres (OFIFC, n.d.) offers training on this model that aims to:

- Develop a critical analysis of contemporary issues in order to increase cultural competency.
- Provide an overall perspective of Indigenous people in Ontario.
- Provide an Indigenous Cultural Competency Framework for addressing different levels of cultural competence.
- Explore how organisations and agencies can begin to engage with urban Indigenous Peoples and organizations to provide relevant services.
- Provide participants with a basic understanding of how to interact with Indigenous communities.
- Share culture-based strategic planning methods for improved organisational cultural competence.

Not unlike anthropology, cultural competency creates a set of attributes that are assigned to "the other" and then catalogued and managed as collective cultural profiles or identities. This emphasis on management and service provision is assumed to provide mostly White social service and health-care providers with an increased ability to communicate with non-dominant populations. As Nestel and Razack (n.d.) articulate, "the cultural competence approach proceeds on the assumption that what may be wrong in encounters between lawyers, educators, physicians and other health care providers, and their non-white, non-western clients, patients, or students, is that the professionals lack knowledge about how to manage these populations, and thus cannot adequately serve them" (p. 2).

Various scholars have critiqued the cultural competency model, taking the position that it reproduces simplistic assumptions about the various populations that are reminiscent of the imperialism, racism, and paternalism of an earlier social work era (Baskin, 2006; Dyche & Zayas, 1995; Gelfand & Fandetti, 1986; Gross, 2000; Jeffery, 2005, 2009; Miller & Maiter, 2008; Nestel & Razack, n.d.; Pon, 2009; Razack, 1998; Sakamoto, 2007; Yee & Dumbrill, 2003). For example, in African, Indigenous, and South Asian cultures, there are numerous languages spoken, several forms of spirituality, and multiple traditions which are further complicated by class, gender, age, sexual orientation, and context. Without an understanding of this complexity, ideas about cultures can then become simplified and practitioners can fall into the trap of seeing culture as the only variable in the lives of individuals, families, or communities. Furthermore, an emphasis on attempting to learn about cultures may also create generalizations that limit rather than enhance cross-cultural encounters.

A cultural competency model can also reduce the understanding of the difficulties that particular individuals face when accessing social services to cultural differences, rather than attending to the social, economic, and political realities that support systemic inequalities. Thus, when structural power inequities are conceptually removed from our understanding, oppression may easily be attributed to individual prejudice and/or attributed to "cultural barriers." Needless to say, the cultural competency model is limited because it doesn't take into account power differences and the ways that power is maintained through a social hierarchy that marginalizes particular groups of people.

There is also an assumption within the cultural competency model that the practitioner is "culture free." The assumption that the practitioner is

White, and therefore has no culture, is prevalent. Only the "other" has culture. However, the reality is that everyone has a culture and is influenced by culture. Those in the helping professions need to examine their own cultural standpoint. The ways that social workers regard service users, understand particular challenges, and work on possible solutions to these challenges is going to be shaped by cultural understandings. Further, the culture of the helping professions is largely shaped by the particular understandings of the dominant group. Even if the social worker is a member of an Indigenous or other minority group, they will inevitably practise social work, at least in some measure, using the cultural understandings of the dominant group. It is likely this social worker has also been educated in these more dominant worldviews and perspectives. Despite the critiques, cultural competency discourse remains popular with some schools of social work and other helping professions and with many social services and health-care providers.

Gordon Pon (2009), a faculty member of the School of Social Work at Ryerson University, describes "cultural competency as new racism" (p. 59). By this, Pon (2009) means that racial discrimination has moved away from exclusion based on biology toward racial discrimination based on culture. Through this notion of cultural competency, the social work profession unwittingly essentializes culture, which leads to a reinforcement of cultural stereotypes and a freezing of culture that renders it fixed or static. Of course, it is Whiteness that constructs cultural "others" who are supposedly different from White Canadians, who do not belong, and who come from somewhere else (Pon, 2009). Despite the fact that the Indigenous Peoples of Turtle Island did not come from anywhere else, they are still most definitely seen as "other" within White Canadian culture. I agree with Pon's (2009) assertion that "when cultural competency constructs knowledge of cultural 'others,' it forgets the history of non-whites in Canada and how this troubles, even renders absurd, any notion of a pure or absolute Canadian culture" (p. 63).

As some social work scholars (Baskin, 2006; Pon, 2009) have written, culture is extremely complicated and there is far too much information that is associated with what constitutes "culture" for anyone to possibly become competent in every aspect of it. I don't think I am fully competent in understanding my own culture, never mind anyone else's. Fortunately, both Indigenous worldviews and postmodern theory challenge the idea of fixed cultures and identities A much more realistic understanding of culture comes from Yon (2000, as cited in Pon, 2009), who states that "postmodern understandings of culture shifted from being 'a stable and knowable set of attributes' to a view of culture as a 'matter of debate about representations and the complex relationships that individuals take up in relation to them'" (p. 64).

Pon (2009) then asks the question why, despite the fact that cultural competency is an outdated theory about culture embedded in modernist and colonialist discourses, do some people within the social work profession continue to engage with ideas and practices of cultural competency? I agree with Pon's (2009) answer to his own question, when he suggests that this clinging to cultural competency is based in Canada's desire to forget about its genocide of Indigenous Peoples and its desire to see itself as a fair and tolerant country. Thus, social work can hold on to an identity of innocence and goodness by focusing its attention on the "other" who is being helped, rather than on itself. Pon (2009) identifies this phenomenon as "a manifestation of a rush to practice" which is, according to Britzman (2000, as cited in Pon, 2009), "often related to a refusal to engage with learning about social violence, such as colonialism, racism and slavery" (p. 69). Such learning can be difficult for both educators and learners since it requires that they examine how they are implicated in benefiting from colonization. Hence, those who benefit from colonization may run to cultural competency, rather than engage in the necessary processes of self-reflexivity that help develop self-knowledge. As this book emphasizes, running away from oneself is the last thing we want to do if creating a better world is our intention.

CULTURAL SAFETY

Cultural safety emerged as a concept in the 1980s in Aotearoa/New Zealand. Much of the development of this concept stems from the work of Dr. Irihapeti Ramsden, an Aotearoa/New Zealand nurse of Ngai Tahupotiki and Rangitane descent, or, "if expressed in colonial identity markers, she was a Maori woman" (Koptie, 2009, p. 30). Although Dr. Ramsden passed into the spirit world in 2003, her work continues to be built upon. In academia, there have been some examinations of cultural safety in the United States and the United Kingdom, but most have come out of New Zealand, Australia, and Canada (Smye, Josewski, & Kendall, 2010). The concept has expanded beyond health-care professions and is now being applied in other fields such as social services, particularly social work and child welfare (Fulcher, 2001; Milliken, 2008).

Though the exact definition of culturally safe practices remains elusive, one approach has been to define them as they relate to practices that are found to be "culturally unsafe" (Anderson, Perry, Blue, & Browne, 2003). Wood and Schwass (1993, cited in Polaschek, 1998) define culturally unsafe practices as "any actions which diminish, demean or disempower the cultural identity and wellbeing of an individual" (p. 5). Culture, in relation to this concept, is not restricted to ethnicity, but includes class, race, sex, age, and so on, and the intersection of these identities (Baker & Giles, 2012; De & Richardson, 2008; Papps & Ramsden, 1996). Further, cultural safety encompasses not only the principles of equality and equity, but also calls awareness to the ways in which "historical, economical, and social contexts" influence our position (Gerlach, 2012, p. 152; Fulcher, 2001; Health Council of Canada [HCC], 2012).

There is an important distinction to be made between cultural safety and concepts such as cultural sensitivity, awareness, and competence. The latter concepts were developed in relation to diversity and though these are a part of its composition, cultural safety moves beyond these ideas and involves reflection on racism, power relations, and one's own privilege and status, as well as the oppression/marginalization and status of those we service. More specifically, cultural safety allows the service user to guide the practice according to what is safe for them (Fulcher, 2001; HCC, 2012; Kirmayer, 2012; Koptie, 2009; National Aboriginal Health Organization [NAHO], 2006; Nguyen, 2008; Papps & Ramsden, 1996). NAHO (2006) expands on this differentiation, stating that cultural safety takes into account relationships between two cultures, which relates specifically to colonizer and colonized peoples in countries such as Aotearoa/New Zealand and, more recently, Canada. This bicultural relationship is taken into account through the practitioner's reflection of their own position and subsequent ability to adjust their care according to the needs, expectations, and standards of the service user (Anderson et al., 2003; Browne et al., 2009; Gerlach, Sullivan, Valavaara, & McNeil, 2014; NAHO, 2006). Of note is the fact that cultural safety has been embraced by the Assembly of First Nations and NAHO as being an ideal approach to working with Indigenous Peoples (Gerlach et al., 2014; NAHO, 2006; HCC, 2012; Smye et al., 2010).

Cultural safety has been used to deepen understandings of how relationships between Indigenous and non-Indigenous peoples are experienced in Canada (Milliken, 2008; NAHO, 2006; Shah & Reeves, 2012). Eveline J. Milliken (2008) identifies common experiences of cultural unsafety as well as concepts contributing to culturally safe experiences in these relationships. The lived experiences of Indigenous Peoples include both their own cultures and the domination of their cultures by mainstream, Euro-Canadian culture. Such experiences of domination, along with encounters of overt and covert racism, result in the requirement of Indigenous Peoples to maintain "a constant vigilance" to ensure the safety of their cultures (Milliken, 2008, p. 197; HCC, 2012). However, making Indigenous worldviews visible; addressing individuals as multi-dimensional beings, which includes mind, body, spirit, and emotions, as well as past, present, and future experiences; and raising awareness of the history of colonization, with its current effects, are examples of cultural safety at work in social services contexts (Milliken, 2008; Nguyen, 2008; Shah & Reeves, 2012).

Within education, the Aboriginal Nurses Association of Canada (2009) stresses the need for cultural safety curriculum, due to the lasting impacts of colonization, historical and current government policies, the residential school system, the sixties scoop, and intergenerational trauma. Similarly, Brascoupé and Waters (2009) outline recommendations for the training of all professionals who work with Indigenous communities, including community leaders, teachers, and professionals in, for example, health, law, and politics, regarding Indigenous histories, cultural awareness, and the concept and practice of cultural safety. However, they advocate for the creation of teaching materials specific to the communities with which professionals are working and recommend ongoing research into cultural safety by Indigenous communities, organizations, and service users. In addition, these authors emphasize building stronger relationships between Indigenous Peoples and postsecondary institutions to ensure accountability of the latter to the former. They add that the fostering of learning culturally safe practices could also improve the rate of attendance by Indigenous Peoples within educational institutions (Brascoupé & Waters, 2009).

There is a growing collection of research on cultural safety as it pertains to social work, but the pool is still quite limited. A much deeper understanding of colonization, differing worldviews, diversity among Indigenous cultures, and involvement of communities in the development of policies and programs is needed.

INDIGENOUS WORLDVIEWS GUIDE APPROACHES TO HELPING

In 1995, Chickasaw academic Eber Hampton published an article in the *Canadian Journal of Native Education* titled "Memory Comes Before

Knowledge: Research May Improve if Researchers Remember Their Motives." For me, this magical, mysterious, and completely sensible title continues to capture the connections inherent in Indigenous worldviews. It is inclusive of spirit, blood memory, respect, interconnectedness, story-telling, feelings, experiences, and guidance. It also reminds me that I do not need to know about or understand everything with a sense of absolute certainty. It reinforces the concept that it is perfectly acceptable and appropriate to believe that there is much that I am aware of and rationally cannot explain. I am also aware that this is the way it is supposed to be. I accept and am comfortable with what cannot be known, and I recognize that this is part of my worldview.

In order to find meanings in the world around us, we must continuously explore our inner selves. Indigenous worldviews incorporate ways of turning inward for the purpose of finding meanings through, for example, prayer, fasting, dream interpretation, ceremonies, and silence. Our ancestors left us these methods through the generational teachings that are passed on by our Elders and through our blood memories. Within Indigenous epistemologies, there is an explicit acceptance that each individual has the inherent ability for introspection. Although there is great community guidance, this inward journey is conducted alone and is unique to each of us. It provides us with our purpose and, therefore, what we have to offer the whole of Creation. Knowledge, then, is based on experience. One's experiences, through inward journeys and living life, provide both individual learning and teachings for the collective. Within Indigenous worldviews, the personal experiences of helpers contribute to the helping process. There is an understanding that experience, rather than "book learning," leads to knowledge that will benefit others. For example, it is often those healing from substance misuse who are the best addictions counsellors, or those who have survived domestic violence who are the most informed about making positive policy changes for the safety of women and children. Furthermore, within Indigenous societies worldwide, it is the older people, often called Elders, rather than people with Ph.D.s, who are held in the highest regard. Why? It is because Elders have knowledge based on experience rather than merely on theory. It would be wonderful if Western societies and the helping professions valued elderly people in this way.

Collective Indigenous cultural and spiritual experiences across the globe strongly emphasize this notion of connection. Over the years, many Indigenous writers (Baskin, 2002, 2005, 2006; Battiste & Youngblood

Henderson, 2000; Cajete, 1994; Couture, 1991; Fitznor, 1998; Hart, 2009; Shilling, 2002) have spoken to the idea of interconnectedness as an important concept within our worldviews. Thus, I am connected to my family, community, Mi'kmaq Nation, and to everything and everyone on Mother Earth and to everything in the spirit world. To divide any of these realities into separate categories is a dishonour to Indigenous ways of thinking (as well as the teachings of Buddhism).

This understanding of interrelatedness applies to each individual as well. We cannot separate our spiritual teachings, beliefs, and values from everything else that we are learning. Hence, all of the aspects of a person—spiritual, physical, emotional, and psychological—are connected and cannot be viewed in isolation. This concept of holism, then, applies to the well-being of each of us, and reminds us that we are all related and have a responsibility to one another's healing and growth. In turn, this concept of interconnectedness, which leads to a holistic approach to healing and learning, means that all of one's senses, intuition, and spiritual experiences are necessary.

When someone can live as a whole person, then they can connect to everything around them and attend to their responsibilities. In Indigenous worldviews, a focus on individual and collective responsibility for all members of one's community is highlighted. Many years ago, Blood scholar Leroy Little Bear (2000) articulated this focus beautifully:

> Wholeness is like a flower with four petals. When it opens, one discovers strength, sharing, honesty, and kindness. Together these four petals create balance, harmony, and beauty. Wholeness works in the same interconnected way. The whole strength speaks to the idea of sustaining balance. If a person is whole and balanced, then he or she is in a position to fulfill his or her individual responsibilities to the whole. If a person is not balanced, then he or she is sick and weak—physically, mentally or both—and cannot fulfill his or her individual responsibilities. (p. 79)

Is it not possible that teachings of connectedness can lead to a sense of responsibility and greater compassion for all? Is compassion not a deeply rooted value of the helping professions? I would guess that the vast majority of social service and health-care users who seek the assistance of professionals may come away from the experience not feeling connected to much of anything. It is this disconnect or lack of wholeness, which leads to the exclusion of some populations, that causes so much pain for so many people. A focus on connecting marginalized people, both to their own inner worlds and to the worlds of other people, needs to be a major focus of the profession of social work. After all, we as educators and practitioners need to keep in mind that the work we are involved in is "social," which clearly includes facilitating connections between people.

Writing about their work in a Dine community in southwestern Turtle Island (North America), Dine social work practitioners Margaret Waller and Shirley Patterson (2002) focus on what it means to offer and receive help within Indigenous worldviews. According to these writers, helping one another is a way of life; there is no distinction between the helper and the person in need, and no stigma attached to the need for help. Unlike the stigma that is often attached to need in a Western context, in this Dine community, it is "assumed that everyone has problems at one time or another and therefore that everyone will be a recipient of help as well as a helper" (Waller & Patterson, 2002, p. 11). Hence, there is no sense of social distance between people in need and those who are helping. In addition, the writers highlight the importance of natural helpers, such as family, clan members, and friends, as people who may greatly support those in need.

This concept of a reciprocal relationship amongst people speaks to the notions of connectedness and compassion outlined previously. It also suggests an egalitarian way of living in which helping is understood through values of sharing. Today, I will help you simply because I can. Next week, next year, when I am in need, you will help me because you can. This way, the well-being of everyone is considered. When each individual is doing okay, then it follows that the whole community benefits. In addition, many peoples throughout the world share the belief that help comes from natural networks such as family, friends, and other community members. In fact, social work is a Western concept that is foreign to many societies. It must be rather puzzling to some people to hear that they would have to go to a stranger who is paid a salary through government funding to help them sort out particular personal concerns.

Spirituality, of course, is another significant component of Indigenous worldviews. My understanding of Indigenous spirituality, according to the teachings that have been passed on to me, is that it is about our inter-connectedness and interrelationship with all life. Everything in the world (both "animate" and "inanimate") is seen as being an equal. Everything has a spirit and is also an interdependent part of the great whole. This inclusive view permeates the entire Indigenous vision of life and the universe. Often, this reclaiming of spirituality begins in healing processes with Indigenous social workers and other helpers. It is important that these helpers adopt this work because the spiritual aspect of Indigenous identity has suffered greatly from the impacts of colonization. Thus, some healing programs ensure that emphasis is placed on activism, resistance, and social change as well as community recovery (Absolon, 2009; Crooks, Chiodo, Thomas, & Hughes, 2009, 2011; Reid, 2009; Sium & Ritskes, 2013). Within Indigenous worldviews, spirituality has a central place in healing. In fact, I do not believe that healing can occur apart from spirituality. Within specific Indigenous cultures, traditional teachings, ceremonies, rituals, stones, water, pipes, herbs, sitting on the earth, fasting, prayer, dreams, visions, channelling, out-of-body experiences, touch, and food may be part of the journey to spiritual balance and well-being. In addition, those who are the helpers are said to be containers or channels for healing. Their abilities come from the spirits and live inside them through blood memory. The assistance that helpers or healers pass on to others is more spiritual than anything else. Thus, helping practices from Indigenous worldviews deeply involve spirituality and cannot be truly effective without it.

A significant area that I believe to be of great concern within helping processes is the connection, and confusion, between mental health and spirituality. I think that the line between a spiritual and a psychotic experience can be blurred. However, some practitioners may diagnose some spiritual experiences and practices as delusions or neurosis. In fact, what some people see as spiritual strength is often pathologized by practitioners. Often, service users learn that they cannot discuss their spiritual beliefs and experiences with practitioners for fear of being judged or pathologized as "crazy." This is a problematic situation for many Indigenous Peoples. For example, within Indigenous worldviews, a major focus of spirituality is the ability to communicate with the spirit world. There are many practices, such as fasting and ceremonies, that are designed to help us enhance this ability. To hear the voices of spirits is considered to be a strength. However, in the dominant society, the spiritual experiences of Indigenous Peoples may be constructed as schizophrenia by medical professionals who are supported by social workers (Baskin, 2007a, 2007b).

Another issue that concerns the connection between spirituality and mental health is depression. According to many Indigenous Elders and healers, the roots of depression are due to a lack of spirituality in the lives of people. Close to 30 years ago, a group of Indigenous helpers in northern Ontario explained this as an "abandonment of respect for a spiritual way of life in exchange for materialistic things which overwhelm people, preventing them from looking at themselves as they really are" (Timpson et al., 1988, p. 6). Abandoning spirituality involves losing conscious contact with the Creator and the spiritual parts of all life. The more this conscious contact is lost, the more our consciousness becomes numb. We lose our sense of where we come from and the direction in which we are going. However, I caution readers in how they interpret what the authors are saying, as words such as "abandonment" may come across to some that a lack of spirituality in the lives of Indigenous peoples is their sole responsibility, which can sound judgemental or blaming. We need to ensure that such explanations are placed in the context of the impacts of colonization, particularly the impacts of the residential school system and the imposition of Christianity on people, which forcefully did their best to eradicate Indigenous spirituality. In addition, I would argue that, due to material depravity, spiritual abuse, and countless forms of oppression, many Indigenous Peoples are suffering from spirit injuries that often manifest as depression. In all of these situations, however, depression is considered to be a spiritual illness and, therefore, spiritual practices must be a part of the healing process. Nevertheless, practitioners must also be open to the fact that, in some cases, chemical imbalances in the brain may be at the root of depression and other mental health challenges, which are exasperated by both individual and collective trauma.

Once again, I am reminded that many societies of the world, such as those in Africa and the Far East, incorporate spirituality within their helping and healing practices. In fact, like the Indigenous Peoples of Turtle Island, these societies do not separate spirituality from day-to-day living. A chapter in this book is dedicated to the topic of spirituality and this commonality will be explored.

CONCLUSION

This chapter briefly explored critical, structural, postmodern, and post-colonial social work theories as they relate to Indigenous approaches to helping. Viewed through an Indigenous lens, this exploration concludes that the first three theories have both strengths and challenges as they relate to Indigenous approaches. Post-colonial, or anti-colonial, theory fits best with Indigenous approaches as it originates with and is written by

Indigenous Peoples. I believe, however, that all of these theories, when applied to the area of social work, can operate alongside Indigenous approaches toward common goals. All of these theories can strengthen the work that social work students, educators, researchers, and practitioners do. Having allies helps everyone to create a more credible public position.

However, critical social work perspectives continue to be critiqued for their day-to-day usefulness and applicability to social work practice because they are thought to be too sociological in nature. Indigenous worldviews attempt to extend beyond critical theory to include processes of agency, resistance, and transformation, which are just as important to social work theory and practice as critical perspectives. Social work educators, students, and practitioners are encouraged to explore these processes within their own practices.

The chapter also critiqued the cultural competency model, concluding that it fails both service users as a helpful approach to practice and helpers as it sets practitioners up to do the impossible. The cultural competency model also allows helpers to ignore the role that their own identities and positionalities play in practice and obscures social justice concerns. This critique from an Indigenous lens can be considered by all educators, students, and practitioners in the helping professions in how they work with those who do not come from a similar social location.

Finally, some aspects of Indigenous worldviews were described as being the foundation for helping approaches. This book takes the position that Indigenous approaches to helping are theories that do not belong to any other theory. As theory is transferred into practice, the value of Indigenous approaches to helping practices will be demonstrated in the chapters that follow in this book.

REFERENCES

Aboriginal Nurses Association of Canada. (2009). *Cultural competence and cultural safety in First Nations, Inuit and Métis nursing education: An integrated review of the literature.* Retrieved from https://docs.google.com/file/d/0B9KOzMT_mKCmRFFiRzVDai12NkE/edit.

Absolon, K. (2009). Navigating the landscape of practice: Dbaagmowin of a helper. In R. Sinclair, M.A. Hart, & G. Bruyere (Eds.), *Wicihitowin: Aboriginal social work in Canada* (pp. 172–199). Winnipeg: Fernwood Publishing.

Anderson, J., Perry, J., Blue, C., & Browne, A. (2003). "Rewriting" cultural safety within the postcolonial and postnational feminist project: Toward new epistemologies of healing. *Advances in Nursing Science, 26*(3), 196–213.

Appiah, A.K. (1992). *In my father's house: Africa in the philosophy of culture.* London: Methuen.

Ashcroft, B. (2001). *Post-colonial transformation.* New York: Routledge.

Baker, A., & Giles, A. (2012). Cultural safety: A framework for interactions between Aboriginal patients and Canadian family medicine practitioners. *Journal of Aboriginal Health, 9*(1), 15–22.

Baskin, C. (2002). Circles of resistance: Spirituality in social work practice, education and transformative change. *Currents: New Scholarship in the Human Services, 1*(1). Retrieved from http://wcmprod2.ucalgary.ca/currents/.

Baskin, C. (2005). Centring Indigenous world views in social work education. *Australian Journal of Indigenous Education, 34,* 96–106.

Baskin, C. (2006). Indigenous world views as challenges and possibilities in social work education. *Critical Social Work, 7*(2). Retrieved from http://www.uwindsor.ca/criticalsocialwork/.

Baskin. C. (2007a). Conceptualizing, framing and politicizing Indigenous ethics in mental health. *Journal of Ethics in Mental Health, 2*(2), 1–5. Retrieved from http://www.jemh.ca.

Baskin, C. (2007b). Working together in the circle: Challenges and possibilities within mental health ethics. *Journal of Ethics in Mental Health, 2*(2), 1–4. Retrieved from http://www.jemh.ca.

Battiste, M., & Youngblood Henderson, J. (2000). *Protecting Indigenous knowledge and heritage: A global challenge.* Saskatoon: Purich Publishing.

Bhabha, H. (1994). *The location of culture.* London: Routledge.

Bishop, A. (2015). *Becoming an ally: Breaking the cycle of oppression* (3rd ed.). Halifax: Fernwood Publishing.

Blackstock, C., Cross, T., George, J., Brown, I., & Formsma, J. (2006). *Reconciliation in child welfare: Touchstones of hope for Indigenous children, youth, and families.* Ottawa: First Nations Child & Family Caring Society of Canada. Retrieved from http://www.reconciliationmovement.org.

Brascoupé, S., & Waters, C. (2009). Cultural safety: Exploring the applicability of the concept of cultural safety to Aboriginal health and community wellness. *Journal of Aboriginal Health, 5*(2), 6–41.

Browne, A.J., Varcoe, C., Smye, V., Reimer-Kirkham, S., Lynam, J.M., & Wong, S. (2009). Cultural safety and the challenges of translating critically oriented knowledge in practice. *Nursing Philosophy: An International Journal for Healthcare Professionals, 10*(3), 167–179.

Cajete, G. (1994). *Look to the mountain: An ecology of Indigenous education.* Durando, CO: Kivaki Press.

Couture, J. (1991). Explorations in Native knowing. In J.W. Friesen (Ed.), *The cultural maze: Complex questions on Native destiny in Western Canada* (pp. 201–215). Calgary: Detselig Enterprises.

Crooks, C.V., Chiodo, D., Thomas, D., & Hughes, R. (2009). Strengths-based programming for First Nations youth in school: Building engagement through healthy relationships and leadership skills. *International Journal of Mental Health and Addiction, 8*, 160–173.

Crooks, C.V., Chiodo, D., Thomas, D., & Hughes, R. (2011). Strength-based violence prevention programming for First Nations youth within a mainstream school setting. In D. Pepler, J. Cummings, & W. Craig (Eds.), *Creating a world without bullying* (pp. 43–62). Ottawa: National Printers.

CUPE. (2009). First anniversary of residential schools apology.

De, D., & Richardson, J. (2008). Cultural safety: An introduction. *Paediatric Nursing, 20*(2), 39–43.

Deloria Jr., V. (1969). *Custer died for your sins: An Indian manifesto.* New York: Avon Books.

Dyche, L., & Zayas, L.H. (1995). The value of curiosity and naiveté for the cross-cultural psychotherapist. *Family Process, 34*, 389–399. doi: 10.1111/j.1545-5300.1995.00389.x

Fanon, F. (1963). *The wretched of the earth.* New York: Grove Weidenfeld.

Fanon, F. (1967). *Black skin, white masks.* New York: Grove Press.

First Nations Drum. (2000). Crisis inspired many Native people. Retrieved from http://firstnationsdrum.com.

Fitznor, L. (1998). The circle of life: Affirming Indigenous philosophies in everyday living. In D. McCane (Ed.), *Life ethics in world religions* (pp. 21–40). Winnipeg: University of Manitoba.

Foucault, M. (1965). *Madness and civilization: A history of insanity in the age of reason.* New York: Vintage Press.

Foucault, M. (1980a). Two lectures. In C. Gordon (Ed.), *Power/knowledge: Selected interviews and other writings, 1972–1977* (pp. 78–108). New York: Pantheon.

Foucault, M. (1980b). *Language, counter memory, practice.* Ithaca, NY: Cornell University Press.

Foucault, M. (1985). *The history of sexuality. Vol 2. The uses of pleasure.* New York: Pantheon.

Fulcher, L. (2001). Cultural safety: Lessons from Maori wisdom. *Reclaiming Children and Youth, 10*(3), 153–157.

Gelfand, D., & Fandetti, D. (1986). The emergent nature of ethnicity: Dilemmas in assessment. *Social Casework, 67*, 542–550.

Gerlach, A.J. (2012). A critical reflection on the concept of cultural safety. *Canadian Journal of Occupational Therapy, 79*(3), 151–158.

Gerlach, A.J., Sullivan, T., Valavaara, K., & McNeil, C. (2014). Turning the gaze inward: Relational practices with Aboriginal peoples informed by cultural safety. *Occupational Therapy Now, 16*(1), 20–21.

Gross, G.D. (2000). Gatekeeping for cultural competence: Ready or not? Some post and modernist doubts. *Journal of Baccalaureate Social Work, 5*(2), 47–66.

Hampton, E. (1995). Memory comes before knowledge: Research may improve if researchers remember their motives. *Canadian Journal of Native Education, 21*(Suppl.), 46–54.

Hart, M.A. (2009). Anti-colonial Indigenous social work. In R. Sinclair, M.A. Hart, & G. Bruyere (Eds.), *Wicihitowin: Aboriginal social work in Canada* (pp. 25–41). Winnipeg: Fernwood Publishing.

Health Council of Canada (HCC). (2012, December). *Empathy, dignity, and respect: Creating cultural safety for Aboriginal people in urban health care.* Retrieved from http://www.healthcouncilcanada.ca/rpt_det.php?id=437.

Hines, P.M., Garcia-Preto, N., McGoldrick M., Almeida, R., & Weltman, S. (1999). Culture and the family life cycle. In B. Carter & M. McGolrick (Eds.), *The expanded family life cycle* (3rd ed., pp. 69–87). Boston: Allyn & Bacon.

Jeffery, D. (2005). "What good is anti-racist social work if you can't master it"?: Exploring a paradox in social work education. *Race, Ethnicity and Education, 8*, 409–425. doi: 10.1080/13613320500324011

Jeffery, D. (2009). Meeting here and now: Reflections on racial and cultural difference in social work encounters. In S. Strega & J. Carrière (Eds.), *Walking this path together: Anti-racist and anti-opppressive child welfare practice* (pp. 45–61). Black Point, NS: Fernwood Publications.

Kirmayer, L.J. (2012). Rethinking cultural competence. *Transcultural Psychiatry, 49*(2), 149–164.

Koptie, S. (2009). Irihapeti Ramsden: The public narrative on cultural safety. *First Peoples Child & Family Review, 4*(2), 30–43.

Little Bear, L. (2000). Jagged worldviews colliding. In M. Battiste (Ed.), *Reclaiming Indigenous voice and vision* (pp. 77–85). Vancouver: University of British Columbia Press.

Lundy, C. (2011). *Social work, social justice and human rights: A structural approach to practice* (2nd ed.). Toronto: University of Toronto Press.

Martell, B. (2013). Information sheet: Structural interventions in child welfare. Ottawa: First Nations Child and Family Caring Society of Canada. Retrieved from

http://www.fncaringsociety.com/sites/default/files/Information%20Sheet%20
_%20Structural%20Intervention%20in%20Child%20Welfare.pdf.

Miller, W., & Maiter, S. (2008). Fatherhood and culture: Moving beyond stereotypical understanding. *Journal of Ethnic and Cultural Diversity in Social Work*,
17, 279–300. doi: 10.1080/15313200802258216

Milliken, E.J. (2008). Toward cultural safety: An exploration of the concept for
social work education with Canadian Aboriginal peoples. (Doctoral dissertation).
Memorial University of Newfoundland.

Moosa-Mitha, M. (2005). Situating anti-oppressive theories within critical and
difference-centered perspectives. In L. Brown & S. Strega (Eds.), *Research
as resistance: Critical, Indigenous, and anti-oppressive approaches* (pp. 37–72).
Toronto: Canadian Scholars' Press Inc.

Mullaly, B. (2002). *Challenging oppression: A critical social work approach.* Don
Mills, ON: Oxford University Press.

National Aboriginal Health Organization (NAHO). (2006). Fact sheet: Cultural
safety. Retrieved from http://www.naho.ca/jah/english/jah05_02/V5_I2_
Cultural_01.pdf.

Nestel, S., & Razack, S. (n.d.). Wrestling with the "ghost of anthropology past":
Cultural competency approaches in medical education. Unpublished manuscript, 1–58.

Nguyen, H. (2008). Patient centered care: Cultural safety in indigenous health.
Australian Family Physician, 37(12), 990–994.

Ontario Federation of Indigenous Friendship Centres (OFIFC). (n.d.). Aboriginal
Cultural Competency Training (ACCT). Retrieved from http://www.ofifc.org/
aboriginal-cultural-competency-training-acct.

Papps, E., & Ramsden, I. (1996). Cultural safety in nursing: The New Zealand
experience. *International Journal for Quality in Health Care, 8*(5), 491–497.

Polaschek, N.R. (1998). Cultural safety: A new concept in nursing people of different ethnicities. *Journal of Advanced Nursing, 27*, 452–457.

Pon, G. (2009). Cultural competency as new racism: An ontology of
forgetting. *Journal of Progressive Human Services, 20*(1), 59–71. doi:
10.1080/10428230902871173

Razack, S. (1998). *Looking white people in the eye: Gender, race and culture in
courtrooms and classrooms.* Toronto: University of Toronto Press.

Reid, M. (2009). Kaxlaya Gvila: Upholding traditional Heiltsuk laws. In R.
Sinclair, M.A. Hart, & G. Bruyere (Eds.), *Wicihitowin: Aboriginal social work
in Canada.* Winnipeg: Fernwood Publishing.

Said, E. (1978). *Orientalism.* New York: Vintage Books.

Said, E. (1993). *Culture and imperialism*. London: Chatto & Windus.

Sakamoto, I. (2007). An anti-oppressive approach to cultural competence. *Canadian Social Work Review, 24*(1), 105–118.

Shah, C., & Reeves, A. (2012). Increasing Aboriginal cultural safety among health care practitioners. *Canadian Journal of Public Health, 103*(6), 397.

Shilling, R. (2002). Journey of our spirits: Challenges for adult Indigenous learners. In E.V. O'Sullivan, A. Morrell, & M.A. O'Connor (Eds.), *Expanding the boundaries of transformative learning: Essays on theory and practice* (pp. 151–158). Toronto: Palgrave.

Sium, A., & Ritskes, E. (2013). Speaking truth to power: Indigenous storytelling as an act of living resistance. *Decolonization, Indigenity, Education & Society, 2*(1), i–x.

Smye, V., Josewski, V., & Kendall, E. (2010, April 6). Cultural safety: An overview. Retrieved from http://www.mooddisorderscanada.ca/documents/Publications/CULTURAL%20SAFETY%20AN%20OVERVIEW%20(draft%20mar%202010).pdf.

Spivak, G. (1999). *A critique of postcolonial reason: Toward a history of the vanishing present*. Cambridge, MA: Harvard University Press.

Strega, S. (2005). The view from the poststructural margins: Epistemology and methodology reconsidered. In L. Brown & S. Strega (Eds.), *Research as resistance: Critical, Indigenous, and anti-oppressive approaches* (pp. 199–235). Toronto: Canadian Scholars' Press Inc.

Tamburro, A. (2013). Including decolonization in social work education and practice. *Journal of Indigenous Social Development, 2*(1). Retrieved from http://scholarspace.manoa.hawaii.edu/ handle/10125/29811.

Timpson, J., McKay, S., Kakegamic, S., Roundhead, D., Cohen, C., & Matewapit, G. (1988). Depression in a Native Canadian in northwestern Ontario: Sadness, grief or spiritual illness? *Canada's Mental Health*, June/September, 5–8.

Truth and Reconciliation Commission (TRC). (2015). *It's time for reconciliation*. Retrieved from http://www.trc.ca/websites/trcinstitution/index.php?p=3.

Waller, M., & Patterson, S. (2002). Natural helping and resilience in a Diné (Navajo) community. *Families in Society, 83*, 73–88. doi: 10.1606/1044-3894.46

Yee, J.Y., & Dumbrill, G. (2003). Whiteout: Looking for race in Canadian social work practice. In A. Al-Krenawi & J.R. Graham (Eds.), *Multicultural social work in Canada* (pp. 98–121). Don Mills, ON: Oxford University Press.

Chapter Five

CENTRING
ALL HELPING
APPROACHES

INTRODUCTION

During ongoing self-reflexivity, helping professionals create space for themselves to explore who they are and what they bring to their work. Through these opportunities, helpers can consider ideas of universalism, difference, essentialism, and knowledge, which will be discussed in this chapter. Through self-reflexivity, social workers and other helping professionals can also consider what might be the challenges to incorporating Indigenous knowledges into their work and explore possible solutions to such challenges.

BEING SECURE IN WHO YOU ARE

To be an effective helper, particularly with service users who are not members of one's specific population or subjectivity, each of us needs to understand *our own* values, beliefs, and cultures. It is culture that informs how we frame the helping professions, which are never neutral or objective. Rather, feelings, thoughts, and experiences all contribute to what we see as good practice.

Then there is the larger, dominant culture of the country in which one lives. It is this dominant culture that sets community standards of what is acceptable within the areas of social workers' practice, areas such as child welfare or what happens when a person commits a crime or when someone has an addiction. However, the views of the dominant culture are rarely discussed and analyzed, as they are widely seen as what is "normal" and "right" within that dominant culture.

In some of my courses, one of the assignments for students is to write about how they are influenced by their values, beliefs, cultures, and experiences and how this may impact on their practice with Indigenous Peoples. An initial response to this assignment from many White students is, "But I'm Canadian. I don't have a culture." I would guess that White students across countries such as the United States, Australia, and New Zealand would have similar initial responses to such an assignment. This response, however, is really a denial that the dominant culture is actually a culture, because it is so taken for granted and rarely "seen," even though it is all around us. Dominant White culture informs all of our institutions—education; media; law, government; the holidays that are officially recognized (Christmas, Easter, etc.); how we shop; how we are entertained; advertising; how our families, streets, and communities are designed; what is valued (youthful appearances, materialism, etc.); and who are considered to be the carriers of knowledge.

Becoming aware of one's own culture, which includes recognition of the values, beliefs, and practices inherent in this culture, comes about through critical self-reflexivity and questioning. This involves an ongoing process of looking inward and being open to learning more about the self and how we might practice our professions. This is an ongoing process that focuses on questions about how one sees their world, the wider society around them, and how these two do and do not connect. Based on this, we can ask questions such as the following:

- Why am I working with this specific population (e.g., street-involved youth of colour, Indigenous single mothers) in this particular place (e.g., agency, organization)?
- What do I have to offer (e.g., knowledge of appropriate resources, advocacy skills) to this population?
- Will I stand by these service users when the work becomes difficult?
- What are the areas of my work that challenge my values and beliefs and why?
- Am I committed to ongoing learning from service users and through self-reflection?
- What social policies and social work practices do I see as oppressive in the context of my work with this population, including within my place of employment, and how can I work toward changing these practices?

Knowing who you are in terms of your culture requires ongoing self-reflexivity that can help you as a social worker become more secure in your own identity. Security in knowing who you are and what your purpose is helps you resist appropriating cultures that are not your own. There is no need to search other cultural practices in order to fill up emptiness inside you. This sense of security also leads to a greater openness to many ways of knowing, rather than sticking to only one way or your way of knowing. Often, it is insecurity about who one is that leads one to view the "other" as being inferior.

Charlene Avalos, who was first introduced in Chapter Two, is a good example of a non-Indigenous social worker who successfully works with Indigenous Peoples. The following is some of Charlene's story about her early days working in the Bela Bela First Nation in B.C.:

My social work education did not prepare me for doing social work out in a community. However, my learning was balanced out when I moved to the First Nations community where I gained an understanding of the teachings there which led to my deep respect for the people. This was my first social work job—being the first band social worker in the community. The people saw me as "the welfare lady" who could take children away. The people were not much interested in my degree. They were more interested in who I was, what I could do for them and would I stay there. For a while, most people didn't like me. They asked what I was doing in their community; told me I didn't know anything about them or their lives; they were unfriendly, cold and they excluded me. I was pushed to the extreme where I was asking myself why I was there and what I was doing. (C. Avalos, personal communication, February 14, 2009)

Needless to say, these were exactly the kind of questions Charlene needed to ask herself. Once she began, she was able to uncover what the issues were:

I realized that when I first got to the community, I wanted to jump in and do the kind of social work I was taught to do through my education. This did not work! I suggest to all social workers that instead of doing this, you watch, observe, take your time, learn and receive when people want to teach you. When I started to do this, I arrived at a place of collaboration with the people of the community. I joined committees to help get people what they needed such as a day care. I gradually became a part of helping to build back the community after the destruction of the residential schools. (C. Avalos, personal communication, February 14, 2009)

Charlene's process of self-reflexivity assisted her in coming to some important insights into her work with Indigenous people:

I was insecure when I came to Bela Bela. As a non-Aboriginal social worker in an Aboriginal community, I carried guilt about what had been done to Aboriginal people in the past. I also had to learn about not taking things personally. One time I was at a party where some of the people were cutting down White people. I began to pull away, but when someone asked what was wrong, I told them. Everyone was surprised and saying, "We don't mean you." This taught me that when Aboriginal people talk about what White people have done, it's not directed at any individual one of us. (C. Avalos, personal communication, February 14, 2009)

This example refers to the concept of "Whiteness," which is succinctly explained by social work educator June Ying Yee (2015):

Around the Western world, power and privilege is given to those who hold a white racial identity. Even though the definition of white, as a racial identity, is socially constructed, past and present-day political, social, and economic arrangements reaffirm the power of the white race. It is no accident that many examples exist of the differential and negative treatment of those who are non-white and Aboriginal. This process of differential treatment is known as racialization. Behind all processes of racialization rests the ability of those who hold power through the white race to grant power or take away power from people. In the Western world, the white race has garnered power through acts of colonialism that are ultimately rooted in notions of superiority and used to justify the economic exploitation of those who are non-white. The legacy of colonialism inflicted upon Aboriginal peoples and people of color continues into present day institutional systems and structures without people being aware of it happening. The way it manifests is not always readily apparent or detectable. This is because the enactment of racism itself has been routinized, and naturalized through the strategies and processes of whiteness. (p. 570)

What is being critiqued here is not Charlene or any other individual White person, but rather discourses of power that maintain Whiteness in a privileged position. The Indigenous people in Charlene's story were referring to the colonizing power that is a part of Whiteness, but is not inherent within any individual who is a member of this race.

Most of us, both social workers and service users, carry multiple identities that carry a combination of power and oppression. For example, I am oppressed as an Indigenous woman who has little power in society. However, as a university professor with a Ph.D., I hold significant power in my classroom and my knowledge is sought after and valued (as evidenced by my writing this text!). A low-income, female White social service user may hold very little power. In some aspects of her identity, she may be oppressed. However, she also may exert power if she refuses the services of a Black, Muslim helper. A White, female social worker may carry power in her work with service users, but perhaps the power that she exerts may be reduced when the service users with whom she interacts are male. Further, the power that she exerts may be significantly reduced when she interacts with a male executive director of her agency.

Of course, awareness of one's privileges does not always lead to action. However, action is what is needed. The next section of this chapter takes up the action of privileging Indigenous worldviews and ways of helping so that they occupy a position of equality with respect to other ways of helping. Please read on, but be kind to yourself while doing so. A process of self-reflexivity also requires one to be kind to oneself.

SAMENESS OR ACCEPTANCE OF DIFFERENCE?

Centring all helping approaches involves creating space for all of us in the circle. It asks Western knowledge to move over so that Indigenous knowledges can occupy a place in the circle that is neither in front nor behind. Everyone's knowledge is not the same and everyone also has something of value to offer to the whole. People are not the same. We are all different. This stand, then, rejects universalism within the helping professions. This universalism is currently being challenged not only by Indigenous voices, but also by many marginalized peoples.

When we come to understand one another's worldviews, then we will be more likely to accept differences and begin to value them. Valuing differences means letting go of one's comfort zone and arrogance about the "right" way to help or practice our disciplines. Valuing differences asks us to listen to what others have to say, keep our minds open to new learning, and consider how we can be enriched by these teachings.

Challenging universalism involves questioning whether or not Western theories and practices are relevant within all contexts. It is unlikely that these practices can simply be dug up and transplanted within non-Western communities. Like plants, if they are not indigenous to their environment, they may not survive. This challenge involves "authentication," which means in this case "to become genuine" or "to go back to one's roots to seek direction" (Gray, Coates, & Hetherington, 2007, p. 61). This is precisely what I am advocating for *all* peoples. It is important that we all look toward the values and beliefs of *all* of our worldviews in order to guide us in shaping our practice. In doing so, we will come to realize that many people around the world do not support Western concepts such as individualism, professionalism, and objectivity. In fact, I have met many non-Indigenous peoples from India to Australia to Canada working in the helping professions who do not base their practice on these concepts.

Gray, Coates, and Hetherington (2007) write about Indigenous perspectives on helping, which they believe can enrich social work practice regardless of who the service users are. Some of these aspects are:

- Everyone has a common humanity
- There are many ways of knowing and all are significant
- Helping inherently carries humanistic goals
- Context needs to always be kept in mind
- Connecting with service users and ensuring that our practices are meaningful to them
- Self-fulfillment can only be truly realized when there is group/community fulfillment

Our differences may be large or small, but do not have to be based on binaries. I encourage readers to have deep discussions about these seven points and keep them in mind when reading the rest of this book.

Undoubtedly, there is an interest in Indigenous worldviews as sites of assistance in several areas of concern to the West. A literature review in this area revealed a number of examples of the importance of Indigenous worldviews within diverse professions, places, and publications. Here are some examples:

- Documentation of the positive impacts of culturally based programming rooted in Indigenous worldviews for survivors of Indian Residential Schools in *Australasian Psychiatry* (DeGagne, 2007)
- The work of the Aboriginal Healing Foundation in the *Canadian Public Administration Journal* not only in the area of culturally based practices, but also in the field of administration where its high standards were emphasized (DeGagne, 2008)
- Increased concern for the environment has resulted in more openness to worldviews other than those of the dominant society, including an openness to Indigenous ways of healing (Coates, Gray, & Hetherington, 2006)
- A holistic approach is becoming more valued in health-care education (Hunter, Logan, Goulet, & Barton, 2006)
- Indigenous and non-Indigenous helping approaches have been combined and used in healing work. For example, the Wellbriety Movement blends the teachings of the Medicine Wheel with the 12-step Alcoholics Anonymous program (Coyhis & Simonelli, 2005)
- The Canadian International Development Agency (CIDA)'s policy document on Indigenous knowledge and sustainable development (2002) states that "some see Indigenous knowledge as a last hope in implementation of a sustainable future" (p. 3)

According to Schaefer (2006), Indigenous worldviews can guide humanity. More than 25 years ago, research was conducted with Russell Willier, a Cree Medicine Man from Sucker Creek First Nation in northern Alberta. Swartz (1987) documented Willier's treatment of non-Indigenous participants suffering from psoriasis. Willier permitted researchers to conduct an intrusive investigation, including a chemical analysis of the plants used in his treatments and both photographs and videotaping of participants' skin conditions before and after treatments (Swartz, 1987). This example is evidence of an Indigenous value of knowledge sharing. According to Willier, the earth offers many medicines for human beings including plants, animals, water, and soil. At the same time, the earth is also suffering. Some argue that pollutants, the destruction of ecosystems, and the genocide of some animal species has resulted in a state of chronic sickness for human beings (Swartz, 1987).

Within social work specifically, Gray and colleagues (2007) take a similar position to the writers above, stating that "Indigenous beliefs and values have gained recognition and credibility among the worldviews that provide a re-conceptualization of the universe and humanity's relationship to it. In social work this has opened avenues of acceptance toward Indigenous approaches to helping" (p. 60). I believe that the social work profession is not only ready to listen to Indigenous worldviews, but is actually taking the lead within the helping professions to create a space for these worldviews. Indigenous worldviews are acknowledged by a rising number of Indigenous and non-Indigenous people, both students and educators within social work education. There is also a growing amount of literature by Indigenous writers that has been included within peer-reviewed journals, and Indigenous content is included within the curriculum of a number of college- and university-level social work programs. In fact, in 2014, the Canadian Association for Social Work Education added to their *Principles Guiding Accreditation of Social Work Education Programs*, "Social work programs acknowledge and challenge the injustices of Canada's colonial history and continuing colonization efforts as they relate to the role of social work education in Canada and the self-determination of the Indigenous peoples" (p. 3). The number of Indigenous social work practitioners both within Indigenous and other social services agencies has also increased. It may be said that we are beginning to Indigenize the profession of social work in numerous pockets throughout the West!

CHALLENGES TO INCORPORATING INDIGENOUS APPROACHES

First, let me tell you about one of the challenges I am having right now while writing this book. No, it's not the one I have already mentioned about walking the fine line between worldviews and cultures. This one is about writing about Indigenous approaches on topics of helping as though they are separate from one another. Indigenous approaches in helping areas cannot be separate, which is the whole point!

Within Indigenous worldviews, everything is connected. Therefore, it is difficult to write chapters about chosen topics such as values and ethics, caring for families and children, and research without saying something from other chapters about areas that include holistic approaches and spirituality. Should I include a disclaimer here?

Spirituality, holistic approaches, and values and ethics are all part of the knowledge that is taught, learned, and practised within Indigenous helping approaches. They are woven into our helping practices and so will show up in every chapter of this book. Therefore, I may repeat myself many times, causing readers to exclaim, perhaps in frustration, "She already said that!"

I fear I have no choice but to refer to these foundational aspects of Indigenous worldviews repeatedly and hope that I do not bore you. I will do my best to not repeat exactly the same words, but to instead explain in a variety of ways how these aspects apply to each particular chapter.

Wendy Martin is a non-Indigenous ally with an MSW who has taken social work courses with Indigenous professors on the history of colonization and on Indigenous worldviews in both her undergraduate and graduate education. She works in areas such as youth in conflict with the law and community mental health. She is also one of my dearest friends. When I asked Wendy what her greatest challenge was in terms of her work regarding Indigenous Peoples, she responded:

> Educating colleagues! I do a lot of this, especially when I talk about the impacts of colonization for example. I'm often tuned out, negated, ignored; others don't want to hear at times, they get angry, shut me down. Then I get hurt. It gets so that I feel I'm doing more of a disservice to Aboriginal people if I'm not listened to. I don't want to ever invalidate Aboriginal people's pain, but being an ally can give one a bit of an idea of what it's like to be shut out and pushed away all the time which is what Aboriginal peoples experience daily. I can get apathetic at times: there are times when I just can't muster up the strength to address colleagues' ignorant statements, so I'm now learning how to choose my battles and be strategic. It seems that successful strategies are often about timing. Sometimes I use my intuition or ask myself "Will I be helping with Aboriginal causes by saying something right now or will I actually be alienating non-Aboriginal people from them?" (W. Martin, personal communication, February 8, 2009)

Doing the "right thing" is not always doing the easiest thing, which is clearly what Wendy is experiencing. No doubt non-Indigenous practitioners everywhere face similar practice challenges. However, White people standing beside Indigenous Peoples by educating other White people is exactly the work that is required of a true ally—especially when the work gets tough. As Indigenous people, it is not our responsibility to do all the educating. However, our allies need to be kind to themselves, take care of themselves, and receive support, so that they too can continue their important work of helping to educate others. Wendy spoke to me about how she does this:

> I have a support group, which I believe is essential to doing the work of an ally. I have a circle of Aboriginal friends who are also in the helping professions who support me and who I support. I also have non-Aboriginal people in my life who think similarly to me. These supports are vital to the work of an ally. When I need some guidance about a particular situation, my Aboriginal friends and colleagues are there to help me in the moment. We support each other which helps prevent burnout and compassionate fatigue. Being an ally in an agency or working in an institution often means you are alone in the work you are trying to do. Sometimes when you are on your own, you just feel like giving up, but when I connect with Aboriginal helpers, I get energized again! (W. Martin, personal communication, February 8, 2009)

The students from a course that I teach, Indigenous Knowledges in Social Work, participated in a sharing circle for this book, as mentioned in an earlier chapter. One area I asked them to talk about was what they saw as challenges to incorporating Indigenous approaches within social work, which I believe students in many other parts of the world will relate to. The following is their discussion on some of the challenges they identified and suggestions on how to address them.

> *Eddy:* I see it as a struggle to figure out where to fit within Indigenous social work. This is my second Indigenous knowledges in social work course in the School of Social Work at Ryerson and I believe that continuous learning is crucial. I never want to feel like I know enough, that I can stop learning.

Flo: I agree with Eddy that as non-Indigenous social workers we need to continue to learn in the future. We need to be diligent about de-constructing and really take a good look at things like I had to do regarding the song *Onward Christian Soldiers*. Let me remind you about that learning for me.

I was raised in a Christian family and grew up in church singing the song *Onward Christian Soldiers* on occasion. I never considered its meaning. The song is a popular one and is sung in church, so I never thought of questioning it. Why should I? After all, all hymns have a good meaning or so I thought. But then, I read an article about this hymn for the presentation I was doing for our course and found out about the origins of the song. This had quite an emotional impact on me, but the experience taught me to see how important it is for all of us to continuously aim to gain new knowledge which brings awareness. I think if we are not aware then we can easily be manipulated by, or influenced about, what is taught to us. It became important then for me to take some sort of action by talking to others who attend my church to see what we could do about not having it sung there.

But it turned out that there was another layer to my experience that Cyndy taught me which led me to understand that it is not this hymn or any other hymn that I have a relationship with since, after all, they have been manmade, but my relationship is with God.

Meliza: My greatest challenge is when do we as non-Indigenous social workers pass on information that we have learned about Indigenous worldviews? When do we as non-Indigenous social workers call people on their inaccurate information or racist comments about Indigenous peoples? Those we challenge may respond with "who made you the expert?" or "what makes you think you can speak on this?"

Carolina: We need to listen to our inner voices when they tell us to speak up and resist. We need to listen to our own ancestral voices inside us. Indigenous ways speak to those of us who are searching for better ways, so we need to do this.

Karen: I agree. Intuition is our cue as to when to speak up or not. And we can speak up without having to know it all.

Lorraine: Our work can be to engage people who don't care by showing them they need to care because we are all connected. The work of non-Indigenous people is to dedicate ourselves to creating equitable partnerships with Indigenous people and deal with whatever arises in a productive way. An example is appropriation—to challenge ourselves about it and to initiate conversations, rather than simply rejecting what people do or walking away all the time.

It's easy to be critical, but not so easy to form partnerships. This is what I started to understand in this course in the middle of a critically focused, anti-oppressive curriculum. It is a quick decision to reject or dismiss something that is not working or will not work or should not work. I think this is about expecting perfect plans and rejecting messy processes, but we don't know if something will work at first glance. There isn't enough time to make this judgement, so it often seems easier to just reject something at the first sign that it does not fit with what one knows. I think the message for us non-Indigenous people is you made this mess, so you stay and be a part of cleaning it up; you stay and work at relationships and partnerships. (Eddy, Flo, Meliza, Carolina, Karen, & Lorraine, personal communication, April 6, 2009)

A strong and gifted Two-Spirited Anishnawbe Kwe (woman) from Couchching First Nation also contributed her thoughts on what are the most challenging aspects of bringing Indigenous helping approaches into social work. Charlene Catchpole, Bear Clan, lives in Toronto and is currently the Executive Director of North York Women's Shelter. When I raised this topic with her, she immediately took up the issue of appropriation:

This is an ongoing struggle and it happens in many ways. I feel that I am being appropriated when I'm asked to do a smudge at an event and nothing else as though this is my only possible contribution.

Also, because of appropriation, I don't identify my specific Aboriginal teachings as I believe they will be appropriated by others. My preference is to go with what is generic, what is common for many Indigenous peoples globally which represents the women and children in the shelter. This way, many women can share their beliefs, which is empowering for them, as they feel respected and welcomed. I encourage and support women to bring their worldviews into the shelter through, for example, their ways of cleansing the building and feasting, so that there is a collective response rather than only a focus on my beliefs.

I do wonder from time to time whether I am honouring my teachings by not sharing specific ones or if I'm protecting them. I tend to go with my intuition when it comes to sharing and know that is the right way to do things. I believe being two spirit helps me with all of this because I have male energy which is my gut reaction which helps me to protect what I feel needs to be protected and I have female energy which helps me to decide what to share and what not to. I have a balance of these two. (C. Catchpole, personal communication, March 20, 2009)

Charlene went on to speak about a few other significant challenges that she often encounters, which may sound familiar to Indigenous service providers in many other countries: lack of acknowledgement for Indigenous knowledges and people's motivation for wanting to learn about them. She suggests,

Recognize, first and foremost, that you are on our land. Work with an understanding that Aboriginal peoples need to have credit for their knowledges as these teachings have survived because of the diligence of Aboriginal peoples.

Our knowledges can help many communities of social workers and non-Aboriginal helpers can work with Aboriginal people, but these can only happen if they acknowledge

our approaches. If society would do more honouring of Aboriginal worldviews, then perhaps Aboriginal people would
be more likely to share more of their teachings.

When students want to learn about Aboriginal worldviews and teachings, I ask them why. If a non-Aboriginal
person wants to learn about our ways of helping, they need
to be sincere and express evidence of this. They need to be
aware that they cannot learn Aboriginal ways of helping in
a few sittings, rather this learning is forever. Plus, one needs
to learn as a whole being —not only from school—because
Aboriginal teachings cannot be taught in a classroom.
Learn from life and those you seek to assist. (C. Catchpole,
personal communication, March 20, 2009)

Despite the support from some for the inclusion of Indigenous worldviews
within social work education, there also remain challenges to such inclusion. Non-Indigenous social work educator Gary Dumbrill and Jacquie
Green (2008), who is of the Haisla Nation and is also a social work educator, propose that before there can be inclusion of Indigenous knowledges
in the academy, there needs to be a willingness to disrupt the continued
dominance of Western knowledges. I agree that this is a case where the
knowledges and practices of non-Western peoples remain relegated to a
secondary status in social work curricula. However, I also believe that the
disruption has begun, which is highlighted throughout this book.

One area in the academy that receives little attention involves how
students are evaluated. Charlene Avalos, in addition to her work as a practitioner, also teaches part-time in the School of Social Work at Ryerson.
She notes,

Each time we develop a course, there's always the chance
of reinforcing assimilation because certain standards of
evaluation are set by educational institutions that everyone must adhere to. This is just as true for courses on
Aboriginal approaches in social work as with any other
courses. For example, perhaps someone doesn't do so well
at writing a 10 page essay on healing work with children,
but the same person may be *doing* amazing healing work
with children. How can a student's inherent strengths be

built upon rather than them being tested according to certain standards and why must testing be exactly the same for all students? (C. Avalos, personal communication, February 14, 2009)

CONCLUSION

The voices in this chapter have all shared how they work at centring Indigenous worldviews alongside other knowledges in social work education and practice. These practitioners, students, and educators all noted the value of Indigenous knowledges not only in the work they do, but also in their own personal development. Centring knowledges that have been marginalized for centuries is challenging, but, according to those who were interviewed for this book, definitely worth doing. The interviewees offered valuable suggestions on how to overcome these challenges, respectfully learn about Indigenous worldviews, and work as allies with Indigenous Peoples, which is one of the fundamental teachings of this book and will be taken up at greater length in a later chapter. I also encourage readers to come up with their own suggestions to centring all helping approaches and share these with others.

REFERENCES

Canadian Association for Social Work Education. (2014). Standards for accreditation. Retrieved from http://caswe-acfts.ca/wp-content/uploads/2013/03/CASWE-ACFTS-Standards-11-2014.pdf.

Canadian International Development Agency (CIDA). (2002). *The human development draft—CIDA policy on Indigenous knowledge and sustainable human development*. Ottawa: Author.

Coates, J., Gray, M., & Hetherington, T. (2006). An "ecospiritual" perspective: Finally, a place for Indigenous social work. *British Journal of Social Work, 36*, 381–399. doi: 10.1093/bjsw/bcl005

Coyhis, D., & Simonelli, R. (2008). The Native American healing experience. *Substance Use & Misuse, 43*, 1927–1949. doi: 10.1080/10826080802292584

DeGagne, M. (2007). Toward an Aboriginal paradigm of healing: Addressing the legacy of residential schools. *Australasian Psychiatry, 15*(1), 49–53. doi: 10.1080/10398560701701114

DeGagne, M. (2008). Administration in a national Aboriginal organization: Impacts of cultural adaptation. *Canadian Public Administration, 51*(4), 659–672. doi: 10.1111/j.1754-7121.2008.00046.x

Dumbrill, G., & Green, J. (2008). Indigenous knowledge in the social work academy. *Social Work Education, 27,* 489–503. doi: 10.1080/02615470701379891

Gray, M., Coates, J., & Hetherington, T. (2007). Hearing Indigenous voices in mainstream social work. *Families in Society, 88*(1), 55–66. doi: 10.1606/1044-3894.3592

Hunter, L.M., Logan J., Goulet J., & Barton, S. (2006). Aboriginal healing: Regaining balance and culture. *Journal of Transcultural Nursing, 17*(1), 13–22. doi: 10.1177/1043659605278937

Schaefer, C. (2006). *Grandmothers counsel the world: Women Elders offer their vision for our planet.* Boston: Trumpeter Books.

Swartz, L. (1987). *A Cree healer in role transition.* Unpublished Master's thesis, University of Alberta, Calgary.

Yee, J.Y. (2015). Whiteness and white supremacy. *International Encyclopedia of the Social & Behavioral Sciences 25* (2nd ed.). doi: 10.1016/B978-0-08-097086-8.28099-9

Chapter Six

FROM AN ETHICAL PLACE

INTRODUCTION

It is not possible for this chapter to take up *all* possible Indigenous values. Rather, it will centre on the values that most guide processes of helping and relate to the topics of this book. Once again, because within Indigenous worldviews everything is interwoven into the whole, values and ethics are not seen as separate from anything else. Thus, I will not attempt to separate values from ethics by defining them as might be done in more conventional writing. Values and ethics are vital to people's worldviews. Our behaviours are based on our values and ethics. Values and ethics also hold very little relevance if they are not brought into action.

FRAMEWORK FOR WRITING ABOUT VALUES AND ETHICS

I want to begin with a piece written by Kovach, Thomas, Montgomery, Green, and Brown (2007), who eloquently express how important Indigenous values are in the work of helping. Although they are referring specifically to the area of child welfare, these values apply to all areas of helping work:

> It is our values that matter most in protecting children. To reiterate an important message by Debbie Foxcroft, the process is not just about having control of the resources, but also about including Aboriginal values. Our chapter has been a compilation of voices presenting this same theme in different words, contexts and stories. Throughout British Columbia—and Canada—[there are a] myriad of Aboriginal voices on protecting and keeping Aboriginal children safe.... There is no one story, no one standard account, no singular perspective, nor one all-encompassing model for Aboriginal child welfare—but there is a commonality of vision about values.... This is akin to the creation-story about the earth resting on the turtle's back. In his book *The Truth About Stories*, Thomas King tells the story of a little girl who, on hearing this story, asks the storyteller a question: "if the earth rests on the turtle, then what is below the turtle?" The storyteller tells the little girl, that all he can say for sure is "it's turtles all

the way down" (King, 2003, p. 1). It is much the same with Aboriginal child welfare—for Aboriginal people and their allies it's Aboriginal values all the way down. (Kovach, Thomas, Montgomery, Green, & Brown, 2007, p. 116)

Although I risk being accused of making generalizations, I do believe that there are vast differences between Indigenous values and ethics and Western values and ethics. It is important to state that I am not referring to the values and ethics of individual people, as I am well aware that many White people are disillusioned with Western values such as individualism and materialism. Certainly, the White people who participated in the interviews for this book and those I surround myself with as friends do not support such values. However, there is no doubt that the colonization of Indigenous Peoples globally by the West was, and continues to be, based on particular values that persist to this day in all institutions that direct our lives. These values are embedded within our government, our economy, our education, and our justice systems, and in every other system in this country, and have their roots in racist, sexist, classist, and heterosexist values.

In my social work classes on Indigenous worldviews within social work theories, research, and practice, I sometimes introduce a values comparison chart to students for discussion. I then ask them to do an exercise for themselves, which is not graded or shared (unless they wish to share it). The only direction I give them is to be honest with themselves. I ask that they pull out the values from the chart that they believe are a part of their worldviews and come up with concrete behaviours that express those values. I invite you, readers, to do the same now.

When students are able to share the results of this exercise, they are often surprised to find out that they are moving toward rejecting some of these Western values. Students also express an intuitive sense that things are not well in a world that has been largely run based on Western values, and that Indigenous perspectives and values need to be considered and offer something different. Students are also able to understand how Indigenous values and ethics are very much aligned with anti-oppression social work theory and practice, and with social justice values.

Indigenous	Western
Permissive	Coercive
Extended family	Nuclear family
Interdependence	Independence
Cooperation	Competition
Non-materialistic	Materialistic
Non-aggressive	Aggressive
Humility	Confidence
Non-interference	Interference
Respect for Elders	Respect for youthful appearances
Children are gifts	Children are owned
Communal living	Isolation
Silence	Noise
Emphasis on group/clan	Emphasis on individual
Time based on nature	Time based on clock
Emphasis on giving	Emphasis on acquiring
Patience	Action
Harmony with nature	Control of nature

David Hodge, a non-Indigenous scholar who writes on the importance of including spiritual perspectives in mainstream discourse, and Gordon Limb, a scholar who is affiliated with the Ho-Chunk (Winnebago) Nation, have written, both together and separately, on spirituality. According to Limb and Hodge (2008), common values for Indigenous Peoples are community (taking care of one another); viewing time as relative; respect for age (Elders); cooperation; patience; listening; generosity and sharing; living in harmony; giving indirect criticism; humility; spiritual existence, intuition; and the interconnectedness of the mind, body, and spirit. In the Mi'kmaq worldview, all things, all animate and inanimate beings, have spirit, so people are obligated to respect and honour everything around them. Understanding of the relationships with the environment is demonstrated in songs, stories, dances, art, and practices. Such respect requires people to develop a special consciousness that discourages careless treatment of everything. Thus, for example, a person gathering plants for medicinal purposes honours the spirit of the plant by placing an offering of tobacco before picking it.

Western values, as stated by these authors, are individualism (taking care of oneself); timeliness; an emphasis on looking young; competitiveness; aggressiveness; speaking up and being heard; materialism; conquest over nature; giving direct criticism; self-attention (egocentric); religion; logic; and the separation of the mind, body, and spirit.

Let me explain how I interpret some of these comparisons based on the teachings of several Elders and Traditional Teachers of many Nations from around the world who have shared their wisdom with me, plus my own observations and experiences. When it comes to teaching the concept of non-interference according to Mi'kmaq ways, the practice is to allow people to learn through their own experiences. By Elders giving advice or telling stories that are similar to the person's problem or situation, they listen, watch, and think about everything they hear. They then must come to realizations themselves whereby they make up their own minds, without being told what to do. This way of teaching is similar to the concept of experiential learning.

Another example is how the value of permissiveness can be applied to the raising of children. Within Indigenous worldviews, children tend to learn from observing what parents and older siblings do. Adults serve as role models for children showing them, rather than telling them, how to behave. Children are taught in non-directive ways through, for example, the telling of stories that contain moral teachings. They are allowed some freedom to make choices for themselves, with natural consequences, both positive and negative. A coercive way of raising and teaching children is based on a rewards and punishment framework. If a child does what is required of them by their parents, they might receive a weekly allowance and be allowed certain privileges. If they do not do what is required of them, privileges will likely be taken away. In the area of formal teaching, children live with threats from teachers all the time. If children do not conform to particular norms, they may face exclusion that could include being required to leave the classroom or being expelled from the school. In Canada, children are evaluated according to standardized testing, which sets out exactly what is expected. If children do not learn what is expected, then they "fail."

Jennifer Ajandi, who was previously introduced, shared with me how some of the teachings on Indigenous ways of raising children influenced her in her parenting:

I appreciate the information I have received on raising children within Aboriginal worldviews: an understanding that there are many ways of parenting, that it does not have to be so directive and authoritarian as in mainstream practices. It allows for a child to think through challenges, learn from experiences and understand that there are natural consequences to one's behaviour. I have an example of this with my own daughter who is three and a half years old which was truly a learning moment for me. When she asked to bring something to school that could break, instead of answering "no, go find something else" which is what I usually do when we're rushing in the morning, I discussed with her what I thought might happen if she chose to bring this snow globe with her to school—that it was not a toy in the same way her other stuff was, it could break, that maybe she could bring it but put it in her locker. She stood for a moment and thought about it and then said, "I will go put it back and get something else instead." That moment made me realize how we had just had a discussion about her options and that I provided the space for her to make her own decision and feel confident with it. This was an approach I had learned in class with you Cyndy about Aboriginal ways of parenting which are more non-directive and come about through discussion or storytelling. (J. Ajandi, personal communication, January 10, 2009)

Further, Indigenous worldviews emphasize that children are gifts from the Creator. Indigenous worldviews emphasize that children do not belong to us. We may borrow them for a while and we have responsibility for them. In addition, biological parents are not the only ones who are expected to raise children. Rather, extended families and entire communities share a responsibility for the raising of children. Children are seen as precious because it is believed that they come directly from the spirit world. Today, within Western worldviews, children are not so much owned any longer as in parents doing whatever they wish with them, but there is still this notion of "my" children. This notion of "my" children implies a value, that the parent is the sole one responsible for the raising of a child. Whatever that child does or does not do, the parent is responsible. It is possible to hear stressed-out single mothers saying, "Don't tell me how to raise my child!"

There are many societies that view the raising of children in similar ways to Indigenous people. According to Flo, one of the students in the class that participated in the sharing circle,

> There are many similarities between Aboriginal world-views and those of the peoples of the Caribbean. In both of these worldviews, the community raises children. Why can't everyone practice this so that everyone is looking out for each other and taking care of children? (Flo, personal communication, April 6, 2009)

Non-interference is an Indigenous value that Liz Arger referred to in one of my earlier chapters. This value is about not getting in the way of another person's journey or process, or preventing someone from doing something simply because we do not agree with it. It means not giving advice, not being directive, and not participating in another person's process unless invited to do so. In the West, however, most helping professions do not adopt these kinds of values. There is a great deal of interference. People who require assistance are told what services to access with very little consultation. People are told how to take care of themselves, how to raise their children, and how to manage their relationships. There is also a considerable amount of entertainment on national television that focuses on people's misery and how people ought to be dealing with it.

Another significant value within Indigenous worldviews is the conception of time or timeliness. There is a saying, "Indian time," that is used by many Indigenous Peoples throughout Turtle Island. Some believe this saying means that we are always late, but this is false. There is no "late" and there is no "early." Rather, it means that things will be done when they are meant to be or when they are supposed to be.

In traditional societies, time was gauged by nature and the movement of the sun, moon, and stars. For example, the moon was used to measure time; for instance, it will be many moons (months made up of 28 days each) before we see each other again (Giago, 2009; Gibson, 2011; M. Switzer, personal communication, April 1, 2015). I particularly like Kelly Gibson's (2011), a non-Indigenous contributor to the National Relief Charities Blog, explanation of this concept because of the humour he includes at the end of it:

Traditionally Indian people were very good students of nature. They studied the seasons and the animals to learn how to live well in their environments. Given this, they learned that it's important to be patient and to act when circumstances were "ripe" rather than to try and force things to happen when circumstances did not support them. I have come to understand it's a Western idea that we can control most circumstances. The control we think we have over circumstances is frequently an illusion and can lead to a lot of wasted energy. Much can be gained by watching, listening, waiting and then acting when the time is right. "Indian time" is really about respecting the "timeliness" of an action. It makes more sense to plant crops when the weather is right than when the calendar says it is time. What a mistake it would be to take this traditional concept of timeliness and develop a misperception that contemporary Indian people are frequently late. I am one of the few non-Indian people working in my office, and if someone is running late for a meeting, it's usually me.

FROM AN ETHICAL PLACE

A review of the literature reveals that very little has been published on the subject of Indigenous ethics in the area of social work. This may be, in part, because Indigenous ethics are rooted in the context of oral history and storytelling. Indigenous ethics are framed within a process rather than as a specific code. Ethical decisions are always related to context and involve collaboration with community members and families.

In defining ethics generally from an Indigenous worldview, Brant-Castellano (2004) states,

> Ethics, the rules of right behaviour, are intimately related to who you are, the deep values you subscribe to, and your understanding of your place in the spiritual order of reality. Ethics is integral to the way of life of a people. The fullest expression of a people's ethics is presented in the lives of the most knowledgeable and honourable members of the community. Imposition of rules derived from other

ways of life in other communities will inevitably cause problems, although common understandings and shared interests can be negotiated. (p. 103)

Indigenous worldviews inherently include an epistemology that has ethical and moral dimensions. For example, when a person enters into a relationship with particular knowledge, that person is not only honoured and changed by it, but must also take responsibility for it as well. A relational perspective teaches individuals to take social responsibility for living an ethical and moral life in the present, to honour the past through the spiritual care of those who have passed on, and to always keep the future in mind by taking care of the earth for the next seven generations to come as stated in the Great Law of the Haudenosaunee (A. Jock, personal communication, May 1986). Living an ethical life is particularly important for Elders, healers, and other service providers as they are known and respected within both rural and urban communities. Their efficacy and moral behaviour must be open to scrutiny. Being a healer or helper involves issues of power and there needs to be open and ongoing critical examination of these issues by everyone involved, including those accessing services, community members, and the helper themself.

Another issue that needs to be considered in our work is the idea of objectivity. I do not think objectivity, as defined in conventional usage, exists. We bring who we are and what we believe—our values and ethics—into everything we do. Everything, from an assessment of a family living in poverty or the approach that we might take when working with a child who has been sexually abused, is affected by our values and ethics. The decisions we make are neither neutral nor objective. Rather, they are based on our values and ethics and on the ways that we express our values and ethics through our actions. It is important to ask questions about what kind of lens we are using, where our particular values come from, and what these values really mean. The helping professions are not neutral or objective and neither are the people who do this kind of work.

I would argue that what is needed is respect, rather than holding on to a notion that objectivity exists. At its roots, the meaning of respect involves "looking twice" at something, which allows for an open mind (M. Thrasher, personal communication, October 1991). It means moving beyond one's own initial reactions or assessment and looking at a situation again in a closer, deeper way, taking as many dimensions into account as possible.

MOVING AWAY FROM INDIVIDUALISM

One of the most fascinating activities I am currently engaged in is learning about different ways of knowing. I am interested in the diverse and connected worldviews of the peoples of the world. And I am particularly struck by the common values that many of us coming from non-Western societies share. For example, I meditate, which is a common spiritual practice for many people around the globe. I meditate when I go fasting, but I also meditate almost every day for anywhere between one hour to five minutes in a sitting. I meditate because it's good for me. It helps me as an individual to focus, relax, and stay in the moment. If I don't meditate, I don't feel grounded and balanced. I believe meditation is one way of knowing myself and my relationship to the world I live in.

However, like prayer and my participation in the spiritual ceremonies of my Mi'kmaq Nation or those of the Anishnawbe whose territory I live in, I also mediate because it helps the planet. I do it because I believe that it helps all people who are ill or who are in difficult situations. For me, meditation is a move away from individualism and toward caring for the collective, all people, and for the planet that we all share.

Pema Chodron is a Buddhist nun whose teachings I relate to because they connect closely with those of my Indigenous worldview. In one of her books, *When Things Fall Apart: Heart Advice for Difficult Times*, Chodron (1997) writes about a breathing practice called *tonglen*, which involves breathing in the pain of others and breathing out relief to all those who are feeling pain. She provides a touching example of this practice:

> For instance, if we know of a child who is being hurt, we breathe in with the wish to take away all of that child's pain and fear. Then as we breathe out, we send happiness, joy, or whatever would relieve the child. This is the core of the practice: breathing in others' pain so they can be well and have more space to relax and open—breathing out, sending them relaxation or whatever we feel would bring them relief and happiness. (p. 94)

Such teachings that emphasize connectedness and the well-being of all who make up the collective, rather than the well-being of the self or those who are part of one's inner circle, such as family and friends, have existed since the beginning of time in many non-Western societies.

Within the helping professions, individualism is often manifested in the ways that we choose to work with people. Perhaps we might individualize a person's difficulties. We might choose to work with that individual on a one-on-one basis, but avoid actively engaging in community outreach and practice. We might have rigid guidelines about confidentiality. It also might be that by focusing on one person or one family we are reinforcing a condition of isolation, which is also often a large part of the problems that people are dealing with. By focusing on individual concerns, are we putting the larger community at risk? By seeing the world in a more narrow way, are we hurting ourselves and others? By not bringing the collective together, are we missing out on many helpful possibilities, suggestions, and opportunities that might help us to assist one another?

Helpers are also impacted. Are we not imposing an impossible amount of work on the role of individual helpers? Because social workers often work in isolation, how many of these workers see themselves as part of a larger collective or part of movement toward social justice? By working with one individual or one family at a time, how many see themselves as contributing to significant social justice initiatives? How many see themselves as caring for all peoples and the earth we share?

Such questions can be explored in large part from a values and ethics perspective. Indigenous knowledges and spiritual beliefs, which exist throughout the world on many continents and have no boundaries in terms of "race," teach us that to focus only on the self has long-lasting, negative consequences. For centuries, many countries of the world have focused solely on their own national well-being without any thought for other peoples on the earth. Today, because the globalization of mass media has engendered an increased awareness of global issues, many of us are faced with the consequences of the selfishness of individualism. The values of individualism and competition are not working for most of the earth's people and many of us know this. Rather than continuing on this path, perhaps it may help us all if we begin to look at how we relate to others, to the world, and to our professions in ways that honour and care for collective well-being.

In her contribution to the student sharing circle, Sondra took up the idea of how the mentality of those in the West is problematic, as she sees that, a lot of un-learning is now happening. People in the West have been taught about survival of the fittest; that one needs to be a conqueror or will be conquered. There has been a mentality of faster, better, stronger, but this is making people sick. Aboriginal ways have healing in them, such as medicines, which could be helpful for all people. (Sondra, personal communication, April 6, 2009)

Rupert Ross is an Assistant Crown Attorney in Kenora, Ontario. He has been working with, and writing about, Indigenous Peoples and the justice system for many years. Not Indigenous, Ross has written a number of progressively insightful pieces over the years, some on what he calls "the relational lens" in his attempts to understand Indigenous worldviews. Ross (2007) states that within these worldviews,

the world can be understood as primarily composed of ever-changing relationships of dependency, as all things are seen as essential to a healthy whole. That basic conviction drives a further conclusion: our relationships are fundamentally centred on dependencies, and human beings are not, as the western view seems to hold, fundamentally a collection of rights against others, but a bundle of responsibilities towards others, towards all aspects of Creation. (p. 24)

Ross goes on to speak to how these connections and responsibilities are expressed to community members:

To be told, especially within powerful ceremonies, of your intrinsic worth within Creation, and of the importance of your contribution to maintain its healthy equilibrium, is to be given a precious gift indeed.... They [teenage girls] were ... almost desperately grateful for being told that they were important somewhere, that they had roles to play, that they were part of something larger than themselves—especially something as huge and magical as the universe itself! (pp. 24–25).

Jacquie Green of the Haisla Nation and Robina Thomas of the Lyackson of the Coast Salish Nation (2007) conducted research with Indigenous social work practitioners on what they saw as "best practices" in the area of child welfare. Throughout their interviews, Green and Thomas report, almost all of the social workers described their work as "family-centred," working with families to "collectively make decisions" (p. 182). As one worker explained,

> Our workers include, as much as we can, family, community and anyone the child feels connected to ... because once we have community, once we have family, they have control, and that's where it belongs, with the family, not with us. (p. 182)

RELATIONSHIPS

Charlene Avalos strongly advocates that Indigenous values and ethics have much strength and can be applied to all peoples. In talking about relationships as a significant value within Indigenous ways of helping, she first begins with understandings of a relationship with the self:

> Aboriginal helping approaches are holistic, always viewing a person in relationship with their family and community. I believe every social worker can learn from this. The holistic approach is also about the four aspects of a person which, of course, applies to all peoples. Let me explain this according to the teachings of the four directions as I have been taught about them. The eastern doorway represents vision which means having a purpose in life. Each of us needs a sense of the future and our role in it. We can't get healthy without this. The doorway of the south is all about relationships and connections which are the foundation of helping approaches or social work for all people. Then in the west are emotions. Aboriginal ways of helping have always looked at trauma and how to release it. It's understood and accepted that people need to do this. Social work has begun to do the same. And finally in the northern direction is the area of the physical such as nutrition and exercise. If a person doesn't eat properly

and exercise, then this affects everything else so there will
be a greater chance that the person will be unbalanced.

For all human beings, these aspects are interconnected
and healing needs to take place in all areas so balance
can be achieved. (C. Avalos, personal communication,
February 14, 2009)

When Charlene shares her understandings of the four directions, she is
referring to the teachings of the Medicine Wheel, a much-used symbol
in many Indigenous Nations, which is often employed in teaching and
healing processes. I am quite familiar with the Anishnawbe version of the
Wheel that Charlene is speaking about, as I have used it in my teaching
and healing practices as well. From a Mi'kmaq perspective, the Wheel has
seven directions rather than four. It includes east, south, west, and north,
as well as:

- Up, which is to honour the direction of the Creator, the
  sky, Grandfather Sun, and Grandmother Moon;
- Down, which is the direction of Mother Earth; and
- Inward, which is a recognition of the self and the spirit
  that exists within each of us.

When we have acknowledged each of the seven directions, we have acknowledged everything that is.

I then asked Charlene about her understanding and experiences about
the relationship between a social worker and a service user from an
Indigenous view. Her response focussed on trust:

Service users are supposed to trust social workers, but
we don't trust them since we don't reveal anything about
ourselves to them. This creates a hierarchy and inequality
with an expert-client relationship. Within an Aboriginal
perspective, we are all equal, but each of us can be at a
different place in our healing journey. Sharing one's journey with a client helps to balance out the playing field
while deepening the relationship and connection between
the two. It wasn't until I lived and practiced social work
in an Aboriginal community that I realized how the dis-

closure of a helper's story can greatly increase trust. In Aboriginal helping processes, there is often some form of disclosure between client and worker because this helps to balance out the relationship while normalizing and de-stigmatizing the need for help. (C. Avalos, personal communication, February 14, 2009)

Cree Elder Joanne Dallaire, from Attawapiskat First Nation, is a Traditional Counsellor/Healer with 30 years of experience. She is an adviser to many Indigenous agencies and programs throughout Ontario. Joanne supports what Charlene emphasizes about self-disclosure and trust:

> Actually, I told a woman today who was in an abusive relationship for 8 years that I had been in one for 14 years and know how difficult it is to get out of such a situation. Service providers need to give service users a reason to trust them. This is why I share some of myself with them. If one is recovering from drug abuse, for example, it helps to see someone who had this issue in the past and overcame it. (J. Dallaire, personal communication, July 23, 2009)

I agree with Joanne that a helper's disclosure about how she overcame adversity, what helped her, and what she may still struggle with at times can be encouraging for those who come to us for assistance. If, for example, a worker discloses that she was once a victim of domestic violence, then the woman sitting across from her, who is attempting to stay out of the same situation, may believe that the worker understands her ambivalent feelings and, therefore, see her as more credible. When a worker says to a service user, "I know what you mean," there must be authenticity to this. I also believe that when such a woman hears how the worker got help and created a different story for herself, she may begin to have hope that she will be able to do the same.

However, both service users and helpers need to *choose* what they wish to share with one another. The time helpers spend with service users is not about the helper. It is not a space for them to go into detail about their life experiences or to disclose information that is not directly intended to assist the service user about a specific concern. The service user is not the worker's sounding board or therapist, and disclosure is not to be used as a way to be liked by the service user.

In their research, Green and Thomas (2007) also heard from their participants about "building trusting relationships with the community" (p. 183). They share how one worker stated "that she approaches all relationships as if they will be lifelong relationships ... [which] requires commitment and time" (p. 183). Green and Thomas stress how connection such as knowing "the community, the kinships, the history, [and] the culture ... help us in establishing powerful helping relationships" (p. 187). Such relationships are crucial when helping work becomes difficult:

> We might have to go into a family member's home to "protect" a child and are met with rage. This anger is not easy to overlook. And then, we have to know that we have done everything right when we walk in our communities and face the rest of the family and community. This is when the importance of building "relationships" is critical—the stronger the relationship, the more able we are as workers to work through the anger. (p. 187)

Ross (2008) writes about the relationship between service provider and service user using his observations from his work in Indigenous communities. He states that there are no concepts that express the grey areas that exist between service provider and service user. The relationship between service provider and service user is defined by the idea of "I [the service provider] am well, but you [the service user] are ill" (p. 22). Rather, from an Indigenous perspective,

> The distinction between healer and patient seems to lose its force, as do the boundaries between them. Instead, the sense that "we are all on this journey together" seems to characterize most interactions, and gives people the critical message that they are not some lower order of humanity destined never to rise above their pain or their sins. (p. 22)

Like Avalos, Ross (2008) also raises issues of power, hierarchy, and inequality within Western approaches to helping. He states that "western therapies ... engage patient and therapist in one-on-one relationships conducted within strict professional boundaries" (p. 23). He goes on to quote Judith Herman (1992):

> The Patient enters therapy in need of help and care. By virtue of this fact, she voluntarily submits herself to an unequal relationship in which the therapist has superior status and power (p. 134).... The dynamics of dominance and submission are re-enacted in all subsequent relationships, including the therapy. (p. 138; page numbers in Herman)

Ross (2008) then raises the use of Healing Circles as part of Indigenous approaches to helping and how they may achieve something different from one-on-one counselling:

> I find myself wondering whether the circle, as opposed to the therapist's couch, is a *qualitatively* different place, and whether the circle participants, all speaking of their own healing journeys, are not *qualitatively* different from the single therapist forced by her profession to maintain strict boundaries ... is it possible that aboriginal healing circles can be seen as potentially powerful processes with perhaps a *lesser* risk of obstructions like transference? (pp. 24–25)

Ross concludes from his observations and understandings of Healing Circles that

> it seems that the stories in the circle send another critical message, that healing is indeed *possible*, for every person speaking [has] been exactly where the victim now [sits]....
> I also suggest that no one, even the best-trained therapist, can simply *tell* them that it could be different; instead, they have to feel it to believe it. And if they feel the celebration of others, maybe that's a source of optimism and celebration for them as well. (p. 25)

In Chapter Seven, I take up Ross's ideas about the efficacy of the Healing Circle as a powerful place of learning, sharing, and hope.

Liz Arger sees Indigenous ways of helping as focusing primarily on the value of holism, which can be applied to all people. Arger has been taught by the Cree and Anishnawbe Elders and colleagues where she has worked over the years how to use the Medicine Wheel as a holistic assessment tool. She explained some of her understanding about how the Medicine Wheel works:

> The Medicine Wheel helps practitioners to keep all aspects of a person in mind, especially if they have a tendency to focus on only one or two of them. As an example, if a person is challenged with depression, it will affect all four of their aspects. A person is not compartmentalized nor is their life, so all areas need to be respected. A holistic approach to helping asks how a person is doing physically— for example, asking how sugar affects the person's moods. (L. Arger, personal communication, June 18, 2009)

Liz gave another example that if one takes up a cognitive behavioural approach, then the psychological aspect is being looked at, but what about the person's spirit? This can't be addressed by only talking about it. There's actual research now that shows how all aspects of a person are interconnected and impact upon one another, but this has been a part of Indigenous worldviews forever. This is only one example of how Indigenous people have so much of value to contribute to the world.

LEARNING

I invited Liz Arger to speak about her experiences of how helpers are taught to help within Indigenous worldviews. She shared,

> An Elder that I worked with often said, "We are involved in the university of the universe," which means learning how to live with everything around us. It means learning about values, principles, relationships, roles, the importance of family and how to be with each other in a healthy way.
>
> Helpers are taught that service to others is thoughtful; that they are students of life who learn through paying attention and truly listening. They are taught to respond, rather than react. They develop leadership which is about giving of themselves and what they learn to the commun-

ity through their actions. They learn how *not* to interfere in someone else's journey, growth and development
through the values of respect and non-interference. (L.
Arger, personal communication, June 18, 2009)

I then invited Liz to reflect on why she believes such learning for Indigenous helpers can be of value to non-Indigenous ones. She responded with
the following:

> This learning process I'm talking about means immersing
> oneself subjectively or from the inside out. It entails letting
> go of comfort zones of what is familiar and feels safe. This
> enriches a person and teaches them to respect their own pro-
> cess so that they are better able to do the same for others. It is
> a process of coming to *know* rather than believing something
> that is outside of the self. Believing is a mental concept that
> can be about looking to the future for an idea, hope or vision.
> Yet this is often prescriptive where we are asked to suspend
> an aspect of our intuitive intelligence or pass our process over
> to some "authority." Knowing is lived experiences and comes
> from deep inside of ourselves. It needs to be nurtured to ma-
> ture into an insightful and knowledgeable tool. All helpers
> would benefit from this way of learning. (L. Arger, personal
> communication, June 18, 2009)

Listening to Liz, I thought about how the learning process she speaks of
could be applied to service users as well as helpers, as each individual is
their own expert. I recall hearing from somewhere the phrase that "the
client is the expert on their own life." I think this is what Liz is referring
to when she speaks of "intuitive intelligence"; each of us has the capacity
for insight and healing within ourselves. We do not need to believe in or
take advice from anyone with authority, from social workers to nurses to
psychiatrists. Rather, a helper will learn through their own experiences
and they will in turn assist others to do the same. This fits nicely with what
Charlene Avalos spoke of earlier about avoiding hierarchy and inequality
within the service user–social worker relationship.

I also think that this way of learning teaches the Indigenous value that
everyone has a role and purpose for their life and that each individual can

contribute to the betterment of the community. There is also an understanding that everyone has something to give back in return for what they receive or, as Liz creatively puts it, "everyone is a part of the giveaway." As well, this notion of giving and receiving represents the Indigenous value of reciprocity.

Ross (2007) would appear to agree. This is his description of the role of a helper within healing circles:

> In aboriginal processes, the professional seems to act not so much as an author, but as a process-provider, not as a creator of remedies but as prompter of creation, and not as a prescriber of choices but as the provider of a context in which healthy choices can be discovered and adopted by those directly involved.... the aboriginal professional retreats very substantially from the spotlight to become only a single member of a multi-party process, and that ... as well as the exploration processes undertaken by everyone together, [is what] lend the circles their power to heal. (pp. 34–35)

Jennifer Ajandi also spoke about learning how to become a helper who adopts an Indigenous perspective:

> Aboriginal worldviews teach social work students and practitioners how to practice anti-oppressive social work in terms of being non-judgemental, linking individual issues with structural causes or contributions, that behaviour is learned and can be changed, and that there are many different paths a person can take. There is no *one* right answer, options depend on the person, family, and their community at the particular time. Self-determination has always been a part of Aboriginal worldviews and it is an important part of social work's code of ethics as well.
>
> Aboriginal approaches tend to be non-judgemental. There is much more of an equalizing dynamic between people. There is a strong emphasis on building relationships with those seeking help rather than mechanically running through a list of questions. Trust building happens before talking about personal issues. "Intakes" and

"assessments" are discussions rather than standardized forms to complete. (J. Ajandi, personal communication, January 10, 2009)

Wendy Martin and I had a conversation about Indigenous values and ethics in an interview we did together. Wendy believes, practises, and lives many Indigenous values. She is adamant that the helping professions would be greatly enriched if helpers could pay more attention to these values. She listed those that she implements in her work:

- Developing relationships with the families and communities of a client.
- Being more non-directive.
- Focusing on a client's strengths.
- Emphasizing wellness and what that means to clients.
- Being creative in the helping process, such as using visual representations to discuss concerns or wellness (W. Martin, personal communication, February 8, 2009)

Most of Wendy's social work experience is in the area of youth justice. She challenges mainstream notions of justice and believes that Indigenous approaches to justice are more effective because they focus on the value of community responsibility for young people:

> It's helpful for everyone to take some responsibility when a youth becomes in conflict with the law. Society is letting these youth down. We all need to look at how we have contributed to the problems of a young person; why have we allowed youth to struggle so much for their whole lives by, for example, putting them in foster homes, then group homes, pushing them out of school? Is it any big surprise that they then end up in the youth justice system? (W. Martin, personal communication, February 8, 2009)

Flo supports Wendy's position here about the importance of considering both strengths and responsibilities in our work with people:

Each of us has some kind of strength and I believe that we can learn from each other according to our strengths. At the same time, however, we cannot forget about the systemic barriers we face. How do we learn from each other or even begin to teach others with all the different forms of oppression that are weighing us down? Most marginalized people already know what they would like to achieve, but they cannot obtain them because of systemic issues, such as institutionalized racism. When we work with people, we need to take into consideration that it is not that they do not have strengths or that they are not trying to achieve their goals, but that they have to face obstacles way beyond their control. We need to acknowledge social injustice and not down play structural forms of oppression when we talk about resiliency or strengths. I believe this is what Indigenous peoples do when they work with one another and the rest of us can learn from that. (Flo, personal communication, April 6, 2009)

In pulling together and concluding this section on learning, I will finish with the words of Lindsay, another student who participated in the student sharing circle. She spoke about the value of Indigenous teachings and also asks that social workers be cautious in their approach:

Indigenous ways teach that helping is *who* a person is, rather than that it's a job. As social workers we need to keep this in mind and pay attention to where we are going as a helping profession. We do not want to be disconnected from those we seek to assist which is the danger of becoming professionalized. (Lindsay, personal communication, April 6, 2009)

SEVEN SACRED TEACHINGS

One of the major purposes of helping work is to assist people to restore relationships with other people and with everything around them. (This holistic approach is the topic of the next chapter). Healthy relationships need to be based on what I would say are universal Indigenous values. For instance, central to Mi'kmaq teachings are principles of kindness, honesty, sharing, strength, bravery, wisdom, and humility. Interestingly enough, within Anishnawbe teachings, these values are called "the Seven Grandfathers" or the "Seven Sacred Teachings." I prefer the second phrase as it, unlike the first one, is gender neutral. These teachings are:

1. To cherish knowledge is to know WISDOM.
2. To know LOVE is to know peace.
3. To honour all of Creation is to have RESPECT.
4. BRAVERY is to face the foe with integrity.
5. HONESTY in facing a situation is to be brave.
6. HUMILITY is to know yourself as a sacred part of Creation.
7. TRUTH is to know all of these things.

My understanding is that the Seven Sacred Teachings are about ethics. Love is one of these ethics, but it has a different connotation than it has for mainstream society. In Indigenous worldviews, love is about connectedness. In my experience, students can relate to this concept of love within the helping professions and discuss it. They acknowledge that a relationship is being built between the social worker and service user and they acknowledge that it is okay to care about people we are working with.

CONCLUSION
Values and ethics frame how we conceptualize helping. This chapter has looked at differences between Western and Indigenous values. It is clear that there are some similarities amongst Indigenous values and those of non-Western societies as well as spiritual practices, such as meditation. The chapter also provided ideas for opportunities where social work educators, students, and practitioners, as well as those in other helping professions, can come together to begin a dialogue about values and ethics.

Both Indigenous and non-Indigenous voices in this chapter emphasized the significance of Indigenous values such as connectedness to everything around us, the importance of relationships, wholeness, learning through introspection and experience, and basing all our interactions on foundational principles such as love. Since values underpin all that we do as helping professionals, including theories and practice, it may be that this is one of the areas of Indigenous worldviews that has the most applicability for the helping professions. It would appear that many helpers agree, as evidenced from their contributions to this chapter. Chapter Seven explores the values of connectedness and wholeness in deeper ways, through what is often referred to as a "holistic approach."

REFERENCES

Brant-Castellano, M. (2004). Ethics of Aboriginal research. *Journal of Aboriginal Health, 1*(1), 98–114.

Chodron, P. (1997). *When things fall apart: Heart advice for difficult times.* Boston: Shambhala Publications.

Giago, T. (2009). Is there still a place for Indian time in this busy world? *The Huffington Post.* Retrieved from http://www.huffingtonpost.com/tim-giago/is-there-still-a-place-to_b_381809.html.

Gibson, K. (2011). Stereotypes: "Indian time." *National Relief Charities Blog: Building Strong, Self-Sufficient American Indian Communities.* Retrieved from http://blog.nrcprograms.org/my-thoughts-on-stereotypes/.

Green, J., & Thomas, R. (2007). Learning through our children, healing for our children: Best practices in First Nations communities. In L. Dominelli (Ed.), *Revitalizing communities in a globalizing world* (pp. 175–192). Aldershot: Ashgate.

Herman, J. (1992). *Trauma and recovery: The aftermath of violence—from domestic abuse to political terror.* New York: Basic Books.

Kovach, M., Thomas, R., Montgomery, M., Green, J., & Brown, L. (2007). Witnessing wild woman: Resistance and resilience in Aboriginal child welfare. In L.T. Foster & B. Wharf (Eds.), *People, politics, and child welfare in British Columbia* (pp. 97–116). Vancouver: University of British Columbia Press.

Limb, G., & Hodge, D. (2008). Developing spiritual competency with Native Americans: Promoting wellness through balance and harmony. *Families in Society, 89*(4), 615–622. doi: 10.1606/1044-3894.3816

Ross, R. (2007). *Discussion paper: Exploring criminal justice and the Aboriginal healing paradigm.* Unpublished manuscript. Retrieved from http://www.lsuc.on.ca.

Ross, R. (2008). Colonization, complex PTSD and Aboriginal healing: Exploring diagnoses and strategies for recovery. Adult Custody Division Health Care Conference. Vancouver: British Columbia Ministry of Public Safety and Solicitor General.

Chapter Seven

HOLISTIC OR WHOLISTIC APPROACH

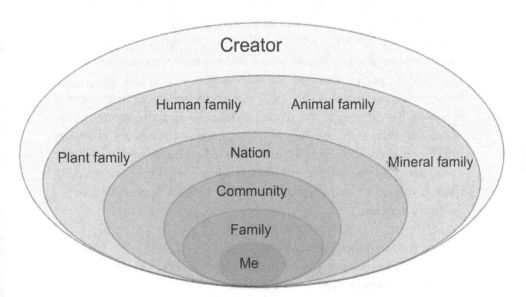

Creator

Human family   Animal family

Plant family   Nation   Mineral family

Community

Family

Me

INTRODUCTION

I have seen both spellings of this word in the literature a o give them the same meaning, but there is some recent literature that explains them as having different connotations. According to Anishnawbe scholar Renee Linklater (2010), wholism refers to wholeness and is, therefore, an "all encompassing term" (p. 230). The author goes on to explain that she has been told by Elders that holism refers to what is holy and, therefore, is seemingly linked to patriarchal power and force. One Elder also shared with Linklater that she believes holism to be "an empty space word" (p. 230). Although not mentioned by Linklater, I also wonder if some people associate the word "holy" with Christianity.

I myself have never been told these differences between the two spellings from any of the Elders I know, nor have I read about it by anyone other than Linklater. Research via a dictionary and a thesaurus states that the two are alternative spellings for the same meaning, but cites holistic as the more common usage and defines its meaning as the view that a whole system of beliefs needs to be taken into consideration, rather than individual components. That is what I mean when I use the term holism. I am used to spelling the word like this—holistic—so this is the spelling I will use throughout this chapter. The concept, and concepts connected to holism, has come up repeatedly in previous chapters. (Remember I cautioned that this might happen!) However, because the concept of holism is so foundational to helping approaches based on Indigenous worldviews and so many authors include this idea in their writing, I believe it needs its space in this book. This chapter will explore a holistic approach based on the following areas:

- The four aspects of a person
- Interdependency of individuals, families, and communities
- Interconnectedness of all Creation
- Healing

THE PERSON

According to a holistic approach, each person is made up of four aspects: spiritual, physical, emotional, and psychological (Hart, 2002; Sterling-Collins, 2009; Verniest, 2006). This is often represented within the Medicine Wheel teachings. It appears that most Indigenous Nations on Turtle Island have a version of the Wheel, typically with the same colours, animals, and gifts associated with the four directions. However, where on the Wheel these show up is different from Nation to Nation. For example, in Anishnawbe teachings, the colour white is in the northern direction, but in Mi'kmaq teachings, it is in the east. Yet some of the teachings of the Medicine Wheel match up exactly for the Anishnawbe and Mi'kmaq. For example, within both of these Nations—because the Wheel represents the passage of the sun and the seasons—when basing discussions or teachings on the Wheel, we begin in the eastern direction, where the sun rises, and travel in a clockwise direction. The east, then, is seen as a direction of beginnings, including infancy, which is the beginning of life, and spring, which is the beginning of a new year. The west is seen as a direction of endings and is the direction the spirit travels when it leaves the earth.

In terms of the four aspects of a person, the Medicine Wheel teaches us that the ideal state of well-being is to be balanced in all of these areas. However, this ideal state of balance is rarely the case for many people, which means that we need to be involved in activities that assist us in our attempts to stay balanced. Because the four aspects—spiritual, physical, emotional, and psychological—are connected, they constantly impact one another. Should a person become ill or be harmed in one area, then the other three areas will also be affected. For example, should someone slip into a depression (emotional aspect), their body (physical) may be impacted because they are not eating or sleeping properly; their mind (psychological) can be affected as they may have self-deprecating thoughts, or might be forgetful and have trouble focusing. On a spiritual level, they may begin to lose hope, and they might stop praying and avoid practices that ordinarily sustain them, such as ceremonies and meditation.

It could be said that such a person is out of balance. In order to return to a place of balance, since all four aspects of this individual are affected, all four aspects must be engaged in a process of returning to balance. In other words, the *whole* person must be included in the healing process. Using the example of a person experiencing depression, it is not enough to only focus on the emotional aspect of healing. Hence, Indigenous methods of restoring balance include ceremonies that address all four aspects. An example of this integrated approach to addressing all aspects of healing is the sweat lodge ceremony, practised by such Nations as the Cree, Lakota, and Anishnawbe. Within this ceremony, one sweats (physical), releases feelings (emotional), hears teachings (psychological), and prays and sings for spirits to come into the lodge to help (spiritual).

Some research studies show the possibilities of how a holistic approach can assist people with physical illnesses. For example, Mehl-Madrona (2008) conducted research with 47 Indigenous people living with cancer who, at the outset of the study, had received a prognosis of five years to live by their Western doctors. Although it was only a preliminary study, the results are promising for those who wish to adopt Indigenous holistic healing approaches. The life expectancy of the participants who had adopted traditional Indigenous healing methods taught by traditional Indigenous healers changed from a range of 5 to 21 years. Mehl-Madrona (2008) points out that these results show a plausible relationship between the mind and body, which also influenced the life expectancy of the study participants.

Consider how what I have written thus far compares to the following writing about behavioural medicine:

> Behavioural medicine represents a new current within medicine itself, one that is rapidly expanding our ideas and knowledge about health and illness. New research findings and new ways of thinking about health and illness in behavioural medicine are rapidly producing a more comprehensive perspective within medicine, one that recognizes the fundamental unit of mind and body…. Perhaps the most fundamental development in behavioural medicine is the recognition that we can no longer think about health as being solely a characteristic of the body or the mind because body and mind are interconnected. The new perspective acknowledges the central importance of thinking in terms of *wholeness* and *interconnectedness* and the need to pay attention to the interactions of mind, body, and behaviour in efforts to understand and treat illness. (Kabat-Zinn, 2005, pp. 150–151)

Dr. Kabat-Zinn is a renowned scientist, writer, and meditation teacher who focuses on mindfulness, which is one of the types of meditation I practise. He is the founder and former director of the world-renowned Stress Reduction Clinic at the Centre for Mindfulness in Medicine, Health Care and Society. He is also a board member of the Mind and Life Institute, which works to establish collaborative partnerships between modern scientists and Buddhists such as the Dalai Lama. Dr. Kabat-Zinn is someone who I admire very much and is someone who is making incredible contributions to our planet. It is clear that there are important connections between the work of Dr. Kabat-Zinn and an Indigenous approach to well-being that make connections between the mind and body. At the same time, I noticed that Dr. Kabat-Zinn (2005) uses the word "new" three times in his description of behavioural medicine in the above quote, and he also talks about "new ways of thinking" (p. 150). I am disappointed because Dr. Kabat-Zinn does not acknowledge that the mind-body connection has existed in Indigenous worldviews since the beginning of time. Even those who position themselves as enlightened allies of Indigenous Peoples can fail to acknowledge where their "new" ideas originate.

THE FAMILY AND COMMUNITY

Every person starts life as a connected being. Each one of us exists because of a connectedness between two people. This connection could exist because of a sexual relationship, a loving relationship, or a giving or donor relationship. Each of us was once entirely connected—spiritually, physically, emotionally and psychologically—to another human being. An Indigenous perspective would say that we come from the spirit world into the physical world through the bodies of our mothers. This connectedness is physically symbolized by the belly button. This is why there are many spiritual practices around the world that are associated with the severing of the umbilical cord (Gonzales, 2007).

Within a holistic framework, each individual is connected to all other people around them. First there are connections to one's family and then connections to the members of one's community. The interconnectedness of all Creation means that everyone is both dependent upon and connected with other people and the environment. Each person has unique contributions to make, which also affect the whole. Every contribution—positive or negative—has an impact on all other people and on her or his physical environment in some way.

But who constitutes one's family? For Indigenous Peoples, as it is in many other worldviews, family can include a wide group of people, some of whom may be biologically related and also people who are not biologically related. Family is made up of parents, grandparents, siblings, aunties and uncles, and cousins. In some Indigenous traditions, such as those of the Anishnawbe,

Haudenosaunee, and Mi'kmaq, family includes members of one's clan and our sponsors, who are there when we receive our spirit names or get married. In my own life, my Elder refers to me as her younger sister and, in my community, many people call female Elders they are particularly connected to "grandmother." Many of my friends' children refer to me as auntie and to my son as cousin. These are all important and unique relationships.

Further, Indigenous Peoples have always had family adoptions within their societies. This not only occurred with children, but also took place in order to replace relationships that were severed through death. Many years ago when my only brother passed on, the Elders who assisted my family and I with the ceremony and grieving process told me something that I initially could not comprehend. They said that at some point in the future, a young man would enter my life and that I would immediately recognize him as my brother. In that moment, I wondered how it could be possible that another person would come along and replace my brother. But that wasn't what the Elders were trying to say. The Elders were not saying that *my brother* could be replaced. They meant that the *relationship* needed to be replaced. Sure enough, in time a young man did came along. I knew he was the one and I adopted him through ceremony as my brother. He is my brother forever, just as my blood relatives are. He is my brother, and I cannot divorce him even if our relationship isn't going well, like I might if he was a marriage partner.

In Indigenous traditions, this concept of replacing relationships is an expression of the value of interconnectedness. It seems to me that this understanding is valuable for all peoples to understand, because many people face the loss of familial relationships through death, conflict, estrangement, lack of safety, abuse, and prejudice. Having the freedom to *choose* some family members for ourselves can be both a source of support and healing.

Another connection to Buddhism, meditation, and other spiritual traditions can be made with respect to the connections between family and community. According to Kabat-Zinn (2005),

> The web of interconnectedness goes beyond our individual psychological self. While we are whole ourselves as individual beings, we are also part of a larger whole, interconnected through our family and our friends and acquaintances to the larger society and ultimately to the whole of humanity and life on the planet. (p. 157)

Many major research studies conducted in several countries demonstrate the importance of social connections and health. This is also explained by Kabat-Zinn (2005):

> Social factors, which of course are related to psychological factors, also play an important role in health and illness. It has long been known, for instance, that, statistically speaking, people who are socially isolated tend to be less healthy, psychologically and physically, and more likely to die prematurely than people who have extensive social relationships. (p. 215)

There seems to be something about having ties to others that is basic to health. Of course, this is intuitively understandable. We all have a strong need to belong, feel a part of something, and associate with other people. However, Indigenous worldviews about holism take the connection between one's individual health and relationships to other people to a deeper level.

These teachings on holism emphasize that family and community members play a direct role in helping to heal individuals. Ross (2007) explains that his collective experiences in Healing Circles and ceremonies gave him

> a powerful, emotional certainty of intimate and healthy connection with other humans struggling through common human challenges that I can only describe them as experiences of spiritual connection. It was not just that we joined each other, but that we all felt joined to something much larger than our collective sum. The challenge seems to involve nourishing a conviction of healthy and meaningful connection in the hearts, minds and spirits of all of us, regardless of whether, in a particular instant of our lives, the world wants to describe us as a victim, an offender, a healer—or a supposedly disinterested stranger. (p. 26)

Ross's experiences speak to the belief that the healing of any one person is dependent on the health of other community members. Thus, the community heals the individual and the individual contributes to the healing of the community. Reliance on the "expertise" of one person, for example a doctor or counsellor, might not be enough (McCabe, 2008). In addition, community members have a duty to help others take responsibility (Hill, 2008). This may involve taking responsibility for harmful behaviour or for actively participating in one's healing journey.

ALL OF CREATION

From the individual to the family, to the community, and then to all of Creation—*all* of the peoples of the world, the plants and animals that feed and sustain us, the water, the rocks, the air, the planet, and the cosmos—*everything* is connected. From an Indigenous perspective, everything has a spirit and impacts upon everything else. Part of the human condition is that we have a kinship to *all* living things, and also to those things that are considered to be inanimate objects.

From a holistic and Indigenous perspective, rocks have a spirit. I have been taught that rocks are the oldest and strongest part of Creation. When we are in need of strength, we go to the mountains. I carry a small stone from a sacred place where I have attended many ceremonies in a pouch around my neck. This stone helps me be strong when I need to be. Should you ever see me clutching my medicine pouch, you will know it is because I am asking for strength in that particular moment!

Knowing that everything on the planet is related and connected has been written about for many years by numerous Indigenous authors. Battiste and Youngblood Henderson (2000), Cajete (1994), Couture (1991), Fitznor (1998), and Shilling (2002) all emphasize interconnectedness as an important concept within Indigenous worldviews. As Paula Gunn Allen (1986) says, "all things are related and are of one family" (p. 60). Thus, I am connected to my family, my community, the Mi'kmaq Nation, and to everything on Mother Earth and in the spirit world. To divide any of these realities into separate categories is a dishonour to Indigenous ways of thinking.

When someone can live as a whole person, then they can connect to everyone and everything around them and be able to attend to their responsibilities. In Indigenous worldviews, a focus on individual and collective responsibility for all members of one's community is highlighted. We can turn again to Blood scholar Leroy Little Bear's (2000) beautiful articulation of this perspective:

> Wholeness is like a flower with four petals. When it opens,
> one discovers strength, sharing, honesty, and kindness.

Together these four petals create balance, harmony, and beauty. Wholeness works in the same interconnected way. The whole strength speaks to the idea of sustaining balance. If a person is whole and balanced, then he or she is in a position to fulfill his or her individual responsibilities to the whole. If a person is not balanced, then he or she is sick and weak—physically, mentally or both—and cannot fulfill his or her individual responsibilities. (p. 79)

Again, I turn to the writing of Dr. Kabat-Zinn (2005) to show that there are other peoples of the world alongside Indigenous Peoples who share similar understandings of wholeness and connectedness. Dr. Kabat-Zinn (2005) states that there are

larger patterns and cycles of nature that we only know about through science and thinking (although even here traditional peoples always knew and respected these aspects of interconnectedness in their own ways as natural ways).... one scientific view known as the Gaia hypothesis, is that the earth as a whole behaves as one self-regulating living organism, given the name Gaia after the Greek goddess of the earth. This hypothesis affirms a view based on scientific reasoning, that was, in essence, also held by all traditional cultures and peoples, a world in which humans were interconnected and interdependent with all beings and with the earth itself. (p. 157)

I am certain that if these knowings were a part of the worldviews of *all* peoples of the world, then collectively we would never have participated in the literal slow death of our Mother the Earth. People everywhere need to awake to the reality that if we do not stop this death of our Mother, we will *all* die as well. The colour of one's skin or how much money one has in the bank will not matter if the earth dies. If She dies, we *all* die. Ross (2007) echoes that, even though many people might still think so, people are not the masters of Creation:

The Bible puts us right at the top, set on earth to rule all the fishes in the sea, everything. Aboriginal teachings seem to present an opposite hierarchy. Mother Earth

(with her life-blood, the waters) plays the most important role in Creation, for without the soil and water there
would be no plant realm. Without the plants there would
be no animal realm, and without soil, water, plants and
animals, there would be no us.... human creatures are
understood to be the least essential and the most dependent aspects of Creation; no longer its Masters, we are its
humble servants instead. (p. 14)

EVER-CHANGING

In viewing all of Creation through a holistic lens, one also comes to appreciate that everything is continually changing. One season moves into another;
day becomes night; babies become children, then youth, then adults, and
eventually, when they are old, they leave this world. Thoughts, feelings,
understandings, our bodies, and relationships all change, sometimes over the
long-term and at other times from moment to moment. Mountains, beaches,
oceans, stars, and galaxies change over time. Everything on the planet and
in the universe is in a state of perpetual change. Everything comes full circle as well—babies come from the spirit world and when they become old
people, they eventually return to the spirit world. Change is inevitable and
everything is constantly evolving. Nothing is permanent. Nothing is forever.

If we choose not to fight against impermanence, then we will begin to
understand that impermanence is another aspect of a holistic understanding where balance and harmony are continually in flux. Change is part of
connectedness. Many worldviews appreciate and celebrate the impermanent
aspect of connectedness. Within Indigenous worldviews, changes are often
marked with ceremonies. There are a lot of ceremonies! There are ceremonies
for the birth of a baby, the naming of a baby, for the changes that occur when
a child begins to grow into a youth, and ceremonies for marriage, adoption,
initiations, and passing on into the spirit world. There are ceremonies for
the full moon, planting and harvesting, and the changing of each season.
Every significant change is acknowledged and celebrated. Impermanence
is the essence of all of Creation, but unfortunately, many people have no
respect for this. Pema Chodron (2000) notes this when she writes, "in the
process of trying to deny that things are always changing, we lose our sense
of the sacredness of life. We tend to forget that we are part of the natural
scheme of things" (p. 61). We also tend to forget that we are the land and
the land is us. The Mi'kmaq way of harvesting resources is done without

jeopardizing the integrity, diversity, or productivity of the environment. The land is always the custodial responsibility of the community and is held "in trust" for future generations. It ensures that the present generation can survive without threatening future generations. Hence, when Mi'kmaq people make a decision, they must think about its impact on future generations.

CONCLUSION

Perhaps what stands out the most from the insights contained in this chapter is that Indigenous Peoples have always lived using a holistic approach. Now, when the entire world is in crisis, the West is searching for possible solutions that may have been here all along. Rather than continue the same behaviours that have led to the current crisis, those who make up dominant societies could perhaps pause and consider for a moment other ways of viewing Creation and living within it.

Many changes happening in the world today support the current global crisis; however, there are also many changes that are helping us move in a direction of balance, understanding, and healing. As we are all able to bring our collective knowledge together—spiritual, physical, emotional, and psychological—a healing movement can begin to grow. I believe that Indigenous Peoples are moving toward healing for themselves and the planet, and they have a desire to share their knowledges to accomplish this with other peoples of the world. Apparently, many non-Indigenous people are also starting to see the world in a similar way that views all life on the planet as connected. Viewing everything in Creation from a holistic lens is one of the gifts that Indigenous knowledges have given to the world.

REFERENCES

Allen, P.G. (1986). *The sacred hoop: Recovering the feminine in American Indian traditions*. Boston: Beacon.

Battiste, M., & Youngblood Henderson, J. (2000). *Protecting Indigenous knowledge and heritage: A global challenge*. Saskatoon: Purich Publishing.

Cajete, G. (1994). *Look to the mountain: An ecology of Indigenous education*. Durando, CO: Kivaki Press.

Chodron, P. (2000). *When things fall apart: Heart advice for difficult times*. Boston: Shambhala Publications.

Couture, J. (1991). Explorations in Native knowing. In J.W. Friesen (Ed.), *The cultural maze: Complex questions on Native destiny in Western Canada* (pp. 201–215). Calgary: Detselig Enterprises.

Fitznor, L. (1998). The circle of life: Affirming Indigenous philosophies in everyday living. In D. McCane (Ed.), *Life ethics in world religions* (pp. 21–40). Winnipeg: University of Manitoba.

Gonzales, P. (2007). *Birth is a ceremony: Story and formulas of thought in Indigenous medicine and Indigenous communications.* (Doctoral dissertation). University of Wisconsin-Madison.

Hart, M.A. (2002). *Seeking mino-pimatisiwin. An Aboriginal approach to helping.* Halifax: Fernwood Publishing.

Hill, L.P. (2008). *Understanding Indigenous Canadian traditional health and healing.* Unpublished Manuscript. Department of Social Work, Wilfrid Laurier University, Waterloo, ON, Canada.

Kabat-Zinn, J. (2005). *Full catastrophe living: Using the wisdom of your body and mind to face stress, pain and illness.* New York: Bantam Dell.

Linklater, R. (2010). Decolonizing our spirits: Cultural knowledge and Indigenous healing. In S. Marcos (Ed.), *Women and Indigenous religions* (pp. 217–232). Santa Barbara, CA: Praeger.

Little Bear, L. (2000). Jagged worldviews colliding. In M. Battiste (Ed.), *Reclaiming Indigenous voice and vision* (pp. 77–85). Vancouver: University of British Columbia Press.

McCabe, G. (2008). Mind, body, emotions and spirit: Reaching to the ancestors for healing. *Counselling Psychology Quarterly, 21,* 143–152. doi: 10.1080/09515070802066847

Mehl-Madrona, L. (2008). Narratives of exceptional survivors who work with Aboriginal healers. *Journal of Complementary and Alternative Medicine, 14*(5), 497–504. doi: 10.1089/acm.2007.0578

Ross, R. (2007). *Discussion paper: Exploring criminal justice and the Aboriginal healing paradigm.* Retrieved from http://www.lsuc.on.ca/media/third_colloquium_rupert_ross.pdf.

Shilling, R. (2002). Journey of our spirits: Challenges for adult Indigenous learners. In E.V. O'Sullivan, A. Morrell, & M.A. O'Connor (Eds.), *Expanding the boundaries of transformative learning: Essays on theory and practice* (pp. 151–158). Toronto: Palgrave.

Sterling-Collins, R. (2009). A holistic approach to supporting children with special needs. In R. Sinclair, M.A. Hart, & G. Bruyere (Eds.), *Wicihitowin: Aboriginal social work in Canada* (pp. 65–88). Winnipeg: Fernwood Publishing.

Verniest, L. (2006). Allying with the medicine wheel: Social work practice with Aboriginal peoples. *Critical Social Work, 7*(1). Retrieved from http://www.uwindsor.ca/criticalsocialwork/.

Chapter Eight

THE ANSWERS ARE IN THE COMMUNITY

INTRODUCTION

In all of my reading and what was shared with me through the interviews I conducted for this book, I heard that community was significant for people regardless of what particular topic was focused on. Because individuals, families, and communities are so connected, it is not possible to write about any one of them without the other.

WHY COMMUNITY FIRST?

I have chosen to place this chapter on community before the one on families and children. This is because I see community first and families and children second, rather than the other way around. This is due to an emphasis that is placed on the collective rather than the individual. Within Indigenous worldviews, the well-being of the community takes precedence over any individual. Collectivism is central, and Indigenous people across the globe have been taught to conduct themselves in ways that creates positive relationships with everyone in their community.

In many Indigenous languages, there is a phrase that translates into "all my relations." It is intended to express that one's community is an extension of one's family, that interdependence is valued, that we must care for one another, and that it is important to focus all our efforts on the betterment of our community. Everyone is viewed as having the ability to participate in the well-being of the community. It is expected that each of us will put the community before our individual gain and that we will take into account everyone's well-being in all that we do.

This emphasis on collective well-being is based on Indigenous values such as caring for all, sharing what one has, and interdependence. But it is also based on necessity and logic. Centuries ago, the original people of this land endured often harsh environmental conditions such as extreme cold and shortages of food. Families gathered to live together so they could support one another by working together for the betterment of all. They needed each other.

Communal living meant sharing the raising of children and providing for old people. It meant that when food was plentiful, everyone had enough and when it was not, no one had more than any other member of the community. No one had more than anyone else. No one moved ahead of anyone else. There were ceremonies in place to ensure this. If any one family accumulated a lot of things, then this family was required to give away things to others; this is what we call the "giveaway" today. In this way, what everyone had was more or less the same.

For the work and betterment of the community, there were hereditary clan systems. Each clan had a specific purpose. Some clans were protectors, others were carriers of medicines, some were mediators. Every person belonged to a clan and, therefore, contributed to the whole.

PEOPLE KNOW WHAT IS NEEDED

If we pay attention, listen, and watch what people are doing in their communities today, we will learn that sustainable development by communities is needed and is being addressed. Indigenous communities are leading the way in terms of healing and transformation. According to activist and academic Jim Silver (2006), who is non-Indigenous,

> The process of people's healing, of their rebuilding or recreating themselves, is rooted in a revived sense of community and a revitalization of Aboriginal cultures; this in turn requires the building of Aboriginal organizations. The process of reclaiming an Aboriginal identity takes place, therefore, at an individual, community, organizational and ultimately political level. This is a process of decolonization that, if it can continue to be rooted in traditional Aboriginal values of sharing and community, will be the foundation upon which healing and rebuilding are based. (p. 133)

When it comes to community rebuilding, many Indigenous authors focus on children and women. When it comes to the power to protect children, communities take up the role of parents, because in an Indigenous community everyone is understood to have a connection to *all* children, can participate in the raising of children, and needs to be involved in decisions that affect children. When it comes to child protection, the community can take responsibility for the safety of its children, including meeting such legal obligations as conducting "risk assessments" and developing "safety plans."

Several Indigenous women, including Kim Anderson (2000, 2006, 2011), who is Cree/Métis; Leanne Simpson (2006), an Anishnawbe kwe; the Anishnawbe mother-daughter team Jeannette Corbiere-Lavell and D. Memee Lavell-Harvard (2006); and Renee Elizabeth Bédard (2006), who is Anishnawbe/Métis, write about women and motherhood in relation to community revitalization. According to the writers for the National Collaborating Centre for Aboriginal Health (2012),

> Mothering is not limited to relationships between a female parent and her biological offspring. Mothering, as a relationship and practice, is a social and cultural act that occurs between multiple configurations of people of many generations—individually and communally. This is something Indigenous peoples have always known, celebrating extended families and lauding the wisdom of matriarchs as it applied and was transmitted to all the younger generations of a community. Mothering, understood in this way as a complex web of relational practices, was and is fundamental to life. This is perhaps also why mothering has often been so threatened while simultaneously holding the potential for (re)building the inherent strengths in our communities. (p. 3)

WHAT'S MISSING?

There are a number of theories about identity formation in children and youth. Indigenous worldviews have a "theory" about this as well. According to Gregory Cajete (2000) of the Tewa Nation, the importance of a community identity needs to be recognized. Cajete explains that "Relationship is the cornerstone of tribal community, and the nature and expression of community is the foundation of tribal identity. Through community, Indian people come to understand their 'personhood' and their connection to the communal soul of their people" (p. 86).

Many other Indigenous writers speak about identity as being inexplicably connected to one's community. Jeannine Carrière (2008), a Métis woman originally from the Red River area of Manitoba, states that "this collective view of identity is linked to the traditional view of children. When children are viewed as gifts from the Creator, their identity is recognized as having a critical place in the family and community they are from" (pp. 70–71).

In a research study with 90 Inuit, Kral (2003) identified that family and kinship are viewed as a determinant of well-being. Kral (2003) states that this research taught him that the Inuit are "collective selves [who] see group membership as central to their identity whereas individualistic selves are more autonomous from any particular group and may value individualism quite highly" (p. 8). Kral's observation applies to other Indigenous Peoples as well.

This sense of a collective self or community identity is place-based identity, which refers to the connectedness to a place of origin and the history connected to it. This, too, is a critical piece of Indigenous worldviews in that identity is strongly linked to a person's original territory, the history of that territory, and how this connection stays intact regardless of where the person lives. As Carrière (2008) reminds us, when it comes to the raising of children, "it takes a community.... How often have we heard this in different circles? It is, however, the core of Aboriginal child development and identity" (p. 77). I believe that community is the core of identity development for *all* children of the world.

WEALTH OF RESOURCES

Several Elders participated in interviews for this book and some focused on their views of community. Each of their contributions fit well together.

Dan (Oneida Nation) and his partner Mary Lou Smoke (Anishnawbe Nation) travel mostly around southern Ontario sharing their teachings with others. They also teach a course in the School of Journalism at the University of Western Ontario. Dan explained to me that he has been a part of many communities throughout his life, several of which were created by groups of Indigenous Peoples who came together for a united purpose. As a young man in the 1970s, Dan began to volunteer for a community newspaper in Akwesasne, a Mohawk community whose territory straddles the Ontario, Quebec, and New York borders. The building in New York where the newspaper was published was called "Nation House" and many Indigenous people from all across the United States lived there. Each person contributed to the Nation House community by chopping wood, cleaning, and cooking. Everyone did their part to ensure that the community functioned well. Dan described this experience as an immersion into a sense of community.

Dan also shared another example of this sense of community. He explained that he and Mary Lou travelled to Alberta to attend a Sundance ceremony, but before the ceremony could begin, everyone present spent a week clearing the land to prepare for the ceremony. This experience taught Dan and Mary Lou about the importance of a strong sense of community, as everyone worked hard together to make the Sundance ceremony happen.

After the work was completed, everyone who helped participated in a sweat lodge ceremony together, which further reinforced a sense of community.

I easily relate to what Dan is talking about here. A great deal of preparation goes into holding a ceremony and the preparation is an integral part of the experience. Preparations that I have participated in have included cooking traditional foods, gathering medicines such as cedar, and building a fasting lodge. Sometimes these activities are done alone and sometimes they are done with others. Sometimes these activities are done in silent prayer, using mindfulness meditation, or in conversation with others. For me, these activities were usually done with other women. I have participated in activities with people that I know well, people that I do not know so well, and people that I have just met.

I would say that, in many ways, once the preparation begins, the ceremony has already begun. The preparation is like part one of a series of parts. During the preparation, people come together on all four levels: spiritual, physical, emotional, and psychological. They share teachings, songs, stories, and information about themselves with each other and a connection is formed that deepens as the ceremony progresses.

For me, there is a huge difference in my experience participating in a ceremony when I am unable to participate in the preparation for that ceremony. When I am unable to participate in the preparation for a ceremony, I feel like I've missed out on something. I can't help feeling that the workers/helpers have bonded and I'm a bit on the outside. I'm just not quite as connected to the others if I am not able to participate in the preparation. There is something about being a part of building something, whether it is for a single ceremony or for the creation of community, that brings people together in a connected way that goes far beyond just being physically present. This kind of connected participation seems to help us *know* in a deeper way that we are an integral part of whatever is happening, that we belong, and that we have a right to have the experiences that we do. This experience of community-building has a direct bearing on social work if we choose to practise from a place of inclusiveness and social justice. Helping work is *social*, meaning that this work isn't just about talking, it's about doing, and that there is also a focus on societies or communities. Indigenous worldviews about working with communities can be valuable to all social workers. These worldviews focus on working *with* groups of people to assist them to move toward what they want and need. Helpers are not expected to do all of the work. Everyone who makes up a community is invited to participate in rebuilding that community because there is recognition that everyone has a contribution to make. We are reminded to consider one of the Seven Sacred Teachings, humility, which teaches that each of us is merely one tiny part of Creation. No individual is an expert on other people's lives. We listen and learn from the people who make up the community we are attempting to assist. Perhaps most importantly, we take the time to connect with the community, develop relationships, get to know people, and people get to know us. We also work hard at reminding everyone that they belong, that they are important, and that no work can be accomplished without them.

As a social worker working within a particular community, are you really a part of that community? Community can be many things—a geographical area, a group of people with similar concerns, a group of people with similar subjectivities. Do you live in the community you work in or do you leave that community at the end of each working day? Are the concerns of the community that you work in your concerns? Although different approaches will be necessary, it is not what is most important. I do not have to be a part of the Muslim, Two-Spirit, or youth population to care about how Muslims, Two-Spirit people, or youth are doing. I do not have to live in Iraq or Guatemala or northern Ontario to care about what is happening in these communities. It all matters to me because, like everyone else, I am a human being. We are all connected and what happens to everyone on the planet affects my humanity. This is why I care.

Eileen Antone is an Oneida woman, originally from Oneida of the Thames First Nation, who lived and worked in Toronto for many years, but has recently moved back home with her partner. As an academic, she took on a great deal of responsibility as an Associate Professor at the University of Toronto's Transitional Year Programme; an Associate Professor in the Department of Adult Education and Counselling Psychology, which is located in the university's Ontario Institute for Studies in Education (OISE); the Director of Aboriginal Studies; and the Director of the Centre for Aboriginal Initiatives. Eileen shared a great story about her experiences growing up in a community that embraced two distinct spiritual traditions found in the longhouse and in a Christian church. She told me:

> My grandfather was such a peaceful person and I wanted to have what he had. He went to church so I thought that was where he got it. When I was six years old, I started to go to the Baptist Church in my community. For awhile I walked until someone started taking me. I saw that church

was about teaching love. An Aboriginal person was the pastor at this church; we sang hymns in Oneida, but everything else was in English. At the Longhouse, everything was spoken in Oneida, so I couldn't understand most of it as my parents chose not to teach me the language so I wouldn't have as much trouble in school. I started going to the Longhouse as a teenager to learn the social songs and dances. Other teenagers who attended churches such as Baptist and Pentecostal like me also went. When I went to church I was told not to sing and dance. I decided to not sing and dance *in church*, but I would in the Longhouse. The teaching for me in all this was that God loves everyone. If a particular church accepted me, then it was good, but if it didn't, then it wasn't good. Both the Longhouse and the church taught me that community and family is vitally important—no one gets left behind. Community is about team work, responsibility and cooperation. People must work together. And through the support one gets, what needs to happen, happens. (E. Antone, personal communication, July 10, 2009)

Three other women who were interviewed also spoke about the importance of community in Indigenous worldviews. These women include Charlene Catchpole, who we heard from earlier in this book; Traditional Teacher Mary Lou Smoke, mentioned above; and Joanne Dallaire, who also appeared earlier. All three women focused on community within urban centres. Mary Lou related:

Community is about people taking care of one another, it is about a sense of belonging. A sense of community can be lost in urban centres. In Toronto, for example, there are many Nations and we need to listen to all of them. We need to welcome and share all the gifts that come with diversity. "Cultural gatekeepers" who want things to always be done their way are not helpful. Community is also about people coming together to deconstruct stereotypes, myths and misrepresentations. (M.L. Smoke, personal communication, February 20, 2009)

Joanne shares a similar message:

> Everyone wants to belong somewhere. Toronto is made
> up of pockets of communities of various populations.
> Many people go to cities because they are looking for
> something better for themselves and their families or
> they are running away from something harmful. This
> is true of many people who immigrate here, as well as
> with Indigenous Peoples, which is one of the many com-
> monalities amongst human beings. It may be difficult in
> North America to hold on to one's community when you
> are coming from another part of the world. When people
> come here, they want to hold onto their identities, so
> they create communities. It's healthy for people of many
> communities to come together to learn from each other;
> to educate ourselves about other peoples' experiences.
> Coming together is not a compromise of self, but rather
> about a common humanity and finding common ground.
> (J. Dallaire, personal communication, July 23, 2009)

Charlene Catchpole offers an example of what Mary Lou and Joanne are
speaking about from the shelter where she works:

> Ideas and values which focus on the importance of com-
> munity, the collective and ways of raising children work
> as many women who are in the shelter are newcomers to
> Canada and/or Indigenous, so these values often apply to
> them as well—for example, that women are the centre of
> the community and children are seen as gifts. (C. Catch-
> pole, personal communication, February 16, 2009)

As a social work practitioner, I have worked for many years in the violence
against women (VAW) movement. Although my direct practice has been
working with Indigenous communities, I have been a part of creating alliances with other populations of women as well, such as women of colour
and newcomers to Canada. Through these alliances, I have learned that perspectives about community may differ between groups of women who are
newcomers to Canada and women who have lived here for generations and,

therefore, have had their identities shaped by Western norms. A newcomer woman's identity tends to be strongly linked to the identity of her community. Value conflicts can arise because many violence against women services often focus on individual women. VAW services often provide women with one-on-one counselling and family issues are not adequately addressed because of limited organizational mandates. This is often the case when a woman seeks support for both herself and her partner. There are very few social service agencies that are able to meet the needs of women's partners, even though many frontline workers report that this kind of assistance has been requested by women over and over (Fong, 2010). It is true that concerns have arisen around maintaining safety while doing couple interventions and family-based support work. These concerns must be taken into consideration. Providing services to the abusing partner challenges the ways that mainstream services are typically delivered to women who have experienced or continue to experience violence. However, this does not mean we should ignore what women are asking from us. Fortunately, there are some communities that are currently exploring this issue. For example, social services agencies in Toronto such as the Family Services Association of Toronto, Abrigo Centre, Native Child and Family Services of Toronto, and the Family Group Conferencing Model at the George Hull Centre are now offering more integrated services (Alcalde & Caragata, 2007; Baskin, 2010, 2012; George Hull Centre, 2007).

It is also important to acknowledge that interventions such as family group conferencing and community-based support in the area of violence prevention have been a part of the work of Indigenous communities and urban agencies for quite some time. In fact, other communities and services are often learning how to do their work through implementing Indigenous practice examples. I have an example from a community program that I worked in for several years that focused on violence prevention. This program, called Mino-Yaa-Daa (meaning "Healing Together" in the Anishnawbe language), followed Indigenous worldviews that emphasize the value of the well-being of the community and the family above that of the individual. The individual is seen in the context of the family, which is seen in the context of the community. Thus, from this holistic perspective, when an individual is harmed, it is believed that this affects all other individuals in that person's family and community.

A major purpose of the Mino-Yaa-Daa program's services for women was to bring the community's women together. Only through women joining together can the disempowering silence around issues related to family violence be broken. By coming together in a circle, women learned that they were not alone, and that their situations and feelings were similar to those of other women. The women learned how to trust, take risks, and both give and receive support, while building relationships and a community of empowered women. This can only be achieved by individuals coming together in a circle. This kind of community-building cannot happen through individual counselling or therapy.

Two important elements were emphasized in the women's circles. The first was a focus on tools that women learned in the circle, which they then took with them to help them in their daily lives. It was important that what was learned in the circle had value to women in practical ways. There was also a need for women to support each other and develop friendships outside of the program. This kind of community-building was significant because it reinforced the Indigenous value of interdependency, which emphasizes an understanding that everyone has gifts and resources inside them and a natural ability to help others. Incorporated into all program services for women was a belief in the healing powers of laughter. We had fun!

When it comes to the importance of a community focus in anti-violence work, no one says it better than Andrea Gunraj (2005), who at the time was the outreach manager at the Metropolitan Action Committee on Violence Against Women and Children (METRAC) in Toronto:

> True safety doesn't come from individuals. I can buy security gadgets and learn how to defend myself, but it won't do anything to make the world a safer place. And it definitely won't benefit those who are most vulnerable to experiencing violence. True safety comes from community, from diverse people creating an inclusive vision for safety and working together to make a difference. (p. 8)

To close this section, I encourage all helpers to question the assumptions of universal standardized forms of their professions and begin to build multiple approaches to helping. Mainstream services in areas such as child protection and youth justice are evidence of how non-Indigenous practitioners can learn from Indigenous ways. Indigenous knowledges are significant sites of learning and are much more progressive than Western theories and practice in many areas. I am open and committed to sharing these knowledges for the good of all humanity.

HELPERS AS WARRIORS

Sharon Big Plume (2008) is an Anishnawbe/Métis woman who has written about the role of the warrior within Indigenous societies prior to colonization. She explores how the roles of warriors are akin to the ideals of social justice, which she defines simply and succinctly as "the ability to determine when something is not right, along with willingness to do something positive about it" (p. 235). Big Plume (2008) proposes that the role of the warrior can be understood in the context of setting standards for social work practice in Indigenous communities. She states that warriors have a mission that originates from their agreement with the Creator. Warriors prepare themselves to complete their mission through ceremonies and through their own ongoing healing, as it is understood that they will face challenges and adversities. Big Plume (2008) believes that both warriors and social workers have a vested interest in "strengthening people so the community can survive, flourish, and thrive" (p. 248).

Let's have a look at what Big Plume is advocating. Like warriors, part of what social workers do is to identify what is not right within societies, particularly regarding how certain populations are marginalized. As mentioned earlier, similar to a group of warriors, we are a helping profession whose role is tied to the notion of "doing." More on this will be taken up in the chapter on spirituality, but for now, within social work, choosing to have a relationship with one's Creator is an individual choice. Within Western social work codes of ethics, for example, there is no reference to spirituality as a guiding principle for practice. Social workers certainly prepare themselves for their work by attending university and participating in professional development which, in part, offers people direction about how to address specific challenges. Social workers are also encouraged to engage in ongoing self-reflexivity and self-care which relates to the warriors' teaching about the importance of personal healing. And, like warriors, one of the roles of a social worker is to help strengthen people in many areas, using many different methods. As this chapter emphasizes, social work with individuals and families cannot be separated from our work within communities.

I believe there are, and always have been, many types of warriors: academic ones, spiritual ones, and helping ones. In my opinion, social workers are a type of warrior and I am happy to report that I am not the only one who thinks so. We, as in myself and some members of Toronto's Indigenous community who make up the Aboriginal Advisory Committee in the School of

Social Work where I teach, named one of my courses *Ogitchita Lu Wa Ti Li Hu Nyu Nih*. *Ogitchita* means "warriors" or "strong helpers" in Anishnawbe and *Lu Wa Ti Li Hu Nyu Nih* means "teachings" in Oneida.

CONCLUSION

This chapter attempts to emphasize the overarching significance of community as the beginning point for helping within Indigenous worldviews. This means that the overall well-being of everyone must be considered rather than the well-being of only a few. Communal societies around the world carry this perspective and within these multiple communal spaces, it may be possible to come together to share our commonalities and form alliances and partnerships within helping.

The teachings are clear: a person cannot be viewed as separate from their community—however that community may be defined. Every community has a wealth of resources—teachers, natural helpers, warriors—and the answers to what we seek are there. This is a valuable Indigenous perspective that is influencing the area of social work more and more, as seen by the profession's willingness to take up practices such as family group conferencing and kinship placements within child welfare, which are based on the importance of community in the lives of people. For the good of the world, we must always keep in mind that every one of us is a part of the human community. We *are* all related.

REFERENCES

Alcalde, J., & Caragata, L. (2007). Environmental scan of services and service coordination for woman abuse in Toronto: Final report. *Toronto Public Health*. Retrieved from http://www.womanabuse.ca.

Anderson, K. (2000). *A recognition of being: Reconstructing Native womanhood*. Toronto: Sumach Press.

Anderson, K. (2006). New life stirring: Mothering, transformation and Aboriginal womanhood. In D. Lavell-Harvard & J. Lavell (Eds.), *"Until our hearts are on the ground": Aboriginal mothering, oppression, resistance and rebirth* (pp. 13–24). Bradford, ON: Demeter Press.

Anderson, K. (2011). *Life stages and Native women: Memory, teachings, and story medicine*. Winnipeg: University of Manitoba Press.

Baskin, C. (2010). Challenges, connections and creativity: Anti-violence work with racialized women. In J. Fong (Ed.), *Out of the shadows: Woman abuse in ethnic, immigrant and Aboriginal communities* (pp. 73–98). Toronto: Women's Press.

Baskin, C. (2012). Systemic oppression, violence and healing in Aboriginal families and communities. In R. Alaggia & C. Vine (Eds.), *Cruel but not unusual: Violence in Canadian families. A sourcebook for educators & practitioners* (pp. 147–178). Waterloo, ON: Wilfrid Laurier University Press.

Bédard, R.E.M. (2006). An Anishinaabe-kwe ideology on mothering and motherhood. In D. Lavell-Harvard & J. Lavell (Eds.), *"Until our hearts are on the ground": Aboriginal mothering, oppression, resistance and rebirth* (pp. 65–75). Bradford, ON: Demeter Press.

Big Plume, S. (2008). *Warriors, empowerment and social work* (Doctoral dissertation). University of Calgary.

Cajete, G. (2000). *Native science: Natural laws of interdependence.* Santa Fe, NM: Clear Light.

Carrière, J. (2008). Maintaining identities: The soul work of adoption and Aboriginal children. *Pimatisiwin: A Journal of Aboriginal and Indigenous Community Health, 6*(1), 61–80. Retrieved from http://www.pimatisiwin.com.

Corbiere-Lavell, J., & Lavell-Harvard, D.M. (2006). *"Until our hearts are on the ground": Aboriginal mothering, oppression, resistance and rebirth.* Bradford, ON: Demeter Press.

Fong, F. (2010). *Out of the shadows: Woman abuse in ethnic, immigrant, and Aboriginal communities.* Toronto: Women's Press.

George Hull Centre. (2007). *About the George Hull Centre.* Retrieved from http://www.georgehullcentre.on.ca/FamilyGroupConferencing.

Gunraj, A. (2005, Fall). Reaching out for safer communities. *Metropolitan Action Committee on Violence Against Women and Children.* Retrieved from http://www.metrac.org/wp-content/uploads/2014/07/newsletter.fall_.10.pdf.

Kral, M.J. (2003). *Unikaartuit: Meanings of well-being, sadness, suicide and change in two Inuit communities.* Final report to the National Health Research and Development.

National Collaborating Centre for Aboriginal Health. (2012). The sacred space of motherhood: Mothering across the generations. Ottawa: Author. Retrieved from http://www.nccah-ccnsa.ca/docs/child%20and%20youth/The%20Sacred%20Space%20of%20Womanhood%20-%20Mothering%20Across%20the%20Generations%20(EN%20-%20web).pdf.

Silver, J. (2006). *In their own voices: Building urban Aboriginal communities.* Black Point, NS: Fernwood Publications.

Simpson, L. (2006). Birthing an Indigenous resurgence: Decolonizing our pregnancy and birthing ceremonies. In D. Lavell-Harvard & J. Lavell (Eds.), *"Until our hearts are on the ground": Aboriginal mothering, oppression, resistance and rebirth* (pp. 25–33). Bradford, ON: Demeter Press.

Chapter Nine

SPIRITUALITY: THE CORE OF INDIGENOUS WORLDVIEWS

INTRODUCTION

In the early 2000s when I began to write and publish about spirituality in social work practice, education, and transformative change, there were few social work scholars, let alone Indigenous ones, who were publishing in this area (Baskin, 2002). Less than 15 years later, as I conduct a literature review on this topic, I am encouraged by the amount of information I find. Clearly, spirituality is emerging as an area of interest within the helping professions, including social work, psychology, psychiatry, and the health sciences. I would like to think that such interest in spirituality also means that more helpers and educators are listening to the needs of service users and students who practise some form of spirituality. I also believe that this interest in spirituality means that practitioners and educators are beginning to see people and the world around them in more holistic ways, a view that has been influenced by Indigenous worldviews.

The literature on spirituality in social work states that, historically, spirituality has been excluded due to the

> [s]eparation of church and state, which has a huge impact since most social workers are employed in agencies funded by the government; drive toward professionalism and evidence based scientific practice where spiritual issues are viewed as unscientific; and tendency to link spirituality to pathology rather than seeing it as a strength and resource. (Zapf, 2005)

Why the rising interest in spirituality within the helping professions of today, then? Authors such as Zapf (2005) argue that this interest is due to the fact that the Western mindset of individualism and materialism is not working for many people any longer. Many people are realizing that spirituality that encompasses connections to others, to community, and to the land may bring some meaning and fulfillment into their lives.

HOW IS SPIRITUALITY DEFINED?

Over the years, the social work and religious studies literature has remained consistent and similar in their definitions of spirituality as encompassing an individual's values, relationships with others, and a perception of the sacred (Baskin, 2002; Canda, 1989; Gilbert, 2000; O'Rouke, 1997; Pellebon & Anderson, 1999; Zapf, 2005). Although challenging to articulate, spirituality is about wholeness, making meaning, and creating inner peace. It is a sense of being one with both one's inner and outer worlds.

Although religion can be a part of spirituality, religion and spirituality are not interchangeable. And, despite scholars from diverse disciplines working on a definition for over a century, no single definition has ever been produced that pleases everyone (Brodd, Little, Nystrom, Platzner, Shek, & Stiles, 2013). In their recent work, Brodd and colleagues (2013) decided on this definition of religion: "it is a cultural system integrating teachings, practices, modes of experience, institutions, and artistic expressions that relates people to what they perceive to be transcendent" (p. 9). The significant difference between religion and spirituality is that religion is a structured form of spirituality that usually has a group following, whereas spirituality can include individual experiences with or without a structured belief system (Baskin, 2002).

My understanding of Indigenous spirituality, according to the teachings that have been passed on to me, is that spirituality embodies an interconnectedness and interrelationship with all life. Everyone and everything (both "animate" and "inanimate") is seen as being equal and interdependent, as part of the great whole, and as having a spirit. This view permeates the entire Indigenous vision of life, land, and the universe.

According to Ruth Koleszar-Green, who was introduced in Chapter One, spirituality as viewed through a Haudenosaunee lens emphasizes that:

> Our teachings are not only spiritual, they're about everything; about the Great Law of Peace and the Two Row Wampum which talk about peace, love and respect in all of our interactions. We can't separate the spiritual from any of the other aspects. Mentally taking the time to speak in a good way is an example of how the spiritual influences the mind. The Great Law of Peace is about the traditional ways of interacting and acting within the Haudenosaunee Confederacy based on peace, unity and the power of the good mind.
>
> Everything in one's body knows spirit. Spirituality is difficult to put into words. It's difficult to articulate on its own, to try and talk about it as separate from everything else when it isn't. This is an artificial way to discuss it. Spirituality isn't just about attending ceremonies; it's

about how we walk in the world, what we believe, how we connect, how we practice our beliefs.

Spirituality isn't stagnant. The ways in which we celebrate and acknowledge our existence and experiences change as we advance as a species. The underlying core or values of spirituality are always the same, but how this comes to fruition always changes. For example, our ways of practicing spirituality had to change as our people went into hiding when spirituality was legislated illegal by the colonization process. Sometimes we just understand why some things are done, such as ceremonies, but not exactly how to do all of the things that are involved.

Humility is paramount: we can't learn everything there is to know about spirituality, nor are we meant to. If we knew everything there is to know, then we would not have anything left to learn. Learning is important even when one is already a teacher. (R. Koleszar-Green, personal communication, November 26, 2008)

Joanne Dallaire sees spirituality as a relationship with what one believes in. She shared that:

There is a sense or connection to community through spirituality. Spirituality brings people together which is wanted and needed by all people. It is a way of expressing the self. Spirituality can create a bigger trust of the self. It is a process of going inward to look for answers.

Spirituality is a way of living that shows us that all is connected; everyone and everything has a reason, purpose and value for being here, even though we may not know what this is in the moment.

Experiencing a health or emotional crisis is seriously difficult. Everyone needs something that will help with this. It is comforting for people to believe in something. The power of faith is much known to heal the body. This helps us to understand the spiritual piece of healing. Spirituality is about turning it over to faith or one's beliefs when one cannot solve things alone. Spiritual practices are designed to heal in many cultures of the world. It is humanity's quest to seek things spiritual; to have something outside of the self to believe in, to help explain things that happen. (J. Dallaire, personal communication, July 23, 2009)

After more than 30 years at the School of Social Work at Ryerson University in Toronto, Dennis J. Haubrich is now Professor Emeritus. He has conducted research in the psychosocial dimensions of HIV disease, and has done work with AIDS caregivers in the area of spirituality. He now lives in Thornbury, Ontario, on southern Georgian Bay. Dennis started out as a colleague of mine, but over time, he became a friend. He is one of only a few White men that I have been able to discuss spirituality with. So, needless to say, I asked him to share his thoughts with me for this chapter. Dennis explains spirituality like this:

Getting to the core of who you are and validating this. It's so difficult to always try to be who everyone else wants us to be, like doing what you are told and blindly obeying, so spirituality is about letting go of all the roles and expectations that others have of us. Spirituality is engagement with all around us, but it is too often constructed as a private matter. We complicate our lives with social expectations: being part of the status quo, making money, getting married, having children. Although these things are neither positive nor negative, we construct ourselves according to what we are told to do, which includes these things usually.

Sometimes we cannot do anything to change the physical or outside of us, but we can change the inside of us. Spirituality is a search for the sacredness inside. It's about trying to find one's relationship with the world. It's a search for meaning and purpose. Making meaning of one's life is central to the spiritual endeavour.

Spirituality is relational: person to person, person to earth. It tells us that the answers we search for are inside us and in nature around us. Spirituality is recognition of our connectedness to all things, including things past. It means that I am part of this very earth—"remember that thou art dust and to dust thou shall return." (D. Haubrich, personal communication, November 26, 2008)

Dennis also shared his notions about the impacts of not having spirituality and how it can be of help:

> Most people are missing the spiritual dimension. They're searching for it, but they are not listened to by others when they try to speak of this because public social discourse is largely devoid of spirituality apart from the formal spiritual discourses generated by religions. Depression, despair, and suicide: these come from not having spirituality. We need to listen to people who want to speak about their spirituality, about the things that others in their ordinary lives don't want to hear.
>
> Spirituality is so significant for people who need to be released from addictions, trauma and resentments. It is healing. It unburdens us from what harms us. There are journeys that are unchosen in life and spirituality can help us get through these challenging ones such as a serious illness. (D. Haubrich, personal communication, November 26, 2008)

LAND-BASED SPIRITUALITY

Although Indigenous scholars who write about spirituality such as Kim Anderson (Métis) (2006, 2011), Michael Hart (Cree) (2002, 2009), Rod McCormick (Haudenosaunee) (2009), and myself (2002, 2009) include the land in their discussions, Western scholars rarely do. Within Indigenous worldviews and spirituality, there is no separation between people and the land. Place, or the physical environment, shapes Indigenous people's entire lives and everyone else's lives too, even though in Western culture people are largely removed and unaware of the connections between themselves and the physical environment in which they live. Place or physical environment directly influences cultures, education, relationships, food security, transportation, and spiritual beliefs. Around the globe there are sacred physical places that Indigenous Peoples fight to protect and where they conduct their ceremonies. The earth is often referred to as our Mother for She gives birth to us and provides all that we need.

Rarely do Indigenous Peoples anywhere in the world need buildings to conduct their ceremonies or offer prayers. Ceremonies are held on the land; all sacred objects used for prayer and ceremony come from the land;

the people sit directly on the land. When answers to questions are sought or healing is needed, many Indigenous Peoples go off by themselves and sit with their Mother in a fast or enter her womb through a sweat lodge.

It is often the land that awakens blood memories within us, such as being in a certain place and knowing down to our core that we have been here before. The land has the ability to calm and restore us and to inspire creativity. The land is home. The land is in us. The land *is* us.

I am originally from a tiny community on the Atlantic coast, but currently live in Toronto. It is the land that I miss the most: the contrast of woods and fields, the smell of the salt from the ocean, my feet sinking in the sand, and the ocean itself which goes on forever. As soon as I step onto the beach down home, my breathing begins to slow down, my muscles relax, and calmness begins. This physical state is not what I feel in myself and those around me as I go about my daily life in the city of Toronto, a place that always pushes at me to go faster and do more.

My best writing happens when I am on the land and water. I am able to tap into my creativity more easily. I have fewer distractions. I do everything at a slower pace. I feel as though I am as much a part of the place as the chipmunks who befriend me. It is not merely that the beauty of my surroundings inspires me to write, but that my connection to place takes over and allows access to what I am *supposed* to be writing. A good part of my Ph.D. dissertation was written while I was down home on the ocean and some of this book was written while I was on Manitoulin Island on Lake Huron. My writing is part of my spirituality.

Of course, there is land everywhere, even under the cement of cities. Indigenous spirituality goes with us wherever we go. It teaches that a person is a spiritual being and can practise spirituality anywhere. Spirituality is inside us, in a tree in a park, a flower in a garden, and the sunset at the end of each day. Land-based ceremony and prayer can happen every day in cities such as Toronto if we want it to.

Some forms of spirituality have many similarities. I have been meditating and practising mindfulness meditation for many years now. More recently, I have been drawn more and more to Buddhism because I see its similarities to my Indigenous spirituality. I have been very fortunate to explore a few retreats along my journey, but five years ago I had the experience of "when a student is ready, the teacher will appear." The Wisdom Master that I am learning from has a beautiful retreat in the mountains of southern British Columbia, with acres of land to walk along and a clean, fresh river running through it. I know that I am so attracted to this place because of the land and the river. When I am there, much of my teachings and meditating are directly on the earth, just as with my Indigenous ones. What I particularly am happy about is I did not have to give up any of my teachings and spiritual practices to become a Buddhist (of course, I would not have done so if that was a requirement). Rather, my spirituality is enhanced by practising Buddhism. We are all connected. In the summer of 2014, I took my vows. I could very likely be the only Mi'kmaq and Celtic Buddhist on the planet!

Before becoming a faculty member in the School of Social Work at York University in 2015, Koleszar-Green worked as a helper while attending postsecondary education. In one of her previous workplaces, the agency had a backyard where she would bring service users to talk. Notes Koleszar-Green, "I don't think about this. I just do it" (R. Koleszar-Green, personal communication, November 26, 2008). Spirituality is also a major aspect of Ruth's role as a member of the Aboriginal Legal Services of Toronto's Community Council, which will be elaborated on in the chapter "Healing Justice." As she sees it,

> Council members see people through eyes with love and respect. The Council creates a space where people can begin to connect with the Aboriginal community in Toronto and with their spirituality. Many of the people who come though the Council have not had Aboriginal spirituality in their lives and state that they feel disconnected from it and the community. In many of the hearings that I have participated in youth have expressed an interest in exploring Aboriginal spirituality and some specifically ask to speak to an Elder or Traditional Teacher. It's amazing to bear witness to them beginning to connect to medicines, beliefs and ceremonies that are a part of Aboriginal spirituality. For many people, being through the Council has been the best thing that's happened to them as it has helped them to connect, to belong, and to be a part of something that is so much bigger than them as individuals. Spirituality heals. (R. Koleszar-Green, personal communication, November 26, 2008)

As emphasized above and throughout this book, connection and relationships between service providers and service users may be the most important aspect of any healing process. This can be viewed as not only an individual relationship, but the one that is created between society and those who are struggling, such as people who are addicted to substances. Spirituality lies at the heart of caring relationships and connections. It guides our answers to questions such as do we see people who are addicted "as human beings who are legitimately part of the social fabric, deserving of compassion and respect?" (Maté, 2008, p. 297).

In writing about addictions, it is important to note that drugs or alcohol are not the only things that people struggle with, as sex, work, and food can also become addictions. For example, the obesity that so many people are living with can be seen as a way to deal with spiritual emptiness. As a bestselling author and well-respected medical doctor who has worked with addicted people in Vancouver's Downtown Eastside, Gabor Maté (2008) writes, "food is the universal soother, and many are driven to eat themselves into psychological oblivion" (p. 234).

Maté (2008) also makes some fascinating connections between spirituality, addictions, and the brain, which he believes can be far-reaching in the healing of addictions. As he notes, "brain research is demonstrating that mindful awareness is able to release the grip of harmful thoughts and also to change positively the physiology of the brain circuits where those thoughts originate" (p. 345). Maté is, of course, referring to mindfulness here. I appreciate how he frames mindfulness as something all helpers could be trained in so that we could observe our mind-states and reactions to those who are addicted. He suggests, and I could not agree more, that helpers in all areas, including medicine and psychiatry, would

> spare ourselves a lot of tension and stress, and protect our patients from further psychological trauma, if we learned to take responsibility for what we bring to our encounters with them. Five minutes of mindful meditation in the middle of a shift in the context of an emergency ward may seem like an absurd luxury, but the time saved and the bruised and inflamed emotions prevented would be a rich payoff. We may not be responsible for another's addiction or the life history that preceded it, but many painful situations could be avoided if we recognized that we are responsible for the way we ourselves enter into the interaction. (p. 385)

Groen, Coholic, and Graham (2012) and Gause and Coholic (2007) conducted literature reviews on spirituality in the social work literature. Neither of the reviews includes mention of a connection to place or the physical environment in the definitions of spirituality that are presented. This is taken up by Hunkpapa Lakota scholar Vine Deloria Jr., who wrote in 1999 that Western society can "attribute to the landscape only the aesthetic and not the sacred perspective" because it relates to the environment through technology such as photography or television (p. 257). When people have been in a particular place for generation after generation, their identities include that place and their connection to it. No one yet has explained this better than Spretnak (1991), who a quarter of a century ago wrote, "a people rooted in the land over time have exchanged their tears, their breath, their bones, all of their elements—oxygen, carbon, nitrogen, hydrogen, phosphorus, sulphur, all the rest—with their habitat many times over. *Here nature knows us*" (p. 19).

Generally speaking, Western social work and other helping professions focus on person–environment relationships. From this perspective, the person and the environment are viewed as two separate entities that relate to each other. It is this relationship that needs to be changed in order to assist the person, family, or group to gain greater stability, health, or well-being. However, within the helping professions, environment refers to systems such as the school, workplace, or services. It does not tend to include the physical environment or nature. As non-Indigenous social work educator Michael Zapf (2005) explains,

> We view the physical environment as separate from ourselves, as an objective thing, as a commodity to be developed or traded or wasted or exploited, as an economic unit, as property. The dominant western culture has been described as "hostile to nature" (Spretnak, 1991, p. 102) and antagonistic to any concept of personhood beyond individualism. It is little wonder that the treatment of spirituality in the social work literature has been limited to a narrow person-centered perspective. Yet there are alternatives. If we are open to exploring the connection of person and environment from a different worldview, we might have much to learn from the developing written knowledge base for Aboriginal social work. (p. 636)

My friend Dennis is certainly someone who understands the connection between himself and the environment. In 2005, Dennis went on a spiritual walk through France and Spain. He began walking on his 58th birthday— April 12. He arrived in Camino de Santiago de Compostela (the Way of St. James, as it is the alleged burial place of St. James the Apostle) on June 18 and in Finisterre, which is the medieval end of the world, on June 22. He walked 1,600 kilometres in three months.

Dennis explained to me that people from many parts of the world go on this pilgrimage for all sorts of reasons: to be healed, to be forgiven, or to simplify their lives. He went on this walk just as he was coming out of a dark place of despair and addictions due to the many losses he had in his life. He lost both his partner and his best friend and was wondering why he was still here. The walk was about coming into the light, choosing life rather than a slow death.

He walked for all of his friends who had died of AIDS. Dennis said that they were all with him as he walked. He was never alone and there was much healing in this for him. Dennis became much more aware of the physical earth he inhabits as he walked through Europe. He learned that the earth is sacred and that everything on it is sacred. He explained that he came to realize that he is only a speck on the earth, but a speck which is part of a much bigger existence:

> I believe that I am a part of something much greater than myself, albeit a small part, but a part nevertheless. When I was walking, I became aware that I was not alone in what I was doing, but that I was walking in the footsteps of thousands upon thousands of others. However, I was also not alone in another way for I was walking this journey for the people in my life that I had so loved and lost to AIDS. I was walking for them because they were no longer here to walk for themselves. My walk was also representative of putting the capstone on the journey out of sorrow, grief and addiction. (D. Haubrich, personal communication, November 26, 2008)

Dennis also built a different relationship with himself on the walk, with his body, and with his spirit, and he came to understand that body and spirit are integrated. He said he believes that as he became more and more aware of all the relationships he had with everything around him, he became clearer to himself about who he truly is. Considering his relationships to others who walked the pilgrimage at the same time as he did, Dennis explained,

> On the pilgrimage, everyone is on the same playing field. The freedom is that they don't have to be who they are in the rest of the world of work and all that. Equality doesn't have to be taught on the walk; people don't even ask what you do back home—this tends to only come out at the end—everyone is the same, a child of creation, connected by humanity. People let go of defences and methods of protection while on the walk. The pilgrimage allows for the authentic person to come out. People from all over the world go on this pilgrimage. There was an 18 year old youth from L.A., a social worker from Holland, a judge from Germany, a middle aged woman from Australia. Youth are sent by their parents as they are beginning to get in trouble. There is a program where youth walk the pilgrimage instead of going to jail. People are walking through the problems they have in order to find solutions inside themselves. I think that as a metaphor for life the Camino de Santiago Compostela is representative of helping people find their way, thus it's called "The Way." As such, it may be seen as providing direction, assisting in life decisions. (D. Haubrich, personal communication, November 26, 2008)

Dennis concluded our conversation about his life-changing spiritual journey:

> One only truly learns why one went on the walk, why and what one learned, when the walk is finished. It ended at Finisterre—the end of the world—which is a fishing village on the Costa de Morte—coast of the dead. It was believed that this was the literal end of the world in the days when people there believed that the world was flat and that the stars that shone above the sea were the souls of the dead. When I came to the end of the walk, I felt

that I had been given the greatest gift in the world: the gift was having been able to walk the Camino, to finally reach the end which is yet another beginning. I felt that I had been blessed to be able to do this walk. (D. Haubrich, personal communication, November 26, 2008)

On the walk, Dennis made the decision to leave academia and take early retirement. He knew it was the right decision as he felt out of place when he returned to his ordinary life there. He knew he was different from how he was before he went on the walk. He could no longer relate to the values of academia such as "rugged individualism rather than collectivism."

WHERE ARE WE HEADING?

I think Zapf (2005) would agree that there is a slightly different thought emerging in the typical person–environment social work literature of late. This comes from writing on eco-spiritualism. One of the more prominent writers on this subject is social work scholar John Coates (2003, 2004; Coates, Gray, & Hetherington, 2006). At this point in our history, it is beyond doubt that we are living amidst an environmental catastrophe whereby humans are slowly killing the earth. We are being warned through climate change and the increasingly frequent and horrendous "natural disasters" that are taking place around the globe. The industrial and agricultural practices that exploit both the physical environment and human beings are supported by the values and beliefs of a Western society that believes that economic well-being, which often translates into having more things and gaining material wealth, will lead to overall well-being. In other words, materialism and consumerism equals happiness. These beliefs also stress that technology will solve all of our problems. However, the kinds of material benefits that these claims support are not within reach of 80 percent of the earth's population, nor is our current rate of consumption sustainable (Chossudovsky, 1998).

The destruction of our planet ought to be of concern to the profession of social work because "progress" has contributed to vast social injustices such as racism, sexism, and the abuse of women and children. Overproduction in the name of progress has generated both pollution and increasing human exploitation as people engaged in low-paid and often dangerous jobs struggle to keep up with an increasing demand for products. Coates (2003) writes that humanitarian values that are also social work values can play a leading role in the struggle to assert new perspectives about how the West currently operates. Coates (2003) then goes on to discuss what he refers to as "new foundational assumptions" (New Foundational Assumptions, para. 3), which are: all things are connected, everyone and everything has inherent value, there is wisdom in nature, diversity is natural, and identity and fulfillment happen within community. Sound familiar? Coates (2003) does mention that these beliefs are consistent with those of Indigenous Peoples at least. He then offers a number of tasks for social workers to consider, based on the above assumptions:

> Nurture an understanding and appreciation of the connectedness of all things, and the hope and direction that can flow from this. This step is perhaps the most essential as it will involve, for many, the emergence of a transformed consciousness—the acceptance of an alternative world view. This is particularly significant in today's modern culture where politicians, transnational corporations, and mainstream economics preach from the same modernist book—neo-liberalism and market forces. An unfolding worldview moves away from an exclusively human-centered, materialistic, individualistic, and consumerist value system to one that is based on interdependence, community, the sacredness of all life, and sustainability. (New Tasks for Social Work, para. 3)

This time, however, Coates does not make reference to Indigenous worldviews although the connection is obvious. In another article by Coates, Gray, and Hetherington (2006), entitled "An 'Ecospiritual' Perspective: Finally, a Place for Indigenous Approaches," the authors advocate for the foundation of a new system of beliefs and values that is needed to guide human behaviour so that people become more in harmony with the earth. The authors further point out that several scholars now "recognize the important contribution made by traditional indigenous beliefs and values" (pp. 389–391). In another article, these same authors state that "Indigenous beliefs and values have gained recognition and credibility among the worldviews that provide a reconceptualization of the universe and humanity's relationship to it. In social work this has opened avenues of acceptance toward Indigenous approaches to helping"

(Gray, Coates, & Hetherington, 2007, p. 60). Increasing environmental concerns and a renewed interest in spirituality within the social work field, which has been expressed by scholars in the dominant culture, have perhaps resulted in greater openness to alternative worldviews. However, it is also problematic that Indigenous worldviews and understandings about spirituality and the interconnectedness of all life, including the earth, that have been a part of Indigenous belief systems for centuries, have been renamed "eco-spirituality" and have now only gained favour under the auspices of Western scholarship. The authors even go so far as to use the term "indigenous ecospiritual approaches" (Coates, Gray, & Hetherington, 2006, p. 395).

I suggest that an alternative way to look at the significance of Indigenous worldviews and their connection to the area of spirituality is within the helping professions. Rather than insisting that Indigenous knowledges be adapted to Western concepts such as eco-spiritualism, why not listen to what Indigenous Peoples are saying and learn from them? Trying to force these knowledges into Western constructs can never work as this changes these knowledges into something they are not.

In some ways, I see hopeful inspirations that humanity is heading toward making spirituality a part of everyday life and work. In 2014, I came across a call for proposals to present at a conference on spirituality and creativity in business management. I was sincerely shocked! Spirituality in business sounded like an oxymoron to me, but, of course, I had to find out more. There is an organization called the International Association of Management, Spirituality & Religion that puts on an international conference every two years. This is described as:

> The first global congress that invites both academics and leading executives to bring spirituality (aided and/ or fuelled by creativity) to the forefront of management research and practice. Our goal is to integrate spiritual practice within the daily work of professionals.... [We] explore new views of spirituality [and] creativity and [their] connection with management research, education and practice. [We] bring together academics, global spiritual leaders, practitioners and leading executives of many companies throughout the world to present, discuss and debate multiple angles of spirituality and creativity in the

broad field of management. (International Association of Management, Spirituality & Religion, 2015)

The conference for 2015 was titled "Spirituality and Creativity in Management World Congress: Challenges for the Future." Out of great curiosity and a desire to attend the conference, I decided to submit a proposal to present called "The Role of Spirituality in Indigenous Leadership." My proposal was accepted.

I was in a constant state of awe for the entire time I was in attendance at the conference. I listened to CEOs and managers with business degrees of all sorts of companies. I heard them ask questions such as "why am I here," "how do we determine the spiritual needs of staff members," and "how might we incorporate spirituality into training and professional development?" I participated in workshops about spiritual intelligence, daily reflections, individuals who have a light about them that attracts people to them, the power of the collective unconscious, and how we need leaders who are grounded in spirituality. How exciting and inspiring to know that there are people in business who care about the greater good and the state of our planet.

ASSESSING SPIRITUALITY

A fascinating approach is emerging within the area of spirituality and the helping professions—methods that can be used to assess a person's spirituality. There are verbal models, spiritual histories, and visual tools such as spiritual life maps, spiritual genograms, spiritual eco-maps, and spiritual eco-grams (Hodge, 2005a, 2005b). These methods are used to assist service users to explain their spiritual life journeys. Some of these methods are similar to art therapy and these methods support creativity and self-expression, and facilitate the process of making meaning of life experiences (Hodge, 2005a, 2005b). The methods are meant to explore spiritual resources and strengths.

I believe that including a person's spirituality in an assessment is a positive addition to the practice of all helping professions. I have always found it confusing that as helpers we are expected to access multiple areas of a service user's life, including whether a person has experienced physical and/or sexual abuse, yet have shied away from exploring spiritual beliefs. Why is it easier to ask a person if she has been sexually abused than to ask if, for example, she believes in a Creator or God? Thus, if methods for spiritual assessments are helpful to practitioners, I am in favour of them. Nevertheless, if we wish to send the message to service users that their spirituality is important in the helping process, why don't we simply ask them about their beliefs and practices? I believe that Indigenous methods of sincerely and respectfully inquiring about a person's spirituality can offer guidance to the helping professions. Ruth Koleszar-Green agrees:

> Students are not taught to ask service users about their spiritual beliefs or even to ask if this is a space where an individual or family can draw strength in a time of struggle. There is spiritual space everywhere and students need to connect their spirituality with their practice. They need ways to ground themselves while practicing; they need introspection; to have an understanding of how their beliefs have been harmed or lessened. Some clients want workers who practice spirituality. It can bring people from marginalized spaces together—we don't have to believe the same things—just believe. Students want spirituality in education. I found that in talking with my classmates they had a desire to have a space where speaking about spirituality within the classroom was okay; that they shouldn't have to park their identities at the classroom door, but should be able to bring their whole selves in. (R. Koleszar-Green, personal communication, November 26, 2008)

Assessing a person's spirituality may go a long way in helping them to understand their purpose on earth in this particular lifetime. According to Mi'kmaq teachings, Kisu'lk (the Creator)

> created the world for us to come to, in order to grow and to heal as spirits through the experiences we have as humans. Each of us has a particular purpose or goal when we come here, and our lives will be steered in such a way that the experiences we require will be made to happen. We will meet certain people, or be present at a particular place and time to witness a certain event. However, we always have free will, so we can choose to benefit from

our experiences or not, and we can resist the urges that try to steer us in the right direction. (Muin'iskw [Jean] & Crowfeather [Dan], 2013)

Furthermore, should we decide not to pick up the offer the first time around, or perhaps the second or the fifth,

> It is possible to find that preferred road again. If a person realizes that they are off-track and wishes to return to their path, help is provided by the spirits to make that happen. Once again, the right person will show up, or another opportunity will arise to have a particular learning experience that was missed previously. (Muin'iskw [Jean] & Crowfeather [Dan], 2013)

Even if we make it through an entire lifetime without accomplishing the things we need to accomplish, we simply come back in a new body to try again. This spiritual outlook is suggesting that we can uncover the reasons for us being here at this particular time and the direction that we can go should we choose to. For me, that element of choice is critical to understanding Mi'kmaq spirituality. There are no worries if we make the choice not to follow the suggested path because we can just come back later to do it. Thus, there are no judgements. It is important to note, however, that when you are walking your intended path, you find that all things you need, but not necessarily those you want, are made available to you. Wow, I think I hear the Wisdom Master's voice telling me this as well. Once again, the similarities in Indigenous and Buddhist spiritual teachings are amazing.

Another important part of Mi'kmaq spirituality that is non-judgemental and very practical is explained by teachers Muin'iskw (Jean) and Crowfeather (Dan) (2013):

> One of the hardest things to master can be the art of finding a balance between the things we must do in daily life, and the things we must do for spiritual reasons. It is not always appropriate, or even possible, to do all the spiritual things we would like to do. Smudging in public, for example, can attract unwanted attention that will ruin the effect of calm that we are trying to achieve. We may also have to delay

fasts or other ceremonies, because it is necessary to do some work-related task instead. Perhaps the toughest conflict comes from our modern lifestyle.... Always remember that we must live in both worlds, the spiritual and the mundane, just as our Ancestors did, and sometimes we must make compromises. As in all things, we simply do the best we can, and incorporate our spirituality as much as possible in our daily lives while still living in the modern world.

It is crucial that we accept these realities and talk to others about them. There is no point in feeling guilty about what we cannot do. Rather, we need to focus on what we can do. Incorporating spirituality into our lives is not a contest amongst us. If you have wooden matches to light your sweetgrass, excellent; if you do not, but have paper matches, great; however, if you only have a lighter, use it. If you have a bundle of home-grown tobacco to offer an Elder for a teaching, wonderful; if you have a pouch of tobacco you bought at the convenience store, use it; if all you have is a cigarette, offer it to the Elder. If you have the money to purchase a lot of cotton cloth to make your tobacco ties for a full moon ceremony, be thankful you are so fortunate; if what you have is a small square of cloth, also be thankful. Each of us does the best we can with what we have and that is okay. Should someone tell you it is not, then I strongly suggest you consider being with other people.

A significant challenge in enquiring about a service user's or a student's spirituality may arise if spiritual beliefs are discriminatory. For example, how does a practitioner or educator respond to spiritual beliefs that are patriarchal or heterosexist? Both Indigenous worldviews and the profession of social work support values and practices of inclusion and respect for diversity. However, if some people are being harmed by others' spiritual beliefs, perhaps there need to be limits to inclusion. Of course, this in turn leads to questions around who decides what beliefs ought to be included or excluded within education and practice. Such a decision is valuable for educators; students; practitioners; and organizations that govern the helping professions, education, and practice. Nevertheless, social work, in all of its components, is supposed to be committed to social justice. It is social justice that guides our values and ethics. Therefore, as social workers, we must be prepared to take a stand against what creates injustice.

CONCLUSION

Research from around the globe tells us that a respect for life and an acknowledgement of the interconnectedness of all beings, everything on the earth, and the earth herself is central to Indigenous worldviews (Richardson & Blanchet-Cohen, 2000). Recognition of what the spirit can teach us through dreams and meditation, for example, are simply a part of natural life. Spiritual experiences, and the learning that comes from these experiences, are significant to each person's life journey.

The interpretation of spirituality as presented in this chapter, however, is not the sole domain of Indigenous people. We do not have a monopoly on spirituality. What we do have is a spirituality that is connected to place. It is this connection that many of us would like to share with *all* peoples of the earth because without her, there is nothing.

There is absolutely no doubt that land-based spirituality can be lived by anyone regardless of one's perspective, adherence to a formalized religion, or one's belief in a God or Creator. Dennis Haubrich and the diverse people he met while on his pilgrimage show us this. However, each person needs to find their own way in connecting to the land and to the spiritual aspect of themselves rather than imitating the specific ceremonies of Indigenous Peoples. Certainly, guidance can come from the worldviews and knowledges of the Indigenous Peoples of whatever land we are on, but specific practices in developing a relationship with the land and one's spirit are connected to one's own particular roots. There are many ways to meditate other than through fasting in a lodge made of willow branches in the bush. There are many ways to cleanse and purify other than smudging. There are many ways to heal one's spirit other than through the sweat lodge. Look inside yourself, find out who you are, and listen to your dreams and blood memories as these will lead you to your own practices of connection.

But most importantly, please consider that if human beings continue to destroy our Mother the Earth, the colour of one's skin or the amount of money in one's bank account is not going to matter. If She dies, we all die. If there is only one thing that you learn about and decide to implement in your life that comes out of reading this book, let it be a belief in land-based spirituality which, at the end of the day, is caring for the earth and everything on Her.

REFERENCES

Anderson, K. (2006). New life stirring: Mothering, transformation and Aboriginal womanhood. In D. Lavell-Harvard & J. Lavell (Eds.), *"Until our hearts are on the ground": Aboriginal mothering, oppression, resistance and rebirth* (pp. 13–24). Bradford, ON: Demeter Press.

Anderson, K. (2011). *Life stages and Native women: Memory, teachings, and story medicine*. Winnipeg: University of Manitoba Press.

Baskin, C. (2002). Circles of resistance: Spirituality in social work practice, education and transformative change. *Currents: New Scholarship in the Human Services*. Retrieved from http://www.ucalgary.ca/SW/currents/.

Baskin, C. (2009). Evolution and revolution: Healing approaches with Aboriginal adults. In R. Sinclair, M.A. Hart, & G. Bruyere (Eds.), *Wicihitowin: Aboriginal social work in Canada* (pp. 133–152). Halifax: Fernwood Publishing.

Brodd, J., Little, L., Nystrom, B., Platzner, R., Shek, R., & Stiles, E. (2013). *Invitation to world religions*. New York: Oxford University Press.

Canda, E. (1989). Religious content in social work education: A comparative approach. *Journal of Social Work Education, 25*(1), 36–45.

Chossudovsky, M. (1998). *The globalisation of poverty*. Halifax: Fernwood Publishing.

Coates, J. (2003). Exploring the roots of the environmental crisis: Opportunity for social transformation. *Critical Social Work, 4*(1). Retrieved from http://www.uwindsor.ca/criticalsocialwork/.

Coates, J. (2004). From ecology to spirituality and social justice. *Currents: New Scholarship in the Human Services, 3*(1). Retrieved from http://fsw.ucalgary.ca/currents/.

Coates, J., Gray, M., & Hetherington, T. (2006). An "ecospiritual" perspective: Finally, a place for Indigenous approaches. *British Journal of Social Work, 36*(3), 381–399.

Deloria Jr., V. (1999). *For this land: Writings of religion in America*. New York: Routledge.

Gause, R., & Coholic, D. (2007). *Spirituality-influenced social work practice: A descriptive overview of recent literature*. Unpublished manuscript, Laurentian University, Sudbury, Ontario, Canada.

Gilbert, M.C. (2000). Spirituality in social work groups: Practitioners speak out. *Social Work with Groups, 22*(4), 67–84. doi: 10.1300/J009v22n04_06

Gray, M., Coates, J., & Hetherington, T. (2007). Hearing Indigenous voices in mainstream social work. *Families in Society, 88*(1), 55–66.

Groen, J., Coholic, D., & Graham, J.R. (2012). *Spirituality in social work and education: Theory, practice, and pedagogies*. Waterloo, ON: Wilfrid Laurier University Press.

Hart, M.A. (2002). *Seeking mino-pimatisiwin: An Aboriginal approach to helping*. Halifax: Fernwood Publishing.

Hart, M.A. (2009). Anti-colonial Indigenous social work. In R. Sinclair, M.A. Hart, & G. Bruyere (Eds.), *Wicihitowin: Aboriginal social work in Canada* (pp. 25–41). Winnipeg: Fernwood Publishing.

Hodge, D.R. (2005a). Developing a spiritual assessment toolbox: A discussion of the strengths and limitations of five different assessment methods. *Health and Social Work, 30*(4), 314–323. Retrieved from http://www.ingentaconnect.com.

Hodge, D.R. (2005b). Spiritual lifemaps: A client-centered pictorial instrument for spiritual assessment, planning, and intervention. *Social Work, 50*(1), 77–87. Retrieved from http://www.ingentaconnect.com.

International Association of Management, Spirituality & Religion. (2015). *Spirituality and Creativity in Management World Congress: Challenges for the Future.* (Conference.) Retrieved from http://www.esade.edu/homesite/eng/scmwc/.

Maté, G. (2008). *In the realm of hungry ghosts: Close encounters with addiction*. Toronto: Vintage Canada.

McCormick, R. (2009). Aboriginal approaches to counselling. In L.J. Kirmayer & G.G. Valaskakis (Eds.), *Healing traditions: The mental health of Aboriginal peoples in Canada* (pp. 337–354). Vancouver: University of British Columbia Press.

Muin'iskw (Jean), & Crowfeather (Dan). (2013). *The human experience*. Retrieved from http://www.muiniskw.org/pgCulture2.html.

O'Rouke, C. (1997). Listening for the sacred: Addressing spiritual issues in the group treatment of adults with mental illness. *Smith College Studies in Social Work, 67*(2), 177–195.

Pellebon, D.A., & Anderson, S.C. (1999). Understanding the life issues of spiritually-based clients. *Families in Society, 80*(3), 229–239. doi: 10.1606/1044-3894.676

Richardson, C., & Blanchet-Cohen, N. (2000). *Survey of post-secondary education programs in Canada for Aboriginal peoples*. University of Victoria, Institute for Child Rights and Development, and First Nations Partnerships Program. Retrieved from http://www.nvit.ca.

Spretnak, C. (1991). *States of grace: The recovery of meaning in the postmodern age*. San Francisco: Harper.

Zapf, M.K. (2005). The spiritual dimension of person and environment: Perspectives from social work and traditional knowledge. *International Social Work, 48*(5), 633–642. doi: 10.1177/0020872805055328

Chapter Ten

Mental Health as Connected to the Whole

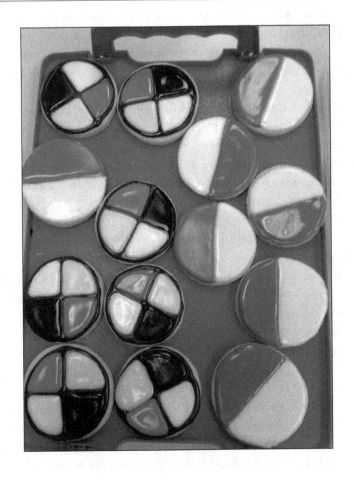

INTRODUCTION

There are two reasons for sharing parts of my personal story in my writing: one is to provide examples of the theories, worldviews, and practices I am discussing; and the other is intended to let readers know that anyone can be living with challenges. As mentioned at the beginning of this book, I am a person living with mental health challenges, but for this chapter, I would like to say a little more about this.

Since the first edition of this book, I have been given an additional diagnosis, an extra medication, and have had to take a second medical leave from work. Apparently, I am now also "somewhat" bipolar, but lean more to the depression end of the pole. Perhaps I now have an answer to the often asked question, "how can you do so much?" I will reply, "I did my Ph.D., got tenure and promotion while raising a pre-school son in four years because I was manic much of the time" or "I wrote all of those articles when I was manic as I was awake for days at a time." For me, this attitude is about taking a challenge and putting it to good use, although I am certainly not able to do so all the time. I sincerely hope, though, that the work I do also comes from a place of insightfulness and creativity. After all, I do not want to give my "mental health illness" all the credit!

As for medication, I now take three kinds every day. I have been told by my psychiatrist that this is a lot. The third one was added during my leave of absence from work and I know it is necessary for me to function as I wish, without extreme highs and lows which are so hard on my body and brain. I have accepted that I will be on medication for the rest of my life here and I will not be ashamed about it. I have come a long way from the young practitioner who felt judged and incompetent when I heard a co-worker say to another, "I don't know about that Cyndy. She's nuts and takes pills you know." I do not know how she knew about the medication, but clearly my confidentiality about the medication had been breached. Unfortunately at the time, I internalized this comment, rather than holding the agency accountable. That would not happen today!

Am I fine with having these mental health challenges? Absolutely not; if they could be taken away tomorrow, I would be thrilled. But I have come to believe, through my spirituality, that they have been given to me for a reason. I have many helpers in my life, some human and many of the earth and cosmos. I believe it is my responsibility to share how I have been helped with others because teachings are meant to be shared and perhaps I can encourage others like me to share their stories of what helps and what does not.

This chapter will define mental health in terms of wellness and difficulties, explain the role of colonization as a cause of such difficulties, address the tension between Indigenous and Western approaches to mental health, and explore how the two approaches may work together.

DEFINITIONS AND CAUSES

Consistent with Indigenous perspectives generally, mental health is broadly viewed through a holistic lens that takes into consideration the well-being of spirit, body, emotions, and the mind. This lens also includes how human beings are connected to and have a relationship with their environment (Carrière & Richardson, 2013). In addition as declared by the United Nations (2009), justice is just as important as healthy food, clean water, and love to the overall mental well-being of Indigenous Peoples. Mental health includes knowing one's purpose for being here and connecting this to a sense of belonging to a culture or community (Haskell & Randall, 2009; Vickers, 2009). Each of us is on a lifelong journey to achieve as much balance as we can within all aspects of ourselves, gain as much cultural pride as possible, and connect to all of Creation in whatever ways we can.

In a research project with Indigenous women who identified as having mental health challenges, participants describe mental health in the following ways:

- being happy;
- having a spirit that is not broken;
- peace of mind;
- stable within oneself and family;
- being in the moment; and
- being in balance (Roy, 2014).

Also in keeping with Indigenous worldviews is the notion of mental health and well-being as connected to community. A mentally healthy community is one that is on its Nation's traditional lands; shares language concepts; and practises ceremonial processes around birth and rites of passages such as puberty, marriage, adoption, divorce, and death (Brasfield, 2009). Of course, such communities value the experiences and wisdom of their Elders who teach younger people; are financially stable over the long term, with their members earning appropriate income; and have strong leadership that represents the interests of their membership (Brasfield, 2009). In addition, it would be enormously helpful if Canadian governments were also mentally healthy in that they would be "aware and respectful of [First Nations communities'] values and activities" (Brasfield, 2009).

According to the literature, the most common manifestations of mental health challenges are depression, anxiety, PTSD, suicidality, self-harm, and substance misuse (Briere & Jordan, 2004; First Nations Centre, 2005; Haskell & Randall, 2009; Matheson & Anisman, 2009; Tjepkema, 2002). Of note is the fact that Indigenous women living in First Nations communities experience particularly high rates of depression compared to Canadian women, at 18 percent versus 9 percent, respectively (Macmillan, Jamieson, Walsh, Wong, Faries, & McCue, 2008). Furthermore, 64 percent of survivors of the residential school system have been diagnosed with PTSD (Bombay, Matheson, & Anisman, 2009; Corrado & Cohen, 2003).

Regarding substance misuse, it is important to state that, although Indigenous Peoples are often stereotyped as alcoholics, compared to the general Canadian population, they are more likely to not consume alcohol at all (34 percent vs. 21 percent) and are less likely to consume alcohol on a weekly or daily basis (18 percent vs. 44 percent) (First Nations Centre, 2005). The only instance where Indigenous Peoples have a higher percentage of consuming alcohol than the general population regards binge drinking one or more times a week (16 percent vs. 6 percent) (First Nations Centre, 2005).

Although there is no dearth of materials published on the causes of mental health challenges for Indigenous Peoples, a main theme emerges. The impacts of colonization are referred to as intergenerational, historical, or collective trauma as these impacts are the experiences of all Indigenous Peoples, rather than individual ones. Populations with a history of long-lasting collective traumas can be vulnerable to many challenges, which certainly includes Indigenous groups who have been facing these challenges for the past few centuries.

The term "historical trauma," which emerged in the mid-1990s (Brave Heart, 1998, 2003; Duran & Duran, 1995; Duran, Duran, Brave Heart, & Yellow Horse-Davis, 1998; Wesley-Esquimaux & Smolewski, 2004), is explained as psychological, emotional, and spiritual wounding over the lifespan and across generations, resulting in group trauma leading to high rates of mental health and social challenges for Indigenous Peoples (Brave Heart-Jordan & DeBruyn, 1995; Evans-Campbell, 2008; Robin,

Chester, & Goldman, 1996; Stamm, 1995; Stamm, Stamm, Hudnall, & Higson-Smith, 2004).

As stated throughout this book, language is critically important, thus words describing the long-term, cumulative trauma associated with Indigenous Peoples needs examining. Even though several generations have experienced the unique trauma of Indigenous Peoples, I do not favour the term "intergenerational" as it seems to place responsibility on a generation, or group of parents, for "passing on" their trauma to their children, who then grow up to do the same with their children. Although better, "historical" trauma, which distances itself from focusing on parents, may not take into account that colonization has not ended and people are experiencing such trauma every day. These terms are intended to help explain extremely complex experiences, but as I have just highlighted, how they are interpreted can be problematic. At the present time, I use the term "collective trauma" as it implies that all Indigenous Peoples are burdened with the impacts of colonization, even though, for example, they may not be survivors of the residential school system. This term includes a historical perspective and how this impacts the present, and it acknowledges that the racism faced by Indigenous Peoples today continues to traumatize them.

The impacts of colonization can be included in the social determinants of health or, as I call them, the structural determinants of health (Baskin, 2007a, 2012). One of these determinants is racism, which is a psychosocial stressor and is experienced by the vast majority of Indigenous Peoples in areas such as education, employment, health care, and the justice system. In fact, research by Bombay, Matheson, and Anisman (2009) indicates that 99 percent of urban Indigenous Peoples face at least one racist incident over a one-year period. Other research associates depression, alcohol misuse, and suicidal ideation and attempts with ongoing racism (Bombay, Matheson, & Anisman, 2008a, 2008b; Carrière & Richardson, 2013; Czyzewski, 2011; Walls, Chapple, & Johnson, 2007; Whitbeck, Chen, Hoyt, & Adams, 2004; Yoder, Whitbeck, Hoyt, & LaFromboise, 2006).

Addressing the overall collective trauma of Indigenous Peoples and that of individuals and families are equally important. The first lessens the tendency for a person to blame themselves and those around them for the behaviours they have adopted to cope with the trauma that is beyond their control, while highlighting the value of political and social movements to address the injustices of the past and the structural violence that continues today (Kirmayer, Brass, & Valaskakis, 2009; Wesley-Esquimaux

& Smolewski, 2004). Society's recognition of colonization and its current impacts will assist Indigenous Peoples in a "process of personal and collective transformation from helpless victim, through courageous survivor, to creative thriver" (Kirmayer, Brass, & Valaskakis, 2009, p. 455). This is also important because the structural violence against Indigenous Peoples may not be revealed through individual stories.

However, "although the personal is political, it is not *only* political" (Kirmayer, Brass, & Valaskakis, 2009, p. 456). Thus, focusing on only colonization and collective trauma may overshadow the all too real stress and losses that an individual and family is going through. This can be a dilemma for education in the helping professions, in that they focus on either critical theories and models, such as anti-colonialism and anti-oppression, or on clinical practices. Rather, since both of these are important in the helping professions, both need to be taken up in education.

INDIGENOUS VIEWS

Perhaps the most significant understanding of an Indigenous view of mental health challenges is that they are seen as existing within relationships rather than within individuals, and that respect, reciprocity, and responsibility maintain positive mental health (McCormick, Thira, Arvay, & Rinaldis, 2014; Mehl-Madrona, 2009). Currently, Indigenous Peoples are on a healing journey that encompasses community empowerment and self-determination, which leads to healthy and responsible relationships. This journey, which emphasizes a holistic approach, reminds us that there is no separation between physical health and mental health. Hence, depression and anxiety, for example, are states of health like a physical injury or malnutrition due to a poor diet (Brasfield, 2009).

The work of Chandler and Lalonde (1998) regarding suicide rates of Indigenous youth is well-known for its findings about how the more self-determination a community has, the lower suicide rates it has. Lalonde (2009) makes some pertinent remarks on this, challenging the much-believed idea that there is an epidemic of youth suicides across all communities. He states that, in fact, suicide rates differ from one community to another. Hence, First Nations communities should not be painted with the same brush as the risk of suicide is not the same in each community, which suggests that resources for suicide prevention ought not to be going into all communities, but rather to those that need them (Lalonde, 2009). Healthy First Nations communities have access to traditional lands, promote original languages, create cultural facilities, have control of health services and education, and ensure that women are meaningfully involved in local governance (Lalonde, 2009). Communities that have success in some of these areas have lower rates of youth suicide and higher school completion rates, and those that have all of these in place have no suicides (Lalonde, 2009). There is other research that supports the practising of one's culture as being a significant strength (Chandler & Lalonde, 1998, 2009; LaFromboise, Hoyt, Oliver, & Whitbeck, 2006; National Council of Welfare, 2007; Yoder, Whitbeck, Hoyt, & LaFromboise, 2006). Over several years, many researchers have demonstrated that communities that have protective factors of cultural continuity had no suicides over a six-year period, whereas communities that had none of these factors present suffered a suicide rate ten times the national average (Chandler & Lalonde, 2009). Obviously, then, healing needs to focus on the strengths of communities and the building of further capacities.

In his research with Indigenous Elders, Mehl-Madrona (2009) identified 12 key concepts of Indigenous knowledges regarding mental health well-being. These are:

1. genuinely listen;
2. incorporate a relational model of the self;
3. help communities find their own solutions;
4. know that people can heal themselves;
5. place emphasis on the community;
6. use own experiences to help relate to others;
7. be passionate and care about the work you do;
8. maintain some independence from politics;
9. remember hope, faith and the power of the mind;
10. focus on empowerment over treatment;
11. recognize the teachings and messages that come from difficult experiences; and
12. all healing is spiritual healing.

These concepts are important for students and practitioners in the mental health field to learn. As Mehl-Madrona (2009) concludes from his research,

> mainstream training programs currently offered ... are often concerned with teaching students how to be expert professionals who apply solutions to fix or treat problems,

expecting their patients to comply with expert advice. Spirituality is rarely discussed. Clinical detachment and professionalism is emphasized. Humour is rarely encouraged ... [plus] our trainees need to be more humble. (p. 27)

I have noted other differences in both my social work practice and that of other helpers. For example, Indigenous helpers do not necessarily use an individual appointment model within an office, but are more likely to meet with people where they are, such as in their homes, in schools, or at gatherings. They may also include family and community members in the discussions. Healers from other communities may come to assist people in need of help and stay at their homes while doing so, which contradicts the boundaries of mainstream mental health services. Another important aspect of providing mental health services to Indigenous Peoples is the telling of stories. Storytelling is not only a way to pass on teachings and cultures, but is also significant in the healing of mental imbalances in the context of holistic understandings, which include all aspects of a person and their interconnectedness with everyone and everything around them. The significance of stories emerged in Mehl-Madrona's (2009) research with Elders, whereby he learned that

suffering [exists] within the context of a story, for all we are is story ... all that is left when we die are the stories told about us ... the self we believe we are is just the story we tell ourselves to make sense of all the stories that have been told about us ... to understand an illness, it is necessary to place it within the context of the story that the person is living. To help a person, we must hear as many stories that are being, or have been, told about that person as is possible. (p. 23)

Often, people do not associate their harmful current behaviours with the trauma they have experienced in the past and which may be continuing today. Hence, part of the healing process is to assist with coming to a place where we tell a different story about who we are and the people we have relationships with. Such new stories can first be ones that we are thinking, then ones we are telling and, finally, those we are living. Stories then, and Indigenous healing methods generally, are strengths that reframe "problems" and "symptoms" into adaptations. In other words, traumatized people are not collections of symptoms, but rather are coping as best they can, which needs to be seen as "courageous attempts to survive."

TENSIONS

When examining the tensions between Indigenous and mainstream ways of seeing and addressing mental health challenges, the first acknowledgement must be that the latter continues to deny any responsibility for producing the conditions that cause mental health challenges for Indigenous Peoples. Instead of acknowledging their role in this, mainstream society prefers to blame the victims, deny any responsibility for the current situations of Indigenous Peoples and communities, and feign ignorance of Canada's history. The dominant view, then, holds Indigenous Peoples responsible for the traumatic events that mainstream society inflicts on them. Thus, services that ignore the historical and current social and political context will not address the needs of Indigenous Peoples.

A second important consideration is how the values of mainstream mental health treatment tend to focus on individuation, self-actualization, and independence, which are not part of Indigenous worldviews (McCormick, 2009). Hence, as Stewart (2008) suggests, mental health services may be underused due to different understandings. However, Indigenous understandings are needed as communities wish to promote mental health and healing, which calls for these understandings to be included in research on this topic. Unfortunately, much of the research to date builds upon, and is influenced by, assumptions about Indigenous Peoples, which makes any findings questionable (Nelson, 2012). Western society has no way of defining mental health challenges other than through its perceived ideas of what is "normal." Norms, beliefs, and ways of defining such challenges that do not conform to these ideas are then often viewed as problematic for mainstream psychiatry and psychology (Nelson, 2012). As noted in other parts of this book, many valuable sources of knowledge and understandings, such as that of Elders, are often discredited, rather than seen as helpful to all people.

Research with Indigenous women has identified a number of barriers they have in accessing mainstream mental health services (Baskin, Strike, & McPherson, 2015; Roy, 2014). The most common ones identified are:

- lack of confidentiality and trust;
- fear of losing their children;

- lack of child care within programming;
- cookie-cutter approaches;
- lack of training of mental health workers;
- waiting lists;
- lack of validation;
- problems with medication;
- stigma; and
- racism (Baskin, Strike, & McPherson, 2015; Roy, 2014).

For Indigenous mothers, the fear of having their children apprehended by child welfare far outweighs their need for help for their mental health challenges. Some research findings outline women's concerns regarding this dilemma, which included not liking to tell people about the medications they take, being viewed as addicts, and being afraid that they will be reported to child protection services, which can lead to their children being apprehended, rather than receiving help (Baskin, Strike, & McPherson, 2015; Roy, 2014). Another common concern expressed by Indigenous women was how mental health workers linked their challenges to substance misuse even though they did not consume alcohol or drugs or had not had a drink in years. This is a perfect example of how workers stereotype Indigenous Peoples, as seen earlier in this chapter. Overall, women often do not feel validated for what they tell workers, making them feel like they are being abused by the systems that are supposed to help them (Baskin, Strike, & McPherson, 2015; Roy, 2014). By the way, I use the term "substance misuse" deliberately despite the fact that some of my well-respected colleagues take the position that "terms and language often change over time as learning evolves, [thus] the preferred term in 2015 is 'substance use.' It replaces descriptors that relay stigma, like 'substance abuse' or 'misuse'" (Goodman, Baker-Lai, Ussher, Coutu, & Smylie, 2015). I do not use the term "substance abuse," of course, because that certainly does sound stigmatizing, but I actually see the term "substance use" as being problematic as well. To me, this term covers everyone, as who does not use any substances? People use Tylenol for a headache and caffeine to stay awake. However, I do not see "substance misuse" as stigmatizing at all. Rather, I see it as referring to misusing substances, as in using Tylenol when one does not have a headache.

Some of the literature focuses on assessment and diagnosis for mental health challenges, which can both be barriers to seeking assistance.

Sometimes, the problem is the failure of clinicians to get information about a person's trauma history, which leads to the person not getting the help they need (Bombay, Matheson, & Anisman, 2009). In other situations, psychiatry assesses mental health challenges as neurobiological in nature. While this may be accurate since trauma and stress can cause neurochemical changes in several areas of the brain, including serotonin levels (Anisman, Merali, & Hayley, 2008), it fails to include aspects of the body, emotions, and spirit, as well as a person's interconnectedness with family, community, and land (Vickers, 2009; Vukic, Gregory, Martin-Misener, & Etowa, 2011).

In Western mental health services, an assessment leads to a diagnosis, which typically includes a label. Often, one needs the label to access services, but they can also be restrictive, rather than fluid and descriptive. Furthermore, assessment tools themselves can be hindering if they are viewed as intrusive to building a helping relationship or taking on stereotypical assumptions about Indigenous Peoples.

As emphasized earlier, it is also important to take into consideration the impact of language. For example, the use of words such as "pathology," "dysfunction," "symptoms," and "disorder" can be stigmatizing, as though a person has a disease or some personal flaw, rather than a socially created experience (Haskell & Randall, 2009). Instead of such language, words such as "adoption," "strategic," and "responses" reflect how traumatized people courageously survive their circumstances (Haskell & Randall, 2009). As Vukic, Gregory, Martin-Misener, and Etowa (2011) suggest, "if psychiatry took into account Aboriginal ways of knowing or understandings of the wholistic nature of mental health and healing, it would broaden the assessment, diagnosis and care of individuals with mental illness" (p. 73). I strongly agree with this, but would not use the word "illness" to refer to those who have such challenges. In addition, mainstream mental health services often focus on what is "wrong" with a person, rather than what has happened to them. This creates a deficits approach to helping when it would be more helpful to emphasize a person's strengths and potential.

COMING TOGETHER

I believe that clinical and Indigenous approaches to mental health can work together to assist Indigenous Peoples and communities, but, of course, this comes with conditions. I have experienced this combination from the lens of both a service user and a service provider. I have in mind one psychiatrist and one clinical social worker who helped me with my mental health challenges over the many years that I have accessed mainstream services. They had several things in common that helped me:

- They did not assume I followed Indigenous worldviews or spirituality, but once they knew, they encouraged, rather than only supported me in doing so.
- They encouraged that I see Elders and attend ceremonies.
- When they did not understand something regarding my beliefs and practices, they asked.
- Neither told me that they had an Indigenous friend, that their great-great-grandmother was part Cherokee, or that I didn't look Indigenous.
- They put my access to Indigenous methods first; for example, if I got an appointment to see an Indigenous healer on the same day that I had one with them, they insisted I go to the former.
- They did not assume I had a substance misuse problem, which led to my telling them early on that I had a drug addiction primarily to cocaine.
- They talked to each other, so they could be on the same page with helping me.
- The psychiatrist did not push medication on me and shared whatever was known about the different options, what might work best for me, and the side effects of each.
- When I expressed concern over taking medication, they asked, "if you were seriously diabetic, would you take insulin?" When I replied "yes," they then asked, "so why is this any different?"
- Both were able to frame my experiences as part of the bigger picture regarding the impacts of colonization on my mental health.
- They never tried to take my power away or tried to impose their beliefs on me.
- From time to time, they shared bits of information about themselves, such as the social worker who also grew up in a family impacted by alcoholism and the psychiatrist who asked me what I thought of certain schools of social

work as one of his daughters was considering which ones
to apply to.
- Because of my positive experience with the social worker,
this had a role to play in my decision to go into this profession.

The limited literature that speaks to collaborative relationships between
Indigenous and non-Indigenous mental health workers emphasizes ethics.
Ethical space requires cooperation between these two groups in connection
to cultural safety, which "prompts us to ask a series of questions to unmask
the ways in which current mental health policies, research, and practices
may be perpetuating neocolonial approaches to healthcare for Aboriginal
peoples" (Smye & Browne, 2002, p. 47).

When it comes to considering collaborations between mainstream mental health services and Indigenous agencies and communities, Smye and
Brown (2002) suggest exploring questions together, such as:

> Do current mental health services fit well with Aborig-
> inal understandings of health, illness and healing, or are
> they at odds with them given the current sociopolitical
> environment? How are the myriad social issues such as
> poverty and homelessness, that serve to curtail the life
> opportunities of many Aboriginal people, and, as such,
> their health, being addressed...? (p. 49)

Collaboratively addressing these questions could likely inform all levels of
health ministries and policy makers in creating and funding appropriate prevention, promotion, and services for Indigenous Peoples and communities.

It is vitally important that Indigenous communities take back the
responsibility for their mental health well-being, which requires cultural
safety, self-determination, and the incorporation of principles of social
justice. As Vukic, Gregory, Martin-Misener, and Etowa (2011) suggest,
Indigenous and Western conceptions of mental health and illness are vastly
different. However, as their article stresses, this "does not mean a complete
rejection of Western models of care, but rather seeks to incorporate what
is valuable from these models even while recognizing that they are im-
bedded within colonialist structures and processes" (p. 46). This is a clear
message of the need to work together. In addition, in a research project

with Indigenous Elders about mental health, these participants supported a combination of both approaches. "The Elders spoke of the need to respect both Western and Traditional approaches to healing and self-care, including the use of prescription pills, when necessary, combined with ceremonies, when requested" (Stout, 2010, p. 33).

If Elders are so willing to work with mainstream mental health services, then the latter must be willing to work with them. Such services need to support capacity building and the development of sustainable structures in Indigenous communities that will promote mental health. This is also built on research that shows that the strengths of social bonds in these communities, and the emphasis on benefits for the whole, provides a network for community-based mental health services (Native Association of Health Organizations [NAHO], 2011; Vickers, 2009). This position is also taken up by Joseph P. Gone (2009) of the Gros Ventre Tribal Nation of Montana, who is an Associate Professor of Psychology and American Culture (Native American Studies) at the University of Michigan:

> If the low number of mental health professionals—especially Native mental health professionals who presumably have a greater commitment to working in often isolated indigenous settings—can barely begin to meet the needs of our peoples, how might psychologists cultivate and expand the non-professional "mental health" resources available to Native communities without either repudiating our years of training and experience or rendering our roles obsolete? (p. 431)

Gone (2009) answers his question by stating that a new generation of helpers (he refers specifically to psychologists) is necessary. These new helpers are not needed so much for direct clinical practice as they are for creative program development, training for Indigenous helpers, mentorship, clinical supervision, and writing proposals for funding grants. All of these methods of support, however, must be in partnership with local Indigenous people, such as Elders, healers, and other natural helpers.

There are some core concepts that need to be taken up when it comes to collaborations and relationships in delivering services for mental health well-being. A basic one is how service users are viewed and named. In mainstream practices, these people are referred to as clients (consumers) or patients (passive receivers), which conflicts with Indigenous perspectives in which a person is seen as an equal partner in the helping relationship. According to the Native Association of Health Organizations (NAHO, 2011), such a person is referred to as a "relative" (p. 21). NAHO's (2011) research found that many Indigenous people wondered if the clinician actually believed in Indigenous healing practices since the subtleties of their words did not match their actions.

This input from Indigenous service providers speaks to the need for humility, a critical value within Indigenous worldviews. This value is described by Minkler and Wallerstein (2008) as "a lifelong commitment to self-evaluation and self-critique in order to redress power imbalances and to develop and maintain mutually respectful dynamic partnerships based on mutual trust" (p. 11). Significantly, as emphasized throughout this book, the mental health worker needs to engage in self-reflexivity whereby their culture, and all that comes with it, are acknowledged in the work they do with Indigenous people. They are also required to always consider the historical and current social contexts of the mental health challenges of Indigenous Peoples, as well as their incredible strengths and resiliency to survive despite such adversity. An example of this is the way in which fetal alcohol spectrum effects (FASE) is depicted in media campaigns, which typically state that FASE is 100 percent preventable—don't drink alcohol and your baby will be fine. However, this is a blame-the-victim message as it does not connect the many systemic barriers that impede pregnant Indigenous women from accessing services (Baskin, Strike, & McPherson, 2015; Carrière & Richardson, 2013).

During my years as a practitioner, I collaborated with many mental health workers, and those who I had strong working relations with had approaches similar to those I referred to earlier. What stands out about them was a bit of humility, meaning that they knew that they did not know everything and were not self-conscious about this; they respected my input and often acted upon it; we had clear roles in how we worked with individuals and families that they did not overstep; and they often took a backseat so that I could take the lead in the work. They may not have had the same values as me, such as sharing personal information, but acknowledged that, as an Indigenous practitioner, my values likely mirrored those of the people we served. These psychiatrists and mental health nurses were also willing to answer my questions and educate me on the approaches of their professions. I was privileged to learn a great deal from them and continue to be grateful for their generosity.

Through these relationships over the years, I came to a number of realizations. For example, for someone struggling with mental health challenges, part of the role of medications, crisis intervention, and hospitalization in a Western framework is to re-establish needed connections to the here and now and alleviate distress. The goal of a ceremony, such as the sweat lodge, the meals that follow them, and the use of herbal medicines with Indigenous frameworks, is to activate a new relationship between the body, mind, emotions, and spirit. Both approaches may calm people and ground them in human relationships, so they can make informed choices about treatment and/or healing (Baskin, 2007b, 2007c).

Within Indigenous worldviews, the individual and the community are not separate. Relatives, community members, and support people need to work together in order for health and well-being to be re-established for the person. Thus, it is necessary for everyone to work toward common goals. Ceremonies often help to achieve these connections. In fact, family members often speak about how ceremonies help them understand how they can help their loved one (Baskin, 2007b, 2007c). Mainstream mental health workers can also work with families using modelling in their responses to those who are struggling with mental health challenges. For example, modelling calmness for people who are experiencing anxiety attacks can help them to cope with ongoing symptoms of anxiety. Such modelling can also help to increase the skills of the family while assisting them in building the confidence to know they can help (Baskin, 2007b, 2007c).

SOME SUGGESTIONS

Some authors offer recommendations to both Indigenous and non-Indigenous mental health workers in their collaborations, and for policy implications. Those recommendations stressed most often in the literature are:

- listen to communities as they will tell you what is helpful for them;
- highlight protective factors for children and youth;
- raise awareness about mental health in ways that community members understand and can relate to;
- create around-the-clock mental health services and programming, particularly for women and youth, that they help create;

- organize people to leverage their collectivity to protect themselves and ensure ethical standards of services;
- create community women's groups that do activities together unrelated to mental health;
- conduct research on and document what is working, as well as the resiliency and human agency of people living with mental health challenges, and the consequences of trauma on the collective;
- educate the Canadian public about the causes of mental health challenges and the many strengths of Indigenous Peoples (Barry & Jenkins, 2007; Haskell & Randall, 2009; National Council of Welfare, 2007; Roy, 2014).

It is critically important, however, that all of us be mindful of the diversity amongst Indigenous Peoples, as nicely explained by Michael Hart (2014):

> We must shift from the attitude that Indigenous people need to choose between either Indigenous or mainstream ways of being and move toward a more nuanced understanding that people can express themselves in various ways. Through my interactions with many Indigenous people I have learned that some are strong in their Christian faith, others are steeped in Indigenous spirituality, and still others have been denied the opportunity to understand themselves as members of a people. Some Indigenous people are strict followers of non-Aboriginal ways of being in the world, whereas others know only their Indigenous traditions and culture. Still others combine these two ways of being in the world, for example, an Indigenous teenager who listens to rap music, dances pow wow, practices Buddhist meditation and participates in sweat lodge ceremonies with her grandparents. (pp. 81–82)

I completely agree with Michael. I myself am a person of much diversity. I do all of the activities mentioned above, but am also a grandmother!

CONCLUSION

The professions of psychology and psychiatry, when implementing un-critical knowledge and practices, can obviously be problematic in terms of pathologizing and individualizing the mental health challenges of Indigenous Peoples. However, they do not have to be. As Haskell and Randall (2009) write,

> within these professions (and others) a small but critical mass of non-traditional clinicians, scholars, researchers, and practitioners are engaging in ways of understanding and approaching mental health and healing which are contextualized, expressly acknowledge social injustice, colonialism and the social relations of inequality, and which interpret and apply the insights of the psychological and neuro-sciences in a social context framework. (p. 78)

This is encouraging to hear and I sincerely hope that those working in the mental health field open their minds and hearts to exploring partnerships with their counterparts in Indigenous communities and urban agencies. These opportunities to learn from one another and, more importantly, better serve Indigenous Peoples, are available to those who are willing to take risks, be creative, and welcome diverse ways of looking at mental health wellness.

Indigenous and Western worldviews may or may not agree about the origins or meanings of mental health challenges or about specific practices to address them. However, the intentions of the helping practices are certainly similar and include:

- calming the person and grounding them in human relationships;
- ensuring informed choice about decisions regarding healing;
- acknowledging that mental health challenges are not only within a person, but are connected to relationships;
- restoring relatedness to others; and
- acting as a role model for others.

These observations can be a starting point for Western and Indigenous helping practices within the mental health field.

REFERENCES

Anisman, H., Merali, Z., & Hayley, S. (2008). Depressive disorders: Contribution of cytokines and other growth factors. In M. Hersen & A.M. Gross (Eds.), *Handbook of clinical psychology* (pp. 779–809). New York: Wiley.

Barry, M., & Jenkins, R. (2007). *Implementing mental health promotion.* Philadelphia: Elsevier.

Baskin, C. (2007a). Structural determinants as the cause of homelessness for Aboriginal youth. *Critical Social Work, 8*(1). Retrieved from www.criticalsocialwork.com.

Baskin, C. (2007b). Conceptualizing, framing and politicizing Aboriginal ethics in mental health. *Journal of Ethics in Mental Health, 2*(2). Retrieved from http://www.jemh.ca/.

Baskin, C. (2007c). Working together in the circle: Challenges and possibilities within mental health ethics. *Journal of Ethics in Mental Health, 2*(2). Retrieved from http://www.jemh.ca/.

Baskin, C. (2012). Aboriginal youth talk about structural determinants as the cause of their homelessness. In M.J. Cannon & L. Sunseri (Eds.), *Racism, colonialism and Indigeneity in Canada.* Toronto: Oxford University Press.

Baskin, C., Strike, C., & McPherson, B. (2015). Long time overdue: An examination of the destructive impacts of policy and legislation on pregnant and parenting Aboriginal women and their children. *International Indigenous Policy Journal, 6*(1). Retrieved from http://ir.lib.uwo.ca/iipj/vol6/iss1/5.

Bombay, A., Matheson, K., & Anisman, H. (2008a). Resilience and vulnerability to depressive symptoms associated with perceived discrimination among First Nations people in Canada. Poster presented at the Annual Meeting of the Society for Personality and Social Psychology, Albuquerque, New Mexico.

Bombay, A., Matheson, K., & Anisman, H. (2008b). The impact of stressors on second generation Indian Residential School survivors. Poster presented at the Annual Meeting of the National Network for Aboriginal Mental Health Research, Montreal, Quebec.

Bombay, A., Matheson, K., & Anisman, H. (2009). Intergenerational trauma: Convergence of multiple processes among First Nations peoples in Canada. *Journal of Aboriginal Health, 5*(3). Retrieved from http://www.naho.ca/journal/2009/11/03/intergenerational-trauma-convergence-of-multiple-processes-among-first-nations-peoples-in-canada/.

Brasfield, C. (2009). Polar bears and fireweed. In Canadian Institute for Health Information (Ed.), *Mentally Healthy Communities: Aboriginal Perspectives* (pp. 21–23). Ottawa: Author. Retrieved from http://cahr.uvic.ca/nearbc/documents/2009/MentallyHealthyCommunities.pdf.

Brave Heart, M.Y.H. (1998). The return to the sacred path: Healing the historical trauma response among the Lakota. *Smith College Studies in Social Work, 68,* 287–305.

Brave Heart, M.Y.H. (2003). The historical trauma response among natives and its relationship with substance abuse: A Lakota illustration. *Journal of Psychoactive Drugs, 35,* 7–13.

Brave Heart-Jordan, M., & DeBruyn, L. (1995). So she may walk in back: Integrating the impact of historical trauma in the treatment of Native American women. In J. Adlerman & G.M. Enguidanos (Eds.), *Racism in therapy of women: Testimony, theory, and guides to antiracist practice* (pp. 345–362). New York: Haworth.

Briere, J., & Jordan, C.E. (2004). Violence against women: Outcome complexity and implications for treatment. *Journal of Interpersonal Violence, 19,* 1252–1276.

Carrière, J., & Richardson, C. (2013). Relationship is everything: Holistic approaches to Aboriginal child and youth mental health. *First Peoples Child & Family Review, 7*(2), 8–26.

Chandler, M.J., & Lalonde, C.E. (1998). Cultural continuity as a hedge against suicide in Canada's First Nations. *Transcultural Psychiatry, 35*(2), 191–219.

Chandler, M.J., & Lalonde, C.E. (2009). Cultural continuity as a moderator of suicide risk among Canada's First Nations. In L.J. Kirmayer & G.G. Valaskakis (Eds.), *Healing traditions: The mental health of Aboriginal peoples of Canada.* Vancouver: University of British Columbia Press.

Corrado, R.R. & Cohen, I.M. (2003). Mental health profiles for a sample of British Columbia's Aboriginal survivors of the Canadian residential school system. Ottawa: Aboriginal Healing Foundation. Retrieved from http://www.ahf.ca/downloads/mental-health.pdf.

Czyzewski, K. (2011). Colonialism as a broader social determinant of health. *International Indigenous Policy Journal, 2*(1). Retrieved from http://ir.lib.uwo.ca/iipj/vol2/iss1/5. doi: 10.18584/iipj.2011.2.1.5

Duran, E., & Duran, B. (1995). *Native American postcolonial psychology.* Albany: New York Press.

Duran, E., Duran, B., Brave Heart, M.Y.H., & Yellow Horse-Davis, S. (1998). Healing the American Indian soul wound. In Y. Danieli (Ed.), *International handbook of multigenerational legacies of trauma* (pp. 341–354). New York: Plenum.

Evans-Campbell, T.J. (2008). Historical trauma in American Indian/Native Alaska communities: A multilevel framework for exploring impacts on individuals, families, and communities. *Journal of Interpersonal Violence, 23,* 316–338.

First Nations Centre. (2005). *First Nations regional longitudinal health survey (RHS) 2002/03: Results for adults, youth, and children living in First Nations communities*. Ottawa: Author.

Gone, J.P. (2009). Re-envisioning mental health services for Native North America. In L.J. Kirmayer, G.M. Brass, & G.G Valaskakis (Eds.), *Healing traditions* (pp. 419–439). Vancouver: University of British Columbia Press.

Goodman, D., Baker-Lai, C., Ussher, C., Coutu, M., & Smylie, D. (2015). Evidence-informed practice in intervening with children affected by substance abuse (CASA). *Ontario Association of Children's Aid Societies Journal, 59*(1), 2–11.

Hart, M.A. (2014). Indigenous ways of helping. In P. Menzies & L. Lavallée (Eds.), *Journey to healing: Aboriginal people with addiction and mental health issues* (pp. 73–85). Toronto: CAMH.

Haskell, L., & Randall, M. (2009). Disrupted attachments: A social context complex trauma framework and the lives of Aboriginal peoples in Canada. *Journal of Aboriginal Health, 5*(3), 48–99. Retrieved from http://www.naho.ca/journal/2009/11/02/disrupted-attachments-a-social-context-complex-trauma-framework-and-the-lives-of-aboriginal-peoples-in-canada/.

Kirmayer, L.J., Brass, G.M., & Valaskakis, G.G. (2009). Conclusion: Healing/invention/tradition. In L.J. Kirmayer, G.M. Brass, & G.G. Valaskakis (Eds.), *Healing traditions* (pp. 440–472). Vancouver: University of British Columbia Press.

LaFromboise, T.D., Hoyt, D.R., Oliver, L., & Whitbeck, L.B. (2006). Family, community, and school influences on resilience among American Indian adolescents in the upper Midwest. *Journal of Community Psychology, 34*(2), 193–209.

Lalonde, C.E. (2009). Can a community be called "mentally healthy"? Maybe, but only when the whole really is greater than the sum of its parts. In Canadian Institute for Health Information (Ed.), *Mentally healthy communities: Aboriginal perspectives* (pp. 3–37). Retrieved from http://cahr.uvic.ca/nearbc/documents/2009/MentallyHealthyCommunities.pdf.

Macmillan, H., Jamieson, E., Walsh, C., Wong, M., Faries, E., & McCue, H. (2008). First Nations women's mental health: Results from an Ontario survey. *Archives of Women's Mental Health, 11*, 109–115. doi: 10.1007/s00737-008-0004-y

Matheson, K., & Anisman, H. (2009). Anger and shame elicited by discrimination: Moderating role of coping on action endorsements and salivary cortisol. *European Journal of Social Psychology, 39*, 163–185.

McCormick, R.M. (2009). All my relations. In Canadian Institute for Health Information (Ed.), *Mentally healthy communities: Aboriginal Perspectives* (pp. 3–7). Retrieved from http://cahr.uvic.ca/nearbc/documents/2009/MentallyHealthyCommunities.pdf.

McCormick, R., Thira, S., Arvay, M., & Rinaldis, S. (2014). The facilitation of healing for Indigenous youth who are suicidal: A retrospective exploratory study. In J.R. Cutcliffe, J. Santos, P.S. Links, J. Zaheer, H.G. Harder, F. Campbell ... R. Eynan (Eds.), *Routledge International Handbook of Clinical Suicide Research* (pp. 351–363). New York: Routledge. Retrieved from http://www.tru.ca/research/publications.html.

Mehl-Madrona, L. (2009). What Traditional Indigenous Elders say about cross-cultural mental health training. *Journal of Science and Healing, 5*(1), 20–29.

Minkler, M., & Wallerstein, N. (2008). Introduction to community-based participatory research: New issues and emphases. In M. Minkler & N. Wallerstein (Eds.), *Community-based participatory research for health: From process to outcomes* (pp. 5–23). San Francisco: John Wiley & Sons.

National Council of Welfare. (2007). *First Nations, Métis and Inuit children and youth: Time to act.* Ottawa: Author. Retrieved from http://publications.gc.ca/collections/collection_2007/hrsdc-rhdsc/HS54-1-2007E.pdf.

Native Association of Health Organizations (NAHO). (2011). Traditional Anishinabe healing in a clinical setting. *Pimatisiwin: A Journal of Aboriginal and Indigenous Community Health, 9*(1), 65–86.

Nelson, S. (2012). *Challenging hidden assumptions: Colonial norms as determinants of Aboriginal mental health.* Ottawa: National Collaborating Centre for Aboriginal Health. Retrieved from http://www.nccah-ccnsa.ca/Publications/Lists/Publications/Attachments/70/colonial_norms_EN_web.pdf.

Robin, R.W., Chester, B., & Goldman, D.M. (1996). Cumulative trauma and PTSD in American Indian communities. In J. Anthony, M.J. Friedman, E.T. Gerrity, & R.M. Scurfield (Eds.), *Ethnocultural aspects of posttraumatic stress disorder: Issues, research, and clinical applications* (pp. 239–253). Washington, DC: American Psychological Association. doi: 10.1037/10555-009

Roy, A. (2014). Intergenerational trauma and Aboriginal women: Implications for mental health during pregnancy. *First Peoples Child & Family Review, 9*(1), 7–21. Retrieved from http://journals.sfu.ca/fpcfr/index.php/FPCFR/article/view/189/214.

Smye, V., & Browne, A.J. (2002). Cultural safety and the analysis of the health policy affecting Aboriginal people. *Nurse Researcher, 9*(3), 42–56.

Stamm, B.H. (Ed). (1995). *Secondary traumatic stress: Self-care issues for clinicians, researchers, and educators.* Baltimore: Sidran Press.

Stamm, B.H., Stamm, H.E., Hudnall, A.C., & Higson-Smith, C. (2004). Considering a theory of cultural trauma and loss. *Journal of Loss and Trauma, 9*(1), 89–111.

Stewart, S. (2008). Promoting Indigenous mental health: Cultural perspectives on healing from Native counselors in Canada. *International Journal of Health Promotion & Education, 48*(2), 49–56.

Stout, R. (2010). Kiskâyitamawin miyo-mamitonecikan: Urban Aboriginal women and mental health. Winnipeg: Prairie Women's Health Centre of Excellence. Retrieved from http://www.pwhce.ca/pdf/urbanAboriginalWomenMentalHealth.pdf.

Tjepkema, M. (2002). The health of the off-reserve Aboriginal population. *Health Reports Supplement, 13*, 1–17.

United Nations. (2009). *State of the world's Indigenous peoples.* Retrieved from http://www.un.org/esa/socdev/unpfii/documents/SOWIP/en/SOWIP_web.pdf.

Vickers, P.J. (2009). Ancestral law and community mental health. In Canadian Institute for Health Information (Ed.), *Mentally healthy communities: Aboriginal perspectives* (pp. 17–20). Ottawa: Author. Retrieved from http://cahr.uvic.ca/nearbc/documents/2009/MentallyHealthyCommunities.pdf.

Vukic, A., Gregory, D., Martin-Misener, R., & Etowa, J. (2011). Aboriginal and Western conceptions of mental health and illness. *Pimatisiwin: A Journal of Aboriginal and Indigenous Community Health, 9*(1), 65–86. Retrieved from http://www.pimatisiwin.com/online/wp-content/uploads/2011/08/04VukicGregory.pdf.

Walls, M.L., Chapple, C.L., & Johnson, K.D. (2007). Strain, emotion, and suicide among American Indian youth. *Deviant Behavior, 28*, 219–246.

Wesley-Esquimaux, C.C., & Smolewski, M. (2004). Historic trauma and Aboriginal healing. Ottawa: Aboriginal Healing Foundation.

Whitbeck, L.B., Chen, X., Hoyt, D.R., & Adams, G.W. (2004). Discrimination, historical loss and enculturation: Culturally specific risk and resiliency factors for alcohol abuse among American Indians. *Journal of Studies on Alcohol, 65*, 409–418.

Yoder, K.A., Whitbeck, L.B, Hoyt, D.R, & LaFromboise, T. (2006). Suicidal ideation among American Indian youths. *Archives of Suicide Research, 10*, 177–190.

Chapter Eleven

HEALING JUSTICE

INTRODUCTION

Perhaps justice as seen through an Indigenous lens is one of the more well-known topics within Canadian mainstream society. Such recognition of Indigenous forms of justice can be seen in the justice system's diversion programs for youth in conflict with the law and child welfare's family group conferencing as a way of finding alternatives to state-care for children. This chapter explores how Indigenous Peoples and communities are leaders in the area of restorative types of justice, and what others can learn from their knowledge and experience in this area.

THERE'S ALWAYS A STORY

I have been using the term *healing justice* for more than 20 years since I first became interested in how to help people who hurt others, particularly in the form of family violence, including sexual abuse. At that time, I had worked with people who had survived violence for several years. There was a specific moment which I remember clearly to this day that propelled me on the journey of learning about and practising how to help those who harm others. I had been working with a 13-year-old survivor of familial sexual abuse for a few months. One day, she said to me, "If what you are telling me is right, that I'm not responsible for what he did to me, then why am I in healing and he isn't?" I had no answer for her, but knew I had to do something.

What I did first was approach some of the Elders and Traditional Teachers I knew to ask them about what was done about people who hurt others historically. They taught me about what they called *customary laws* or *natural laws*.

I spoke with Elders and Traditional Teachers (e.g., Rebecca Martel, Edna Manitowabi, Vera Martin, Lily and Paul Bourgeois, Gertie Beaucage, Jim Dumont, Eva Cardinal, Sylvia Maracle, Michael Thrasher, Herb Nabigon, and Jan Longboat) from a diversity of Nations such as Anishnawbe, Haudenosaunee, Cree, and Métis, and found consistencies among their responses. They told me that prior to contact, violence within families and communities was rare due to a number of factors. For example, the necessity of people being able to get along was critical as each person's survival depended on the other. Communities were small and people lived in close quarters, so cooperation was vital. Also, due to these living arrangements, plus the purpose of some of the clans—for example, the bear clan had the job of looking out for others and members of the fish clan were the mediators when problems arose—many eyes and ears were on each other.

I was also told that children were rarely alone with any adult. Instead, as children learned by observing and doing, girls, for example, tended to spend most of their time with the women of the community. In addition, since many Nations were matrilineal (e.g., Haudenosaunee and Mi'kmaq), through customary laws, women were the bosses of their homes. This meant that if a man was to hurt his partner and she no longer wanted to be with him, he would have to leave the home. Any children would stay with her and he would continue to have the responsibility of providing for them.

Aside from practicalities, Indigenous worldviews as expressed through values and spiritual teachings also played a crucial role in ensuring that harm to others was minimal. Such values and teachings have been discussed in earlier chapters, so I will simply mention them here: balance within and amongst people, harmony with all around them, children are gifts from the Creator, every person is valued as each has a role and purpose within their community, and everything one does has an impact on others.

It was explained to me that due to these practicalities and spiritual beliefs, incidents of harm were rare. If a person harmed another, it became a matter of community concern. The idea was to uncover why the incident occurred and what harm was caused. Both the person who did the harm and the one who had been harmed were now seen as being out of balance, which impacted everyone in the community. Thus, balance needed to be restored through means such as accountability on the part of the one who caused the harm, compensation provided to the person who had been harmed, and healing ceremonies. Once harmony within the community had been restored, everyone moved on.

For most Indigenous people, the most severe consequence was being ostracized, which could occur if the harm caused was extreme. This was a powerful deterrent within customary law that no individual would have wanted to face. Being ostracized from the community likely equalled death, as it would have been difficult to survive in such harsh environmental conditions on one's own.

All of the Elders and Traditional Teachers I spoke with were adamant that aspects of their customary laws needed to be brought into today's world when harm was caused. They all spoke of carrying the same spiritual teachings and worldviews of their ancestors regarding balance and harmony. Each emphasized how out of balance those who harmed others were and how they needed to be accountable to the person they hurt, that person's family, and the community. They also emphasized healing for both the harmed person and the one who caused the harm. They consistently pointed out that situations such as woman and child abuse originated from the impacts of colonization, through which violence had been learned and passed on from one generation to the next. Some of these Elders and Traditional Teachers were actively involved in processes of restoring customary laws within their communities and Indigenous agencies in urban centres. They were overwhelmingly supportive of me doing the same.

Then I turned to the literature, where I found little on the topic. However, I did find a report written in 1999 by A.C. Hamilton and Murray Sinclair—a traditional Anishnawbe man who just happens to be a judge in Canada, was a member of the Truth and Reconciliation Commission of Canada on the residential school system, and, as of 2016, is a Senator. Their report was based on an inquiry into Indigenous Peoples and the criminal justice system in Manitoba. Not only did this report confirm what I already knew about racism in the system as evidenced by overpolicing of Indigenous Peoples in urban centres, higher arrests, higher incarceration rates, longer sentences, higher denial of parole rates, and longer parole and probation sentences, it also echoed what the Elders and Traditional Teachers had shared with me about customary laws.

In the following sections I describe some key components of Indigenous justice, how they work in practice, and why many believe the principles can be applied to other populations.

VALUES BEHIND THE PRACTICES

As has been referred to in each chapter of this book, everything is related or connected within Indigenous worldviews. There is nothing that is not viewed through a relational lens. Thus, customary laws, natural laws, community-based justice, restorative justice, and alternative justice are all terms meant to describe processes that restore balance and harmony between people, communities, and all of Creation.

When one person harms another, they have created an imbalance within people and communities. They have negatively impacted upon numerous relationships: between the harmed person and their sense of self; between them and their own sense of self; among both their family members and other community members. The person who has been harmed does not see themself in the same way. They may blame themself for what happened, and lose confidence, and they are often afraid. They no longer view their environment in the same way. Perhaps the home is no longer safe, or they fear being out after dark or cannot tolerate being alone. In other words, their relationships with all that they have been connected to have been damaged.

The person who has done the harm has likely been disconnected from themself, other people, and their community for some time due to the harms that have been done to them in the past. And the community may no longer trust them or they may shun them, as they do not feel safe. The energy around the whole community is tense and can be felt between people and in the air; everyone and everything is out of sorts—all is out of balance.

Many processes can help at this point: Sentencing Circles, Healing Circles, ceremonies, one-on-one work with the people involved, family circles, and removing the person who has done the harm for a time. But if these methods do not centre on the restoration of balance for everyone from a relational lens, they likely will not heal. And healing is the overall goal of Indigenous worldviews of justice.

WHAT NEEDS TO BE LEARNED?

Many people—both professionals, such as social workers and psychologists, and family members, such as partners—would agree that incarceration often further develops harmful behaviours rather than the opposite. Those returning home after spending time in jails or prisons are often more hardened, distanced from their emotions, violent, skilled in criminal behaviours, intimidating, and, at times, connected to drug transportation networks.

Such a phenomenon is eloquently taken up by a Cree Grandmother in northern Quebec, who asked Rupert Ross (2008), "What kinds of values they built relationships upon inside" jails (p. 11). According to Ross, this Grandmother "then expressed her fear that being in jail might make it even harder for her community to teach those men, when they came back, how to live in relationships built on values and sharing instead" (p.11).

Living in relationships also invites us to see a person as separate from their behaviour. From this lens, a person is not an offender or perpetrator, but rather someone who has caused harm. Other examples of seeing people through this wholeness lens are as a person who smokes crack rather than a "crackhead," or someone who is homeless rather than a "homeless guy." This can be applied to those who have been harmed as well: rather than calling someone a "victim," this is a person who has been victimized. In fact,

I would say that most people who have been victimized prefer to be viewed as survivors over the long term rather than being identified as victims, which could be viewed as a negative label. My experiences working with men who have hurt women and children through physical and sexual abuse has taught me that most of them have little understanding of the impact they have had as viewed through a relational negative lens. This seems to be so because those who hurt others tend to have been hurt themselves in similar ways. They are not open to the pain of others because, when they experienced their own pain, they learned how to shut down and turn off their feelings. They taught themselves to control, minimize, or deny what they were feeling when they were abused and they do the same when they hurt others. Shutting down goes hand in hand with a deep sense of isolation, and with a sense of having no purpose other than being used by others. Hence, people who were abused as children often grow up to abuse children themselves. They are behaving within the same sort of relationships they knew as children, except now they are the ones in positions of power.

Those who harm others, however, are capable of empathy. This is why the healing process with them must focus on ways that will chip away their layers of denial and minimization to eventually reach a place where empathetic connections can be accessed. No healing can begin until there is an understanding that the way they are relating to other people is causing harm.

POWER OF THE CIRCLE

Bringing people together in a circle to look at how a person has been harmed, hold the one who did the harm accountable, and begin a healing process for all the relationships involved is the foundation of Indigenous justice.

Family members and friends of the person who has been hurt can make powerful contributions to raising the awareness of the one who has caused the harm and helping to create empathy within them. Because they are close to the one who has been harmed, they can offer first-hand stories of how they have been struggling to relate to others and the world around them since the harm occurred.

Within a circle, surrounded by those who love and support them, a person who has been hurt can talk about the impacts they are now living with and ask questions of the one who hurt them. This is a remarkably different experience than sitting in a courtroom where unknown "experts" such as lawyers and judges decide what is best for those involved based on intrusive questions, "evidence," and "the truth." As Ross (2009) wonders,

When victims complain that the court has never really "heard" them, is it because neither the court nor the offender have ever defined the crime in the same way that victims experience it, as causing an enduring injury to central relationships in their lives? Are victims even able to articulate their injury in that way, or has our "thing-centred" way of looking at the world kept us from recognizing that what is truly injured by crime is our capacity for maintaining or creating healthy relationships? (p. 6)

Family and friends of the person who has done harm are also present in the circle, not only to support the individual, but also to offer relevant information about them. They may share their own experiences and insights as to how their relative came to do what they did. They may also share stories about their relationships with them and speak about them as a whole person, rather than a one-dimensional person who has hurt another. On an emotional level, those family members and friends may feel pain for what their relative has done and wish to express remorse to the person harmed and that person's family. Emotions are, in large part, the meat of these circles. I was fortunate to meet and hear the Honourable Robert Yazzie, Chief Justice Emeritus of the Navajo Nation who is now retired, speak at a conference in 2009. He concisely explained, "Until I know how you feel and you know how I feel, we'll never move beyond those feelings." Is this not the beginning stage of healing for all involved?

My observation from being present in these types of circles is that many significant questions are asked and answered for all that attend them. Family and friends of the person who has been hurt learn that the one who did the harm is not a monster or a psychopath, but a human being who is capable of empathy and remorse.

For those who have been harmed, perhaps the most important question is "why me?" Unfortunately, this tends to lead to other self-blaming questions such as, "Did I do something wrong?" "Was it because of the way I dressed or something I said?" "I shouldn't have been at that house party, right?" or "It was because I was drinking, wasn't it?" Of course, family, friends, and helpers will say repeatedly that it was not their fault, but this will never equal the impact of responsibility on the part of the one who did the harm when they say, for example, "You just happened to be there," "You were the first one I saw," "I was in a rage and wanted to hurt someone—anyone," or "I wanted to take my frustration out on you because I knew you wouldn't be able to stop me," or "I took advantage of you because you're a child."

It is also remarkably helpful for both the one who did the harm and the person who has been harmed to directly hear the impact of what has been done. The harmed person needs to tell the one who hurt them what it feels like to be them right now. The one who did the harm needs to know what has been done to the other person, who may be the only one who can get the former to understand.

There are times, however, when a harmed person does not want to participate in a circle of this kind. Reasons for this may be that they never want to see the person who hurt them again; they are too afraid, angry, or intimidated; or they do not support the process. When this has been the case, I have held circles without the harmed person, where their family, friends, and helpers speak on the person's behalf. This is not as powerful as having the harmed person present, but still goes a long way in getting the one who has done the abuse to understand what they have done and helping all family members and friends to begin to heal.

RELATIONAL LENS

Viewing harmful acts through a Western lens means focusing on the acts alone, dealing with those referred to as "offenders" entirely as individuals, and promoting that "rehabilitation" will happen as long as these individuals choose to change themselves and their behaviour. I'm not sure it's that simple for the majority of people. Rather, I am certain that most will need help from others in their lives, so that making better choices becomes a group effort.

A relationship has formed between the person who has been harmed and the one responsible for it. It is a relationship that has been forced on someone, which inevitably involves violence or the threat of violence. The threat is always present as one wonders, "What will he do to me if I don't do what he says?" This relationship must be changed in order for both people to move forward. In particular, the harmed person will likely need to return to a place where they can have, once again, open and trusting relationships. This can happen if they are provided with the opportunity to ask the person who hurt them, face to face, the questions only they can answer, and then decide for themselves if the person is sincere. As helping professionals, we can tell hurt people over and over that what happened is not their fault, but this can never come close to hearing it from the person who hurt them. They can listen to defence lawyers and court workers talk about how sorry the person who hurt them is, but they need to hear it directly from that person.

My work experience with those who have created harm has taught me that, for the most part, they tend to have a superficial understanding of the damage they have caused. They need to become aware through a relational lens that they have caused emotional, psychological, spiritual, and sometimes physical damage to the person they have hurt and all those who have a significant relationship with them. In order for them to be truly emotionally accountable for the harm caused, they need to move past the facade they show the world of not feeling or caring and be able to feel someone else's pain. More often than not, they begin to feel another person's feelings only after they begin to feel their own. Through a relational lens, this is why there is a focus on learning about the person who has created harm for others—who are you? How do you identify yourself? How would you describe yourself? What was your childhood like? How do you deal with anger? How do you feel about yourself? Through telling their story in this relational way, they can come to a place where they allow themselves to feel and what they usually feel are the same emotions as the one they have hurt. This is a remarkably different experience from the one in a courtroom, which focuses only on the facts and is over within minutes.

The healing process, through a relational lens, is not about trying to change someone, but rather about helping a person to relate differently to other people. What will help this person to see that they are not alone, that they can form relationships based on respect, and what will assist them in moving forward? I am convinced that if our aim is to help people stop hurting others, then this is the most promising way to go. For those who have been hurt, listening to others who were once hurt in similar ways is a powerful tool for healing. They come to understand that their responses to being hurt, such as secrecy, shutting down, or misusing substances, are normal given what happened. They can hear the stories of others who also once thought that they would be stuck in feelings of shame and fear forever but they were able to heal at their own pace and in their own ways, arriving at a place of new ways of seeing themselves and relating to others. Sometimes these stories come from one's own family members and friends. Other times, they may come from the family and friends of the person who has caused the hurt who were once hurt in similar ways. This can be a powerful tool for healing. Such stories are never intended as advice or what one should do. Rather, they are offered as encouragement and examples of what is possible.

In a similar way, it is helpful for those who have hurt others to participate in circles with people who once did the same, but have been on their healing path for a long time. Their stories help to communicate that healing can occur and one can learn to relate to other people in much healthier ways. Another important reason for participating in processes where others are just beginning is because the former, more than any helper regardless of their experience, will be the fastest to catch the latter minimizing what they have done, coming up with excuses, or blaming others. It is important to note that the majority of those who harm others are men, and women are the ones who are most often harmed. This is because even though women do harm other people, the vast majority of reported physical and sexual assaults are committed by men upon women. According to Statistics Canada (2013), most victims of violence across the country continue to be women who have been harmed by men, and they experience more serious types of violence than men. Furthermore, the Canadian Research Institute on the Advancement of Women (CRIAW, 2013) reported that

> In 2010, 70% of dating violence victims and 81% of marital violence victims were female. Altogether, intimate partners account for a much larger share of all violent crimes against women (55% for women and 22% for men). Canadian women reported 460,000 incidents of sexual violence by persons other than marital partners during the one-year period studied. This rate of 33 per 1,000 women has not changed since the early 1990s. In over half of these sexual assaults, the perpetrator was a friend, acquaintance, or neighbour of the victim. Among adult victims of sexual assault reported to police, 92% are women. (pp. 4–5)

In addition, the United Nations (2006) states that around the world, one in three women suffer serious violence at the hands of males, while the CRIAW (2013) reported that

> Rape and intimate partner violence are tolerated violations of women's human rights in all countries. In addi-

tion to the International Violence Against Women Survey (IVAWS), carried out in 11 countries, and the 10-country study conducted by the World Health Organization, additional details are provided in country statements prepared for the 2013 UN Commission on the Status of Women. (p. 5)

It is also important to note that transgender people are the targets of specifically directed violence. According to research data from 2015, in Ontario alone, 20 percent of trans people had been physically or sexually assaulted for being trans, and 34 percent had been verbally threatened or harassed. In addition, 24 percent reported having been harassed by police (Bauer & Scheim, 2015). Of course, when it comes to violence toward women and transgendered people who are Indigenous, the statistics are going to be higher due to colonialism and racism. Furthermore, the above statistics are based only on violence that has been reported, and all research tells us that the majority of these incidents go unreported (Bauer & Scheim, 2015).

Those who have been harmed and those who have created harm need to spend time with people "who have been there." One of the most powerful ways in which this happens is when those who have had these experiences and have been through their particular healing journey wish to assist others. This may happen by them participating in Healing Circles as facilitators or by speaking at conferences, in classrooms, or to those who are incarcerated. These are incredible, brave, and unselfish acts on the part of both those who have been hurt and those who have caused the hurt. Their stories educate others while, at the same time, bringing them closer to being free of the hold the experiences have had on them.

ROLE OF THE HELPER

Interestingly enough, despite the significant roles, such as advocacy and direct practice, that helpers can have in the area of justice, there seems to be little in the literature or within education about this. I believe this is a serious gap in our education and practice.

Ultimately, it is the members of each group—whether that be a family, members of a Sentencing Circle, or those within a Healing Circle—that come up with more positive and healthy ways of relating to one another, which is in turn taken out into the rest of the world.

The helper is present as a guide who assists participants in creating respectful processes; identifying and releasing emotions such as fear, anger, and shame; relating to one another in open and honest ways; and exploring what led to hurtful behaviours in the first place. The helper provides a context in which all of these processes become possible.

THE COMMUNITY COUNCIL

Aboriginal Legal Services of Toronto (ALST) was established in 1990, following a needs assessment by the Native Canadian Centre of Toronto in the mid-1980s. The Centre had been operating justice-related programs for Indigenous people in Toronto, but concluded an agency dedicated to this area was needed. ALST's mission is to strengthen the capacity of the Indigenous community to deal with justice issues and provide Indigenous-controlled, culture-based alternatives. Services offered at ALST include a court worker program, legal clinic, Gladue (Indigenous person's court), community council program, test case litigation, and advocacy and law reform activities.

Rene Timleck, Anishnawbe and a member of Beausoleil First Nation who was born and raised in Toronto, has been an addictions counsellor for the past 30 years. She is the mother of five children, grandmother of ten, and great-grandmother of two. Rene has been a member of ALST's Community Council for Adults and Youth for over ten years. A staff person at ALST whom she had known for a few years asked her if she would be interested in being a member of the Community Council. Rene agreed, motivated by the fact that she had a grandson who had been in and out of trouble with the law. A few years previously, he and another boy stole a car and were killed in an accident. She hoped that if she got involved in the Council, she could help keep another youth from a similar fate.

Rene's process to become a member included completing an application, going through an interview with existing Council members and Elders of the community, attending an information session where all the aspects of the Council were explained, and speaking with existing Council members who shared their experiences with her. She then learned about the criteria for diversion, the history of Indigenous Peoples and the criminal justice system, the discrimination against Indigenous Peoples in Canada, and the objectives of the Council.

Rene meets many diverse people through her involvement with the Council—some who have been in as many as 22 foster homes, who were abused or neglected as children, who may be challenged by fetal alcohol spectrum effects (FASE), and who have never received care from others. Perhaps some of the participants are homeless and without families or other support systems. Rene sees these community members as never having had a chance and she is touched by this. She hopes that those who come through the Council as participants are touched by Council members such as her, that they know others care about them, and that they don't have to be alone.

In my interview with Rene, I first asked her to describe how the Community Council works. She explained,

> Participants coming before their own community members are facing their own people rather than strangers. This touches their emotions as it provides an environment where everyone sits together. Council members introduce themselves and give the participant some personal information about themselves which is intended to show the participant that they are part of this community; we are their peers rather than an unknown judge. Council members ask not only about the charges that brought them to the hearing, but also about their lives and circumstances, about their hopes and dreams. We try to assess the whole person, not just the crime, but also the reasons behind it. This is not about punishment, but rather the Council tries to assist participants in changing some of the things that might have been contributing factors to committing the offense, such as lack of education or shelter or unresolved issues from the past. In other words, the Council looks at what contributed to a participant ending up in the place of having to be at a hearing. (R. Timleck, personal communication, April 22, 2009)

I then invited Rene to share her thoughts on how the Council process benefits participants. She was happy to oblige:

> Participants have been shown (hopefully) that they are part of the community and not just a "case." We call on their pride and responsibility to deal with the problem at hand. I believe the process builds a relationship between

Council members and participants. Participants experience shame as they are in front of their community and truly have to face what they have done. After the shame comes pride because they have been able to go through this process of facing themselves and others. I can see that participants try not to disappoint or let down the Council members. Council members suggest ways of assisting participants such as counselling, returning to school, entering apprenticeships, volunteering, writing a letter of apology and financial compensation for what was stolen for example. They can create paintings or sculptures if they have this talent which helps them feel like they're a part of the community and that they're giving back to the community that is helping them. The art or other creative assignments have been donated to many different places in Toronto. Suggestions for participants must be realistic: they need to know that they can meet the expectations that the Council members suggest for them. If these expectations are too high, participants are set up for failure. There is a strong emphasis on finding a solution that can be accomplished which involves taking into consideration all aspects of the information received and an exploration of the participant's capabilities, interests and gifts. Once the agreement is completed it gives the participant a concrete circumstance under which they have accomplished something ... and maybe they can take another step. I believe if the justice system did more of this sort of intervention, there would be less re-offending. (R. Timleck, personal communication, April 22, 2009)

ALST also has a Community Council specifically for youth. It began in 2000 and serves youth 12 to 18 years old. Funders for this Council are the Ministry of the Attorney General, the Ministry of Child and Youth Services, and the Department of Justice. A protocol is in place between ALST and provincial Crown Attorneys whereby youth in Toronto, Newmarket, and Brampton are eligible for services.

This is how the Youth Community Council works: a youth is charged; an Indigenous court worker from ALST at the court talks to them about

ALST's Community Council, explaining how all charges can be diverted except driving under the influence, domestic assault, and murder; and that the Crown Attorney must agree to the diversion. The youth who is charged must admit responsibility, which is different from the mainstream justice system where one can plead guilty and never have to take responsibility for what was done. With diversion to the Council, a youth must take full responsibility, meaning that "I did everything I am being charged with," or partial responsibility, which means "I was there and took part in some of the offence." If the young person takes responsibility, the charges are stayed or withdrawn according to the discretion of the judge in the case. Usually the Crown involved in the case will have a preference of the two, which is communicated to the judge.

A hearing date with the Community Council is set and the participant is given a hearing notice while still at the Court with the date on it to serve as a reminder. Then an intake form is completed with the participant and a synopsis is written about what happened regarding the incident.

If a victim was involved in the offence, the youth must also acknowledge the harm that was done to this person. There is a victim advocate at ALST who talks to the victim, if there is one, for their story of what happened, their feelings, and how the incident has impacted them. Victims can attend the hearing to have the opportunity to tell their stories to the Council and explain how the crime impacted their lives.

I spoke with Colette Pagano, who is Anishnawbe, has a BSW, has been working at ALST since 2005, and is currently Manager of the Community Council Program and High Risk Youth Program. Colette specifically spoke about the Council process for youth, which is much like the process for adults:

> Two or three members of the Aboriginal community sit at each hearing; they are all volunteers representing a diverse group of Aboriginal people such as counsellors, bankers, Elders and students. Any Aboriginal person is welcome to apply to be a member of the Council; a criminal record will not prevent anyone from being on the Council, but they must have a clean record for over one year.
>
> Members hear the stories of the participant and find out if there are any addictions issues, if their parents or grandparents attended residential schools or if there

are any mental health [challenges]. After this, the participant leaves the room while the members discuss the situation and come up with decisions as to what they think will be helpful for the participant. The youth returns to the room and hears the decisions of the Council members.

Decisions can be artwork (the room where hearings are held is full of beautiful artwork created by people who went through the Community Council), community service, writing a letter of apology to the victim or making restitution of some kind. Participants have input into the decisions. If the person doesn't want to do something that has been suggested, then they can negotiate this with the members.

Restoration is the aim: members do not set up participants for failure or give the youth decisions that they cannot do. Rather, they help them access resources and assist them to get on the path to well being—whatever that looks like for each youth. Often this experience is the first time that a youth has met Aboriginal community members in Toronto. (C. Pagano, personal communication, November 27, 2008)

LISTENING TO THE YOUTH

I knew it was important to have some of the youth who have been through the Community Council process represented in this chapter. With Colette's help, in 2008, I held a Talking Circle with her and three youth who have experienced the process within the last few years. The youth identified themselves as:

- JD, who is Anishnawbe, 18 years old, originally from Sault Ste. Marie, and came to Toronto as a youth. He was homeless when he became involved with the Community Council.
- JP, a 19-year-old Mohawk youth born and raised in the Toronto area. He too was homeless when he became involved with the Community Council.

- Midewin, who is Anishnawbe, 20 years old, and was born and raised in Toronto. Like the other two, he was also homeless when he became involved with the Community Council.

These three youth came to ALST's Community Council with charges of unlawfully being in a dwelling, robbery, mischief, break and enter, and possession of burglary tools.

When I asked the youth if they would share with me a little about where they were at during the time they came into contact with ALST and what the process was like for them within the Community Council, this is what they told me:

> *JD:* I wasn't doing much of anything before I got arrested, but once I got involved with the Community Council, I got help with finding housing and returning to school. Coming through the Community Council and con- tinuing to get services at ALST prevents me from doing something wrong again; it keeps our Aboriginal cultures going; it helps me to calm down and stay that way. Before going through the Community Council, I didn't want anything to do with the Aboriginal community [in To- ronto]. I believed Aboriginal people were all disrespected and disrespectful. I thought they would rob me or beat me up. (JD, personal communication, November 27, 2008)

> *JP:* At ALST we got to experience the positive rather than the negative. Workers at ALST helped us do productive things. They smudged with us. They are people who care. I don't remember the police or judges I've had to deal with, but I remember and stay connected to the Com- munity Council members, staff at ALST and all the other helpers who come my way. (JP, personal communication, November 27, 2008)

> *Midewin:* The idea of the Community Council was intro- duced to me when I was in jail. I knew that trying this route was the best choice for me or I'd stay in jail. The

Council is important not only for averting jail, but to not have a criminal record which is something that follows us forever.

One of my decisions through the Community Council was to get help with my G1 [driving] license. I told the members I wanted to get this and they asked me how it would help me. I told them it would be a piece of ID, provide transportation and help me get a job. The decision went through and ALST assisted me by paying for the license.

Going through the Council helped me understand how the past makes the present: we need to see what has happened in the past which can lead to harmful behaviours in the present. If we understand this, we can begin to make positive changes. It also helped me to look at what we've overcome, not just what we've done that's not good.

In the past, I was ashamed to be Aboriginal because of what some other Aboriginal people did. It was also from what I saw on the news which showed Aboriginal people committing bad stuff like sexual abuse and stereotypes like being drunk, making trouble and being poor. (Midewin, personal communication, November 27, 2008)

I then asked the young men if they would tell me a little about what they are doing now and how they are feeling. These are their responses:

JP: I come to ALST still. We can go to the YMCA for two hours a day to exercise, which is healthy, and a stress reliever. We get help with resume writing, anger management, workshops on job training. They have lawyers if we need them such as for help dealing with landlords. Today I have housing. I also attend some of the circles [Drug and Alcohol Abuse Prevention Circle] offered by Colette. (JP, personal communication, November 27, 2008)

JD: I have a problem with alcohol, so I'm involved in a harm reduction program at ALST. This program helps me to drink less, not stop entirely. We look at areas such as admitting we have a problem, peer pressure, the impacts of colonization, anger, relationships and traditional approaches to healing.

I have housing and am in school with the Native Learning Centre doing grades nine and ten work. Now I go to sweat lodge ceremonies and do fire keeping sometimes. Now I'm into everything Aboriginal instead of how I was before not wanting anything to do with it. [ALST listens to] I and the other youth who don't want non-Aboriginal presenters coming into our circles to talk about their recovery stories for example. We only want Aboriginal speakers. What do white people have to teach us? We can better relate to Aboriginal peoples who come to speak about their experiences, how they got out of their destructive lives through their cultures and spirituality. We can learn from them; they're our role models. (JD, personal communication, November 27, 2008)

Midewin: I continue to attend services at ALST. I see the medicine people and Elders who come here which is something I look forward to. I attend the Drug and Alcohol Abuse Prevention Circle. I'm getting to know my family who I never got along with in the past. I'm working on getting my G2 license. (Midewin, personal communication, November 27, 2008)

At the end of the circle, I gave each of the young men an honorarium of $50 as one of the ways to thank them for talking with me. JP repaid Colette $10 he owed her out of his honourarium. JD said he was going to go buy cleaning supplies so he could go home to clean his place. Midewin gave Colette $40 out of his money toward the cost of his G2 test.

INTEREST IN INDIGENOUS JUSTICE

Interestingly enough, most of the literature on Indigenous approaches to justice are written by White authors involved in the area of criminal justice as professors of criminology or lawyers (Aboriginal Justice Directorate, 2005; Braithwaite, 2000; Friedland, 2014; Losoncz & Tyson, 2007; Palys, 2013; Ross, 2008, 2009; Rudin, 2014). These authors write about definitions of justice; descriptions of specific processes such as the Gladue Court in Toronto; reintegrative shaming that is implemented in some non-Western societies; the need for alternatives to the criminal justice system based on the needs of Indigenous people; and both the effectiveness and the controversies of implementing these alternatives. Some significant points are made by these authors, but it is only Ross (2008, 2009) who views Indigenous worldviews on justice through a relational lens.

Bruce Johansen (2007), who I have yet to find out whether he is or is not not Indigenous, writes about the historic ways in which diverse Indigenous Nations dealt with issues of justice. He focuses on the strengths of the views he presents and provides examples of concepts and legal customs that were taken up by dominant North American society that originate in Indigenous worldviews. One of these is the idea of "sleeping on it":

> Nearly everyone knows the custom "sleeping on it" before making an important decision, allowing a night to pass so that all alternatives may be weighed in a balanced and rational fashion. Yet fewer people realize that this custom comes to us directly from the legal debating procedures of the Haudenosaunee (Iroquois) Confederacy. (p. 25)

As an aside, Johansen (2007) also makes note of the fact that the original American constitution and its policies were also based on the teachings of the Haudenosaunee Confederacy.

There are many ways of describing restorative justice since populations and Nations are diverse and can have differing needs and resources, but there is a foundational base to this form of justice, explained simply by Simon Fraser University's School of Criminology Website (2012):

> Restorative Justice is an old idea with a new name. Its roots can be found in Aboriginal healing traditions and the non-retaliatory responses to violence endorsed by many faith communities. It represents a return of the simple wisdom of viewing conflict as an opportunity for a community to learn and grow. It operates on the premise that conflict, even criminal conflict, inflicts harm, and therefore individuals must accept responsibility for

repairing that harm. Communities are empowered to choose their response to conflict. Victims, offenders and communities actively participate in devising mutually beneficial solutions, and implementing those solutions. Conflicts are resolved in a way that restores harmony in the community members' relationships, and allows people to continue to live together in a safer, healthy environment.

Some writers, myself included (Baskin, 2010), believe that restorative justice historically existed in many parts of the world prior to colonization. Some also state that Canada has been at the forefront of the restorative justice field. "We were the first nation in the world to offer a victim/offender reconciliation program, which was initiated by the Mennonite Community in Kitchener, Ontario" is posted on Simon Fraser University's School of Criminology Website (2012). This statement is widely accepted, but I think it is misleading and needs to be qualified as more like "Canada was the first non-Indigenous Nation to offer such reconciliation programs and, although the Mennonite Community was the first to be recognized for these processes, Indigenous communities had been doing them for centuries prior to this."

It is also important to consider that the dominant justice system has been oppressive toward Indigenous Peoples and other racialized populations. Given the attention that police profiling of Black men in Toronto has been given in recent years, I know many who would agree with me that this statement also applies to other racialized populations. It is critical that sentencing judges truly begin considering the systemic and background factors that bring Indigenous people and racialized groups before the criminal courts. Of course, this statement applies to people in urban and rural areas from New Zealand to South Africa to the United States.

In 2000, John Braithwaite, an Australian criminologist, wrote a book about a specific type of restorative justice known as reintegrative shaming. Braithwaite (2000) explains how this form of justice is not at all how shame is applied in contemporary usage:

> Reintegrative shaming communicates disapproval within a continuum of respect for the offender; the offender is treated as a good person who has done a bad deed.

> Stigmatization is disrespectful shaming; the offender is treated as a bad person. Stigmatization is unforgiving—the offender is left with the stigma permanently, whereas reintegrative shaming is forgiving. (p. 282)

> The First Nations of North America have strong traditions of restorative justice that are being revitalized through Healing Circles or Sentencing Circles. These circles put the problem, not the person, in the centre of the community discussion about crime. (Melton, 1995, as cited in Braithwaite, 2000, p. 293)

> Reintegrative shaming, according to the theory, will be more widespread in societies where communities are strong, where citizens are densely enmeshed in loving, trusting, or respectful relationships with others. (p. 291)

In this way, shaming is in fact positive and can promote healing for the one who has been harmed, the one who has done the harm, and the community. Braithwaite (2000) cites several examples of societies that implement this concept of alternative justice and have low crime rates. According to him, "societies that are forgiving and respectful while taking crime seriously have low crime rates; societies that degrade and humiliate criminals have higher crime rates" (p. 282). He cites African societies, the Pushtoon of Afghanistan, and the country of Japan as using reintegrative shaming and having low crime rates. Braithwaite (2000) reports that Japan is the only nation where evidence indicates a sustained decline in the crime rate over the past 50 years accompanied by a low imprisonment rate—37 out of 100,000 people as compared to over 500 in the U.S.

The Pushtoon, the largest ethnic group in Afghanistan, have a ceremony called Nanante, which takes place when someone has done harm to someone else (Braithwaite, 2000). Remarkably similar to processes of justice within Indigenous Nations in North America, the Pushtoon person who did the harm is responsible for bringing food for a community feast. The ceremony usually takes place at the home of the person who has been harmed and they participate in cooking the food that has been brought. Those who conduct the ceremony tell the one who has created harm, "You have done an injustice to this person [but] you are one of us and we accept you back among us" (Braithwaite, 2000, p. 282). The police and courts have no presence in communities that practise the Nanante.

The literature is consistent in the message that Indigenous forms of justice promote healing and are transformative in meeting the needs of Indigenous people in Canada. Authors such as Braithwaite (2000), Johansen (2007), Losoncz and Tyson (2007), and Palys (2013) highlight the strengths of Indigenous forms of justice, but also point out that even though early research shows hopeful outcomes, there is a strong need for further research in the area. I agree.

I asked Rene Timleck, whose words of wisdom appear earlier in this chapter, if she thought that Indigenous forms of justice might be of assistance to other populations. She offered several points on why she believes it can be:

> First off, Community Councils could be a financial blessing to society as there are no court costs such as lawyer's fees or court clerk's pay and all Council members are volunteers. Plus, if the participant is successful in completing the agreement and does not reoffend, how much cost saving is that for society?
>
> Next, for many people being lost and alone has led them into trouble and the Council process aims to change this. Feeling this way is not exclusive to Aboriginal people[;] many other people feel the same way. Participants are more likely to feel regret for the harm they have caused as they are facing their community and they are in an atmosphere that fosters the idea that they are important to it. They are less likely to have their armour on when in the hearings as they tend to when in the courtroom. The process of going through a hearing assists in breaking down that armour.
>
> Council hearings are much more personal and implement a human touch as compared to the court system. In a hearing, Council members introduce themselves and say a little about who they are; then participants are invited to tell the members a little about themselves. This allows the [C]ouncil members to get to know more about the individual, which assists them in finding more concrete, viable solutions which, in turn, may mean less chance of a participant reoffending.

The process of the Council focuses on restitution, recognizing what was wrongly done and taking responsibility for it which is not necessarily the purpose of the criminal justice system. The court system is more about who can present better in the courtroom, which lawyer is the most eloquent—it isn't about what really happened.

By helping Toronto's Aboriginal community, this helps Toronto and the world. The Council process would help people in other communities in the same way. The work is like a pebble in the pond—it is the atmosphere of community and belonging which may initiate the urge to succeed. There are boxes of files at ALST of people who have completed their requirements and never re-offended. Can the criminal justice system make this claim? I know that all the work in the judicial system aims to assist; to help offenders to not repeat their mistakes, but, for the most part, this system never allows for the time to know the individual or what may be the most effective plan to assist him or her to not reoffend. Our work clearly shows that this is exactly what is needed. (R. Timleck, personal communication, April 22, 2009)

Colette and the young men who spoke with me also had a few ideas about non-Indigenous people and Indigenous methods of justice. Colette told me that police officers involved with the charging of the youth who come to the Council can attend the hearings, but separately from the participants. Colette notes that police officers have attended 2 hearings out of 70 in the past year. When I asked her why those officers came to the hearings, she replied, "they were curious about how the program works" (C. Pagano, personal communication, November 27, 2008).

According to JP, some of the Indigenous youth bring non-Indigenous youth to the circles offered at ALST. He relayed that "the non-Aboriginal youth enjoyed being there. I can tell because they laugh with us and keep coming back" (JP, personal communication, November 27, 2008). Midewin believes "it's a good idea to educate non-Aboriginal youth about Aboriginal people so they can tell others the truth and dispel stereotypes" (Midewin, personal communication, November 22, 2008). He also supports other peoples considering Indigenous forms of justice for their young people:

"The ways in which the Community Council helps Aboriginal youth could be helpful to youth from other populations. Other communities could have services that assist their youth like this rather than send them to jail. They could help their youth instead of punishing them" (Midewin, personal communication, November 22, 2008).

NOT WITHOUT CONTROVERSY

Needless to say, in today's world, there is controversy about Indigenous culture-based forms of justice, which comes from both Indigenous and non-Indigenous communities. Thus, non-Indigenous students and practitioners in the helping professions may be particularly challenged or confused by these differing positions on the topic. One concern revolves around how Indigenous culture-based justice fits into the larger goal of self-government and decolonization. For example, perhaps problems will arise if funding is spent on criminal justice reforms rather than on economic development, including the settlement of land claims. Similarly, the majority of public inquiries in Canada involving Indigenous Peoples have focused on justice issues rather than larger economic issues. Such a focus may deflect attention that could be devoted to what some people view as more urgent aspects of self-government such as health care, unemployment, and poverty in addition to land claims.

Hughes and Mossman (2002) raise several questions about the implementation of Indigenous forms of justice, which continue to be applicable today:

> I will briefly address what I see as the three most important areas of concern. One of these questions is around the definition of community: Even where we think the identification of community is easy, as in the case of Aboriginal circles, this may not be the case in urban rather than reserve settings. We need to establish more clearly the meaning and purpose of community in restorative justice initiatives (is the community always the same for purposes of reintegration and restoration, for example?) and develop ways of ensuring that there is some kind of organic connection between the offender and the community which makes the interaction between offender and community meaningful. (p. 46)

I hope that the experiences of some who have participated in the Community Council of Aboriginal Legal Services of Toronto as shared in this chapter, as well as further research, will shed some light on these questions.

In my opinion, the area that we must be the most cautious about when implementing Indigenous forms of justice is in situations of family violence. In cases of family violence, which includes sexual abuse, we must be cautious about bringing the one who has done the harm together with the one who has been hurt. Due to imbalances of power and safety issues, circles with both of these people present may never be appropriate and must never take place if the harmed one is not certain that it is what is wanted. If the harmed and the one who did the harm do come together, it should happen only after separate healing processes have taken place and everyone is seen as ready to go forward with this (Baskin, 2010).

We must understand that in relationships of violence amongst family members or with others a person is close to, there is always an imbalance of power and we must not recreate this in a circle. Should we do so, those who have done the harm will continue their manipulative behaviours, which may be evident only to the harmed person. They will likely apologize profusely and those who have been harmed will do exactly what they always do—feel sorry for the person and tell them it's okay; they accept the apology. Violence between people who have relationships with one another is significantly different from stranger violence. The stakes are much higher when violence comes from someone who a person loves or is connected to in some relevant way. It is not likely that the harmed person will face the other once and then never have to see them again. How can the harmed person feel safe enough to ask the questions they need answers to? How can they express their pain? These are some of the areas that must be thoroughly explored before proceeding with such encounters.

However, this in no way means that nothing can be done to assist those who have harmed others close to them to learn about the pain they have created. In situations when the harmed one does not wish to participate in a circle, I have implemented other ways of attempting to teach empathy to those who have done harm to others. For example, I have brought in movies, letters, and poems by survivors. I have also brought in people who once experienced physical or sexual violence by someone close to them and who want to talk about it to help stop it for others. The purpose of this is to assist the person who has caused harm to begin to see how what they have done has caused the same damage as that suffered by the person speaking in front of them about their own abuse. Although I do not support some of the language used (e.g., "offender" and "victim"), I agree with Rupert Ross (2009), who writes about this form of violence as well:

> I have seen several instances where an offender was brought together with a group of recovering victims of the same kind of crime. In some ways, these encounters with "surrogate victims" may be the most powerful way to begin. Surrogate victims are often able to provide excruciating detail about how their lives have been affected, perhaps because they are not facing their own assailant. At the same time, it seems easier for offenders to listen to such detail when it comes from strangers, to let it penetrate, perhaps because it is not their crime being discussed. When it does finally sink in that their crime must have caused almost identical damage, however, the impact is often significant—and the manifestation of an empathetic reaction is often sudden and extreme. (p. 16)

Another area of concern centres on aspects of power amongst the different people involved in various forms of Indigenous justice—for example, the person who has done the harm, the one who has been harmed, and those who facilitate the process. We must be cognizant of the power imbalances between the harmed person and the one who did the harm, and the ways in which those who facilitate the process can pressure both parties of the circle in certain directions. Helpers must never re-victimize anyone who participates in this process. It is significant to note, though, that these critiques did not seem to come across in the interviews I conducted with those involved with ALST's Community Council. Finally, the bigger picture of structural oppression, as connected to the individual situations of Indigenous Peoples involved in restorative justice, is not apolitical. Social context is important, particularly one's socio-economic condition. There will likely be many challenges for those who participate in this process, including lack of education, employment, and opportunities, that most people in Canada take for granted, all of which will also need to be addressed. I do think, however, that this holistic way of looking at people, families, and communities is exactly what Indigenous forms of justice are trying to address.

CONCLUSION

The removal of people who hurt other people, who do not "conform" or do not behave in ways taught by dominant society, begins early in countries such as Canada. It begins with children in an educational system that "expels" or removes children who fail to behave in ways that are acceptable in such systems. In the province of Ontario for example, the vast majority of children and youth expelled from schools are Indigenous and African-Canadian (Ontario Human Rights Commission, 2004; Veryard, 2014). It also occurs when White adoptive parents cut ties with their adopted Indigenous children because of "acting out" behaviours (Richard, 2004).

Separating people from the community also takes place within the criminal justice system, which segregates those who break laws by incarcerating them in jails and prisons. As with the educational system and adoption breakdowns, the justice system in Canada segregates Indigenous people at much higher rates than it does others, closely followed by African-Canadians (Kroes, 2008; Rudin, 2006, 2014; Zinger, 2006). Perhaps such removals come from dominant society's not wanting to deal with these particular groups of people as if we do not see them, then we do not have to do anything with them. We do not have to ask any of the tough questions as to why certain people are not doing well or consider that they are being targeted based on their membership in certain populations. We do not have to consider whether dominant society's rules, laws, and ways of dealing with those who do not conform are flawed and in need of examination and reform. We do not have to consider that society has some responsibility for creating circumstances and fostering personal, cultural, and structural factors that account for certain groups of people not doing well.

It is worth considering whether removing people from their families and communities is the only way to address their wrongdoing. Is it possible that society is sending people away when they most need to feel that they belong to something, when they most need to be connected to other people, rather than being ostracized? Is it possible that being held accountable directly to the persons harmed, rather than to an anonymous criminal justice system, might be more significant for both the harmed and the one who caused the harm?

These are the questions that supporters of Indigenous forms of justice strive to answer in practical and healing ways. Such an exploration is what we have to offer others who have been particularly targeted by the "just us" system as well. At the very least, I encourage readers, especially those in the helping professions (including the law), to engage in a dialogue that explores the values and concepts behind Indigenous forms of justice as being applicable to all peoples.

REFERENCES

Aboriginal Justice Directorate. (2005). *Aboriginal Justice Strategy annual activities report 2002–2005.* Retrieved from http://www.justice.gc.ca/eng/rp-pr/aj-ja/0205/rep-rap.pdf.

Baskin, C. (2010). The spirit of belonging: Indigenous cultural practices in conflict transformation. *Journal of Community Corrections, XIX*(1–2), 9–14.

Bauer, G.R., & Scheim, A.I. (2015). *Transgender people in Ontario, Canada: Statistics from the Trans PULSE Project to Inform Human Rights Policy.* Retrieved from http://transpulseproject.ca/wp-content/uploads/2015/06/Trans-PULSE-Statistics-Relevant-for-Human-Rights-Policy-June-2015.pdf.

Braithwaite, J. (2000). Shame and criminal justice. *Canadian Journal of Criminology, 42*(3), 281–298. Retrieved from http://www.anu.edu.au.

Canadian Research Institute on the Advancement of Women. (2013). Fact sheet: Violence against women in Canada. Ottawa: Author. Retrieved from http://www.cwhn.ca/sites/default/files/CRIAW%20FACTSHEET%20Violence%20against%20women%20-%20short%20version.pdf.

Friedland, H. (2014). *IBA accessing justice and reconciliation project: Final report.* Retrieved from http://indigenousbar.ca/indigenouslaw/wp-content/uploads/2013/04/iba_ajr_final_report.pdf.

Hamilton, A.C., & Sinclair, M. (1999). *Report of the Aboriginal justice inquiry of Manitoba.* Winnipeg: Aboriginal Justice Implementation Commission. Retrieved from http://www.ajic.mb.ca.

Hughes, P., & Mossman, M. (2002). Re-thinking access to criminal justice in Canada: A critical review of needs and responses. *Windsor Review of Legal and Social Issues, 13*, 1–132. Retrieved from http://www.heinonline.org.

Johansen, B. (2007). Crimes and punishments: Justice in ancient America. *Native Peoples, 20*(2), 24–27. Retrieved from http://vnweb.hwwilsonweb.com.

Kroes, G. (2008). *Aboriginal youth in Canada: Emerging issues, research priorities, and policy implications.* Retrieved from http://www.policyresearch.gc.ca.

Losoncz, I., & Tyson, G. (2007). Parental shaming and adolescent delinquency: A partial test of reintegrative shaming theory. *Australian and New Zealand Journal of Criminology, 40*(2), 161–178. doi: 10.1375/acri.40.2.161

Ontario Human Rights Commission. (2004). *Submission of the Ontario Human Rights Commission to the Toronto District School Board Safe and Compassionate Schools Task Force.* Retrieved from http://www.ohrc.on.ca.

Palys, T. (2013). Is the Government of Canada living up to its responsibilities regarding Indigenous justice systems under the UN Declaration?: A Report to UN Special Rapporteur James Anaya. Retrieved from http://www.sfu.ca/~palys/Palys-2013-ReportForSpecialRapporteur-web.pdf.

Richard, K. (2004). A commentary against Aboriginal to non-Aboriginal adoption. *First Peoples Child and Family Review, 1(1)*, 101–109.

Ross, R. (2008). *Colonization, complex PTSD and Aboriginal healing: Exploring diagnoses and strategies for recovery.* Adult Custody Division Health Care Conference. Vancouver: Ministry of Public Safety and Solicitor General.

Ross, R. (2009). *Discussion paper: Exploring criminal justice and the Aboriginal healing paradigm.* Kenora, ON: Ontario Ministry of the Attorney General.

Rudin, J. (2006). *Brief to the Standing Committee on Justice and Human Rights on Bill C-10.* Retrieved from http://aboriginallegal.ca.

Rudin, J. (2014). The criminal justice system: Addressing Aboriginal over-representation. In P. Menzies & L.F. Lavallée (Eds.), *Journey to healing: Aboriginal people with addiction and mental health issues: What health, social service and justice workers need to know* (pp. 343–358). Toronto: CAMH.

Simon Fraser University. (2012). The Centre for Restorative Justice. Burnaby, B.C.: School of Criminology, Simon Fraser University. Retrieved from http://www.sfu.ca/crj.html.

Statistics Canada. (2013). Measuring violence against women: Statistical trends. Ottawa: Minister of Industry. Retrieved from http://www.statcan.gc.ca/pub/85-002-x/2013001/article/11766-eng.pdf.

United Nations. (2006). Ending violence against women: From words to action. Study of the Secretary-General. Geneva: Author. Retrieved from http://www.un.org/womenwatch/daw/vaw/launch/english/v.a.w-exeE-use.pdf.

Veryard, J.A. (2014). The implementation of suspension and expulsion programs in two Ontario school boards. (Doctoral dissertation). Retrieved from https://tspace.library.utoronto.ca/bitstream/1807/68385/1/Veryard_Joseph_201411_EdD_thesis.pdf.

Zinger, I. (2006). *Report finds evidence of systemic discrimination against Aboriginal inmates in Canada's prisons.* Retrieved from http://www.oci-bec.gc.ca.

Chapter Twelve

PROUD TWO-SPIRIT PRINCESS BOY

The image text reads around the circle: "I AM PART OF THE CIRCLE" and "PART OF THE SOLUTION"

INTRODUCTION

For the second edition of this book, I decided to include a chapter on Two-Spirit people because, particularly in Canada, there is so little written about their experiences with colonization, as well as the oppression many face today from both Indigenous and gay communities. Alongside this is a lack of information on the needs and experiences of Two-Spirit people when they access helping and healing services. As a non-Two-Spirit person, I know I have much to learn about being an ally, so this is one small step in my journey. In this chapter, I will be using the term Two-Spirit as an umbrella term to refer to Indigenous people who identify on a gender continuum, with the understanding that not all Indigenous people choose to identify in this way. The chapter is dedicated to my young friend Two-Spirit Princess Boy, who you will meet later.

WHO ARE TWO-SPIRIT PEOPLE?

"Two-Spirits" is the translation of the Northern Algonquin phrase *niizh manitoag*, generally understood as reflecting an Indigenous person who identifies on a gender continuum outside European/Western binaries or has a balance of both masculine and feminine spirits (Balsam, Huang, Fieland, Simoni, & Walters, 2004; Driskill, 2010; Evans-Campbell, Fredriksen-Goldsen, Walters, & Stately, 2007; Walters, Evans-Campbell, Simoni, Ronquillo, & Bhuyan, 2006). Since many Indigenous societies believed in numerous gender and sexual identities, the "othering" that often occurs today did not exist in the same way prior to contact (Cameron, 2005). Jeffrey McNeil-Seymour, a young Two-Spirit person from Tk'emlups te Secwepemc Nation (Kamloops Indian Band) elaborates on this from his own experience:

> One of my mentors, Garry Gottfriedson [Tk'emlups te Secwepmc Nation], said that our children [Tk'emlups te Secwepmc], up until puberty, remained genderless. They weren't male, they weren't female, they were just children and once puberty hit, that's when they decided what their roles and responsibilities would be and how they would contribute to the community. The sexuality piece was not an issue. [Another example of this is] during one of my university course lectures, Lee Maracle [Sto:Loh Nation] stood up and said, that in

our traditional times, there was no homosexuality, there was no heterosexuality, it's just human sexuality. From my experience, it is very true. I think that this piece is something that has been silenced out of most discourse and so it's a piece that really needs to be brought to the forefront. Not only do non-Native persons need to understand our ways of knowing, but they also need to understand that the conversation has moved beyond just gender and sexuality; that this is a moment of reclaiming our spaces in communities, and it's also us reclaiming our roles and responsibilities. (J. McNeil-Seymour, personal communication, April 7, 2015)

Prior to the acceptance of the term Two-Spirit, those who fell outside of European gender and sexuality norms were often referred to as *berdache* (Wilson, 1996), which is a non-Indigenous term with Persian roots. This term's original meaning, "male prostitute" or "kept boy," was only used within a sexual context (Epple, 1998; Thomas & Jacobs, 1999; Walters et al., 2006) and, thus, many Indigenous Peoples felt that it did not accurately reflect their histories and identities and was, in fact, offensive (Evans-Campbell et al., 2007). The term Two-Spirit first emerged in 1988 at the Native American Gay and Lesbian Movement's first international gathering in Minneapolis, Minnesota, and again at their third gathering in Winnipeg, Manitoba, in 1990. Two-Spirit was chosen to reflect the distinct experiences of Indigenous Peoples and as a way to move away from the use of the word berdache (Greensmith & Giwa, 2013; Thomas & Jacobs, 1999).

Two-Spirit has multiple meanings, which vary depending on context and community. But what is clear is that, since it is applied to Indigenous Peoples, it must be considered within Indigenous frameworks and worldviews. Alex Wilson (1996), Neyonawak Inniwak from the Opaskwayak Cree Nation, Associate Professor, and the Academic Director of the Aboriginal Education Research Centre at the University of Saskatchewan, explains that, "Two-Spirit identity affirms the interrelatedness of all aspects of identity, including sexuality, gender, culture, community, and spirituality. That is, the sexuality of Two-Spirit people cannot be considered as separate from the rest of an individual's identity" (p. 304). The term can also be interpreted as a political positioning or form of resistance. Those who identify with this term are linked to an Indigenous identity that secures a place of uniqueness, but also perhaps separation, from mainstream LGBTQ communities, thereby rooting gender identities to community and history (Driskill, 2010; Passante, 2012; Walters et al., 2006). Certainly, the term Two-Spirit fits well with Indigenous worldviews that are holistic, take both pre- and post-contact history into account, and connect every individual to their community and all of Creation.

It is important to mention, however, that the term Two-Spirit is not accepted by all individuals or communities. Many have their own terminology within their original languages to define people with diverse gender and cultural roles such as *Winkte* (Lakota), *Nádleeh* (Dené/Navajo), and *Ogokwe* (Ojibwe rough translation of "wise woman" in English) (2-Spirited People of the 1st Nations [2SP1N], 2008; Alaers, 2010; Epple, 1998; Frazer & Pruden, 2010; Passante, 2012; Toronto Aboriginal Support Service Council [TASSC], 2011; Thomas & Jacobs, 1999). Thus, the terminology varies greatly and needs to be considered and reconsidered according to each unique person, Nation, and situation (Alaers, 2010; Driskill, 2010; Passante, 2012). Wesley Thomas (Navajo Nation from New Mexico) and Sue-Ellen Jacobs (non-Indigenous) (1999) explain,

> Multiple gendered male-bodied people of the Tewa world, *kwi-sen*, are men empowered with maternal characteristics and, as principle elders of the community, assume the care of the people (their "children"). *Kwi-sen* (woman+man) are "sacred mothers" in their communities; their specialized duties are not public nor are they for public discussion. At specific ceremonial times (closed to non-Tewa people), they will appear in the plaza to conduct appropriate calendrical rituals. On the other hand, there are individuals whose lives approximate those of the previously described *berdaches*: young men who are sexual consorts of heterosexual men. *Kwido'* is a colloquial Tewa term used to refer to both gay males and *berdache* youth, but most young people prefer to use *gay* or *lesbian* or no term at all for their personal/ sexual identity. Just as at Navajo Nation, where the term *Two-Spirit* is seldom used (in deference to *gay, lesbian,* or *nadleeh*), the Tewa people do not refer to themselves as *Two-Spirit* people on the reservation. (p. 99)

Qwo-Li Driskill (2010), a Two-Spirit academic, writer, and activist of Cherokee, African, Irish, Lenape, Lumbee, and Osage descent, elaborates on the use of language to identify oneself, stating:

> The term Two-Spirit is a word that is intentionally complex. It is meant to be an umbrella term for [Indigenous LGBTQ] people as well as a term for people who use words and concepts from their specific traditions to describe themselves. Like other umbrella terms — including queer—it risks erasing difference. But also like queer, it is meant to be inclusive, ambiguous, and fluid. Some [Indigenous LGBTQ] folks have rejected the term Two-Spirit, while others have rejected terms such as gay, lesbian, bi, trans, and queer in favor of Two-Spirit or tribally specific terms. Still others move between terms depending on the specific rhetorical context. (p. 72)

Referring to his understanding of Two-Spirit identity within his community, McNeil-Seymour shares:

> The closest word that I've come across that would some-what correlate to the word Two-Spirit is chakwoya'heis, which is a Secwepemc word that simply means a person who sleeps with the same sex.... One of our roles and responsibilities as chakwoya'heis from a Secwepemc understanding, is that we have the responsibility of yuca-min'min, which means to protect the earth and protect the people. (J. McNeil-Seymour, personal communication, April 7, 2015)

Finally, some Indigenous Peoples reject the term Two-Spirit because of its being based in the English language (Greensmith & Giwa, 2013). Others contest the term because of the notion that an individual body can hold two spirits. For example, it is a Secwépemc belief that all individuals are born with one spirit only (McNeil-Seymour, 2015).

HOW IS TWO-SPIRIT DIFFERENT FROM LGBTQ?

In an attempt to differentiate Two-Spirit people from those who identify as LGBTQ, Michelle Cameron (2005) of the Dakelh-ne (Carrier) Nation writes, "the difference between the modern constructs of gay/lesbian/bi is that they are based on *sexual orientation*, whereas Two-Spiritedness is based on *gender orientation*" (p. 124). For many, Two-Spirit as a gender orientation is connected to the roles and responsibilities one orients themselves with rather than necessarily having to do with sexuality (Driskill, 2010; Passante, 2012). For example, a same-sex couple may not be considered homosexual in terms of sexuality because their sexual identities may not be a reflection of the gender roles they identify with; thus, they may identify as Two-Spirit and not homosexual. Cameron (2005) puts it simply, but uniquely, when she states, "We are not either/or; we are neither/nor. Traditional western discourse is not an adequate framework for the complexities involved in Two-Spiritedness" (p. 124).

One of the concerns that Two-Spirit people have in relation to the mainstream LGBTQ community is the erasure of their unique positioning within the LGBTQ2S acronym (Driskill, 2010; Greensmith & Giwa, 2013; McNeil-Seymour, 2015). McNeil-Seymour shares that "through being consumed into the acronym, the complexities of our identities and our roles and responsibilities become erased or smoothed away because of people thinking that Two-Spirit is really tied to gay and lesbian identities" (J. McNeil-Seymour, personal communication, April 7, 2015). Needless to say, this is a topic that is greatly debated within the Two-Spirit community. On the one hand, some Two-Spirit people see the addition of TS or 2S to the mainstream acronym as an effort toward inclusion and accessibility (Alaers, 2010; McNeil-Seymour, 2015). However, others believe that "on the surface, LGBTQTS appears to be inclusive, but when viewed across various social media and advertising platforms, the acronym reinforces the margins of gender and sexuality, and smooths away the lines of class and race" (McNeil-Seymour, 2015, p. 13). Thus, while the addition of 2S or TS might seem to be a representation of diversity and inclusion within the mainstream LGBTQ community, it is also experienced as an erasure of the racialized, marginalized experience of Two-Spirit people.

Indeed, Two-Spirit people, as with all Indigenous Peoples, face a specific and unique marginalization due to colonization that members of LGBTQ do not. Tied to this is a lack of acknowledgement from mainstream LGBTQ communities that, like all other Canadians, they too have benefited from colonization at ongoing devastating costs to Indigenous Peoples (Cameron, 2005; Driskill, 2010; Greensmith, 2015;

McNeil-Seymour, 2014). Cameron Greensmith (2015), a non-Indigenous postdoctoral researcher and Adjunct Professor in the Gender Studies Department at Queen's University, supports this reality by stating that "the superficial inclusion of Two-Spiritedness within LGBTTIQQ2S culture and politics masks the ongoing settler-colonial violence required for modern Queer formations to exist" (p. 130). This is to say that much of the privilege held, and the gains made, by mainstream LGBTQ communities remain inaccessible to Two-Spirit people and evidence of this is minimized and masked through this superficial inclusion that Greensmith (2015) speaks about. In addition, the rest of the acronym indicates identification within a Western understanding of gender and/or sexuality. McNeil-Seymour explains:

> Through being consumed into the acronym, the complexities of our identities and our roles and responsibilities becomes erased or smoothed away because of people thinking that Two-Spirit is really tied to gay and lesbian identity. Something that we also need to consider is that 150 years ago these words didn't exist, gay, lesbian, bi-sexual, so we need to ask ourselves why are these the available terms and whose purposes do they serve? (J. McNeil-Seymour, personal communication, April 7, 2015)

A major critique of these Western notions then is that, due to categorization, the terms remain unattached to other aspects of an individual's identity and existence. Two-Spirit identity, on the other hand, represents much more of a comprehensive and interwoven aspect of self that is in keeping with Indigenous worldviews.

COMING IN

Wilson (2008) writes that "Two-Spirit identity [is] one that reflects Aboriginal Peoples' process of 'coming in' to an empowered identity that integrates their sexuality, culture, gender and all other aspects of who they understand and know themselves to be" (p. 197). Many scholars refer to the process of "coming in" as one of becoming who they were meant to be or who they always have been, hence they are "coming in" to themselves and their communities (J. McNeil-Seymour, personal communication, April 7, 2015; Passante, 2012; Walters et al., 2006; Wilson, 2008). Wilson (2008) further adds:

For Two-Spirit people, who typically live with sustained racism, homophobia and sexism, the process of "coming in" to their identity is likely to be very different from the conventional "coming out" story circulated in mainstream Canadian [LGBTQ] culture. In these narratives, "coming out" is typically a declaration of an independent identity: an [LGBTQ] person musters their courage and, anticipating conflict, announces their sexuality to a friend or family member—at the risk of being met with anger, resistance, violence or flat-out rejection or abandonment. In the narratives of Two-Spirit people, however, "coming in" is not a declaration or an announcement. Rather, it is an affirmation of interdependent identity: an Aboriginal person who is [LGBTQ] comes to understand their relationship to and place and value in their own family, community, culture, history and present-day world. (p. 197)

In many mainstream LGBTQ communities, there is a discourse of "coming out," which is commonly accepted as a process necessary to identifying oneself and the community one wishes to belong to. However, as described above by some Two-Spirit writers, "coming out" implies an anticipation of separation, independence, and possible contention, as opposed to the affirming process of "coming-in." McNeil-Seymour elaborates:

[People] base so much importance on coming out, however, that's a really Western way of approaching it because you are asserting individuality whereas in a collective community, which is how Indigenous communities are, [asserting individuality] dislocates you from community. "Coming in" to community is about accepting and being responsible for your roles and responsibilities as a Two-Spirit person, whatever they may be, as manifested in these present times. (J. McNeil-Seymour, personal communication, April 7, 2015)

For many Two-Spirit people, then, "coming out" signifies further separation from culture and family because to individualize oneself is in direct conflict with Indigenous values of collectivism, cooperation, and community (Gilley, 2014; J. McNeil-Seymour, personal communication, April 7, 2015; Walters et al., 2006). The rigid constructs of gender and sexuality that make necessary a process of outwardly identifying oneself as "other" are based in Western frameworks, not Indigenous ones, where the acknowledgement of the existence of a wide range of gender and sexual identities renders identification as "other" unnecessary (Cameron, 2005; Epple, 1998; Gilley, 2014).

In researching the literature for this chapter, I read about the term "coming in" for the first time. My immediate response to it was positive, as it brought visual images of a welcoming circle of family and community members smiling, singing, and drumming in celebration of a person coming into their own. I see it as a time of feasting and gift-giving; a time for speeches about the person that highlight the gifts, strengths, and contributions that the person has, how they are viewed by family and community members, and how they are loved. I picture this celebration like the ones when a person receives their spirit name, comes back into the physical world from a fast, or goes through a rite of passage from child to young adult. The one coming in feels a strong sense of belonging, knows they are appreciated for exactly who they are and the roles and responsibilities that they will be picking up, in much the same way as one's clan and spirit name impart these feelings.

Remembering the value of collectivism within Indigenous worldviews, it can be understood that, regardless of the details of responsibilities given within different communities, Two-Spirit people are meant to be contributing members alongside all other community members. There seem to be two views on the way Two-Spirit people were seen prior to colonization. On the one hand, many Indigenous Peoples believe that Two-Spirit people held sacred traditional roles and responsibilities as caregivers within their communities prior to contact (Evans-Campbell et al., 2007; TASSC, 2011; Walters et al., 2006). In addition to this, Wilson (1996) states that they were also "often seen as 'bridge-makers' between male and female, the spiritual and the material" and, after contact, "between Indigenous American and non-Indigenous American" (p. 305). Furthermore, they often fulfilled roles of mediators within the community, facilitating interactions between community members (2SP1N, 2008; McNeil-Seymour, 2015; Miranda, 2010; Urban Native Youth Association [UNYA], 2004).

On the other hand, just as with the differences between "coming out" and "coming in," some scholars argue that, pre-contact, the notion of referring to a Two-Spirit person as special or unique could have caused a separation for them, threatening the cohesion and balance of a community, as well as their place within it (Gilley, 2014; Wilson, 1996). Like all people, Two-Spirit people were integrated into the community and "played vital roles, including medicine people, warriors, healers and visionaries" (Balsam et al., 2004; National Aboriginal Health Organization [NAHO], 2012; TASSC, 2011, p. 176; Thomas & Jacobs, 1999; UNYA, 2004). However, all of these roles could be taken up by all sorts of people within a community, thereby clearly not singling out Two-Spirit people as different or special. I have heard this position from both Two-Spirit and non-Two-Spirit Indigenous people and, to me, it makes good sense since the idea conjures up an attitude of, "Okay, you're Two-Spirit. These will be your roles and responsibilities. You aren't any more special than anyone else. Off you go. Get to work." Hence, there is no separating out of anyone once they have had their coming in ceremony, since everyone participates in ceremonies, and so people remain equal. Further, as highlighted throughout this book, interdependency of all aspects of one's self and one's environment is a concept woven throughout Indigenous worldviews. Thus, with this in mind, it is highly unlikely that identity would traditionally have been categorically based in gender and sexuality as opposed to one's place in the community and the combined nature of all the characteristics or traits of an individual (Alaers, 2010; Baskin, 2011; Walters et al., 2006; Wilson, 1996).

The embracing of fluid and diverse forms of gender and sexuality prior to contact and colonization is also reflected in Wilson's discussion of the value of non-interference and its effect on child-rearing practices in traditional Indigenous communities. Children were free to explore their environment, to learn and grow "without the limitations of punishment and praise" (Wilson, 1996, p. 307). In her own experience, as Wilson (1996) gravitated toward the "masculine," she was taught to hunt and trap alongside her brothers and was given toys that would typically be considered to be geared toward boys, as those were what she wanted. To illuminate sexism as an imposed impact of colonization, Wilson (1996) shares a defining moment in her childhood when she was told by a young person in her community to stop "dancing like a boy" (p. 311). She goes on to explain, however, how the "invitation" to continue dancing, as interpreted from the enjoyment of the Elders observing her dancing, offered her strength while she came to understand that aspect of her identity. The responses of the Elders are representative of how, traditionally, when a child began to show signs of being Two-Spirit, there were always individuals in the community to guide them and offer them the Two-Spirit teachings of their particular culture (Thomas & Jacobs, 1999; UNYA, 2004).

COLONIZATION AND ITS IMPACTS ON TWO-SPIRIT PEOPLE

The imposition of Christian values and the enforcement of homophobia and heterosexism upon Indigenous communities, coupled with the erosion—and sometimes the destruction—of customs, ceremonies, teachings, and languages of Indigenous populations, resulted in devastating challenges for Two-Spirit people. A frightening example of this can be seen in the gender roles, binaries, and constructs created and enforced within the residential school system (Driskill, 2010; NAHO, 2012; Teengs & Travers, 2006; UNYA, 2004; Wilson, 2008). McNeil-Seymour explains,

> Residential schools were sites that imposed settler norms of gender and sexuality. They also disconnected us from our traditionally accepted spaces in community [where] we never were treated as less than. [In fact], there is no word in Secwepemc'stin for discrimination. (J. McNeil-Seymour, personal communication, April 7, 2015)

Wilson (2008), who conducted research with Two-Spirit survivors of the residential school system, quotes a participant, born with female anatomy, describing an initial experience at one of the schools:

> The first thing they did was divide us by boy/girl. Girl go this way, boy go this way. Girl wear pinafores. Boy wear pants. All hair cut.... I didn't really know which side to go to. I just knew that I wanted to be with my sisters and my brother. I had never worn a dress before so I went with my brother.... It was like a little factory—one priest shaved my head while the other tore off my clothes. I was so scared. I covered my area. It didn't take long for them to notice [that I had a vagina].... That was my first beating. (p. 194)

With the domination of heteronormativity and patriarchy came marginalization and discrimination of women and Two-Spirit people within non-Indigenous communities that eventually crept into Indigenous ones (2SP1N, 2008, 2014; Driskill, 2010; Greensmith & Giwa, 2013; McNeil-Seymour, 2015; NAHO, 2012; Ristock, Zoccole, & Passante, 2010). As a result, "Two-Spirited people experience oppression and exclusion from three potential sources: their First Nations community because they are Two-Spirited, [LGBTQ] communities because they are First Nations and mainstream communities for both reasons" (NAHO, 2012, p. 6). In fact, enforcement of homophobia and patriarchy has resulted in a denial of the very existence of Two-Spirit people by some Indigenous and non-Indigenous knowledge keepers within various communities (Alaers, 2010; McNeil-Seymour, 2014; Passante, 2012).

I had an experience of homophobia by a well-known and respected Elder a few years ago. This gifted Elder travels across North America giving teachings and doctoring people. I was part of a team that brought him to Toronto to offer teachings. We held a circle with him that was open to both Indigenous and non-Indigenous people. At one point, the Elder began talking about how, in nature, there are two groups, males and females, and they come together to reproduce. There are no Two-Spirit animals, therefore, there should not be any Two-Spirit people. I was immediately mortified by what he was saying, finding myself in quite a predicament. Do I stay quiet because this is an Elder—someone with vast knowledge, who is revered and honoured in Indigenous communities—as I do not want to offend him, thereby alienating myself from him? Or do I speak up, not only because there are likely some Two-Spirit people in the circle, but because what he is saying is, quite simply, wrong? I agonized for a bit and finally decided to speak up. I knew if I didn't, it would torment me long into the future. With a racing heart, I challenged the Elder in a calm, respectful way, asking how he came about the information he had, as well as offering my understandings of Two-Spirit people as part of our communities. Did I change his thinking? Probably not, but at least I planted a seed which will, I'm sure, be nourished by others who speak up. At the end of it all, we decided to agree not to agree. This was disappointing, but I felt validated after the circle when several people thanked me for speaking up.

As a consequence of the complex web of discrimination, rejection, and isolation, sometimes by our own people, Two-Spirit people are at an extremely heightened risk for contracting HIV/AIDS, and being victims of violence, homelessness, and suicide (2SP1N, 2008; Alaers, 2010; NAHO, 2012; Passante, 2012; UNYA, 2004; Zoccole, Ristock, Barlow, & Seto,

2005). This is caused, in part, by situations such as the one I just relayed, whereby our own Indigenous communities push Two-Spirit people out of our circles. I am not a Two-Spirit person, but that has nothing to do with my speaking out against discrimination toward them. Every single one of us is connected. When any person is harmed, I am harmed, as is everyone else. We cannot remain silent about this as we are all part of the problem, which means we must all be part of the solutions.

ONE CHILD'S STORY

I know a precious young child who is referred to as a "Two-Spirit Princess Boy," which is partially borrowed from a well-liked story, *My Princess Boy*, authored by Cheryl Kilodavis and illustrated by Suzanne DeSimone (2010). The child in this story "loves pink, sparkly things. Sometimes he wears dresses. Sometimes he wears jeans. He likes to wear his princess tiara, even when climbing trees. He's a Princess Boy." This non-fiction storybook, about the author's son, their family, and his school, along with the mother's initial struggles to understand her child, is about unconditional love. Kilodavis is inspiring, not only for the writing of this award-winning book, but for her advocacy work on acceptance, diversity, and inclusion for all children.

My little friend also loves pink and sparkly things and sometimes wears a dress. He is intelligent; vocal; inquisitive (always asking his parents about what words mean when he hears them spoken); super cute; likes dump trucks, dolls, iPads, and dinosaurs; has a pink *Hello Kitty* umbrella; and does not identify as either a boy or a girl. He received the Kilodavis book when his mother decided that, instead of giving children goody bags when they attended one of her other child's birthday parties, she would give them "social justice storybooks." They have read *My Princess Boy* several times, Mom has cried while reading it, and it is carried in the knapsack that goes to day-camp so that the counsellors can read it for all of the children and themselves.

When I visited the Canadian city where this family lives during the summer of 2015, the mother and child agreed to have lunch with me one day and talk about what it means to be a Two-Spirit child. We began talking about how this child makes decisions from day to day about who he wants to be. Each day before going out, this child decides whether or not he will go out as a girl, a boy, or a princess boy. When I asked how this is decided, the response was, "It's quite easy actually. I think about it in my mind," and then Mom and child discuss it. This is the child speaking, by the way, not the mother! There are days when this child does not mind being called a girl for what he is wearing, or wants to assert his male identity, but then there are other days when he wants his big people to help explain to strangers that he is a Two-Spirit person. He walks an interesting path of fluid identities.

I wanted to know what was helpful for this Two-Spirit Princess Boy when he went out in the world to day-camp where his parents would not be. At the start of the camp, Mom asked that his gender-neutral identity not be made a big deal of and this has been followed by the counsellors. She suggests that "children can use accessible washrooms and family change rooms as these are gender neutral and if you mis-gender a child, then just correct yourself once you are informed about it."

Having support and people who accept this child as he is are invaluable and this family has both. Both parents are completely in sync when it comes to their child's multiple identities. They are surrounded by a pair of uncles who are a gay couple and aunties who are Two-Spirit couples. Mom is an auntie for a Two-Spirit circle that she is a part of, but to date, even though she is always asking, they only know one other child, who is a teenager, that identifies as gender neutral. The entire family is excited and patiently waiting to meet other Two-Spirit children, which will likely happen via the mother's group involvement or through her contacts at the Native Youth Sexual Health Network (NYSHN, n.d.), an organization by and for Indigenous youth that works across issues of sexual and reproductive health, rights, and justice throughout the United States and Canada. It is led by and for Indigenous youth 30 years of age and under. In addition to staff, NYSHN is advised by three Youth Councils: the National Indigenous Young Women's Council (NIYWC), the National Indigenous Youth Council on HIV/AIDS (NIYCHA), and the National Native American Youth Council on HIV/AIDS (NNYC-HIV).

Despite the love and support that surrounds Two-Spirit Princess Boy, his mother is very afraid for him as he goes about in the world, especially for when he begins going to school and as he gets older. She worries that people will not accept him for the fabulous person he is. There are glimmers of this when they are out on days Two-Spirit Princess Boy has decided to be a girl, which means wearing a dress and hair done in fancy braids. People stare at times. But it gets worse, as Mom recounts an experience they had on a bus one day:

A man on the bus called him a girl on a day when he had chosen to identify as a boy. I guess it had to do with the fact that the man had his particular views of children who have long hair and wear pink. I politely corrected this man, simply saying that he was a boy. This man freaked out, literally screaming at me, asking me what was I trying to do, make him gay? It was so bad, we had to get off the bus. (Mother, personal communication, July 16, 2015)

On the brink of tears, Mom revealed to me what is one of a mother's greatest fears: "I can't let myself think about the physical violence that might happen to him just because of who he is."

This family also has the support, teachings, and mentorship of a Two-Spirit Elder who recently attended a Sundance ceremony and, while there, it came to her that she needed to begin putting together a sacred bundle for Two-Spirit Princess Boy. Upon returning home, the Elder presented the child with two goose-feather wings to use as fans, which will be dressed later on, perhaps with streamers—a very Two-Spirit Princess Boy idea. This Elder has also assisted them with one of the traditional methods of many Indigenous Nations to see if a child is Two-Spirit or not. According to Sandra Laframboise, who is Algonquin-Cree, and Michael Anhorn, an ally, (2008),

Many tribes had rituals for children to go through if they were recognized as acting different from their birth gender. These rituals ensured the child was truly Two-Spirit. If parents noticed that a son was disinterested in boyish play or manly work, they would set up a ceremony to determine which way the boy would be brought up. They would make an enclosure of brush, and place in the center both a man's bow and a woman's basket. He was told to go inside the circle of brush and to bring something out, and as he entered, the brush would be set on fire. The tribe watched what he took with him as he ran out. (para. 8)

The ceremony works in the following way: if the child comes out of the brush with the basket or both the basket and the bow, then he is given the teachings regarding both genders and will be seen as Two-Spirit. If he comes out with only the bow, he is given the teachings, roles, and responsibilities for males. Thus, the ceremony is about identifying one's gender and roles, and not about sexuality.

Two-Spirit Princess Boy and his mother shared with me the ceremony, complete with tobacco, a sacred fire, and spirit plate that they experienced. The child, with a flashlight, entered his IKEA tent that had been draped with a blanket to make it dark, where two toys were placed. The Elder explained that even though these were not traditional items, it did not matter as what is needed is the energy that is attached to them. Once inside, Two-Spirit Princess Boy shouted out with excitement, "There's toys in here!" One toy was a dump truck and one was My Little Pony, both in the same colours, but not either of his two favourite colours (which are pink and green). He exclaimed, "There is a My Little Pony in here! But I am not going to bring it out, okay?" He was told by the Elder to bring out the item that felt right to him. After sitting in the tent for a bit, he came out with the dump truck, which he put aside and would not play with. The Elder, seeing that Two-Spirit Princess Boy was not playing with the dump truck and was cuddling with his mother on the couch, asked if he could have taken both toys out with him, would he have? He said no, he would have taken out My Little Pony, and then asked his father if he could go back in and get it. Father said yes, so he went in, got it, came out, and played with it.

The Elder and the parents spoke about what was happening and Two-Spirit Princess Boy told them that he was scared to pick the one he wanted, but when he was told that he could have both, he knew that he only wanted the My Little Pony. When asked if he had decided what he wanted to be—a girl, boy, or Two-Spirit—his reply was, "It's not like I decided. It's what I am." (Yes, that is the child speaking again!) The same Elder also conducted a naming ceremony for my young friend, who already had two names, but now has three. The latest one, "Askiy kisik," is in the Cree language and translates into English as "Earth Sky," meaning that he walks with the energy of both the earth, which is our Mother, and the sky, which is our Father.

Two-Spirit Princess Boy is also a fan of the PRIDE parade and has been going to it since he was in his mother's womb, but 2015 was particularly special for him as it was the year that he "came in," as described earlier in this chapter, to the community as Two-Spirit. To commemorate this important occasion, Mom designed a t-shirt and Dad had it made; it says "Proud 2 Spirit Princess Boy." At the end of our chat, Mom said to me,

"He may or may not be Two-Spirit in the future, but this is who he is right now." And, of course, he will always be fabulous. I love you, Two-Spirit Princess Boy.

ACCESSING SERVICES

Research indicates that Two-Spirit community members experience a lack of safe and aware workers in the social services and health sectors, an unmet need for transition houses for people moving into cities across Canada, and few community events and activities that are non-discriminatory and inclusive (NAHO, 2012; Ristock et al., 2010; TASSC, 2011). Once finding themselves in need of access to services, many Two-Spirit people face barriers in the form of institutionalized racism and discrimination within the organizations that are meant to help them (2SP1N, 2008; Zoccole et al., 2005). Greensmith (2015) explains,

> Queer service provision institutionalizes whiteness, which ultimately produces which queer and trans lives are worth caring for. In a sense, queer service provision caters to a particular white queer politic that invites inclusivity and diversity in, and yet maintains that gender and sexuality must be considered as singular, disconnected from other interlocking systems of oppression. (p. 164)

Many Two-Spirit people migrate to urban centres from First Nations or small, rural communities where they were victims of homophobia, violence, and discrimination (Gilley, 2014; NAHO, 2012; TASSC, 2011; Teengs & Travers, 2006). Upon arriving in the city, many are soon faced with the reality that they cannot find the safe and accepting community they thought they would and, instead, experience exclusion and judgement in LGBTQ spaces and at community events in both these communities and Indigenous ones (Greensmith & Giwa, 2013; NAHO, 2012; Passante, 2012). McNeil-Seymour speaks to this, saying,

> Recognizing that your sexuality is a bit different, you look toward the gay and lesbian community as this safe haven where you're going to find community. [And yet] when you come to the city, you're soon reminded of your place which

often means that you're desired, but not desirable enough to be in a relationship. There's exotification and tokenism. Exotification because of mixed identities or because of your Aboriginal identity which then leads into a sexualized piece. Tokenism, as I experienced it, I was the only person of colour within my gay group of friends in Vancouver, and I know there was no ill-will on their behalf because they very much honoured and appreciated where I was coming from, but there were moments of "what's your Indian name" and that sort of thing which, in some instances, is wildly inappropriate or "I dreamt about this, what does it mean?" And there's that level of tokenism that winds up happening as well. So you're confronted with classism, you're confronted with racism, and you're viewed as just a sexual object in a lot of ways. Not having the sense of community that you were hoping to find is the experience of many. Finding work is hard too because you're facing homophobia, racism, transphobia, classism, all kinds of "isms" when you come to the city. (J. McNeil-Seymour, personal communication, April 7, 2015)

There is a real danger of erasing the unique intersections of oppression experienced by Two-Spirit people by assuming that they can access mainstream LGBTQ services in the same way as non-Indigenous people do (Wilson, 1996). Fortunately, research is highlighting ways to move forward in the social services and health sectors in attempts to decolonize organizations and create safer spaces for Two-Spirit people. Some organizations have chosen to incorporate workshops in attempts to educate helpers about anti-discrimination, HIV/AIDS awareness, and homophobia, and many have established protocols to address individual occurrences, though it is difficult to say how effective or culturally safe they are (Canadian Aboriginal AIDS Network [CAAN], 2007; Zoccole et al., 2005). That being said, there is still a great need for sharing circles or support groups, services, and education for both Indigenous and non-Indigenous communities and organizations about Two-Spirit people, their histories and needs (2SP1N, 2008; Greensmith, 2015; UNYA, 2004). And their contributions! Indigenous leadership is crucial to this process. Seeing positive reflections of self in leadership is key to strengthening self-worth and feelings of acceptance (McNeil-Seymour, 2015; NAHO, 2012; Passante, 2012). However, so is "strong ally-ship, and education about issues facing Two-Spirit people [as this] is also imperative to addressing problems" (J. McNeil-Seymour, personal communication, April 7, 2015).

In a 2004–05 environmental scan of Indigenous organizations serving Two-Spirit people in Canada, Zoccole and colleagues (2005) highlighted potential models for use amongst Indigenous organizations. Among these were a model based on leadership and cultural diversity at all levels of an organization, and an anti-homophobia model specifically intended for Indigenous populations. As they reported:

> Activities [within the workshops] include the development of anti-homophobia strategies to be developed by community health staff and Elders in consultation with community members. The emphasis is on outreach to Aboriginal communities and organizations. Anti-homophobia workshops are considered significant when addressing homophobia in Aboriginal organizations and communities and can assist in the elimination of barriers to access services. (p. 106)

McNeil-Seymour (2015) calls on the helping professions to "place more emphasis on finding confluence with Indigenous epistemology and research methods, or risk the continued production of colonized minds" (p. 17), and to consider cultural safety. As discussed in Chapter Four, culturally unsafe practices are any actions which attack, demean, or deny the cultural identity and well-being of an individual, which includes not only ethnicity, but class, race, sex, age, sexual orientation, and so on, and the intersection of these multiple identities. Cultural safety, on the other hand, emphasizes historical and social contexts, including colonization and its current impacts, which influence our positions. As addressed earlier in this chapter, Christianity and patriarchy have infiltrated present-day Indigenous teachings, such as the example of the Elder. When we think and behave in this way, we are feeding into the oppressors' views and internalizing their prejudice. Is this what we want to do? Is this what we want to pass on to our children? If so, we are denying who we are as Indigenous Peoples and continuing the much-used, and greatly successful, tactic of divide and conquer implemented by the oppressors.

To counteract homophobia within Indigenous communities and services, we must ensure the availability and awareness of Indigenous-based knowledges, and Two-Spirit histories and narratives as necessary beginning steps (McNeil-Seymour, 2015; NAHO, 2012; Passante, 2012; Wilson, 1996). Connection with cultures, ceremonies, and traditions—which could be drumming, singing, dancing, being on the land, and participating in healing ceremonies and pow wows—dramatically increases resilience for many Two-Spirit people (NAHO, 2012; Passante, 2012; Ristock, Zoccole, & Passante, 2010; Wilson, 2008). McNeil-Seymour's (2015) *Cross-Dancing as Culturally Restorative Practice* illuminates a perfect example of reinforcing positive spaces and strengths within the community through the practice of cross-dancing. Pow wows provide an opportunity for Two-Spirit people to express their identities and cultures in a way that is not available in mainstream LGBTQ spaces. McNeil-Seymour (2015) explains that a "Cross-Dance (or Switch-Dance in some Nations) is a pow-wow special (a dance held in honour of age, marriage, and other lifespan markers) in which dancers swap regalia" (p. 4). Furthermore,

> It is an opportunity for Indigenous People experiencing their sexuality or gender identity or expression as outside the norm to see, observe and experience an accepting space. As part of culturally restorative practice, social workers could make Indigenous clients aware that Cross-Dancing is performed at pow-wows for some Nations. (p. 6)

I had the privilege of participating in such a dance several years ago with Chris, who is one of my Two-Spirit friends. I had a lot of fun and laughed so much, especially when Chris insisted that we dance in the opposite direction of the other dancers. As everyone danced clockwise in the circle, he and I danced counter-clockwise. We danced against the grain, which was so appropriate given the context.

Gilley (2014) explains that a "gender diversity tradition" (p. 32) is found in Indigenous cultures, and as such cross-dancing is an act representative of an individual adhering to the roles and responsibilities of the gender they are displaying; it is not understood as a woman dancing as a man, or a man dancing as a woman. "Being able to express one's gender identity through the pow-wow is important for Two-Spirit men [women and trans individuals] because the pow-wow is a culturally sanctioned source and reflection of one's Native identity" (Gilley, 2004, p. 90). In addition, when we consider the homophobia that exists in many Indigenous communities as a result of colonization and the imposition of Christian gender and sexuality binaries, cross-dancing at pow wows "acts to give a public space for representations of Two-Spirit identity, a space that is lacking in most contemporary Native ceremonies and practices" (McNeil-Seymour, 2015, p. 91). It can also be seen as a way for Two-Spirit people who identify as LGBTQ to reconnect their identities to an Indigenous framework.

Although many mainstream LGBTQ services explicitly state Two-Spirit inclusion, development of more Two-Spirit-specific programming is needed even in major urban Canadian centres. There are various service providers working toward inclusivity and diversity, but the necessary acknowledge-ment and focus on Indigenous history and experiences of colonization and exclusion is often lacking (Greensmith, 2015; Passante, 2012). In addition, research has shown that regardless of mandates of inclusivity, Indigenous Peoples often report encounters of racism in mainstream LGBTQ agencies and organizations (Balsam et al., 2004; Passante, 2012; Ristock, Zoccole, & Passante, 2010; Teengs & Travers, 2006).

2-Spirited People of the 1st Nations is a non-profit organization that provides counselling, advocacy, education/awareness services, and so-cial and cultural events/activities to Two-Spirit people in the Toronto area. In addition, the organization has developed a curriculum to raise awareness and counter homophobia in Indigenous communities and within organizations serving Two-Spirit people (2SP1N, 2014). Similarly, according to McNeil-Seymour, the organization Native Youth Sexual Health Network,

> is doing really exciting work around creating space for young persons to articulate their own ways of knowing … I think that supporting an organization that is peer-led and youth-led like the Native Youth Sexual Health Network is important because it helps to give agency back to a marginalized population that is often silenced out of so much of the various discourses. As youth who are perceived as sexual and racial minorities as well as [facing] classism, it's really important to foster them as young leaders to step up and trouble these narratives. (J. McNeil-Seymour, personal communication, April 7, 2015)

Passante (2012) writes about services in Vancouver, B.C.:

> There are two Aboriginal organizations with specific ser-
> vices for Two-Spirit people. The Aboriginal Wellness Pro-
> gram has a Two-Spirit group focusing on mental [health]
> wellness and addiction programs. The Urban Native
> Youth Association had a youth drop-in that ran for about
> two years, but recently closed due to non-attendance.
> Vancouver Coastal Health has counseling services avail-
> able to LGBT people and include Two-Spirit people in
> their targets. Healing Our Spirit is an Aboriginal agency
> working to prevent the spread of HIV while also offering
> care and support to those living with infection. (p. 20)

Needless to say, if a city such as Vancouver has so few services for Two-
Spirit people, other Canadian cities have even fewer. One research project
in 2012 showed that Winnipeg, Manitoba, had no Two-Spirit-specific services, although services are offered to them through other agencies, such
as the Rainbow Resource Centre and a few health clinics (Passante, 2012).
There is an online resource called Two-Spirited People of Manitoba Inc.,
whose mission is "to improve the quality of life of Two-Spirit (Aboriginal
gay, lesbian, bisexual and trans) people in Manitoba, which includes raising funds for, and assisting in, providing appropriate advocacy, education,
health services, housing, employment training and cultural development"
(Two-Spirited People of Manitoba, n.d.).

CONCLUSION

Clearly, Two-Spirit people have unmet needs for spaces that foster a sense of
community and opportunities to build service provision, as well as equitable
and safe access to services, along with identity and culturally based programming. Two-Spirit and ally scholars and activists are calling for mainstream
service providers to begin to deconstruct and decolonize their organizations.
Similar to the fact that colonization in Canada is not an Indigenous problem,
but a Canadian one, the marginalization and discrimination faced by Two-
Spirit people is not their burden to carry alone; it is also up to mainstream
society, LGBTQ communities, and Indigenous communities across Turtle
Island to not only carry it, but help to ease it. Little people, such as my friend
Two-Spirit Princess Boy, are counting on us.

REFERENCES

2-Spirited People of the 1st Nations (2SP1N). (2008). *Our relatives said: A wise practices guide; Voices of Aboriginal trans people.* Retrieved from http://www.2spirits.com/PDFolder/2Spirits%20Transgender%20Training%20Manual.pdf.

2-Spirited People of the 1st Nations (2SP1N). (2014). Current Programs. Retrieved from http://www.2spirits.com.

Alaers, J. (2010). Two-Spirited people and social work practice: Exploring the history of Aboriginal gender and sexual diversity. *Critical Social Work, 11*(1), 63–79.

Balsam, K.F., Huang, B., Fieland, K.C., Simoni, J.M., & Walters, K.L. (2004). Culture, trauma, and wellness: A comparison of heterosexual and lesbian, gay, bisexual, and Two-Spirit Native Americans. *Cultural Diversity and Ethnic Minority Psychology, 10*(3), 287–301.

Baskin, C. (2011). *Strong helpers' teachings: The value of Indigenous knowledges in the helping professions.* Toronto: Canadian Scholars' Press Inc.

Cameron, M. (2005). Two-Spirited Aboriginal people: Continuing cultural appropriation by non-Aboriginal society. *Canadian Woman Studies, 24*(2/3), 123–127.

Canadian Aboriginal AIDS Network (CAAN). (2007). *Walk with me: Pathways to health: Harm reduction service delivery model.* Retrieved from http://caan.ca/wp-content/uploads/2012/05/WalkWithMe_en.pdf.

Driskill, Q. (2010). Doubleweaving Two-Spirit critiques: Building alliances between Native and Queer studies. *GLQ: A Journal of Lesbian and Gay Studies, 16*(1–2), 69–92.

Epple, C. (1998). Coming to terms with Navajo "nádleehí": A critique of "berdache," "gay," "alternate gender," and "Two-Spirit." *American Ethnologist, 25*(2), 267–290.

Evans-Campbell, T., Fredriksen-Goldsen, K., Walters, K., & Stately, A. (2007). Caregiving experiences among American Indian Two-Spirit men and women: Contemporary and historical roles. *Journal of Gay & Lesbian Social Services, 18*(3), 75–92.

Frazer, M.S., & Pruden, H. (2010). Reclaiming our voices: Two Spirit health and human service needs in New York state. Albany: New York State Department of Health AIDS Institute.

Gilley, B.J. (2004). Making traditional spaces: Cultural compromise at Two-Spirit gatherings in Oklahoma. *American Indian Culture and Research Journal, 28*(2), 81–95.

Gilley, B.J. (2014). Joyous discipline: Native autonomy and culturally conservative Two-Spirit people. *American Indian Culture and Research Journal, 38*(2), 17–39.

Greensmith, C. (2015). *Diversity is (not) good enough: Unsettling white settler colonialism within Toronto's Queer service sector.* (Doctoral dissertation). University of Toronto, Toronto.

Greensmith, C., & Giwa, S. (2013). Challenging settler colonialism in contemporary Queer politics: Settler homonationalism, pride Toronto, and Two-Spirit subjectivities. *American Indian Culture and Research Journal, 37*(2), 129–148.

Kilodavis, C., & DeSimone, S. (2010). *My Princess Boy.* Retrieved from https://books.google.ca/books/about/My_Princess_Boy.html?id=FodebKRMNuEC&source=kp_cover&redir_esc=y.

Laframboise, S., & Anhorn, M. (2008). The way of the Two-Spirited people: Native American concepts of gender and sexual orientation. Retrieved from http://www.dancingtoeaglespiritsociety.org/twospirit.php.

McNeil-Seymour, J. (2014). Indigenizing the gay agenda: A note on cultural relativism and homonationalism from the colonial margins. In G. Walton (Ed.), *The gay agenda: Creating space, identity, and justice* (pp. 139–154). New York: Peter Lang.

McNeil-Seymour, J. (2015). Cross-dancing as culturally restorative practice. In B.J. O'Neil (Ed.), *Gender and sexual diversity: Social work practice, policy, research and pedagogy* (pp. 87–105). Toronto: Canadian Scholars' Press Inc.

Miranda, D.A. (2010). Extermination of the Joyas: Gendercide in Spanish California. *GLQ: A Journal of Lesbian and Gay Studies, 16*(1–2), 253–284.

National Aboriginal Health Organization (NAHO). (2012). Suicide prevention and Two-Spirited people. Retrieved from http://www.naho.ca/documents/fnc/english/2012_04_%20Guidebook_Suicide_Prevention.pdf.

Native Youth Sexual Health Network (NYSHN). (n.d.). Who we are. Retrieved from http://www.nativeyouthsexualhealth.com/whoweare.html.

Passante, L. (2012). *Aboriginal Two-Spirit and LGBTQ mobility: Meanings of home, community, and belonging in a secondary analysis of qualitative interviews.* (Master's dissertation). University of Manitoba, Winnipeg.

Ristock, J., Zoccole, A., & Passante, L. (2010). Aboriginal Two-Spirit and LGBTQ migration, mobility and health research project: Winnipeg, final report. Retrieved from http://www.2spirits.com/PDFolder/MMHReport.pdf.

Teengs, D.O., & Travers, R. (2006). "River of life, rapids of change": Understanding HIV vulnerability among Two-Spirit youth who migrate to Toronto. *Canadian Journal of Aboriginal Community-Based HIV/AIDS Research, 1,* 17–28.

Thomas, W., & Jacobs, S. (1999). "... And we are still here": From berdache to Two-Spirit people. *American Indian Culture and Research Journal, 23*(2), 91–107.

Toronto Aboriginal Support Services Council (TASSC). (2011). *Toronto Aboriginal research project*. Retrieved from http://www.councilfire.ca/Acrobat/tarp-final-report2011.pdf.

Two-Spirited People of Manitoba. (n.d.). Mission statement. Retrieved from http://www.twospiritmanitoba.ca.

Urban Native Youth Association (UNYA). (2004). *Two-Spirit youth speak out! Analysis of the needs assessment tool*. Retrieved from http://www.unya.bc.ca/downloads/glbtq-twospirit-final-report.pdf.

Walters, K., Evans-Campbell, T., Simoni, J., Ronquillo, T., & Bhuyan, R. (2006). My spirit in my heart: Identity experiences and challenges among American Indian Two-Spirit women. *Journal of Lesbian Studies, 10*(1), 125–149.

Wilson, A. (1996). How we find ourselves: Identity development and Two-Spirit people. *Harvard Educational Review, 66*(2), 303–317.

Wilson, A. (2008). N'tacimowin inna nah': Our coming in stories. *Canadian Woman Studies, 26*(3/4), 193–199.

Zoccole, A., Ristock, J.L., Barlow, K., Seto, J., & Canadian Aboriginal AIDS Network. (2005). *Addressing homophobia in relation to HIV/AIDS in Aboriginal communities: Final report of the environmental scan 2004–05*. Retrieved from http://www.2spirits.com/PDFolder/CAAN_homophobia_Report.pdf.

Chapter Thirteen

CARING FOR FAMILIES, CARING FOR CHILDREN

INTRODUCTION

Within provincial child welfare and practice standards, the principle of "the best interests of the child" guides how social workers work with children and their families. No one would argue that the protection of children is not of paramount importance. Nevertheless, it is a principle based on a Eurocentric worldview, which may not be aligned with the needs of the diverse populations of Canada. From an Indigenous worldview, the guiding principle regarding child welfare would be oriented toward a values base that takes into account the best interests of the community, as this includes children, their families, and all other people around a child.

WHO SAID, "IT TAKES A VILLAGE TO RAISE A CHILD"?

In 1996, Hillary Rodham Clinton, the wife of then American President Bill Clinton and then First Lady, presented a talk on the importance of children and families in our lives and Nations. When speaking about raising a happy, healthy, and hopeful child, Clinton stated, "it takes a village to raise a child" (1996). First Lady Clinton brought this saying to prominence in her speech, but the statement was first coined by the people of the Igbo and Yoruba regions of Nigeria. The statement describes a belief held by numerous Indigenous Peoples around the world since the beginning of time.

What does it mean and what does it look like for all members of a community to be involved in the raising of all children? It means that I as an individual have a contribution to make not only to my biological children, adopted children, nieces and nephews, and children in my care at a particular time, but also to all children who live around me or who belong to whatever "community" I belong to. The value of family is strong amongst Mi'kmaq people. Prior to contact, extended families were well-organized systems that allowed for extra support and cooperation in the sharing of roles and responsibilities, ranging from parenting to providing food. Strong families meant strong communities. Within Mi'kmaq communities, if a child was adopted by a family, they would have the same status and respect as someone related through bloodlines. Such communities may or may not be based on geography as defined by aspects described in earlier chapters about worldviews.

Special respect is shown toward children and Elders since Elders are the grandparents of all and children are the future of the Nation. Elders are the keepers of the past as well as the road to the future. Marshall (1975, as cited in Berneshawi, 1997) states that Mi'kmaq must respect Elders because they not only hold the knowledge of our ancestors, they have the language through which the knowledge must be imparted to youth. Their years of searching, listening, experiencing and understanding all that is bodily, emotionally and spiritually possible, grants them the wisdom and strength needed by our youth to become good Mi'kmaq. Elders were also respected for their abilities to unite families. (p. 119)

As stated by Berneshawi (1997), "when this lifeline is severed, the younger generation's knowledge of their cultural traditions and the relationship with the land which sustains them is lost and the future of the Nation is jeopardized" (p. 120).

One of the ways in which this lifeline is severed is through the child welfare system. There are many Indigenous scholars who focus on research and writing about child welfare. Without a doubt, all these writers emphasize how children are part of families and communities, and must be viewed as such regardless of the struggles of their parents, as children do not learn or form their identities based solely on their contact with parents. This is supported by Greenwood and de Leeuw (2007):

Children, particularly young children, cannot of course be disentangled from the broader families, communities, and Nations that sustain them. Consequently, the process of reconnection with the Indigenous identity and associatively re-building cultural captivity might be understood as being connected to each of these potential learning sites (family, community, and Nation). (p. 51)

As all children learn from their families, communities, and Nations or state, it seems reasonable that their well-being is connected to the support they receive from all of these groups. When we strengthen community life, we can begin to move family matters out of the courtroom and place these matters back into the capable hands of the community. This can be achieved through community members and service providers, such as social workers, creating strong environments that ensure that the responsibility of caring for children lies within the community. Indigenous communities around the globe are undertaking a gradual decolonization process by returning to beliefs such as "it takes a village to raise a child." One such program located in Northern Manitoba is called Meenoostahtan Minisiwin, meaning "pathways to peace" in Cree, and "focuses on promoting families' strengths and capacities while exploring the best interests of children from a family and community perspective, away from the courts" (Pintarics & Sveinunggaard, 2005, p. 70).

Fortunately, a decolonization process is about going beyond raising awareness of how colonization has undermined our communities to care for our children. This process is about how we can go about creating positive changes in our communities. This is the work that is being done, so the literature needs to reflect this work, by exploring, for example, the strengths that exist within communities that help to make communities stronger, and what social workers may need to understand about what helps communities move toward supporting the health of families and children.

THE STORY OF ANDREA AND CHARLENE

Much has been written about the devastation caused by the adoption of Indigenous children into White families (Blackstock, 2008, 2009; Carrière, 2005, 2006, 2008; Carrière & Scarth, 2007; Hughes, 2006; Menzies, 2014; Reid, 2005; Richardson & Nelson, 2007; Sinclair, 2007; Trocme, Knoke, & Blackstock, 2004), which I will not go into here. Rather, I am offering the story of my good friend Charlene, who was introduced earlier, and her daughter Andrea. Theirs is a story that, to me, represents a loving example of the joys and challenges of a White woman mothering an Indigenous child. Now an adult, Andrea has two daughters, and lives in Toronto.

The story of Charlene and Andrea begins at the time when Charlene was the partner of one of Andrea's uncles, and working as the band social worker in Waglisla. Charlene met Andrea when she was four months old, as she and her partner would babysit the young girl. A short time later, Andrea's mother was struggling and having difficulty caring for Andrea. Andrea's mother was splitting up with Andrea's father and trying to figure out how to do that and where to go. She decided to leave her First Nation community and went to Vancouver to take a break. It was then that Andrea came to stay with Charlene and her partner on a full-time basis. Later on, one of Andrea's aunts wanted to care for the child, but it was clear that Andrea did not want to leave Charlene and her uncle. Charlene called Andrea's mother to ask what she wanted regarding where Andrea should live. She replied, "I would love it if you kept her" (C. Avalos, personal communication, February 3, 2009).

In Waglisla, it is common for children to live with relatives other than their parents. Everyone knows the circumstances, and it is an accepted practice. Many traditional adoptions occur as well. Elders will approach young women to see if they need the help of others to care for their children and adoption happens when needed. According to Charlene, "this was the way it was done in the past and is based on the Aboriginal worldview that it takes a village to raise a child" (C. Avalos, personal communication, February 3, 2009).

Andrea's great-grandfather, a hereditary chief, was well respected and listened to by everyone in Waglisla. He approved of Charlene and her partner caring for Andrea, and the rest of the family was cooperative and supportive of this arrangement, so child welfare did not have to be involved. Charlene states matter-of-factly, "I think if child welfare had been involved, it would have complicated the process" (C. Avalos, personal communication, February 3, 2009). The great-grandfather and hereditary chief instructed Charlene that if she was to keep Andrea with her, then she was not to take her for a short time and then pass her on to others. At the time, although there was no traditional ceremony to adopt Andrea as potlatches were only just being reintroduced into Indigenous communities after having been banned under the Indian Act for many years, it was decided that Andrea, then 18 months old, would stay with Charlene and her uncle permanently. About one year later, Andrea's father and his girlfriend wanted to take Andrea to live with them, but Andrea's great-grandfather said no, that Andrea was to stay with Charlene and her uncle.

When Andrea was five years old, she, Charlene, and her uncle moved to Vancouver in order for Charlene to attend university to get her Master's of Social Work degree. They lived in Vancouver for one year, and during this time Andrea had visits with her mother and visits to her home community. When Andrea was six, Andrea and Charlene moved to Toronto, where Charlene is originally from. All of Andrea's family were in agreement with this. However, Charlene needed to get legal guardianship at this point so she could travel with Andrea. Both of Andrea's parents came to the court-house to sign the documents. Charlene was viewed as Andrea's aunt as she was in a relationship with Andrea's uncle for many years. The family knew that Charlene would not disappear with Andrea. They knew they would see Andrea while she was growing up and they knew that Charlene understood how important this was to them.

Andrea talks about a childhood that combined living with Charlene in Toronto during the school year and living with her family in Waglisla during the summer:

> I was always attached to Charlene and always saw her as my mother. When I visited with my biological mother, I felt kind of uncomfortable or it felt strange to call her "mom," like I was betraying Charlene when I called her that. It felt confusing. The visits with my mother were regular. Sometimes I saw my father, but not as often. I had fun with my mother, but I never felt close to her. We never talked about why I was living in Toronto rather than with her. Usually, I'd be a little afraid each time it got close to me leaving for a visit to Waglisla, but after being with them for awhile, I'd get attached and want to stay there rather than go back to Toronto. (A. Peers, personal communication, February 3, 2009)

This desire to stay in both places reflects what Charlene was also experiencing during these years:

> I wanted to ensure that Andrea knew her family and community which is why I sent her to visit there every summer. But it was emotionally hard on me because each time Andrea visited Waglisla, I worried that she would decide to stay there, rather than return to me. (C. Avalos, personal communication, February 3, 2009)

Life was different for Andrea, living in both Waglisla and Toronto:

> My family lived traditionally, so when I was in Waglisla during the summer, what I remember most is food. My family hunted, fished and canned what they caught during that time of the year. They lived off the land. It was during other times of the year that they attended potlatches and other ceremonies.

In Toronto, Charlene's family made me feel loved and accepted and I felt like a part of the Aboriginal community there. But I always had a sense of not quite belonging, for example, I looked so different from Charlene and her family. It was the same at school. Other kids would tell me I didn't look like my mother Charlene. It went fine though when I told them I was adopted. As far as I know I was the only Aboriginal kid at my school and at times, I was referred to as Chinese, Japanese or Mexican which I didn't like. But I did appreciate being different from other kids because once teachers knew I was Aboriginal, I seemed to get a lot of positive attention.

I went to lots of ceremonies and culture camps with Charlene while growing up. I would often tell my friends that my mother was more traditional than I was. I never felt that connected to Aboriginal culture either in Toronto or Waglisla. I just wasn't sure how I fit in with either of them and felt confused. What was taught in Toronto were the teachings of the Ojibway and Cree people which didn't really interest me. There isn't much information in Toronto about Aboriginal people from B.C. (A. Peers, personal communication, February 3, 2009)

Charlene is adamant that Andrea would have struggled much more as a young adult if she had not spent time with her family and community while growing up. Charlene always felt it was important for Andrea to know where she came from, where her roots were, and what contributed to her identity as an Indigenous person, even if she felt confusion at times. She has always felt it was the best choice for Andrea.

Andrea continues to wonder if going back for visits to B.C. was the best for her because her family there did not talk about why she was not living with her biological mother or father. She now thinks it might have been better for her if she had started going for visits when she was a little older, maybe at ten years old, so that she might have had more of an understanding about her situation. However, Charlene points out that Andrea had seven years of visits with her mother, whereas if she had only begun to visit her at the age of ten, she would have only had three years of visits. The difference in the time frame is due to the heartbreaking fact that Andrea's mother was murdered when Andrea was only 13 years old. Charlene emphasizes, "Andrea wouldn't have gotten to know her mother if she hadn't gone out to visit in the summers when she was a young child" (C. Avalos, personal communication, February 3, 2009). Charlene and Andrea do agree that Andrea may have grown up to be more confused and angry if she had not known her mother, who her family is, where she comes from, where her roots are, and what her cultural affiliation is. Charlene and Andrea have a great deal to teach social workers, as well as other helpers, in the area of caring for families and children. Andrea suggests that everyone involved with children who are not going to live with their biological parents needs to tell these children the reasons why they cannot live with their parents at a particular time. Charlene believes that this approach is much better than silence, which leaves a child wondering, confused, and perhaps blaming themself for why they are unable to be with their parents or feeling as though they are not wanted by their families.

As Andrea explains,

> I know it would have helped me if my mother told me why I wasn't with her, if she had shared her feelings with me. If not her, then someone else in my family. I know my family was affected by residential schools which likely had a lot to do with why they had difficulty talking, sharing feelings and connecting, but knowing this while growing up would have helped me to understand. (A. Peers, personal communication, February 3, 2009)

Charlene expands on these thoughts using a broader perspective:

> Adoption always has an element of loss and grief to it and people need to recognize this, but not get stuck in it. Open adoptions require maturity on the part of all involved. In mainstream society, there continues to be more of a position of ownership of a child, but not so in traditional Aboriginal communities. This makes a large difference on how open adoptions operate.
>
> Aboriginal worldviews embrace self-reflection and healing which is so important in adoption arrangements. Adoptive parents need to work on their own issues and accept the fact

that adoptees will have their issues too. If this is accepted from the beginning, then room is available for the biological parents to be involved in some way. Aboriginal communities also recognize the value of raising a child collectively. The idea that it takes a community to raise a child is embedded in the Aboriginal value system and worldview. This idea is valuable to all peoples of the world. (C. Avalos, personal communication, February, 3, 2009)

Both Andrea and Charlene now believe it would have been helpful if there could have been a family circle when Andrea was a child, which would have allowed the family to talk openly about what happened and why. They believe this would have helped everyone express their emotions. Andrea and Charlene think having circles for adoptees, biological parents, and adoptive parents would also be helpful, because circles could assist people in understanding that they are not alone and that what they are experiencing is okay.

Both Andrea and Charlene caution, however, that every situation needs to be looked at on its own. Not all situations are the same and therefore not all solutions will be the same. There cannot be one way for everyone when it comes to families and children. Both Andrea and Charlene strongly encourage social workers to look closely at the values of mainstream society and the profession, in terms of how they view the caring for and raising of children. They agree that it is important not to view children living with others, rather than their biological parents, as negative.

ELIMINATING THE CHILD VS. THE FAMILY DICHOTOMY

When it comes to the area of child welfare, particularly for Indigenous and African/Caribbean peoples living in Western countries such as Canada, the United States, and Australia, the notion of state authority over children needs to be revisited. History needs to inform how child welfare legislation, policies, and practices are created and implemented. It is of critical importance that bureaucracy not be allowed to harm communities, families, and children any longer. Instead, the cultures and identities of these communities need to direct policies and practices on how children are raised and cared for. Resources need to be focused on whatever is needed to keep children within their families and communities, and on supporting families in their personal growth, healing, and empowerment. I agree with Greenwood and de Leeuw (2007), who argue that "through fostering Indigeneity in Aboriginal mothers, there exists the potential to counteract the state's ongoing child welfare intervention into Aboriginal mothers' families" (p. 180).

We need to truly pay attention to what research is telling us about how children need to be a part of their families and communities. According to Richardson and Nelson (2007), "youth in the child welfare system tend to move back to their birth family as soon as they are cut loose from the child welfare authorities—that is if their familial connections were not completely severed by social work practice" (p. 76). We need to challenge the notions that adoption policies, such as confidentiality and cutting ties to birth families, promote greater attachment to adoptive families and that adoptive parents can replace birth parents through an erasure of information about the birth parents. Who is to say that openness in adoption would not have a positive impact on children and youth in terms of, for example, the crucial issue of identity formation? Growing up in the homes of a few extended family members is not harmful or a sign of instability, but can be understood as a way to provide multiple supports and positive social relationships for children and youth.

In my work and research with Indigenous social workers in child welfare, I have observed similar findings to those of Michelle Reid (2005), a member of the Heiltsuk Nation, who writes that Indigenous child welfare social work practitioners "discussed the 'pressure' and the 'pain' of working under delegated models within their communities that are dealing with the ongoing 'impacts of colonization.' These practitioners do not want to be seen as 'perpetrators of colonialism' within their own people" (p. 30). These concerns are supported by Cindy Blackstock (2009) of the Gitksan Nation, director of First Peoples Child and Family Caring Society and an Associate Professor in the School of Social Work at the University of Alberta, who recently won national and international acclaim over the landmark decision by the Canadian Human Rights Commission that successive federal governments have racially discriminated against Indigenous children. Blackstock states, "the concept that we can do harm or even do evil rarely appears on the optical radar screen of professional training, legislation or practice in anything other than a tangential way through procedural mechanisms such as codes of ethics" (pp. 31–32). As social workers, we do not want to discuss, let alone hear, that our work may be causing harm to others, particularly children. After all, aren't we supposed to be the good people? Blackstock (2009) wisely points out, however, that making positive change means "understanding the harm from those who experienced it, it means setting aside the instinct to rationalize it or to turn away from it because it is too difficult to hear" (p. 36).

These voices of Indigenous women in the area of Indigenous child welfare are crucial to hear. I also wanted to hear from a non-Indigenous voice in the area of mainstream child welfare. I thought it would be interesting to talk with a social worker who had worked with Indigenous people in this area to see what their experiences and perceptions were. I spoke with Carolyn Ussher, who has worked for over 20 years in the area of child welfare and is currently a child welfare supervisor at the Children's Aid Society of Toronto. I knew Carolyn from my years at an Indigenous family services agency when we worked with some of the same families.

Carolyn spoke about the ways that family problems are dealt with through mainstream, state-controlled child welfare:

> Mainstream society personalizes and individualizes problems. There is an emphasis on the person to deal with whatever the problem is. Families tend to be isolated and living in silos—isolated and cut off from resources and supports, formal or informal on their own, not connected. Mainstream child welfare tends to simply look at the fact that there is a problem with the parents or mother. The child is the client by law, yet the work has to occur with the parents or mother. Someone did not get into a particular difficult situation just because. Rather there have been many factors involved that have contributed to the situation. The person cannot get out of their difficult situation just because child welfare tells them to or a judge says they have to if they want their children back. (C. Ussher, personal communication, March 10, 2009)

Carolyn thinks that those who work in mainstream child welfare believe that people do not want to reach out to others, because parents who are struggling do not want others to know they are having difficulty caring for their children. However, she also believes that "this is an assumption. It's more authentic, natural, real, to get many people to help rather than not doing so" (C. Ussher, personal communication, March 10, 2009). A thoughtful Carolyn then went on to explain what she saw and learned from having the privilege of speaking with Indigenous Elders and Traditional Teachers, who taught her about their ways of looking at the world and helping people:

> Aboriginal people pull all kinds of people in to support the family which validates people and acknowledges how grandparents, for example, can take responsibility for caring for their grandchildren. In Aboriginal ways of helping, there is a widening of the circle of care for families and children. There are more eyes to see what the family is experiencing and this leads to how others can help. The community is opened up to care for children, rather than the responsibility being only on parents to do so. Indigenous people look at the extended family, the community, the family's ancestors, where the child comes from and the meanings of all of this when trying to assist those who are struggling. Their ways of helping see the bigger picture. A client is more than just a client; she or he is not just a parent who has abused his or her child for example. There is so much more to people; they are part of a community, a circle, a past and a future. Indigenous ways of caring for families and children provides hope for everyone as parents can see themselves as much more than "a problem." These ways also look at the strengths, skills and gifts of people and assures them they are not alone because they are part of a whole. They teach that everyone has a job, purpose, role; that everyone is worthwhile and everyone's life experiences are valued. (C. Ussher, personal communication, March 10, 2009)

As a self-reflexive social worker, Carolyn is able to critique some child welfare practices that she does not see as helpful, such as where children are allowed to live:

> Mainstream child welfare puts too much emphasis on a certain kind of home where children should live. There can be rigid versions of what an "appropriate" home is. Mainstream child welfare rules people out for caring for children because they do not have a Eurocentric way

of seeing the family, like the two-parent, middle-class family. We continue to be judgmental about variations of what families look like. But Indigenous ways emphasize that it is not important what material possessions a person has, but rather that he or she can see that they are connected to other people and everything around him or her. This is good for all people—to feel a connection to others and to place. (C. Ussher, personal communication, March 10, 2009)

Carolyn also critiques the rigidity of child welfare, which often requires parents to participate in programs and services in order to keep their children or have their children returned to them:

> Mainstream child welfare directs clients to attend all sorts of services, but maybe the person just needs to sit with their situation and think about what will help. We can't always direct clients to services without helping them to incorporate the learning, knowledge and change that comes with this. When we overwhelm people with services, it's just checking off a little box to say they went without really incorporating the learning. People need time to change and sitting with things, with supports, can help I think. Give people some space and time which is another teaching from Indigenous people. (C. Ussher, personal communication, March 10, 2009)

CUSTOMARY LAW AND CARE

Obviously, Indigenous Peoples around the globe cared for their children for centuries according to Indigenous values prior to colonization. Indigenous Peoples had ways of caring for children that we are today working to collectively bring back. There are alternatives to the enormously costly and adversarial court processes when it comes to the care of children and preservation of families. Much time, effort, and money is expended when families are required to go to court for child protection issues. In addition, the adversarial nature of the court system usually has a negative impact on the relationship between the child protection worker and the family. Instead of working together in order to protect the best interests of the child, child protection workers and families are "fighting to win." Since the process is so intrusive, rigid, and impersonal, effective communication and trust are unlikely.

Some Indigenous people, such as myself, believe that ideas for alternatives to the court system, such as child protection mediation, kinship care, and family group conferencing, originate within Indigenous worldviews. Some of these initiatives appear promising. For example, child protection mediation that is separate from existing child protection bodies has proven to be effective in Manitoba and Ontario (Crush, 2005).

The overrepresentation of Indigenous children in the care of the Children's Aid Society in northern Ontario caused Nishnawbe-Aski Legal Services (NALSC) in Thunder Bay, Ontario, to implement an initiative called the Talking Together Program (TTP) in 2002 (NALSC, 2015). The program offers an alternative to court proceedings in child protection matters. The program holds Talking Circles with families, social service workers, and Elders to explore creative solutions in a non-judgemental environment. These solutions are then implemented as the Plan of Care for the child. In 2005, 135 children remained in their community following involvement with TTP and 218 remained in their community in 2006 (Mishibinijima, 2006). The participation of families and community members in the process is the cornerstone of TTP and allows for more innovative and appropriate solutions for the care of children, as opposed to the usual and often ineffective addiction and anger management treatment options (Mishibinijima, 2006). In some areas, the TTP has been so effective that it has evolved into a prevention program rather than a crisis intervention service (NALSC, 2015). This means the program is able to address concerns so that child protection services do not have to become involved.

British Columbia operates a Child Protection Mediation Program (CPMP) where families and child protection workers are brought together to negotiate their disputes with the assistance of a neutral third party. Since 1997, 70 percent of participants in CPMP were able to completely or partially resolve their child protection issues out of court (Ministry of Attorney General, 2006). Another effective alternative to the court system is the Meenoostahtan Minisiwin: First Nations Family Justice Program (MM: FNFJP) in Manitoba. This program, developed by a mandated Indigenous child protection agency, brings families, community members, and service providers together to resolve child protection matters. The idea is to reach solutions that will address the long-term protection of children by getting at the roots of family concerns. The process is based on Indigenous traditions of peacemaking and all participants must be fully informed volunteers. Between 2000 and 2013, MM: FNFJP received 1,370 referrals and provided services for 3,205 children (Awasis Agency of Northern Manitoba, 2012/2013).

In a 2004 evaluation, 100 percent of the participants cited satisfaction with the services with 81 percent stating that they were very satisfied (Pintarics & Sveinunggaard, 2005). Participants stated that the program ensures that their voices are heard, that there is clear communication, and that a safe, comfortable environment is provided for families. Ninety percent of service providers who made referrals to the program stated that there were fewer children going into care and there was more effective planning when a child was required to go into care (Pintarics & Sveinunggaard, 2005). Service providers also noted that the process improved collaborative working relationships with everyone involved and that the process helped keep families together. Finally, 95 percent of service providers identified that a family-oriented approach made a positive difference in the service provided, and a family-oriented approach was preferred to the child-oriented focus that is traditionally taken by child protection agencies (Pintarics & Svienunggaard, 2005).

KINSHIP STRUCTURES AND FAMILY GROUP CONFERENCING

Indigenous values about children and families are understood and practised in many areas of the world, particularly when there are child protection concerns. These methods are being implemented in similar and diverse ways by Indigenous Peoples in countries such as the United States, Australia, and New Zealand. I have personally witnessed these approaches being used in countries such as Jamaica, Brazil, Peru, Guatemala, Mozambique, and Ghana, although these approaches may not be formalized or implemented through social service structures.

One of the processes that has gained greater attention is family circles, which have come to be known as the Family Group Conference (FGC), in New Zealand. It was in Aotearoa/New Zealand where FGC originated, following the legislation of the Children, Young Persons and Their Families Act in 1989 (Connelly, 2004; Mishibinijima, 2006). FGC evolved over time, beginning as a part of legislation in the late 1970s when several reports were issued revealing the structural and institutional racism experienced by the Māori, the Indigenous people of this area (Connelly, 2004). Not surprisingly, Māori children and families were experiencing the same difficulties with child protection agencies as children and families in Canada, including overrepresentation in child protection services, alienation from their families and communities, and difficulties with a system that failed to provide long-term security for children. In the early 1980s, the New Zealand government, in partnership with Māori tribal societies, launched Maatua Whangai, which implements "Kinship structures within a fostering framework to care for Māori children, its objectives being to release Māori children from institutional placements and place them into the care of their family and tribal groups" (Connelly, 2004, p. 1).

As with efforts in Canada, FGC is intended to involve families in decisions about children, include extended family members in kinship care, and support empowerment by adopting a less intrusive approach. The FGC "became the legal mechanism through which the dual principles of child protection and the strengthening and maintenance of families would be formally addressed" (Connelly, 2004, 2).

Today, versions of FGC show up in other Western countries' child protection agencies, including Canada. Carolyn Ussher has much to say on this topic:

> Mainstream child welfare has co-opted kinship care and family group conferencing from Indigenous Peoples. However, family case conferencing, which is not the same as family group conferencing, is the procedure in child welfare now. Thirty days after a case is opened, the workers bring people together to widen the circle of care and help create a plan to move forward.
>
> Mainstream child welfare puts a lot of rules on this method. It's more of a structure on how to invite people, how to share the decisions, who will lead the conference, how will people communicate. Conferencing is happening more now and seen as how to implement shared responsibility for children. There is more input from the family on what will help and support them now.
>
> But mainstream child welfare is not thinking creatively about conferencing. Workers only view immediate and extended family as caring for children, while Indigenous people involve the entire community, which is seen as

able to care for children. The mainstream needs to look at how workers translate what conferencing is, for example, are they allowing families to direct the process? Is the process more client focused? If so, there ought to be more agreement amongst all involved.

Something else that I think is really important is: I'm certain that Indigenous ways of supporting families makes it much easier for people to disclose the difficulties they are experiencing, like a mother feeling comfortable enough to say, "I'm afraid I'm going to use [substances]." Workers do not tend to hear this from people as they are afraid of what the child welfare workers will then do. Yet this can be such a helpful and successful way to work with families. I view parents being able to disclose their fears and realities as making so much sense to the helping process and conferencing creates more safety for greater openness for this. The more information a child welfare worker has, the better, as it helps them to make more creative decisions with a family.

Conferencing is a different way of communicating for mainstream child welfare workers. It means not talking to people in silos or individually, but bringing them together to think creatively instead.

Looking at widening the circle of care for families and children can be powerful for child welfare workers because when they do so, they are not the only ones responsible for child protection and safety. Widening the circle means workers can feel that there is a sharing of this responsibility. This is a much more supportive way for workers. (C. Ussher, personal communication, March 10, 2009)

Carolyn finished her conversation with me with a caution to non-Indigenous social workers that want to incorporate Indigenous ways of helping:

Do not co-opt Indigenous ways of helping. Give credit where it is due. When we co-opt something it feels like we take a great idea and tweak it to look like it's our idea. Instead we need to give credit to where ideas and practices come from such as kinship care and family group conferencing.

Try to learn from Indigenous worldviews as I have and see if you connect to the values. Mainstream ways teach everyone to want something else which is whatever we do not have now, but Indigenous teachings help people to focus, stay in the moment, and ground us which are so much more fulfilling than always wanting something else.

All people can connect on a human level. We all need to go to this place, begin there and see where it takes us. (C. Ussher, personal communication, March 10, 2009)

Several studies have been conducted on the effectiveness of FGCs with a number of diverse groups such as African-American, Cherokee, and Latino communities in the southeastern United States. Within this region in the United States, there was a history of enslavement and segregation of African-Americans; the forced removal of the Cherokee, known as the "Trail of Tears"; and high numbers of undocumented Mexican people who continue to be treated punitively by U.S. police and immigration officials. Research has shown that, within all three groups, participants agreed that FGC provided a respectful way for child welfare to involve them in decision making that was congruent with their cultural beliefs (Pennell, 2007a, 2007b). It has also been demonstrated that FGCs are partly effective in countering institutional or structural racism, and FGCs have been associated with a decline in the numbers of children entering state care (Edwards & Tinworth, 2006; Merkel-Holguin, Nixon, & Burford, 2003; Texas Department of Family and Protective Services, 2006).

The question of whether or not FGCs should be implemented in situations of family violence is often raised. Social workers and others who work in this area are often fearful that children and women will be harmed by family group conferencing or violence will occur after the conference. Although the research is limited on FGCs in the area of family violence, what research there is shows promising results. For example, a Canadian study did not find that any violence occurred during or after the meetings (Pennell, 2007a). In fact, this research also found that there were reductions in indicators of child maltreatment and woman abuse for families who participated in family group conferences, while indicators of violence rose for families who did not participate in them (Pennell, 2007a).

Of course, FGCs require thorough preparation and follow-up, especially where family violence has happened, so that all family members are able to feel safe. I agree with Pennell (2007a), who states, "given the benefits of FGCs to children and their families from diverse populations, prohibiting its application in all instances where there is a history of domestic violence would be problematic" (p. 6).

CHILD WELFARE COMMUNITY COUNCIL

State intervention in the relationship between parents and children is only justified when a parent is understood to be placing the child in jeopardy. Within a more mainstream perspective, when a child is viewed as being in need of protection, typically fault is attributed to the parents. Within Indigenous worldviews, the focus is not on finding fault with the parents, but on support and healing. Since fault does not need to be established, parents do not have to feel that they have failed, if they are able to call upon a broader community for assistance. Looking at the needs of children means exploring what children need in order to thrive and finding the resources to ensure that this happens. When all of a child's needs cannot be met by a parent, this does not mean that the child must be taken from that parent. However, it does mean that the needs of a child may not be being met, which needs to be addressed.

Aboriginal Legal Services of Toronto's (ALST) Child Welfare Community Council (CWCC) is the only council of its kind in the world. Like FGC, its concept is not new, but rather rests on an Indigenous understanding and practice that the responsibility for raising children rests with the community, rather than only with the parents. The CWCC falls within the scope of an alternative dispute resolution process under the Child and Family Services Act of Ontario:

> The CWCC process can occur at two stages. For families who are at risk of having children apprehended there is the Talking Circle—a process that occurs with a view to preventing an apprehension from taking place. The Talking Circle process can take place when Native Child and Family Services of Toronto (NCFST), which is the mandated child protection agency for Indigenous families in Toronto, believes that if the relationship between them and a family that they are involved with does not improve, then apprehension will likely occur. A Talking Circle is a body external to NCFST that attempts to help

open or re-open the lines of communication between the family and the agency, so that progress can be made with the apprehension of a child averted. A Talking Circle would involve the family, NCFST, a facilitator from the CWCC members and an Elder.

Community Council hearings take place following the apprehension of a child by NCFST. The hearing can only occur if both the parents and NCFST agree. NCFST will consider participating in a Council hearing where they believe there are circumstances under which they might agree, at some point, to have the child either returned to the parent or to another caregiver suggested by the parent. If NCFST and one parent agree to have the matter heard by the CWCC and one parent does not agree, the hearing will take place with the one parent.

Council hearings will take place as soon as possible following the first appearance of the matter before the court. Council hearings cannot usurp the role of the Court in determining what is in the best interests of the child. However, a Council hearing, as an alternative dispute resolution forum, may arrive at a plan for the child more quickly, and with greater participation from the parties, than the Court process. (ALST, 2015)

All parties with an interest in the matter will be invited to attend the hearing. This will include the parents, a representative from NCFST, the child (if they are over 12 years of age), a representative from the child's First Nation or Indigenous community, and any other individuals who may have something to contribute to the discussion. An Auntie is chosen in advance of the hearing from among the CWCC members. The role of the Auntie is to represent the interests of the child. In order to represent the interests of the child, the Auntie meets the child on at least one occasion, prior to the Council hearing taking place. At the hearing, the Auntie's role is to ensure that the child's interests remain a priority.

The Council members decide how the hearing will be governed. After hearing from everyone and satisfying themselves that they have all the information they require, the Council members, along with the Elder, determine what they consider to be an appropriate plan for the child. If agreement is reached, then everyone signs the written plan. If agreement is not achieved through this process, the matter will be dealt with through the court system whereby the Council's plan is presented to a judge for their consideration (ALST, 2015).

Rene Timleck was introduced to readers in Chapter Eleven, "Healing Justice." Rene is a member of the CCWC and, at times, takes on the role of the Auntie. She sees the purpose of the CCWC Council as "a process that helps to heal families while protecting children." Rene openly shares that she grew up with neglect and substance misuse in her family of origin. Then, as an adult, her own children went into the care of the Children's Aid Society due to neglect and abuse. Today, she wonders why no one did anything to help her when she or her children were growing up. Rene believes that since she was once in a similar position as the parents who come through the Council process, she is able to assist these families:

> My own experiences not only give me insight into many aspects of the cases, but also help me recognize pitfalls or dangers that might not be apparent to others. I understand the fear the parents feel in their dealings with Native Child and Family Services of Toronto. It is almost an inevitable position of being at loggerheads when it comes to the relationship between families and those that have the power to take or keep their children away from them. I also understand the responsibility that the agency's workers feel in keeping the children safe. (R. Timleck, personal communication, April 22, 2009)

Rene explains that it tends to be the parents who ask for a hearing with the Council. She states that there is often much more emotion involved in these kinds of hearings as compared to hearings that concern youth and adults, because the process concerns a child. Parents are often fearful, which makes it more difficult for them to open up. At times there are outbursts. There may be anger directed at the NCFST's workers or the agency itself. There may be crying. As Rene explains, "these are deeply personal cases. Peoples' lives are and may be deeply affected by what happens on the day of the hearing, so there may be a whole gamut of emotions that participants experience" (R. Timleck, personal communication, April 22, 2009).

Rene notes that a participant at a hearing may at first be opposed to what others are suggesting about a plan for the child and family, but through the hearing process will often change what they think and want, and often an agreement can, in the end, be achieved. Rene hopes that "when consensus is achieved and everyone signs the agreement, each party feels heard and that they have truly participated in the process" (R. Timleck, personal communication, April 22, 2009).

Rene believes that this Council has great potential for all people as "each community could take care of its own children allowing for more personal responsibility. It would allow for more people to be involved in the safe keeping of the children in their communities." Rene also notes that in the mainstream system, judges are burdened with the sole responsibility to make decisions regarding children and their families, but "with the Council, decisions are made by a collective, so the onus of responsibility is spread out amongst several people rather than on only one" (R. Timleck, personal communication, April 22, 2009).

Rene also supports alternatives to state child welfare, such as the Council, for all people because:

> Much is revealed in a day long hearing. Everyone involved comes closer to the truth than when they are in a court-room. There is less chance of losing sight of the real issues in the Council process. In court proceedings, it is often how knowledgeable the lawyers are and who presents their case the most eloquently, rather than the real issues at hand—whether it be criminal or family proceedings. The Council process allows for the problem to be dealt with on a more personal level with the people involved being a part of the process. I believe that such councils could be a very effective tool in assisting people of any culture and, therefore, in all society. (R. Timleck, personal communication, April 22, 2009)

CONCLUSION

Perhaps no practices embody the values of a society more than how that society views and treats its children. Indigenous practices of caring for children from a collective, communal perspective are spreading across international boundaries and into the West. Systems of child welfare are beginning to adopt our practices, such as kinship care and family group conferencing, in ways that suit their particular beliefs and needs. Are Indigenous practices regarding families and children being co-opted or appropriated by dominant forms of child welfare? Or is the West beginning to learn from us that sharing power with families and communities helps to serve the best interests of children?

My answer to these questions is that both may be the case, but what I know to be much more important comes from two other authors since I cannot say it any more eloquently than they can: "Sharing good ideas is an essential human endeavour. As we share our gifts, we contribute to the knowledge basket of all who work with children and families" (Connelly, 2004, 3). On a bigger picture level, Richardson and Nelson (2007) summarize what truly matters:

> When we look deeply, we see that we are at a crisis point in the way we are living on the Earth. Most critically, we need to move from a culture of problem solving to one of visioning and creating the world we want…. Through "cleaning up" our practice and working in ways that actually preserve and strengthen extended families and communities, we help families to help themselves. With increased wellness and improved White/Aboriginal relations (free of racism, Eurocentrism and economic marginalization) true collaborations may emerge. Under improved conditions, all individuals will begin to care for the young ones, as well as the Earth, in a loving and thoughtful way. On a spiritual level, separation is the cause of much of our planetary grief; solutions will not come from continuing to separate children from their families, from their community and from their lands, traditions and spiritual practice. (p. 81)

This chapter, and the words of wisdom above, suggest that separating children from their families and communities is, in most cases, not in the best interests of the child. This in no way applies to only Indigenous children; it applies to *all* children.

REFERENCES

Aboriginal Legal Services of Toronto (ALST). (2015). *Aboriginal Legal Services of Toronto's Child Welfare Community Council*. Toronto: Aboriginal Legal Services of Toronto.

Awasis Agency of Northern Manitoba. (2012/2013). Child and Family Services: Year-end final report. Retrieved from http://www.awasisagency.ca/docs/2012-2013_Annual_Report.pdf.

Berneshawi, S. (1997). Resource management and the Mi'kmaq Nation. *Canadian Journal of Native Studies, 17*(1), 115–148.

Blackstock, C. (2008, February). *The breath of life: When everything matters in child welfare.* Paper presented to University of Victoria Aboriginal Child Welfare Research Symposium, Victoria, B.C.

Blackstock, C. (2009). The occasional evil of angels: Learning from the experiences of Aboriginal peoples and social work. *First Peoples Child & Family Review, 4*(1), 28–37. Retrieved from http://www.fncfcs.ca.

Carrière, J. (2005). *Connectedness and health for First Nation adoptees.* (Doctoral dissertation). University of Alberta, Edmonton.

Carrière, J. (2006). Promising practices for maintaining identities in First Nation adoption. *First Peoples Child and Family Review, 3*(1), 46–64. Retrieved from http://www.fncfcs.ca.

Carrière, J. (2008). Maintaining identities: The soul work of adoption and Aboriginal children. *Pimatisiwin: A Journal of Aboriginal and Indigenous Community Health, 6*(1), 61–80. Retrieved from http://www.pimatisiwin.com/online/.

Carrière, J., & Scarth, S. (2007). Aboriginal children: Maintaining connections in adoption. In I. Brown, F. Chaze, D. Fuches, J. Lafrance, S. McKay, & S. Thomas Prokop (Eds.), *Putting a human face on child welfare: Voices from the prairies* (pp. 205–223). Prairie Child Welfare Consortium, Centre of Excellence for Child Welfare. Retrieved from http://www.cecw-cepb.ca.

Clinton, H. R. (1996, August). Speech presented at the Democratic National Convention, Chicago, IL.

Connelly, M. (2004). *A perspective on the origins of family group conferencing.* Englewood, CO: American Humane Association.

Crush, L. (2005). The state of child protection mediation in Canada. *Canadian Family Law Quarterly, 24*(2), 191–219.

Edwards, M., & Tinworth, K. (with Burford, G., & Pennell, J.). (2006). *Family team meeting (FTM) process, outcome, and impact evaluation: Phase II report.* Englewood, CO: American Humane Association.

Greenwood, M., & de Leeuw, S. (2007). Teachings from the land: Indigenous people, our health, our land, our children. *Canadian Journal of Native Education, 30*(1), 48–53.

Hughes, T. (2006). BC Children and youth review: An independent review of BC's child protection system. Retrieved from http://www.mcf.gov.bc.ca.

Menzies, P. (2014). Child welfare. In P. Menzies & L.F. Lavallée (Eds.), *Journey to healing Aboriginal people with addiction and mental health issues: What health, social service and justice and workers need to know* (pp. 43–60). Toronto: CAMH.

Merkel-Holguin, L., Nixon, P., & Burford, G. (2003). Promising results: Potential new directions: International FGDM research and evaluation in child welfare. *Protecting Children, 18*(1–2), 2–11.

Ministry of Attorney General. (2006). Child protection mediation program. Retrieved from http://www.ag.gov.bc.ca.

Mishibinijima, L. (2006). *Aboriginal child protection alternative dispute resolution: Environmental scan.* Toronto: Aboriginal Legal Services of Toronto.

Nishnawbe-Aski Legal Services. (2015). Talking together. Retrieved from http://www.nanlegal.on.ca/article/talking-together-126.asp.

Pennell, J. (2007a). Safeguarding everyone in the family—family group conferences and family violence. *Social Work Now, 37*, 4–8. Retrieved from http://www.cyf.govt.nz/documents/about-us/publications/social-work-now.

Pennell, J. (with King, J., & Spehar, C.). (2007b). *North Carolina family-centered meetings project: Annual report to the North Carolina Division of Social Services, fiscal year 2006–2007.* Raleigh, NC: North Carolina State University, Department of Social Work, North Carolina Family-Centered Meetings Project.

Pintarics, J., & Sveinunggaard, K. (2005). Meenoostahtan Minisiwin: First Nations child welfare and decolonizing stories. *First Peoples Child & Family Review, 2*(1), 67–88. Retrieved from http://www.fncfcs.ca.

Reid, M. (2005). First Nations women: Workers' speak, write, and research back: Child welfare and decolonizing stories. *First Peoples Child & Family Review, 2*(1), 21–40. Retrieved from http://www.fncfcs.ca.

Richardson, C., & Nelson, B. (2007). A change of residence: Government schools and foster homes as sites of forced Aboriginal assimilation—a paper designed to provoke thought and systemic change. *First Peoples Child & Family Review, 3*(2), 75–83. Retrieved from http://www.fncfcs.ca.

Sinclair, R. (2007). Identities lost and found: Lessons from the sixties scoop. *First Peoples Child & Family Review, 13*(1), 65–82. Retrieved from http://www.fncfcs.ca.

Texas Department of Family and Protective Services. (2006, October). Family group decision making: Final evaluation. Retrieved from http://www.dfps.state.tx.us.

Trocme, N., Knoke, D., & Blackstock, C. (2004). Pathways to the overrepresentation of Aboriginal children in Canada's child welfare system. *Social Services Review, 78*(4), 578–599. Retrieved from http://www.jstor.org.

Chapter Fourteen

THE POWER OF PEDAGOGY

INTRODUCTION

Chapter Fourteen focuses on a discussion about teaching and how crucial it is to include multiple knowledges within our classrooms. Both Indigenous educators and students share some of their experiences and perspectives on how to make education in the helping professions more inclusive for Indigenous and other marginalized learners. Contributions from non-Indigenous students and educators are also highlighted in terms of how they value and incorporate Indigenous pedagogy. The message of this chapter is that education can be healing and decolonizing for both Indigenous and non-Indigenous learners and educators.

HOW I TEACH

Fortunately, with a spirit name, in both Mi'kmaq and Anishnawbe, that means something like "The Woman Who Passes on the Teachings," I love being an educator. I enjoy opening doors for learners and watching them walk through on their journeys of self-discovery. I take pride in being a part of helping students gain new understandings; seeing their eyes light up, their heads nod; hearing their questions; and engaging in critical discussions with them. It is a privilege to walk with learners as they transform into critical, caring thinkers over the time they are in the classroom. However, along with this privilege comes responsibility.

As an educator, I must be mindful of what I teach and how I teach. It is no easy task to teach about colonization and oppression, nor is it easy to teach about decolonization and anti-oppression. Learners are looking for solutions and I do not necessarily have any since I am on this search as well. The challenge is one of how to teach these topic areas with integrity, so that nothing is watered down, without shaming learners for their privileges or their lack of knowledge. Walking the journey of teaching with integrity and caring is founded upon the Indigenous worldview and values that I live by. I carry these values with me at all times, so the classroom is no exception, regardless if I am teaching Aboriginal Approaches to Social Work or Strategies for Conflict Resolution or Advanced Social Work Theory and Practice. Over the years, I have been honoured to hear students share with me that I do not make them feel ignorant about what they do not know; that my words offer encouragement without shaming and help them think more deeply about their work; and my down-to-earth style makes learning fun. All of my classrooms are set up in a circle, so that everyone can see everyone else. There is no seat in the circle that represents a place of power.

There are often no desks between me and the learners, which creates an egalitarian energy in the circle. Such a classroom set-up sends out a number of messages that are remarkably different from one where the teacher stands at the front of the room or behind a podium, and learners sit in rows looking at the backs of those in front of them.

Weather permitting, I have also held some classes outdoors. During a recent one-week intensive course, the learners and I sat outdoors the entire time. We tend to share food in my classrooms, along with personal experiences and lots of humour. Laughter lightens the heaviness of some of the material, material that focuses on colonization and oppression. Telling the stories of real people makes the information come alive for learners.

I am a teacher who discloses personal stories to learners. I tell students about my background, where I am from, what I believe in, why I'm in the academy, and the community I am a part of. I include these stories in my talks about Indigenous worldviews and the impacts of colonization. I allow learners to see how these worldviews and the impacts of these worldviews are not only written about in journals or books, but also relate to the lives of real people. Sometimes I also share about my struggles with mental health challenges, past drug addiction, and attempted suicides. I do this because I know there are learners in my classrooms that have similar stories and I want them to believe that they belong in my classroom.

How I physically look is also something that I address in the classroom. My skin is light. I easily "pass" as a White person. When I walk down Yonge Street in downtown Toronto, no one is looking at me and thinking, "there goes an Indigenous woman." The only time that I am followed by a security guard in the grocery store or stared at while eating in a restaurant is when I am with someone who looks like an Indigenous person is "supposed to look like." I must own that I do have some White skin privilege. A recent research project on education and social work programs in university settings by Kovach and colleagues (2015) takes this up briefly by quoting a participant who is referring to students: "One of the things I think I've seen is the students who I think could probably do with a little bit more support are the students who have an Aboriginal look because they stand out, right?" (p. 47). Similar views have come from some of the Indigenous students that I have taught or met over the years. They have expressed that students who identify as Indigenous but look White are the ones who make the most noise, speak more in classrooms, point out concerns within programs and universities, struggle with their identities, and are more sensitive about what is being taught and said by non-Indigenous students and faculty within the classroom. There may indeed be some truth to this position. Perhaps light-skinned Indigenous students have more confidence and have experienced less racism than brown Indigenous ones, which leads to their being more vocal.

This notion also applies to Indigenous faculty, of course. At a recent anti-racist conference where I was a speaker, a racialized, non-Indigenous student remarked that within the postsecondary institutions in Toronto, the vast majority of Indigenous educators were light-skinned or looked White. She wondered why this was. Is it because we are more likely to further our education and get Ph.Ds., and then be hired as tenured faculty members? Although not explicitly saying so, this student was referring to racism. Have us light-skinned people had it easier than our relatives who are brown throughout our childhoods, adolescence, and young adulthoods, making higher education and work in the academy more attainable? There has to be some truth to this since survivors of the residential school system speak about the lighter-skinned children being treated a little better than the darker-skinned ones. In conversations with a few colleagues and friends, I have learned that, in some cases, lighter-skinned siblings seem to have done better in elementary school than their dark-skinned brothers and sisters. For example, the former went through school without being held back while the latter were sometimes put in "special education classes," seen as having learning disabilities, or failed grades. This is certainly an area that I will be thinking more about in the years to come. Perhaps this is a research project in the making.

Previous chapters, such as "Centring All Helping Approaches," "Holistic or Wholistic Approach," and "The Answers Are in the Community," emphasized that there are many diverse ways of looking at the world and all are equally valid. Bringing multiple knowledges into the academy is crucial. I believe that it is harmful and irresponsible of educators to assume that Western ideas, and the values that are associated with these ideas, are universal. Embracing multiple knowledges is particularly important to the helping professions, as both those we seek to assist and those who come into our classrooms come from diverse backgrounds. As educators and practitioners striving to change the world, we need all the help we can get from all of the possible multiple knowledges that are available to us.

As educators, we have a responsibility to ensure that what we are teaching and how we are teaching it is of relevance to learners and the communities in which these learners live and work. Our world is constantly changing and social work is not the profession it was 25 years ago. Our job as educators is to keep up with these changes, including making ourselves aware of the multiple knowledges that we may be privileged to know something about. In fact, in 2013, the Canadian Association for Social Work Education included a requirement under their Education Standards of Accreditation that states, "social work programs acknowledge and challenge the injustices of Canada's colonial history and continuing colonization efforts as they relate to the role of social work education in Canada and the self-determination of the Indigenous peoples." The implication here is that it is possible to not get accreditation if this requirement is not taken up. It will be interesting in the years to come to see if any social work program is denied accreditation based on this.

I believe it is important to include here how Indigenous educators are typically working twice as hard as other educators. Why? Because the service that we do in our communities is often not recognized by the academy. Many of the participants in Kovach and colleagues' (2015) research spoke about the workload pressures that they face on an ongoing basis, such as one who stated, "I feel that a lot of Indigenous scholars are faced with that kind of double—double duty, double work—kind of thing" (p. 66). Another shared:

> I think there could be some people—it won't be me— that try to push for it [community service] to get more credit. I can't see how you can keep your energy to do it. Because the rewards for doing it are different. It's on a different merit system than the university has—and so trying to put them together is sometimes like trying to put restorative justice in a regular criminal system. You have to blow one up to have the other one work. (p. 66)

LEARNING THROUGH STORY

One way to practise inclusive education is to teach through story. Storytelling is an important aspect of Indigenous worldviews as it embodies life's lessons and shows how knowledge is transmitted to all. Stories are not one-dimensional, but are told in order to convey several different lessons depending on when and where they are told and by whom. Storytelling is a powerful medium of life instruction and a means of conveying values. Stories also serve as important links to the past and provide a means of surviving into the future. Indigenous authors, scholars, and educators have been writing and publishing about storytelling for the past few decades. For example, in 1992, Anishnawbe writer Esther Jacko explained that stories teach

> in a way that is warm, entertaining and lots of fun! Storytelling improves speaking skills and listening skills, and provides a novel way to learn. I think people can learn more from something if they are able to enjoy what they are learning, as well as participate in it. Storytelling allows listeners to participate by asking questions and by contributing their personal interpretation of what they have heard afterwards. (p. 42)

According to Cree educator Charles Lanigan (1998), storytelling is the oldest art and is universal to all people:

> It is the basis of all other arts—drama, art, dance and music. It has been and is an important part of every culture. It can be a starting point from moving away from assimilationist to liberationist education. Stories provide the communication of essential ideas. Stories have many layers of meaning, giving the listener the responsibility to listen, reflect and then interpret the message. Stories incorporate several possible explanations for phenomena, allowing listeners to creatively expand their thinking processes so that each problem they encounter in life can be viewed from a variety of angles before a solution is reached. (p. 113)

Lanigan's references to storytelling as a powerful teaching tool also shows up in Mi'kmaq teachings as well, proving how universal this teaching method is. The core of Mi'kmaq ways of teaching allows people to learn through their own experiences. They must come to realizations themselves. By Elders and other teachers telling stories that are similar to the person's situation or areas of learning, people listen, watch, and think about everything they hear. They are then left to make up their own minds about what they are learning based on their own explorations and experiences. This way of teaching is very similar to the concept of experiential learning,

Storytelling is incorporated into research, helping, and healing by many Indigenous writers and practitioners today. From healing from family violence (Lester-Smith, 2011), to youth suicide prevention (Wexler, White, & Trainor, 2015), to truth and reconciliation (Corntassel, 2009; Truth and Reconciliation Commission, 2015), storytelling is a powerful technique that offers inspiration and hope that all of us can make positive changes in our lives. As Lester-Smith (2011) explains in a piece about a three-year research project with the Vancouver, British Columbia, organization called the Warriors Against Violence Society:

> The transformative power of Aboriginal storytelling is evident in Warriors' violence intervention model, whereby facilitators and members alike share their deeply internalized soul-wounds and recovery practices in order to heal their present-day health struggles toward their future well-being. This dynamic living-narration is the cornerstone that WAVS facilitates. (p. 315)

In addition, storytelling is used to teach young children about life and reciprocity. Thus, stories often do not have a conclusion, but are told in ways that help develop critical thinking skills. This allows learners to interpret their own truths and arrive at their own conclusions, which allows learners to see that one way is not the only way.

Storytelling in a classroom setting combines the teachings of the past and adds a new dimension to the political, cultural, and environmental challenges faced by our world today. Everyone has a story, and honouring stories can not only provide an important healing dimension to our lives, but can also inform the formal learning process, especially in cases where people have been deeply impacted by social, political, and economic marginalization.

Storytelling, through music, can also focus on social problems as well as social justice. Music can also build bridges between Indigenous and non-Indigenous communities. By building bridges, contemporary Indigenous music also serves as a healing mechanism in several ways. By building bridges between Indigenous society and the dominant society through telling stories about history, spirituality, and values, contemporary music can educate about misunderstandings, mistrust, and negative stereotypes that are still perpetuated today.

One musical endeavour that promotes social justice and positive images of Indigenous Peoples, which appeals to thousands of youth (and people like me), is the work of A Tribe Called Red. Since 2007, this Indigenous electronic music group—who blend instrumental hip hop, reggae, moombahton, and dubstep-influenced dance music with elements of Indigenous music, such as vocal chanting and drumming—have been vocal supporters of Indigenous movements such as Idle No More. In 2013, they issued a public statement asking non-Indigenous fans to refrain from engaging in cultural appropriation by wearing headdresses and war paint to their shows; filed a human rights complaint against an amateur football team in Ottawa that was using "Redskins" as its name; and, in 2014, they withdrew from a scheduled performance at the official opening ceremonies of the Canadian Museum for Human Rights, citing concerns about the museum's depiction of Indigenous human rights issues (Adams, 2013; Birne, 2013; Boles, 2013; CBC, 2014).

A caution to incorporating many ways of seeing the world is needed, however. Educators must be aware that if multiple knowledges are to be incorporated in educational practices, it is not enough to present parts of multiple worldviews in order to support Western views of helping professions, because once these knowledges become disassembled, they no longer retain their holistic meanings. Thus, learning about multiple worldviews, values, and ways of helping must be explained within a particular context. In terms of education, this means that multiple knowledges need to be considered and taught as complete approaches in and of themselves, not as secondary information to Western knowledges that are added to "sensitize" people who are learning about various helping professions. Incorporating multiple worldviews in education also means that educators need to be careful not to use Western theories to legitimize diverse worldviews.

The knowledges of diverse people need to be included in all aspects of education. This means incorporating multiple knowledges about social policy development and analysis, about research methodologies, and about direct practice. The inclusion of diverse worldviews in each of these areas of interest is based upon the fact that a multiplicity of worldviews influences each area and the fact these worldviews are all interconnected, influencing both helpers and the people with whom they interact.

TEACHING IN CONTEXT

In ancient times, it was the ability to connect knowledge to the world that marked a scholar—not the letter grade given for the production of a text. Text too easily becomes a map that precedes the territory it represents and promotes the notion that knowledge can stand apart from contexts, relationships, and living things (Baudrillard, as cited in Dumbrill & Green, 2008, p. 495). Knowledge comes to us from processes of watching, learning, and doing. Since educators hold power in the academy, they have a responsibility to promote positive change. This may include how learning is evaluated. There is an assumption within the academy that learning must be proven in specified and limited ways, such as through writing papers or memorizing information for an exam. Each learner is individually evaluated and given a letter grade. I often wonder what's more important to students, what they have learned that helps them to make positive changes in the world or the letter grade that they are awarded? I have heard some students say that in forming groups for presentations, they seek out other students they believe will work for an A grade and they inform their peers that this will be the focus. This is not the fault of students, however. It is the academy that has set up an evaluation system, which extends from elementary school to Ph.D. programs, that engenders this kind of competitive attitude.

From an Indigenous perspective, knowledge does not focus on writing, but rather on making live connections within complex, multifaceted contexts and relations. Such connections, I believe, are what we are trying to help learners understand. It is unfortunate that text-based knowledge is privileged over other forms of knowledge, as there is much wisdom that can be learned from people's stories, including the experiences of students.

Leona Wright, BSW, of the Gitanmaxx First Nation, who works in her community in B.C., explains how Indigenous pedagogy contextualizes knowledge:

> Eurocentric education is like opening up one's head and having professors put information in it. Aboriginal education is about learning through hands on experience, never judging and understanding that it is the spiritual aspect that keeps helpers grounded. Learning happens through the whole person according to Aboriginal education, not just through the mind. Education has a ripple effect in

that it not only helps the individual, but it has an effect on families and communities. Perhaps most importantly, there is a healing of the mental, physical, spiritual, and emotional aspects of the individual through learning. Since each individual is unique and no one is better than the next person, we learn from each other and are willing to share our life experiences with one another as a way of teaching others (L. Wright, personal communication, December 4, 2008)

Leona also contextualizes her social work education in terms of both her past life and the person she is today:

I witnessed changes in myself while in social work education. Before I started I just accepted things for the way they were. Now I question things, learn what not to do and am passionate about my work, especially when I really believe in something. I'm no longer the quiet one. Now I have a better understanding of injustices people face in today's society and want to give back to people because of the opportunities that were given to me. By trying to provide opportunities to others, standing beside them and supporting them when they need it, I can be a part of how they empower themselves. (L. Wright, personal communication, December 4, 2008)

Leona's years in a social work program fostered her resourcefulness in how she was able to translate what she was learning into an Indigenous context:

I had to work much harder than most students due to having to translate everything from a Eurocentric worldview, which is still prominent in social work education, into an Aboriginal worldview. This is similar to language translation. I did diagrams for course outlines, circles rather than boxes and other visual representations which were helpful. My mind heads right to circles all the time when I'm trying to figure a concept out. This is how I attempt to make sense of information. I need to be able to make what I learn my own understanding of what is being taught to me and find ways of being able to use it for myself in the context of an Aboriginal perspective. (L. Wright, personal communication, December 4, 2008)

I wonder how many students, Indigenous or not, also have to undertake knowledge translation during their education. I know that some educators work at decreasing the necessity of this translation by incorporating multiple knowledges and ways of learning into classroom teaching.

As a White educator, Jennifer Ajandi has much to contribute about how she has come to critical consciousness about education and the need for diverse worldviews and approaches to pedagogy. She shared some experiences from her childhood and how she later came to see these experiences, through gaining an understanding of her privilege:

> I grew up in a low-income neighbourhood in St. Catharines: poor white people and poor Aboriginal people. I had many Aboriginal friends and didn't see any differences between myself and them. They were all heavily policed, had CAS [Children's Aid Society] involvement, were living with alcoholism, involvement with the criminal justice system. I had a young single mother, was left alone a lot, got into shoplifting and was caught at the age of 12. All that happened was the police officer told me I was bad at shoplifting. He didn't charge me. He brought me home in the police car to my mother who was devastated and grounded me. As an adult I look back and can now see racism which I didn't see while growing up. I believe I was privileged not to see it. I think because at the time I didn't see any differences. I just thought we all grew up with these things like alcoholism, violence, young pregnancies, over policing. It wasn't until I was in university that I saw that because of colonialism these experiences were experienced differently in that I grew up with "resilience factors" that my friends did not have because of racism.
>
> For example, I had supportive White teachers who believed and supported me and was able to access paid employment

without fear of racial discrimination. I had strong teachers in school who were role models, but Aboriginal friends didn't have Aboriginal teachers as role models. I began to think about what got me to where I was in university while my Aboriginal friends didn't make it there. (J. Ajandi, personal communication, December 8, 2008)

Jenn goes on to tell her story of how experiencing Indigenous worldviews in the academy positively impacted upon her education:

I took your [Cyndy Baskin's] elective [Strong Helpers' Teachings] in 2005 and found it to be taught differently from other courses. Everyone was encouraged to learn from one another. There was little hierarchy; everyone's thoughts were appreciated. Attending to the whole person and including spirituality were present in the classroom. Students were encouraged to bring their own experiences into the classroom and all parts of them and their lives were recognised. You also attended to students' differences without outing them by, for example, not having mandatory attendance which accounted for student absences due to mental health issues or the fact that they were single mothers with many responsibilities. Students tended to feel valued and respected in the class. Reflexivity was central in that the teaching was always connected to the students' personal situation or location and their social work practice. Learning about the processes and analysing colonization and its impacts helped me put my own experiences of childhood and youth into context. I then deliberately selected courses based on the fact that they included some Aboriginal content. I had an Aboriginal faculty for my practice course in social work, took a course in graduate education on Philosophical Foundations in Women's Studies which had readings by Aboriginal scholars such as Patricia Monture-Angus and Jean Fyre Graveline and took a PhD course on spirituality which included materials and guest speakers on Indigenous spirituality. (J. Ajandi, personal communication, December 8, 2008)

Now, as an educator, Jenn incorporates what she learned in her own education into her pedagogy. A true ally, she is a wonderful example of how a non-Indigenous scholar can take up the responsibility of ensuring that diverse perspectives can be taught regardless of one's subjectivity:

> Much of what I learned about teaching comes from the class I took with you [Cyndy Baskin]. I ensure that I include Aboriginal content into every course I teach, look at the whole student and encourage them to bring their experiences into the classroom. These are the principles that provide a general framework for my pedagogy. I also strive to help students feel valued and respected in my classes. I notice that marginalized students, in particular those who are queer or have (dis)abilities, feel comfortable in my classes. I notice that these students would spend a lot of time with me after classes, they speak in class, discuss their feelings in the critical reflection assignments[,] tell me after the fact that they learned so much in the class—more than other classes. They state this in their course evaluations of me. There have also been a few Black students who would stay with me after class and disclose how they experienced racial discrimination within the academy and we would talk about strategies to address this. Sometimes, they would raise this in class. (J. Ajandi, personal communication, December, 8, 2008)

I use storytelling in the class that Jenn took and one of the novels—*In Search of April Raintree* by Beatrice Culleton-Mosionier (1999), which is about child welfare—impacted her so much that she used it in a child and youth course that she taught at Brock University in 2008. Students told her they loved this book and could not put it down once they started reading it. Jenn appreciates how instructive and meaningful it can be to bring storytelling, narrative, and novels into a course because these narratives are written by authors who have had the experiences they are writing about. This helps students make links to their own lives and make the links to the lives of those that they will be servicing. These are the kind of readings that impact students because they help students understand the structural issues facing marginalized peoples.

Jenn partners with Indigenous people in the academy who can come into her classrooms to teach on subjects that she needs assistance with. For example, in a class that she taught on ethics in social work she brought in someone to do a teaching on Indigenous ethics because "it's important to look at ethics from many perspectives." She also encourages alternative assignments for students and pushes them "to contribute to knowledge in the classroom as I can't include everything and of course I don't know all of the different perspectives" (J. Ajandi, personal communication, December 8, 2008).

WHO TEACHES WHOM?

From an Indigenous perspective, educators, students, and community members teach one another and learn from each other. Indigenous values of humility and reciprocity are emphasized in the classroom "through recognition of the validity of students' knowledges and experience and through the development of authentic relationships exemplified by acknowledgment that everyone has something to learn" (Harris, 2006, p. 127). Such classrooms depend on recognizing the wealth of information and experience that learners bring with them. In classrooms there needs to be an emphasis on cooperation rather than competition. These classrooms need to include educators who acknowledge their own lack of knowledge or expertise, and who are open to trusting the process that unfolds.

The academy must also meaningfully engage the communities that are the recipients of the services that will be delivered by practitioners in the helping professions. This means that the visions and goals of communities must be reflected in all areas of education programs. This kind of teaching is echoed in Kovach and colleagues' (2015) research report, wherein several scholars suggest that non-Indigenous scholars can co-teach with Indigenous ones and bring in local people as guest speakers. These community people may be known to the instructor or they may ask Indigenous colleagues for suggestions on who to bring in. In this way, embodied Indigenous knowledge can be alive in the classroom. A caution is added, however, that community people be asked what they believe is appropriate to teach in a classroom:

> The desire to avoid becoming anthropologized is strong.
> As such, there are some faculty [and community people]
> who do not wish to speak to all aspects of Indigenous
> Knowledges and who do not necessarily feel that all as-

pects of Indigenous Knowledges need to be brought into
academic classrooms. (Kovach et al., 2015, p. 39)

Consultation between community members and educators can be achieved
through community advisory committees, which can guide program curriculum and help develop strategies for learning that are relevant, empowering, and transformative. Such guidance "foster[s] a sense of responsibility
as students, but also as community members" (Harris, 2006, p. 123) and
this kind of consultation helps to link the needs and abilities of learners
with the needs of communities.

Meaningful community involvement also ensures that there is a place
where members can raise concrete concerns about programs and have these
concerns satisfactorily addressed. This requires educators to be flexible and
learn to see themselves as being in partnership with communities, and as
being students as well as teachers. Willingness to use one's professional status
and skills in the service of others is the foundation of community-based
services and programming. Although helpful and influential, committees
made up of university and community members have no real decision-
making powers, which means that partnerships between the community and
the academy are often unequal, as the academy retains the power to make
decisions. However, if we were to move toward a politics of post-colonialism,
and adopt practices that support the kinds of transformational processes that
are needed within a post-colonial framework, which are those created and
written about by Indigenous thinkers, power-sharing would be addressed in
the relationship between communities and the academy.

In addressing post-colonialism, and the concerns related to practices
within a post-colonial framework, questions about the fairly recent emphasis on anti-oppression in social work theory and practice can be raised.
Cree/Assinboine/Saulteaux scholar Raven Sinclair (2004) offers the following critique of anti-oppressive theory and practice:

> Anti-oppressive practice has an inherent danger. The
> danger lies in proclaiming an anti-oppressive stance, while
> doing little or nothing to address the reality of oppression.
> As a profession, social work can do many things with
> "awareness" of critical issues such as racism including
> nothing. "Awareness itself lacks political substance and is
> sociologically naive" (Dominelli, 1998, p. 13). Awareness

without legitimate action is a cognitive play that risks passing for anti-oppressive and anti-racist pedagogy and practice in social work. It contributes to silence and inactivity about tangible issues of racism and oppression in the field of social work and in society. Contemporary anti-oppressive pedagogy does not address the culture of silence because it does not require anything beyond a theoretical grasping of issues. Neither the personal involvement nor the commitment of the social work student or practitioner is requested or required. Social workers risk falling into the trap of believing that just because they are social workers they are, therefore, non-racist and non-oppressive because the profession has a Code of Ethics to guide practice and because social work institutions proclaim they are committed to this ideology. (p. 36)

Sinclair's critique is well taken. Insight alone doesn't change anything. Knowledge must lead to action. Her analysis comes at an important time when both social work programs and social services agencies are proclaiming anti-oppressive approaches. However, a plaque on the reception area's wall, a two-day training workshop, and a statement on a program's Website do not make for anti-oppressive social work. Such superficiality is merely co-optation. What is required is a common phrase often cited by Indigenous peoples: "walk the talk."

Post-colonial thought may have something to add to a pedagogy that centres the importance of turning knowledge into practice. Post-colonialism involves a critical analysis of history, thereby contextualizing colonization. It also teaches about valuing Indigenous healing and helping approaches, which is part of the decolonization process for all peoples. Post-colonial practice also has the ability to integrate Indigenous knowledges and practices with Eurocentric models of helping. As Sinclair (2004) adds, "Aboriginal social work education ... is charged with the task of imparting this knowledge to students in order that they can effectively work in a de-colonized context" (p. 40). I would add, however, that such a task belongs to *all* social work educators, not just Indigenous educators.

Jennifer Ajandi believes that Indigenous worldviews have much to teach students, practitioners, and educators about practicing anti-oppression within their professions:

Let's consider ethics: self-determination has always been a part of Aboriginal worldviews and is now an important part of social work's code of ethics as well. There is also being non-judgemental, linking individual issues with structural causes or contributions, that behaviour is learned and can be changed, that there are many different paths a person can take, that there is no ONE right answer, options depend on the person, family, and their community at the particular time.

Aboriginal languages tend to be non-judgemental. There is much more of an equalizing dynamic between people. There is a strong emphasis on building relationships with those seeking help rather than mechanically running through a list of questions. "Intakes" and "assessments" are discussions rather than standardized forms to complete, trust building happens before talking about personal issues.

The Seven Grandfather [Sacred] Teachings are ethics as well. Love is one of these, but it has a different connotation than a more typical mainstream society definition. Love is about connectedness. In my experience, I found that students can relate to this concept of love within social work practice and are able to discuss it ... acknowledging that important relationships are built between workers and service users, and that it is okay for [them] to care about the people they are working with. The feminist Ethics of Care Model emphasizes the interconnectedness of people, connections between people, between people and the earth. This model emphasizes that building relationships can be "therapeutic," and it is important to recognize that all of these ideas have been an important part of Aboriginal worldviews since the beginning of time. (J. Ajandi, personal communication, December 8, 2008)

HEALING IN THE CLASSROOM

Education was a particularly destructive tool of colonization for Indigenous Peoples across the globe. Therefore, it is education that needs to take on a role of positive change for today and for the future. Decolonization must include healing and must also take into account the ways that people learn with their entire beings, rather than with only the mind. As the Dalai Lama noted during a visit to Vancouver, B.C., to give a talk on "balancing educating the mind with educating the heart," "too much energy in your country is developing the mind instead of the heart. Develop the heart" (University of British Columbia, 2004, as quoted in Harris, 2006, pp. 125–126).

Robina Thomas practises what the Dalai Lama notes is lacking about education in Canada. She states,

> we ask whether all students are learning to be proud of all aspects of their identities, we question whether they are gaining their own vision and are developing an understanding of why they wish to become social workers. Ultimately, we evaluate whether students are connecting the knowledge entering their heads to the feeling in their heart. (Dumbrill & Green, 2008, p. 496)

Teaching about identity and learning through the heart are two areas of teaching that many Indigenous scholars take up in their classrooms. Kovach and colleagues' research (2015) revealed that teaching about history, policies, and critical thinking are necessary when teaching Indigenous content and that exploring these, along with racist assumptions, must be addressed before introducing Indigenous knowledges and worldviews. In addition, because identities have been impacted by history and policies, within this context students often need assistance to work through their struggles about who they are and what it means to be Indigenous.

Decolonization is emotional work for all students and instructors, but for non-Indigenous ones in particular being in a program that centres "a social justice or anti-oppressive approach, their coursework may present the first opportunity they will have had in their lives to a) be asked to examine their social privilege; and b) develop a significant relationship with an Aboriginal person" (Kovach et al., 2015, p. 25). As one participant stated in this research, settler students cannot "really do authentic work without acknowledging and taking responsibility for where you're positioned and understanding the opportunities and the privileges that come your way" (Kovach et al., 2015, p. 48).

And yet, decolonization and healing can occur in the classroom, as Barbara Harris (2006), a Dené Professor Emeritus of the School of Social Work, University of Victoria, states,

> reconciliation occurs in a holistic learning environment that attends to the emotional effect of the content being addressed. In this sense, the Talking Circle has been an effective strategy in the classroom, as everyone shares his or her own knowledge and experience. (p. 128)

Michael Kim Zapf, a White social work scholar at the University of Calgary, recounts his experience of decolonization, healing, and reconciliation through the Talking Circle. Zapf was co-teaching a social work course with an Indigenous educator. All of the learners in the class were Indigenous. Without Zapf present, they held a circle to discuss internalized colonization. The following day, they held another circle with Zapf in attendance. He relates that,

> Many students had spent the night agonizing over the buried issues that had now been made conscious. It was not enough that I was the only non-Native in the room; I was now a white male authority figure, an easy target.... With Apella's [the co-teacher] support I moved past my initial defensive reactions. I could see that this was not a personal attack; the students needed a target for their new rage. How I would react would be critical for the future of our work together.... This was a slow and very difficult sharing process, with hesitation and tears on both sides. I was involved with this class, with our process, with an immediacy that I had never experienced through prepared lectures, lab exercises or class discussion.... We came to a realization, probably the most powerful and crucial insight to come out of the entire course. If their anger forced them to shut me out and dismiss me, or if my guilt sent me back to the city where I could comfortably ignore the issue, then we would waste a special opportunity to build a bridge that we both needed. (Zapf, as cited in Harris, 2006, p. 125)

Leona Wright shared similar experiences of decolonization and healing in a second-year mandatory course, Aboriginal Approaches to Social Work, in the School of Social Work at Ryerson University:

> Much of what I learned in this course was about me and my experiences and what these have to do with how I practice social work or helping. I learned about how non-Aboriginal students see Aboriginal Peoples. This is what I got out of the course; this was the purpose for me to take it. It was as though I was looking through non-Aboriginal students' eyes and thinking what they think.
>
> The assumptions non-Aboriginal students have came out through the presentations they did in the classroom and through some of the remarks they made. But I watched them grow in this class. I saw that some students were upset in the beginning having to take a course that they felt wasn't important to them and some felt there was favouritism toward Aboriginal people because this was a mandatory class. Some students felt their cultures and traditions were being left out. But as the class continued and they started to get an understanding of what Aboriginal people went through, they came to see the resilience of Aboriginal people in dealing with the struggles and the healing journeys that they are now taking. They soon lost those assumptions that society often portrays about Aboriginal people and they began to heal themselves through tears in the classroom.
>
> This class was held in a circle. It took a while for some students to get used to this. But it eventually became a safe place for all of them to share their feelings. It became a safe place for them by the teachings they received on the sacredness of the circle to Aboriginal people, how no one is higher within the circle and what is said in the circle remains in the circle. Students learned to share their own experiences when they could relate to some of the experiences of Aboriginal people. They learned to respect what they were learning and come to understand the importance of sharing. (L. Wright, personal communication, December 4, 2008)

Interestingly enough, the instructor who taught the section of the course that Leona speaks about is White. As mentioned earlier in this book, there are people inside and outside the academy who stand against non-Indigenous people teaching and practising Indigenous methods of helping. There are others who accept this. I believe the answer to this situation is contextual. If a non-Indigenous person has meaningfully experienced Indigenous teachings and healing, and is accepted by the Indigenous community—which includes sincere relationships with individuals in the community, as well as recognition from those they work with—and this person reflects Indigenous worldviews through their actions, then why not? Leona further shared her experiences with this instructor, which supports my position:

> Having a non-Aboriginal person as an instructor was hard at first. I was disappointed that I had a non-Aboriginal instructor for such a course. I felt that she was just a "wanna-be" [a person who romanticizes being Indigenous and tries to act like one], but as the course went on, I gained respect for this instructor and the way she presented the information. I saw that she did not take credit for what she was teaching, but respected the knowledge that was passed on to her through the Aboriginal community. I saw her as an ally working from the inside out within the Aboriginal community. She was sincere and passionate about wanting all the students to learn about Aboriginal worldviews. I say chi meegwetch [many thanks in Anishnawbe] to this instructor for such a wonderful learning experience. (L. Wright, personal communication, December 4, 2008)

Indeed, today's classrooms can be seen as being in transition for both Indigenous and non-Indigenous students, as the findings of Kovach and colleagues' (2015) work show. With regard to Indigenous students, one participant said, "it used to be the Aboriginal students would sit in the back and hide and now more and more of them are sitting right up in the front and are more vocal" (p. 46). Another shared, "I'm seeing less resistance by the students to take up the Indigenous Knowledges or even anti-racism and I feel that that's just such a positive thing" (p. 46).

CONCLUSION

This chapter shows that multiple knowledges and ways of learning are needed and welcomed in the classroom if all involved are willing to walk the talk of anti-oppression and decolonization. The journey is at times painful, but the rewards are well worth it. Leona Wright explains this beautifully:

> Aboriginal worldviews ought to be taught to all students. Non-Aboriginal people must learn about Aboriginal people, as it is the only way to stop racism and stereotypes. We [Aboriginal people] need to share our ways of understanding and seeing the world to assist non-Aboriginal students to see the great value in our worldviews which can help all peoples. The Seven Grandfather [Sacred] Teachings, which are the Anishnawbe peoples' code of ethics, speaks for itself as it talks about wisdom, love, respect, bravery, honesty, humility and truth—all peoples believe in these, what else is there? (L. Wright, personal communication, December 4, 2008)

More often than not, students come into the helping professions because they want to help people. I see this as a good reason to go into such professions. As educators, our work is to assist students in exploring what help means and how it can be carried out, which means, in part, creating classrooms that welcome diverse worldviews of how to do so. Constantly listening to, and learning from, the students who enter our programs will assist us in accomplishing such inclusion. Incorporating the Seven Sacred Teachings, mentioned by Leona in the quote above, into our pedagogy may be a useful foundation from which to begin.

REFERENCES

Adams, G. (2013, September 5). A Tribe Called Red's Ian Campeau files human rights complaint over Redskins football club name. *Exclaim*. Retrieved from http://exclaim.ca/Music/article/tribe_called_reds_ian_campeau_files_human_rights_complaint_over_redskins_football_club_name.

Birne, S. (2013, September 8). Beats against colonialism: A Tribe Called Red. *Canadian Dimension*. Retrieved from https://canadiandimension.com/articles/view/beats-against-colonialism-a-tribe-called-red.

Boles, B. (2013, February 7). A Tribe Called Red bring politics into the party by reimagining the pow wow tradition, flipping the script on cultural appropriation in electronic dance music. *Now Magazine*. Retrieved from https://nowtoronto.com/music/cover-story/a-tribe-called-red/.

Canadian Association for Social Work Education. (2013). Standards of accreditation. Retrieved from http://caswe-acfts.ca/wp-content/uploads/2013/03/CASWE.ACFTS_.Standards.Oct2013.pdf.

CBC News. (2014, September 18). A Tribe Called Red cancels performance at human rights museum. *CBC News*. Retrieved from http://www.cbc.ca/news/canada/manitoba/a-tribe-called-red-cancels-performance-at-human-rights-museum-1.2771222.

Corntassel, J. (2009). Indigenous storytelling, truth-telling, and community approaches to reconciliation. *English Studies in Canada, 35*(1), 137–159.

Dumbrill, G., & Green, J. (2008). Indigenous knowledge in the social work academy. *Social Work Education, 27*(5), 489–503. doi: 10.1080/02615470701379891

Harris, B. (2006). What can we learn from traditional Aboriginal education? Transforming social work education delivered in First Nations communities. *Canadian Journal of Native Education, 29*(1), 117–134.

Jacko, E. (1992). Traditional Ojibway storytelling. In L. Jaine & D. Hayden Taylor (Eds.), *Being Native in Canada* (pp. 40–51). Saskatoon: University of Saskatchewan, Extension Division.

Kovach, M., Carrière, J., Montgomery, H., Barrett, M.J., & Gilles, C. (2015). *Indigenous presence: Experiencing and envisioning Indigenous knowledges within selected post-secondary sites of education and social work*. Retrieved from http://www.usask.ca/education/profiles/kovach/index.php.

Lanigan, M. (1998). Indigenous pedagogy: Storytelling. In L.A. Stiffarm (Ed.), *As we see .... Indigenous pedagogy* (pp. 103–120). Saskatoon: University of Saskatchewan Press.

Lester-Smith, D. (2011). Healing Aboriginal family violence through Aboriginal storytelling. *Alternative, 19*(4), 309–321. Retrieved from http://www.metismotivations.ca/wp-content/uploads/2011/06/Alternative_Vol9_iss_4_Lester2.pdf.

Sinclair, R. (2004). Aboriginal social work education in Canada: Decolonizing pedagogy for the seventh generation. *First Peoples Child & Family Review, 1*(1), 49–61. Retrieved from http://www.fncfcs.ca.

Truth and Reconciliation Commission. (2015). Truth and Reconciliation Commission of Canada: Calls to Action. Retrieved from http://www.trc.ca/websites/trcinstitution/File/2015/Findings/Calls_to_Action_English2.pdf

Wexler, L., White, J., & Trainor, B. (2015). Why an alternative to suicide pre-
vention gatekeeper training is needed for rural Indigenous communities:
Presenting an empowering community storytelling approach. *Critical Public
Health, 25*(2), 205–217. doi: 10.1080/09581596.2014.904039

Chapter Fifteen

TAKING BACK
RESEARCH

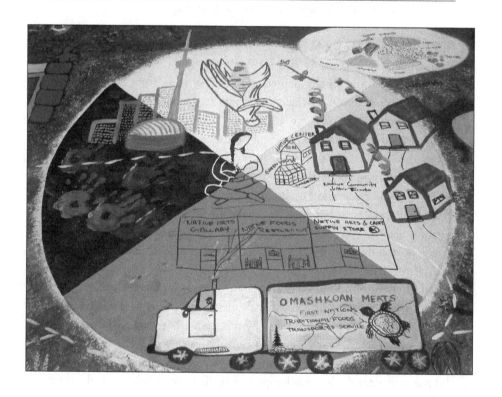

INTRODUCTION

"I spent several weeks going through books, articles and journals trying to find one good definition of Indigenous research methodology, and in the end I realized that I would not find a specific answer" (Steinhauer, 2002, p. 69). This statement remains true despite the explosion of literature in recent years on the topic of research methodologies by Indigenous scholars. This is not surprising given that there are numerous Indigenous Nations and cultures, so there will be many research methodologies. Something that works well in one community may not work in another. However, as with worldviews, there are foundational values and ways of knowing that are contained within these research methodologies.

RESEARCHED TO DEATH

I have heard it said many times that Indigenous Peoples are the most studied population on the planet and that we have been "researched to death." I do not know how accurate these statements are, but I do know that Indigenous Peoples can be greatly suspicious, distrustful and, at times, fearful of mainstream research. Indigenous scholars and researchers have called mainstream research unethical, exploitative, and a misrepresentation of Indigenous Peoples (Coburn, 2013; Kenny, 2004; Menzies, 2004; Ontario Federation of Indian Friendship Centres [OFIFC], 2012). Historically, research has been *done to* Indigenous populations with often harmful results (First Nations Centre, 2007; Steinhauer, 2002). According to a report published by the National Aboriginal Health Organization (NAHO), "past research processes were often disrespectful, damaging and stigmatizing to First Nations people" (First Nations Centre, 2007, p. 3). No wonder these views are widely held since, for hundreds of years, Indigenous Peoples were described by others in whatever way they wished (Deloria Jr., 1997). Much more concerning, however, is the fact that research has been done to Indigenous Peoples without their consent, as they did not understand what was happening or they were children at the time.

An example of such research, known as biomedical experimentation, occurred in several First Nations communities and residential schools across Canada during the 1940s and 1950s. During these decades, government departments and corporations—including Indian and Northern Affairs Canada (INAC), the Royal Canadian Air Force, and the Hudson's Bay Company—conducted nutritional research projects in communities such as Norway House and The Pas in northern Manitoba, Attawapiskat in northern Ontario, and the Great Whale River Inuit community in northern Quebec (Goodman, McElligott & Marks, 2003; McCallum, 2005; Mosby, 2013; Shewell, 2004). Physical examinations, blood tests, and X-rays were conducted on hundreds of Indigenous residents by leading nutrition experts, drawing connections between their hunger and malnutrition to broader health problems such as tuberculosis (Mosby, 2013). However, these same researchers also connected their findings to the so-called Indian Problem, reporting that "it is not unlikely that many characteristics, such as shiftlessness, indolence, improvidence and inertia, so long regarded as inherent or hereditary traits in the Indian race may, at the root, be really the manifestations of malnutrition" (Tisdall & Kruse, 1942, as cited in Mosby, 2013, p. 147).

Such experiments were conducted without the knowledge or informed consent of the Indigenous Peoples involved and viewed communities as laboratories that did nothing more than further the careers of the researchers, some of whom went so far as to provide some residents with vitamin supplements and used others as members of control groups (Mosby, 2013). As Mosby (2013) emphasizes, these research teams knew exactly what they were doing since "vitamin supplements only addressed a small part of the problem and that, if they really wanted to deal with the immediate problem of malnutrition and hunger, emergency food relief that met all of the nutritional needs of the [communities] was badly needed" (p. 152). In addition, researchers also knew that one of the key reasons for such hunger and malnutrition was due to Indigenous Peoples' increasing dependence on food from stores, which, in some cases, was made up of 85 percent "white flour, lard, sugar and jam" (Moore, Kruse, & Tisdall, 1943, 1944, as cited in Mosby, 2013, p. 155). Not surprisingly, INAC blamed this consumption on Indigenous Peoples, stating in a 1948 press release that:

> They have abandoned the native eating habits of their forefathers and adopted a semi civilized, semi native diet which lacks essential food values, brings them to malnutrition and leaves them prey to tuberculosis and other disease. The white man, who unintentionally is responsible for the Indians' changed eating habits, now is trying to salvage the red man by directing him towards proper food channels. (LAC, 1948, as cited in Mosby, 2013, p. 155)

A policy emerging from these research projects that drastically impacted the diets of Indigenous Peoples was the prevention of families from collecting family allowances as cash, which everyone else in Canada was allowed to do. Instead, a separate, in-kind system was created for "Bush Indians" and "Eskimos," under which food purchases were restricted to "foods of high nutritive value over and above their basic subsistence requirements" such as "canned tomatoes …[,] rolled oats, Pablum, pork luncheon meat such as … Klick …[,] dried prunes …[,] and cheese or canned butter" (Mosby, 2013, p. 156). Perhaps even more concerning was another INAC experiment that prevented some Indigenous families from using family allowances to buy flour, even though this had been a food staple, introduced by INAC in the first place, for quite some time. One of the consequences of this was that in 1949–50, many Inuit families had to embark on their annual winter hunt with not enough flour to last the season. Hence, some were hungry enough that they had no choice but to eat their sled dogs and boiled seal skin (Honigmann, 1951, as cited in Mosby, 2013).

During this period, nutrition experiments were also conducted on Indigenous children in residential schools. By 1944, officials within INAC were well aware of the hunger endured by children in the schools and so, with the assistance of the Nutrition Services Division of the Canadian Red Cross Society, inspections began (Mosby, 2013). However, schools were notified in advance of these inspections, with the result being that "instead of lard, there were pats of butter on a tin plate, and the soup was thicker than usual, with more meat and vegetables" (Johnson, 1998, p. 40). Nevertheless, investigations consistently showed seriously poor conditions, with food failing to meet the government's basic nutritional requirements.

One would think that after such investigations, recommendations would be offered and implemented. This is, of course, supposed to be the purpose of research. However, follow-up with investigated schools showed a serious lack of improvement, which led to a lead investigator stating that she was "utterly disgusted" and wondered, "how can a report on each of these schools be effective if it is to be a repetition of the first report?" (LAC, 1947, as cited in Mosby, 2013, p. 160). In addition to hunger, about 1,000 children were used in experiments on nutritional interventions, which meant medical and dental examinations, blood tests, and no "over-all type of dental service" as "any significant dental interventions would interfere with the results of the study" (LAC, 1949, as cited in Mosby, 2013, p. 163).

There is little evidence in any of the records that the researchers involved in these studies ever discussed the ethical implications of their work, which included malnourished children to be used as controls. In fact, some authors suggest that such research was conducted on groups such as those with mental health challenges, the poor, and Indigenous Peoples because they were viewed as public burdens and so, "through medical experimentation, use*less* bodies were rendered use*ful* by being made us*able* in the national project of regeneration, thus gaining a utility they were believed otherwise to lack" (Goodman, McElligott, & Marks, 2003, p. 2). Hence, such social engineering was simply intended to further the political and professional careers of politicians, scientists, and researchers, rather than to assist Indigenous Peoples and address the root causes of their hunger and malnutrition. As Mosby (2013) concludes, such research and experiments need to be "recognized for what they truly were: one among many examples of a larger institutionalized and, ultimately, dehumanizing colonialist racial ideology that has governed Canada's policies towards and treatment of Aboriginal Peoples" (p. 172).

If all of this is not enough, there is more. Most of us believe that the uncovering of the atrocities committed by Nazi scientists and doctors during World War II at the 1947 Nuremberg trials immediately led to a rethinking of how research on human beings was conducted. Not so. According to Mosby (2013), information in the North American context shows that the trials, which led to the ten principles of the Nuremberg Code, actually had little impact on medical research practices. In fact, scientists and doctors who were aware of the Nuremberg Code saw it "as a code for barbarians and not for civilized physician investigators" (Katz, 1996, as cited in Mosby, 2013, p. 166). In typical fashion, those in Canada were clearly quite comfortable with pointing fingers at horrors committed in other parts of the world, while completely denying any responsibility of their own actions.

Is it any wonder then that Indigenous Peoples are wary of research today? Patty Chabbert, Algonquin Nation and lead researcher of a recent two-year research project hosted by the North Bay Indian Friendship Centre (NBIFC) in North Bay, Ontario, refers to this and then explains how the fear was respectfully addressed:

> We could have had a survey, or carried out formal interviews. However, the community was already very hesitant, cautious and closed about having a two year

research project! Many had experienced the negative aspects of research DONE TO them. So we started by asking community members, "what does research mean to you? What would a research project mean to you? If we were to represent this project visually, what would it look like?" Their answers helped guide our next steps. People then shared symbols of what research and this project could mean to the community.

The result was our logo. We worked with an Indigenous graphic designer and Paige, one of the research associates, helped map out the meaning of this project in our logo. Paige's summary of the logo is: the circle incorporates a feather to represent the path that each individual takes. The urban community (in blue) and the teepees (in different colors) are displayed in balance through reflection. The land is represented as sweetgrass in a braid, signifying the strength of communities. The sunburst behind the teepees and in the water represented the "shine," as one Elder commented, "It's our time to shine!" (P. Chabbert, personal communication, August 5, 2015)

SELF-IDENTIFICATION

Indigenous researchers tend to identify themselves within their research projects and publications (Anderson, 2004; Baker, 2008; Baskin, 2005; Green, 2009; Hart, 2007, 2009, 2014; Smith, 2012; Tupola, 2006; Wilson, 2008). This is intended so that we can situate ourselves within the research and show why it is important to us. This practice is also meant to offer legitimacy to projects, where we are reclaiming our knowledges and ways of conducting research. Western approaches to research tend to focus on the research participants, with little or no attention paid to the researcher, other than to her or his academic qualifications. In the area of Indigenous research, it is viewed as problematic not to identify oneself and state why one is conducting a particular research project. The issue of insider-outsider researcher status also needs to be taken into consideration. In other words, who should conduct research with Indigenous Peoples: only Indigenous researchers or only non-Indigenous researchers or both? Indigenous researchers are often personally involved in their projects. Other academics often see us as not being objective when we conduct research with our own communities. They are right as *everyone*, whether Western or non-Western, who conducts research has biases. As human beings, how could it possibly be any other way?

I also believe that there are advantages to biases and we ought to acknowledge them as such rather than pretending that they do not exist. When Indigenous people conduct research with Indigenous communities, it is less likely that those communities will be exploited and more likely that they will benefit from the research findings. When an Indigenous researcher chooses projects within their community, they are not only grounded geographically, culturally, and experientially in that community, but are also personally invested in the research findings because the results may have impacts on their family as much as on the research participants. Thus, when a researcher is personally involved in the research process and its outcomes because the project matters to them as a community member, rather than as a person whose agenda is to advance their career, the integrity of the work may be of higher calibre.

Another area of tension for Indigenous researchers implementing Indigenous research methodologies occurs when we present our findings. Often, the academy criticizes Indigenous writing as subjective, emotional, and personal, rather than adhering to the accepted Eurocentric value of objectivity in the presentation of research findings. In my own research projects, my findings are presented in a subjective way, without apology. I have deliberately chosen to write in this way as this too is in keeping with Indigenous worldviews. My voice is embedded throughout my writing. In addition, I take the position that there is no such thing as objectivity. A lens and value base through which one views the world is inherent in every written work. It is just that some of us are upfront about this, while others pretend that this value base does not exist. I particularly like the assertions made by researchers Ballard, Fernandez-Gimenez, and Sturtevant (2008, as cited in OFIFC, 2012) who write that

> Indigenous research is often viewed as lacking credibility because it is not informed by the Western school of thought with its imposed rules. It is important to note that a key feature of Indigenous knowledge is that it purposefully does not conform to Western technical rationality used by the mainstream in the search for causal models that support universal theories, principles, and tools for establishing the "truth." (p. 65)

HOLISTIC AND RECIPROCAL

Indigenous research methodologies, like Indigenous worldviews, are intrinsically holistic. As Shawn Wilson (2008) of the Opaskwayak Cree from northern Manitoba explains, the knowledge we gain from conducting research needs to be shared with all that is a part of Creation, rather than only the human participants. Communities give researchers the gift of being able to conduct research projects in their spaces and participants give the gift of their knowledge. What gifts do researchers give to communities and participants? Within Indigenous worldviews, it is widely understood that one never takes without giving something back. This applies to research as much as it does to food and relationships. "Engaging in reciprocity allows community members and researchers to remain equal partners. If researchers make use of participants' ideas and time, they must give back by providing resources, skills, employment, and/or training" (Caldwell et al., 2005, p. 9). Capacity-building, as described here, is one form of reciprocity that has always been practised by Indigenous people. Many Indigenous scholars write about this value (Bartlett, Iwasaki, Gottlieb, Hall, & Mannell, 2007; Caldwell et al., 2005; Jones, Crengle, & McCreanor, 2006; Porsanger, 2004; Smith, 2012; Wilson, 2008). As part of this reciprocal capacity-building, community members may be hired as research assistants and project coordinators. Elders may be called in for their wisdom and guidance and community groups may be involved to provide catering services. I have been involved in projects where storytellers and visual artists were hired to help develop research tools and methods of dissemination. It is also crucial to hire research assistants who are part of the population the research is being done with. For example, if youth are the focus of the project, then youth need to be hired as research assistants.

There are other ways to look at Indigenous capacity-building, however. For instance, Métis/Swampy Cree Research Associate Dawn Lamothe, in a research report from the NBIFC (2014), wrote about her holistic way of looking at how sharing circles and ceremonies are

> important for us to attend as we still have much to learn about ceremonies and our roles as women leading youth, and also being able to pass on the knowledge to them about their roles as they mature. For me, this is "building capacity" in its purest form. Having one of our youth from the YAC [Youth Action Circle] be our fire keeper during a ceremony is a great example of the good we can do when

we continue to support and empower our youth. Myself and the other women were very grateful for the fire and the youth agreeing to tend to it during our ceremony. In turn, he was able to gain invaluable experience and build his confidence acting in his role as a man. (p. 31)

Patty Chabbert added to Dawn's writing by stating:

> We talk so often of capacity, as in capacity building which has become a community development term. When we break this down, I think Dawn is also talking about strengthening the self and relationships between people in the community, which therefore builds capacity! If we said we held a program and a young man learned valuable job skills, we could report to a funder that we strengthen our community's capacity in the labor market. Equally, we are strengthening the ability of this young man to function in the community, relate to people, strengthen his self-esteem and contribute. Thus, this is another way in which we are building capacity within our community. (P. Chabbert, personal communication, August 5, 2015)

The research group somewhat resembles an extended family. Members spend time together in order to get to know each other; they make consensus-based decisions. Each group member supports the other, everyone's input is respected, and hospitality is an expected norm. Hence, research projects need to focus on mutual purposes and outcomes for both the researcher and participants. No one to date has explained this mutual relationship as succinctly and simply as Māori scholar Russell Bishop, who wrote in 1998, "there is common understanding and a common basis for such an understanding, where the concerns, interests, and agendas of the researcher become the concerns, interests, and agendas of the researched and vice versa" (p. 203). Non-Indigenous students and researchers in Western countries such as Canada, Australia, and the United States may be challenged by the amount of time it can take to develop relationships with research participants and reach decisions through consensus. Rigid timelines can interfere with such processes, so this needs to be taken into consideration when planning research projects.

Emotional bonding with those who participate in a research project has the ability to generate new insights and knowledge. This is another significant component of Indigenous worldviews. Our holistic way of seeing an individual means that all four aspects of a person—spiritual, emotional, psychological, and physical—are included and these aspects are understood to be connected. It is important to relate to others on all of these levels. Indeed, intellect and emotion cannot be artificially separated, nor can the spirit and the body. I would argue that knowledge comes out of all of these aspects because none of them can be separated.

I believe that research needs to be more than participatory. Rather, it needs to be participant-driven, meaning that it is the participants who come up with the research questions, the design, the distribution of findings, and so on. The researcher is one of the participants in this process. It is not a relationship of "I" and "them." It is a relationship based on "us" as we work together. This focus on the collective will and collective interests assists researchers to avoid the danger of generating research that does not represent the Indigenous community and, instead, producing research from an ideology of individualism that is seen in mainstream society. This notion of individualist, expert professional knowledge reproduces the existing status quo socially, economically, and politically, rather than working toward social justice.

More respectful types of research relationships reposition researchers in ways that no longer seek to give voice, empower, or emancipate people, but rather to listen to, and participate with, those viewed as "others." In this way, research participants become the creators of the meanings of their own experiences, thereby constructing knowledge that is important to them. This is a crucial message for researchers in the helping professions, as it is important to understand that it is not possible for us to empower anyone. The only person I can empower is myself. However, helping professionals as researchers can use their privileges to assist community members to empower themselves through the research projects we choose to take on and the research methodologies that we implement.

Once again, Patty Chabbert and her team put the above concepts into practice:

> We wanted to learn more about youth experiences finding "home" in North Bay. We held a focus group. Only four youth came. They felt unsupported talking about

very challenging topics and basically said it "sucked," so we stopped after 14 minutes. Two of the youth had been very active in other parts of our project, mainly the Youth Action Circle, and they said, "why don't we do this again, but invite an Elder for support, do it in the medicine room with medicines, and hold a sharing circle." At the next gathering, there were 12 youth who participated and the discussion went on for hours. This experience demonstrates what happens when people decide what feels right to them. Youth decided how, where and WHAT they wanted to share about the theme of "finding home." Our role then became one of supporting them to do it themselves! (P. Chabbert, personal communication, August 5, 2015)

CONTROL AND OWNERSHIP

Having control and ownership of research is consistently emphasized by Indigenous scholars (Bartlett et al., 2007; Caldwell et al., 2005; Ermine, Sinclair, & Jeffery, 2004; First Nations Centre, 2007; Hart, 2007, 2009, 2014; Jones et al., 2006; Smith, 2012). I see ownership of research as part of the political project. As explained by the First Nations Centre (2007),

> First Nations need to protect all information concerning themselves, their traditional knowledge and culture, including information resulting from research. The Principles of Ownership, Control, Access, and Possession (OCAP) enables self-determination over all research concerning First Nations. It offers a way for First Nations to make decisions regarding what research will be done, for what purpose information or data will be used, where the information or data will be used, where the information will be physically stored, and who will have access. (p. 1)

This reclamation and taking control of research by Indigenous Peoples is being taken up by Indigenous scholars globally. "Indigenous scholars from Australia, Aotearoa-New Zealand, the US and Canada have brought to academic discussions the indigenous peoples' project of reclaiming control over indigenous ways of knowing and being, a project that implies better control over research on indigenous issues" (Porsanger, 2004, pp.

108–109). Thus, a primary guideline is that research with Indigenous Peoples needs to be community-based and controlled. Out of this primary guideline come several directives that say that research and research findings should:

- be the intellectual property of the community;
- be of direct benefit to families and communities;
- transfer skills;
- include mechanisms for continued gains/work;
- be reviewed to ensure accuracy; and
- include community members as co-authors in publications (Porsanger, 2004, p. 117).

Research that is community-based and -controlled, first and foremost, involves work on areas that are of interest and concern to the local community that is approached. Ideally, the community itself identifies the areas and initiates the projects. Community-based work also involves ensuring that a multiplicity of viewpoints are fairly represented. It means eliminating or at least lessening barriers to community members' participation in the project.

However, as Indigenous researchers, we need to think critically about what "community-based" means and if it is what we want to do. This is taken up by Patty Chabbert, who challenges the term:

> The very word, "based" means founded, grounded, created, constructed, which suggests some pre-fabricated notion of what research is, who the participants are, what the process will look like, etc. The very flaw of community-based research is that it will always remain based or rooted somewhere. Community driven research has no base. When we start to look at "research" in this way, we empower community to take back the gathering and sharing of knowledge processes in their communities. They reclaim the process and the knowledge to change things that they want to change. (P. Chabbert, personal communication, August 5, 2015)

Community control means establishing collaborative processes to support communities to participate in all phases of a research project. It also means hiring community members for paid positions, such as research assistants, within the research project. Self-determination can be facilitated in many ways, including providing financial remuneration and helping people gain new skills, which are of benefit to the community. All too often, Indigenous Peoples' knowledge and work is used, and people are never compensated. Instead, paid positions are given to non-Indigenous people. Not only is this unfair, but it is terribly disrespectful. A shift in thinking could mean that the ongoing work of research can be taken up by community members themselves. I also believe that it is important to include community participants as co-authors of published research.

COMMUNITY-DRIVEN

In the spring of 2015, I was a guest speaker at a gathering in North Bay, Ontario, called "Urban Aboriginal Communities Walking Together, Sharing Together Conference: Stories and Strategies Nurturing Culture, Community & Capacity," hosted by the NBIFC. This gathering, based on a report and action plan for North Bay's Urban Aboriginal Strategy (NBUAS), focused on Indigenous research and taught me a lot about community-driven projects. From the beginning, I was intrigued with Chabbert's statement (NBIFC, 2014), "we didn't want a community-based research project; we wanted one that was community-driven" (p. 25).

But what exactly is community-driven research? How is it different from community-based research? It begins with where the community is in terms of present realities, circumstances, and capacities. This means ensuring that the community drives the entire project through methods by which participants formalize their involvement and the activities and events that they want to see happen. It follows what knowledge the community wishes to gather and supports finding solutions to problems (NBIFC, 2014). It is based on the Utility, Self-Voicing, Access, Inter-Relationality (USAI) research framework created by the Ontario Federation of Indigenous Friendship Centres (OFIFC) (2012), which states that "research, knowledge, and practice are authored by communities" (p. 9).

The researchers in the North Bay project refer to "going with the flow" and working "with the rhythms and dynamics of the community" (NBIFC, 2014, p. 38), thereby being flexible and responsive. This means that the participation of community members will ebb and flow; researchers do not need to be overly concerned about this and, instead, should work with those who wish to at any given time, supporting a person's involvement when they are motivated to be involved. It recognizes that all areas of community life are appropriate for conducting research and taking up research questions. Hence, having tea with an Elder who drops by and activities of all kinds, such as cooking, medicine walks, and drum-making, are all appropriate contexts for exploring research questions.

As important as it was to read the reports and attend the gathering, I also wanted to speak with some of the people who were involved with the research project to gain more of an understanding of community-driven research. Thus, I had conversations with Patty Chabbert and Dawn Lamothe, both of who are mentioned above. Patty generously shared with me what she believes community-driven research is:

> We have gotten so stuck on what research is, but I think we first need to ask, where does the word or the concept of research come from? When we look at the histories (yes plural!) we see many streams of research. Western streams are more prominent and Indigenous Peoples have adopted the [W]estern research language to describe Indigenous research experiences; sometimes it['s] like fitting a square peg in a round hole. But, if we stop and ask, what are Indigenous words for research, they often end up describing the gathering and sharing of knowledge. We realize that community driven or Indigenous research is not new at all, we are just starting to put words to something that has been happening forever!
>
> I've said this so many times to Paige and Dawn [who worked with me on the project] and many other researchers in our community—"throw the language of 'research' out the window." When we ask[ed] people, community members, what research is, they cocked their heads, raised their eyebrows questioningly and said, "well, it's life! Or, history, or teachings! It's searching and learning and sharing—in no particular order!"
>
> My favorite moment was when an Elder at the Friendship Centre held a rock out in his hand and asked, "is this rock alive?" For me, research is the sharing, gathering and sharing of knowledge, it's circular. In community driven research, we make sure there is a space, a foundation, for

this gathering and sharing of knowledge to occur in ways that make sense and respect those participating. In the moment with this Elder, the office we were in was the research space, that interaction was an exchange of knowledge, the Elder and that rock were both sources of knowledge and the rock was also a research tool. The knowledge that was shared would go on to influence my thoughts on research or the process of the project and so much more. This is all research! (Chabbert in NBIFC, 2014)

TELLING STORIES

Storytelling has a long history among Indigenous communities around the world and it stands on its own as a research methodology. Some of the literature regarding research with Indigenous Peoples refers to qualitative research, narrative approaches, and Participatory Action Research (PAR) as methodologies that will capture the experiential knowledge of Indigenous Peoples. Such authors also suggest that participatory research, which is a combination of education, research, and action, contributes to the empowerment of Indigenous Peoples. The problem with such statements is that these research methodologies are viewed as novel in conducting research with Indigenous Peoples and other populations, which is not the case. Storytelling methodologies existed long before narrative approaches and participatory action methods were developed. In fact, I would say that these research methodologies are based on Indigenous ones such as storytelling circles. Some other Indigenous scholars agree, such as Jenny Lee (2009) of the Māori Nation, who describes Māori narratives as being revived within research today, which implies that these are traditional Indigenous approaches or methodologies rather than something new. She uses narrative terminology and discusses the traditional role of narratives or storytelling within Māori worldviews. In her 2009 book *Indigenous Methodologies: Characteristics, Conversations, and Contexts*, Cree educator Maggie Kovach writes about story as not being unique to Indigenous knowledge systems alone, but rather as used in various qualitative methodologies including narrative inquiry. She emphasizes how stories were an intrinsic part of Indigenous oral societies long before the rise of Western education and academic research. Interestingly enough, non-Indigenous academics Roxanne Struthers and Cynthia Peden-McAlpine (2005) directly correlate Indigenous storytelling and oral histories or narratives as a premise to phenomenological research, which uses in-depth narrative accounts and methods.

Often, when there are discussions about Indigenous research, it is described as being "new," "emerging," a "paradigm," or something that is being "reclaimed." In this way, Indigenous research is "othered," rather than seen on its own terms and built on its own knowledges, worldviews, and history. Our forms of research did not simply appear one day in a research textbook, nor are they just being reclaimed. For many, they have not been lost or stolen from us. As Oodgeroo Noonuccal (cited in Martin & Mirraboopa, 2003) tells us,

> Our people did not cut down trees for paper, nor did they mine metals for pencils, typewriters, computer, printouts, phones, facsimiles, photocopiers etc. They successfully sustained our people and environment as they talked, sang and danced the knowledge on to the young, while others used bark, branches, sticks, stones, ochres, fire and smoke for communication. To many, these methods are preferable for the environment.... These methods were shared amongst the many nations through clan gatherings, family gatherings, message stick carriers, story tellers, songs, dance and paintings. (p. 11)

Furthermore, as Stewart-Harawira (2013) emphasizes, "there is, of course, nothing new about the idea that Indigenous people conduct research. Indigenous Peoples have been conducting research since time immemorial, in the sense of investigating and uncovering knowledge and developing new ways of understanding the world" (p. 39).

Dominant writing on research also sees Indigenous research as resembling PAR. Although PAR is encouraging and represents how mainstream research has undergone many positive changes in recent years, it is still limited since

> most PAR research projects do not go far enough to recognize local systems of knowledge and practice as fully authoritative and competent to design, conduct, and evaluate their own research. We also note that the PAR paradigm often fails to recognize a subtle but crucial

difference between "participation" and "authorship," where in the case of the former—Indigenous communities and people remain more "trusted informants, confidants, and advisors," while in the latter—they assume the rightful position of creators and holders of knowledge and praxis. (OFIFC, 2012, p. 7)

Storytelling is a vibrant component of Indigenous research methodologies and exists in all cultures. Still relevant today is Cree educator Charles Lanigan's (1998) suggestion that storytelling

can be a starting point for moving away from assimilationist to liberationist education.... Stories have many layers of meaning, giving the listener the responsibility to listen, reflect and then interpret the message. Stories incorporate several possible explanations for phenomena, allowing listeners to creatively expand their thinking process so that each problem they encounter in life can be viewed from a variety of angles before a solution is reached. (p. 113)

To me, storytelling, as a methodology, fits beautifully with research, as indicated in this quote. It includes responsibility on the part of the listener/ researcher, interpretation/analysis, room for many explanations of the phenomena being researched, a creative search for solutions, and a political act of liberation/self-determination. Storytelling is encouraging for research participants, because it ensures a reflective discussion that enables all participants, including the researcher, to build knowledge together. I believe this is the key to Indigenous research methodology—building knowledge collectively, by focusing on the community in order to create richer understandings. Of utmost importance is that communities are the ones that choose methods of inquiry that are most appropriate within any research context. In fact, instead of using the term "methodology," some researchers prefer the term "orientation to research" (USAI, 2014, as cited in NBIFC, 2014, p. 94).

Storytelling also makes room for healing within the research process. As has already been noted, Indigenous worldviews centre on the notion of holism, which addresses all four dimensions of a human being. From my perspective, it is inevitable that many research topics will elicit strong emotions from participants. Since, as Indigenous persons, we have decolonizing aims, we acknowledge our history and our current situations on the journey toward self-determination and our future. There is much pain woven into our stories, and the circle, along with its protocols, is designed to welcome and address anger and hurt, should these emotions emerge.

Researchers need to be prepared for strong emotions that may come from participants in a storytelling circle. Although these emotions may not intentionally be invited, doorways may be opened for participants in terms of memories, insights, feelings, and spiritual encounters. In my own research work with Indigenous people, I have explained the possibility that emotions may come up through storytelling to potential participants beforehand, in order to encourage participants to assist one another and ask for support outside of the project.

BENEFICIAL

Our work as Indigenous scholars and researchers must lead to action. It is, in my opinion, useless if it does not. Why conduct research that does not originate out of the interests and needs of the community? What is the point of research that is not meaningful or of some benefit to the community? Data that are collected through research projects have the potential to change social policies for the better, which is one of the ways in which educational institutions can help to create positive change for Indigenous Peoples and other marginalized communities.

Completing a research project does not mean ending the relationships established during the research process. Rather, the next phase of research requires that relationships among participants continue. I believe that it is the responsibility of the researcher to ensure that the positive and meaningful intentions of the research project can continue, which means that participants are then potentially able to put their new knowledge into action. An additional responsibility of researchers and writers is taken up by Māori scholar Linda Smith (2012), who refers to a process that she calls "researching back." She states that researching back, in the same tradition of writing back or talking back, "characterizes much of the post-colonial or anti-colonial literature. [This involves] a 'knowing-ness of the colonizer' and a recovery of ourselves, an analysis of colonialism, and a struggle for self-determination" (p. 8). I must admit, however, that I prefer how Smith (1999) stated this in the first edition of her book. At that time, she wrote that "researching back ... is partly about talking back to the West ... and partly about talking to ourselves" (p. 204).

Indigenous research is also especially pertinent to the helping professions. The research conducted by Indigenous researchers proves time and again the competency, capability, and valuable knowledge that is held by Indigenous Peoples and communities (Baker, 2008; Bartlett et al., 2007; Baskin, 2005; Caldwell et al., 2005; First Nations Centre, 2007; Hart, 2007, 2009, 2014; Jones et al., 2006; Lavallée, 2008, 2009; Smith, 2012; Tupola, 2006; Wilson, 2008). Indigenous research produces knowledge that schools of social work use to inform their teaching. It is important for both Indigenous and non-Indigenous students to have access to Indigenous knowledges. Indigenous research methodologies assist populations of over-researched and exploited Indigenous people to empower themselves. These methodologies can also help inform the next generation of students/researchers who wish to work with other historically marginalized and racialized communities.

COLLABORATION

Some of the literature on Indigenous research is written by research teams made up of both Indigenous and non-Indigenous scholars. The work of Bartlett and colleagues (2007) was conducted by two Métis and three non-Indigenous academics. The study by Jones and colleagues (2006) was done by one British and two Māori scholars. I have been involved in a number of collaborative research teams made up of both Indigenous and non-Indigenous researchers, in areas such as food security, homelessness, child welfare, and addictions.

In the literature on collaborative research projects, the favoured research methodologies appear to be combinations of community-based and PAR, as seen in the quote below by a group of non-Indigenous researchers:

> Community-based, collaborative, and participatory research makes tribal people full partners, benefits the communities studied, and empowers people to define and address the issues that affect their lives; in the process, community members set the agenda of research that affects them. Scientists and community members must share equally in the research planning, implementation,

evaluation, and results dissemination phases, as well as in
any resulting benefits. (Caldwell et al., 2005, p. 7)

Many Indigenous writers (Harata Te Aika & Greenwood, 2009; Kovach,
2005; Loppie, 2007; Smith, 2012; Weber-Pillwax, 2009) agree that PAR is
an ally to Indigenous research methodologies. Some go a bit further, alluding
to the position that PAR may actually be based on some of the concepts of
Indigenous worldviews. For example, Māori authors Lynne Harata Te Aika
and Janinka Greenwood (2009) state how, for Western researchers, PAR is a
relatively "recent" engagement, but for Māori traditions "it is embedded" by
way of their *marae*, the people's communal house where issues are debated
and investigated within and by the community (p. 59). Cree/Métis academic
Weber-Pillwax (2009) discusses PAR as a research methodology that is in
support of "the intellectual and spiritual revolution of Indigenous peoples" (p.
48). Although she does not exactly state that PAR is derived from Indigenous
methods, she alludes to this when she states how "fully complementary" it is
with the research process of "ancient" Indigenous knowledges and peoples.
She also cites other Indigenous authors as having said that PAR processes are
"particularly derived and intrinsically connected to the original sources of
their own Indigeneity" (p. 48).

Some Indigenous researchers also use a number of different research
frameworks in combination. For example, one project by Tupola (2006)
used "three different cultural methodological frameworks: indigenous,
cross-cultural and trans-national. These different cultural designs reflect
my shifting positions as an insider researcher during these individual studies as well as the diverse cultural identities of the young people with whom
I collaborated" (p. 293).

I have consistently used Indigenous research methodologies in all of the
research projects I have been involved in. In some of these projects, I have
been the only principal investigator, while in others, I have collaborated
with Indigenous and non-Indigenous researchers. Here I will write about
two successful collaborative research projects that I have been involved in.

Upon the completion of a research project with young Indigenous
mothers on food security in Toronto, I was invited to participate in a
collaborative research project with seven other groups. The invitation
came from social work educator and project coordinator Izumi Sakamoto,
because my work had been noticed by groups that were implementing
community-based, arts-informed research methodologies. These projects

focused on homelessness and/or the threat of becoming homeless, but the researchers did not have an Indigenous-specific project in mind. Since my work was closely connected to the issue of homelessness (I had previously conducted research on homelessness with Indigenous people in Toronto), I implemented Indigenous research methodologies, and the women who participated in the food security project had created a mural of their depiction of a food-secure Indigenous community in Toronto, my work seemed to fit with theirs. However, I did not join this group simply because they asked me to. I first needed to find out more about the people who were involved, and I needed to have many questions answered, such as:

- What perspectives were the groups that I would be working with coming from? Were the researchers anti-oppressive?
- What did the researchers know about Indigenous people in Toronto? Were Indigenous participants working with any of them in their projects?
- How would my project be represented? Would it be given the same amount of space as other projects?
- Would I and the young Indigenous mothers who worked with me have real input into the overall project or would we just be the "token Indians"?

After a few meetings with the group, my questions were answered in ways that showed me these were researchers with a sincere desire to include Indigenous people in the research project in meaningful ways. They heard me when I emphasized that homelessness is different for Indigenous people, as homelessness is connected to colonization, which has led to the kinds of social, economic, and political conditions that have seriously disadvantaged Indigenous Peoples. The group seemed to understand my comment that it is particularly ironic that Indigenous people are homeless in their homeland. We began to build relationships that were necessary in order for us to do this work together.

I liked the group's idea to use community-based, arts-informed, participatory research methodologies to conduct projects in the area of homelessness, because of the ways I felt I could make connections between these research methodologies and Indigenous methodologies. The funding application for the project read as follows:

Homelessness is an enormous issue that must be pursued from different perspectives considering the intersections of gender, race, Aboriginal heritage, disability, and other differences. These factors contextualize the diverse experiences of people who are homeless. Yet, research on homelessness has typically focused on men who are on the street or in shelters (Sakamoto, 2009). To the extent we lack information on these different sub-groups of the homeless, it is imperative to develop a ground-up approach to reflect the diversity of experiences while exploring commonalities of such experiences. Community-based participatory research and arts-informed research value these experiences and provide mechanisms to articulate how different groups of individuals experience homelessness and how they themselves envision solutions to homelessness.

Within the homeless community our respective arts-informed studies have provided project participants an opportunity to use art to capture and express their daily experiences and challenges as they related to health, poverty, social exclusion, and other day-to-day struggles, as well as to their hope, vision and resiliency. Homeless citizens have found arts-informed research useful in order to think critically about problems and solutions from the community's perspective, and to work towards social change (Daiski, Davis-Halifax, Mitchell & Lyn, 2012; Sakamoto, 2009). The arts used in research projects herein elaborate, contextualize and expand upon what has escaped broader social attention: the strengths of people who are homeless.

Community-based participatory research methods (CBR/CBPR) came out of the reflection that traditional social research based in academic institutions does not directly benefit marginalized communities which are often "the researched" in traditional forms of research. Rather, CBR/CBPR recognizes the strengths of the community as the core of the research endeavours, and promotes the equitable involvement of all partners in the research process including academic researchers, community agencies and community members, to make the research more relevant to the community with which they work. (Sakamoto, 2009)

These participatory and emancipatory approaches can sit alongside an anti-colonial research framework that centres emancipatory aims within the research process. An anti-colonial framework is about community control over decision making, over the research agenda, over how resources will be distributed and over ethical practices. It includes a focus on critical questions such as the following:

1. What research is important and worthwhile to carry out?
2. Who will conduct the research?
3. How will it be carried out?
4. Who will own the research?
5. Who will the research benefit and what positive differences will it make?
6. How does conventional research support local capacity to undertake research?

Within an anti-colonial framework, when a research project is undertaken, it must be endorsed by the community, and credit needs to be given to those community members who participate in the research process. Developing relationships is critical, whereby communities decide whether they are interested in a researcher's project, if the researcher is respectful enough for them to share their information with, who will be involved, and what is appropriate to share. Furthermore, an agenda for research with Indigenous Peoples must focus on the goals and processes of decolonization and self-determination. If a research project does not contribute in some way to these objectives, then it is not worth doing. Such a research agenda

becomes a goal of social justice which is expressed through and across a wide range of psychological, social, cultural and economic terrains. It necessarily involves the processes of transformation, of decolonization, of healing and of mobilization as peoples. (Smith, 2012, p. 120)

Community-based participatory research also aims to benefit and mobilize marginalized populations.

The rationale for a collaboration of eight research projects to come together was explained in a way that emphasized that, despite the diversity amongst us, these studies validate the relevance of community-based, arts-informed participatory action research, especially when such diverse projects have all arrived at similar policy and practice recommendations. These projects represent homeless people as the "experts" in their life experiences who know the solutions to mediate their life circumstances. In addition, such research gives voice to a highly stigmatized population that is generally framed in negative, "deficit"-based terms. Community-based, arts-informed, and participatory research can thus break and disturb the fixed stereotypes surrounding homeless people in our society and allow for a dialogue about solutions to poverty and homelessness to begin with people most directly impacted. Although the informed projects in this collaborative employed different arts-based research methods and worked with people with different identities and experiences of homelessness, they came to many of the same conclusions. A consensus was reached across all eight projects on the recommendations about what needs to be done to address homelessness in Toronto, challenged many of the assumptions that exist about homeless people's lives, and confirmed the power of CBR/ CBPR as a tool for social change (Sakamoto, 2009, p. 11).

Upon completion of the eight research projects, we held a five-day exhibit of our work at Metro Hall in Toronto. Indigenous worldviews guided the set-up of the exhibit. We chose to organize our projects according to one of the versions of the teachings of the Medicine Wheel of the Anishnawbe. We recognized that there are many versions of the Medicine Wheel across several Indigenous Nations in Canada and our intention was not to value any particular version over another; our decision to implement this particular version of the Medicine Wheel was based on our commitment to acknowledge and honour those peoples living in Toronto, upon whose territory we were on. This idea was initiated by the project I led, which focused exclusively on Indigenous Peoples in Toronto. The idea was then supported by the Indigenous people who participated in the various projects of the collaborative endeavour.

We came to the agreement that the Medicine Wheel represented a good fit among all of our projects as it signifies unity. The Medicine Wheel symbolizes bringing people together and, in seeking to find solutions to homelessness, this initiative brought together people with experiences of homelessness as well as community agencies and academics. Implementing the Medicine Wheel as a symbol of our collaborative work also seemed appropriate because Indigenous Peoples are overrepresented amongst those with experiences of homelessness due to historical and contemporary forces of colonization, and because many of the people actively involved in many aspects of our collaborative and individual research projects identified as Indigenous.

Another successful collaborative research project I was involved in was one that focused on developing collaborative relationships between pregnant/parenting Indigenous women with substance misuse challenges and drug and alcohol treatment counsellors and child welfare workers. For this project, the team of researchers worked from an anti-colonial theoretical framework, which was written about in an earlier chapter. For some time now, a paradigm shift has been emerging whereby several studies "agree that a significant element of the solution" to the costs of social problems facing Indigenous Peoples "is the need to shift the research paradigm from one in which outsiders seek solutions to the 'Indian problem' to one in which Indigenous people conduct research and facilitate solutions themselves," which highlights Indigenous knowledge traditions and research methodologies (Saskatchewan Indian Federated College, 2002, p. 1). We chose to implement Talking Circles with the women who decided to participate in our projects. We understood that circles have many benefits as a research method such as learning from what is said, respecting what is heard, honouring confidentiality, equalizing all voices, and encouraging interconnectedness.

Hosting and taking care of people, whether they be guests or research participants, is also of great importance within Indigenous worldviews. Those who share their knowledges with a researcher must be given food, drink, honorariums, and gifts of thanks. These exchanges are as natural as breathing, and are also expected. To not carry out these protocols of reciprocity would be considered disrespectful and could even jeopardize the research project and, more importantly, possibly damage relationships. Respecting protocols is also a way of acquiring informed consent from research participants. When the protocol offering, such as tobacco, is accepted by those asked to participate in a project, it represents a deep commitment to the person who is seeking knowledge. According to researchers LaBoucane-Benson and her team (2012, as cited in OFIFC, 2012),

> In the [non-Aboriginal] world, people have to sign a paper to give permission to record on camera. In the traditional way when we make an offering and an offering is accepted—people don't understand that that is our consent—traditionally. I think it's one of the differences of our laws—when we do research in Indian country or when we ask a question of an Elder—when they accept an offering, that's giving consent to give knowledge. (p. 72)

The Teaching Circle of Elders that this team was working with responded to the above by stating:

> It's very important to do that—to make that gesture to give a gift and to receive a gift. In this case, the gift of knowledge and the sharing of that story.... When protocol is done, like in this case, it is opening the door for that relationship—to be open and of giving—sharing. And that's what is very important in our traditions—more important than me signing a piece of paper. Because a paper is a paper to us—it is something that was brought to us—it was foreign. In our way this is what guides us. I think you have done the proper thing—we are willing to share as much as we can with respect to the questions that you have brought before us. (LaBoucane-Benson et al., 2012, as cited in OFIFC, 2012, p. 72)

Some Indigenous Peoples not only do not wish to sign papers, but they also do not want their words to be written down. A staff member of an urban Indigenous organization who agreed to participate in a community research project explained this position in the following way:

> What I am sharing with you right now is within the context of this conversation, this room, this moment. When you write it down, I won't know where it will go, or will not have control over how it is used. I will not know if the next person who reads it is ready to receive this knowledge. I will not be able to share it in a way that will ensure they understand it as it is meant to be for them. (OFIFC, 2012, p. 92)

This is, of course, the case with anything that is written down. Once it leaves the writer, it is open to each reader's interpretation. In the case of research, this would need to be negotiated between the researchers and the participants. If one is going to conduct their research from a community-driven perspective, these concerns would need to be discussed and a consensus arrived at in terms of how to move forward.

Within this research project, as in the others I have been involved in, the team did not ask any direct questions of the participants. Rather, we introduced the research topic to the women, explained why we wanted to do this work, introduced ourselves, and invited them to share their stories about their experiences regarding the topic. Direct questioning can be viewed as intrusive or disrespectful within Indigenous worldviews. In addition, I tend to view direct questions, particularly within a research framework, as potentially leading participants in the direction that the researcher wants to go. However, inviting participants to share whatever is important to them and allowing each to take as much time to speak as they wish expresses respect and caring for the speaker and what they have to say.

We offered suggested areas for discussion to the women in this particular research project, such as:

- Whatever comes to mind when you think about women who are pregnant or have kids and are in substance misuse treatment programs.
- How substance misuse treatment programs help these women.
- How these programs recognize the spiritual, physical, emotional, and psychological aspects of a woman.
- How women are impacted by being involved with substance misuse treatment programs and child welfare services at the same time.

The team for this research project was made up of Indigenous and non-Indigenous women. Some were university professors, others were full-time research scientists. There were women who worked in the areas of child welfare and addictions, and there were students. Some of the team members worked at huge institutions while others were employed in grassroots agencies. Some had personal experiences of child welfare involvement and addictions while others worked directly with women who did. A female

Elder, also a member of the team, was involved in all aspects of the project from planning to participation in circles, to analyzing the information that was shared with us.

As with the previous research project mentioned in this chapter, the team members worked together in a respectful partnership, a partnership in which Indigenous worldviews and research methodologies were privileged. This is critical to collaborative research space because

> invited ally researchers will have to fully adhere to the research principles, procedures, and ethics, and commit to a long-term alliance with a mutually-shared goal to reach an identical objective that directly benefit urban Aboriginal communities [and] the potential biases of ally researchers and their own research interests must be clearly stated and addressed in a principled, self-reflexive way. (OFIFC, 2012, p. 74)

The non-Indigenous ally co-principal investigator in this research project emulated the above by generally standing back, listening more than speaking, offering the resources of her workplace such as space, supporting the leadership of the Indigenous co-principal investigator, and following the protocols specified by the Elder involved in the project. She also politely declined when asked to represent or present information about the project, instead referring the enquirer to me. She did, however, join us in representing the project when we asked her to. In addition, all literature written about our work was authored by the research team.

Again, this was a research project whereby those involved asked me to participate as a co-principal investigator not only because I am an Indigenous researcher, who works from an Indigenous worldview and uses Indigenous research methodologies, but also because I was a well-known and respected community member and social work practitioner. I consistently felt welcomed and appreciated, and I believe all of the other Indigenous team members did as well.

WHAT NON-INDIGENOUS RESEARCHERS CAN LEARN FROM US
All people and everything else in our world is dependent upon, and shares in the work and growth of, everyone and everything else. When there is a healthy interconnected web that exists between individuals, commun-

ities, and all of nature, everyone prospers because we are aligned with our Mother the Earth.

Every decision that each of us makes and everything we do affects all around us, not only our families and communities, but the animals, plants, water, the air we breathe, and the earth we walk on. We are completely dependent on everything else around us. In all that we do, including research, we have relational responsibilities. The following quote by Forbes (1992) will always be applicable to all peoples, Indigenous and non-Indigenous alike:

> I can lose my hands, and still live. I can lose my legs and still live. I can lose my eyes and still live. I can lose my hair, eyebrows, nose, arms, and many other things and still live. But if I lose the air I die. If I lose the sun I die. If I lose the earth I die. If I lose the water I die. If I lose the plants and animals I die. All of these things are more a part of me, more essential to my every breath, than is my so-called body. (pp. 145–146)

Gaining knowledge through research, then, is not an abstract pursuit but is meant to lead to transformative action in all of our relationships.

Another important aspect to consider within Indigenous research methodologies is the ways that knowledge comes to people. Knowledge can come through dreams, intuition, and cellular memories (memories stored in our cells and blood) as much as through interviews, Talking Circles, and observation. Once again, all people dream and carry memories within their blood and bodies.

Relational responsibilities and transformative action are often not part of dominant research paradigms. Rather, dominant paradigms follow the belief that knowledge is individual; a researcher searches for knowledge; they gain the knowledge and therefore own it. An Indigenous paradigm recognizes that knowledge is relational. Knowledge is meant for everyone and everything. What is the point of acquiring knowledge if it is not shared for the benefit of all?

A researcher's honesty within research is another component in an Indigenous paradigm. Research is never objective and there is always a motive for conducting it. This is as true today as it was 20 years ago when Hampton (1995) assertively articulated that the motive is emotional because we feel. We feel because we are hungry, cold, afraid, brave, loving, or hateful. We do what we do for reasons. That is the gift of the Creator of life. Life feels.... Feeling is connected to our intellect and we ignore, hide from, disguise, or suppress that feeling at our peril and at the peril of those around us. Emotionless, passionless, abstract, intellectual, academic research is a goddamn lie, it does not exist. It is a lie to other people. Humans—feeling, living, breathing, thinking humans—do research. When we try to cut ourselves off at the neck and pretend an objectifying that does not exist in the human world, we become dangerous, to ourselves first, and then to people around us. (p. 52)

Every researcher brings her or his own cultural expectations, values, and biases into the research process, and all these influence the ways that research questions are created, the choice of methods, data interpretation, and research recommendations. Thus, it can only be beneficial to all involved that researchers clearly and honestly discuss their emotional reasons for wanting to conduct any research project.

CONCLUSION

There is no such thing as one Indigenous research methodology. Rather, like Indigenous cultures, there are many and we create them as we go about conducting our research projects. They become Indigenous research methodologies as long as they follow Indigenous worldviews, which are the key foundational values and beliefs of our Nations. These values and beliefs, such as a holistic approach, relationship building, and connection to everything around us, apply to everything we do. Research is not exempt from these values and beliefs.

It is not Indigenous research methodologies that I believe can be of value to the world. Rather, it is the values and reasons behind Indigenous methodologies that can be of value. When Indigenous and non-Indigenous researchers work together with Indigenous participants or communities, it is the cultural protocols and specific methodologies of those involved that need to be taken up. But the values of self- identification, reciprocity, benefits, control and ownership, and hearing people's stories can be applied to all peoples of the world. This is particularly the case in the helping professions, such as social work—a profession that seeks, through research, to make the world a better place for all.

REFERENCES

Anderson, K. (2004). Speaking from the heart: Everyday storytelling and adult learning. *Canadian Journal of Native Education, 28*(1/2), 123–129.

Baker, E. (2008). Locating ourselves in the place of creation: The academy as Kitsu'lt melkiko'tin. *Canadian Woman Studies, 26*(3/4), 15–20.

Bartlett, J.G., Iwasaki, Y., Gottlieb, B., Hall, D., & Mannell, R. (2007). Framework for Aboriginal-guided decolonizing research involving Métis and First Nations persons with diabetes. *Social Science & Medicine, 65*, 2371–2382. doi: 10.1016/j.socscimed.2007.06.011

Baskin, C. (2005). Storytelling circles: Reflections of Aboriginal protocols in research. *Social Work Review, 22*(2), 171–187.

Bishop, R. (1998). Freeing ourselves from neo-colonial domination in research: A Maori approach to creating knowledge. *Qualitative Studies in Education, 11*(2), 199–219.

Caldwell, J.Y., Davis, J.D., Du Bois, B., Echo-Hawk, H., Shephard Erickson, J., & Stone, J.B. (2005). Culturally competent research with American Indians and Alaska Natives: Findings and recommendations of the first symposium of the work group on American Indian research and program evaluation. *American Indian and Alaska Native Mental Health Research, 12*(1), 1–21. Retrieved from http://www98.griffith.edu.au.

Coburn, E. (2013). Indigenous research as resistance. *Journal of the Society for Socialist Studies, 9*(1), 52–63. Retrieved from http://www.socialiststudies.com/index.php/sss/article/view/23524/17408.

Daiski, I., Davis-Halifax, N.V., Mitchell, G., & Lyn, A. (2012). Homelessness in the suburbs: Engulfment in the grotto of poverty. *Studies in Social Justice, 6*(1), 103–123.

Deloria Jr., V. (1997). *Red earth, white lies: Native Americans and the myth of scientific fact.* Golden, CO: Fulcrum Publishing.

Ermine, W., Sinclair, R., & Jeffery, B. (2004). *The ethics of research involving Indigenous peoples.* Retrieved from http://www.iphrc.ca.

First Nations Centre. (2007) *OCAP: Ownership, control, access and possession.* Sanctioned by the First Nations Information Governance Committee, Assembly of First Nations. Ottawa: National Aboriginal Health Organization.

Forbes, J.D. (1992). *Columbus and other cannibals: The Wetiko disease of exploitation, imperialism and terrorism.* Brooklyn: Autonomedia.

Goodman, J., McElligott, A., & Marks, L. (2003). *Useful bodies: Humans in the service of medical science in the twentieth century.* Baltimore: Johns Hopkins University Press.

Green, J. (2009). Gyawaglaab (Helping one another): Approaches to best practices through teachings of Oolichan fishing. In R. Sinclair, M.A. Hart, & G. Bruyere (Eds.), *Wicihitowin: Aboriginal social work in Canada* (pp. 222–233). Winnipeg: Fernwood Publishing.

Hampton, E. (1995). Memory comes before knowledge: Research may improve if researchers remember their motives. *Canadian Journal of Native Education, 21,* 46–54.

Harata Te Aika, L., & Greenwood, J. (2009). Ko tatou te rangahau, ko te rangahau, ko tatou: A Maori approach to participatory action research. In D. Kapoor & S. Jordan (Eds.), *Education, participatory action research, and social change: International perspectives* (pp. 59–72). New York: Palgrave Macmillan.

Hart, M. (2007). Indigenous knowledge and research: The mikiwahp as a symbol for reclaiming our knowledge and ways of knowing. *The First Peoples Child & Family Review, 3*(1), 83–90. Retrieved from http://www.fncfcs.ca.

Hart, M.A. (2009). For Indigenous people, by Indigenous people, with Indigenous people. In R. Sinclair, M.A. Hart, & G. Bruyere (Eds.), *Wicihitowin: Aboriginal social work in Canada* (pp. 153-169). Winnipeg: Fernwood Publishing.

Hart, M.A. (2014). Indigenous ways of helping. In P. Menzies & L. Lavallée (Eds.), *Aboriginal people with addiction and mental health issues: What health, social service and justice workers need to know* (pp. 73–86). Toronto: CAMH.

Johnson, B.H. (1998). *Indian school days.* Toronto: Key Porter.

Jones, R., Crengle, S., & McCreanor, T. (2006). How tikanga guides and protects the research process: Insights from the hauora tane project. *Social Policy Journal of New Zealand, 29,* 60–77. Retrieved from https://www.msd.govt.nz.

Kenny, C. (2004). *A holistic framework for Aboriginal policy research.* Ottawa: Status of Women Canada. Retrieved from http://www.publications.gc.ca/collections/Collection/SW21-114-2004E.pdf.

Kovach, M. (2005). Emerging from the margins: Indigenous methodologies. In L. Brown & S. Stretga (Eds.), *Research as resistance* (pp. 19–36). Toronto: Canadian Scholars' Press Inc.

Kovach, M. (2009). *Indigenous methodologies: Characteristics, conversations, and contexts.* Toronto: University of Toronto Press.

Lanigan, M. (1998). Indigenous pedagogy: Storytelling. In L.A. Stiffarm (Ed.), *As we see … Indigenous pedagogy* (pp. 103–120). Saskatoon: University of Saskatchewan Press.

Lavallée, L. (2008). Balancing the medicine wheel through physical activity. *Journal of Aboriginal Health,* 64–71. Retrieved from http://www.naho.ca.

Lavallée, L. (2009). Practical application of an Indigenous research framework and two qualitative Indigenous research methods: Sharing circles and Anishnaabe symbol-based reflection. *International Journal of Qualitative Methods, 8*(1), 21–40.

Lee, J. (2009). Decolonising Maori narratives: Purakau as a method. *MAI Review, 2*, 1–12. Retrieved from http://ojs.review.mai.ac.nz.

Loppie, C. (2007). Learning from the grandmothers: Incorporating Indigenous principles into qualitative research. *Qualitative Health Research, 17*(2), 276–284. doi: 10.1177/1049732306297905

Martin, K., & Mirraboopa, B. (2003). Ways of knowing, ways of being and ways of doing: A theoretical framework and methods for Indigenous re-search and Indigenist research. *Journal of Australian Studies, 76*(27), 203–214.

McCallum, M.J. (2005). This last frontier: Isolation and Aboriginal health. *Canadian Bulletin of Medical History, 22*(1), 103–120.

Menzies, C.R. (2004). Putting words into action: Negotiating collaborative re-search in Gitxaala. *Canadian Journal of Native Education, 28*(1&2), 15–32.

Mosby, I. (2013). Administering colonial science: Nutrition research and human biomedical experimentation in Aboriginal communities and residential schools, 1942–1952. *Social History, 46*(91), 145–172.

North Bay Indian Friendship Centre (NBIFC). (2014). Walking the red road: Our community's journey to help each person live a good life. North Bay, ON: Author. Retrieved from http://online.flipbuilder.com/chcx/edtv/#p=1.

Ontario Federation of Indigenous Friendship Centres (OFIFC). (2012). *USAI research framework*. Retrieved from http://ofifc.org/sites/default/files/docs/USAI%20Research%20Framework%20Booklet%202012.pdf.

Porsanger, J. (2004). An essay about Indigenous methodology. *Nordlit, 15*, 105–120. Retrieved from http://septentrio.uit.no/index.php/nordlit/article/view/1910/1776.

Sakamoto, I. (2009). SSHRC funding application: Mobilizing and leveraging knowledge on homelessness through arts-informed, community-based re-search. Toronto: University of Toronto.

Saskatchewan Indian Federated College. (2002). A brief to propose a national Indigenous research agenda. (Submitted to the Social Science and Humanities Research Council). Retrieved from http://old.fedcan.ca.

Shewell, H. (2004). *"Enough to keep them alive": Indian social welfare in Canada, 1873–1965*. Toronto: University of Toronto Press.

Smith, L.T. (1999). *Decolonizing methodologies: Research and Indigenous peoples*. Dunedin, New Zealand: University of Otago Press.

Smith, L.T. (2012). *Decolonizing methodologies: Research and Indigenous peoples* (2nd ed.). Dunedin, New Zealand: University of Otago Press.

Steinhauer, E. (2002). Thoughts on an Indigenous research methodology. *Canadian Journal of Native Education, 26*(2), 69–81.

Stewart-Harawira, M. (2013). Challenging knowledge capitalism: Indigenous research in the 21st century. *Socialist Studies, 9*(1), 39–51.

Struthers, R., & Peden-McAlpine, C. (2005). Phenomenological research among Canadian and United States Indigenous populations: Oral tradition and quintessence of time. *Qualitative Health Research, 15*(9), 1264–1276. doi: 10.1177/1049732305281329

Tupola, A. (2006). Participatory research, culture and youth identities: An exploration of Indigenous, cross-cultural and trans-national methods. *Children, Youth and Environments, 16*(2), 291–316. Retrieved from http://www.colorado.edu/journals.

Weber-Pillwax, C. (2009). When research becomes a revolution: Participatory action research with Indigenous peoples. In D. Kapoor & S. Jordan (Eds.), *Education, participatory action research, and social change: International perspectives* (pp. 46–58). New York: Palgrave Macmillan.

Wilson, S. (2008). *Research is ceremony: Indigenous research methods.* Halifax: Fernwood Publishing.

Chapter Sixteen

WE ARE ALL RELATED

INTRODUCTION

Peggy Wilson relates a story about how, before the *Exxon Valdez* oil spill, one of her students in Alaska had a dream in which everything was black, and how she felt like she was being strangled by this black mass. The student was moved and shocked into action by this experience because it was the day before the oil spill, and she wondered if anyone else in the world had had that warning. So she placed an ad in a number of newspapers throughout the world. She received responses from as far away as England and Africa with people describing similar dreams before that monumental disaster. She referred to this experience as the collective unconscious (Wilson cited in Steinhauer, 2002, pp. 75–76).

Experiences such as this one send a clear message: we are all connected. Regardless of how we explain such phenomena, whether we refer to the collective unconsciousness or spirituality, the earth ties us together.

CONNECTED THROUGH WORLDVIEWS

As an awareness of global colonization and Indigenous worldviews gradually becomes a part of education in Canada, it is helpful to consider why this might be so. I believe this acceptance is due to a number of positive events around us. One of these is the fact that Canada is a country of many peoples who are represented in our classrooms. Many of these learners are Indigenous to other parts of the world and they are bringing with them remarkably similar worldviews to those of Indigenous Peoples here.

Another reason is likely due to the increasing prevalence of literature on spirituality in social work practice and the interest that some educators have shown in taking spirituality up in their classrooms. The growing awareness of the destruction of the earth and all that lives on Her is a third reason for the growing interest and inclusion of Indigenous knowledges in social work education.

These three causes—similarity in worldviews, spirituality, and caring for the world around us—are impacting the education and practice of the helping professions. Spirituality is viewed as a celebration of diversity that promotes inclusion and, in a similar way, eco-social work draws our attention to our collective interest in protecting our spirituality and our world (Gray, Coates, & Hetherington, 2007). These concepts of interdependence and relatedness to Mother Earth come from global Indigenous worldviews. By embracing interdependence and relatedness, "we end up with multiple forms of interventions" as stated by Gray and colleagues (2007, p. 57), although I would use the term "helping" rather than "interventions."

In combating the ever-increasing destruction of the earth and the effects of this ongoing destruction on the earth's peoples, we need to look toward our commonalities and focus on ways that people can work together to address these potentially life-threatening problems. We need to embark on a journey together to search out alternative ways to live, rather than continuing to embrace ongoing Western development without questioning its effects. The world's Indigenous Peoples may hold the worldviews that will help to heal and protect our earth and everything on Her.

In conducting the research for this book, I found countless examples of commonalities amongst the worldviews of Indigenous Peoples on Turtle Island, New Zealand, Tibet, and the continent of Africa, to name a few. I have also learned about these similarities from relatives, friends, students, and classes for my Ph.D. program at OISE/U of T. My brother-in-law, who is originally from Mozambique, and I have shared many stories about our worldviews, which are similar in their focus on community values rather than individual interests, and on the importance of ceremony for one's well-being. We have similar understandings about the drum, language, and the healing properties of plants, despite the fact that we grew up on opposite sides of the world.

In my class discussions with Dr. George Dei and other learners while at OISE, I was amazed at what I heard about Indigenous knowledges from around the world. My classmates were from many countries throughout Africa, Asia, and South America, but when they spoke about their worldviews, I understood what they were saying. I was able to relate to how they lived their worldviews. For the first time in my education, I participated in class discussions where what I had to say was met with understanding and interest, rather than uncomprehending silence and dismissal. In the classroom, there was both a diverse range of individual perspectives and also a sense of connection that existed through our Indigenous knowledges and identities.

The literature from Indigenous scholars around the world also recognizes commonalities within worldviews. For example, in the area of research, Māori scholar Jelena Porsanger (2004) writes,

> The Maori concept of *whanaungatanga* has been proposed as a methodological frame for research. As a concept, *whanaungatanga* has a great array of meanings, which may

be translated as "relationships," primarily those between kin, the extended family (*whanau*), individuals, ancestors, spirits, the environment and many other aspects of the holistic Maori understandings of connectedness. (p. 111)

Another example is Afrocentricity, which relies on spirituality, appreciates the connectedness of all on the planet and in the cosmos, emphasizes the collective rather than the individual, and promotes harmony amongst all. African-American scholar Mambo Ama Mazama (2002) writes that within African forms of spirituality, "special rituals take place before cutting trees down" (p. 220), which is exactly what happens on Turtle Island as well. Mazama speaks of the connection between human beings and the spirit world, noting that "the ancestors provide guidance; they will send us messages about how we operate in this life, in this world, if we honour them" (p. 222). We are more alike than we are different!

The use of the circle is also prominent in the helping and healing practices of Indigenous Peoples throughout Africa and North America. Mazama (2002) states that the circle "is the African symbol par excellence" (p. 221). Two examples of African-based approaches that focus on the spiritual energy of the circle are the story circle technique (Williams-Clay, Olatunji, & Cooley, 2001, as cited in Garrett, Brubaker, Torres-Rivera, West-Olatunji, & Conwill, 2008) and the dance of the ring about (Spencer, 2001, as cited in Garrett et al., 2008). These approaches offer support to the members of the circle through connectedness and belonging. Similar to the methods of many Indigenous groups on Turtle Island, these approaches help participants to connect with themselves, the world around them, and the ancestors who came before them.

There is a need to instill Indigenous knowledge systems as a tool to rebuild democratic values, ethics, sustainable development, and human liberation free from all forms of oppression. For decades, Black scholars such as hooks (1984), Davis (1974), Odora Hoppers (2002), and Dei (2000) have claimed that only when intellectual production is de-racialized and Black intelligentsia is fuelled by African values will an African renaissance truly take place. Similar thoughts are expressed by Indigenous writers in other parts of the world with respect to Indigenous values.

Similarities in worldviews also extend to spirituality. Kabat-Zinn (2005) explains why mindfulness meditation has spread across the planet:

The systematic cultivation of mindfulness has been called the heart of Buddhist meditation. It has flourished over the past 2500 years in both monastic and secular settings in many Asian countries. In recent years the practice of this kind of meditation has become widespread in the world. This has been due in part to the Chinese invasion of Tibet and the continual war in Southeast Asia, both of which made exiles of many Buddhist monks and teachers; in part to young Westerners who went to Asia to learn and practice mediation in monasteries and then become teachers in the West; and in part to Zen masters and other meditation teachers who have come to the West to visit and teach, drawn by the remarkable interest in this country in meditative practices. Although at this time mindfulness meditation is most commonly taught and practiced within the context of Buddhism, its essence is universal. Mindfulness is basically just a particular way of paying attention. It is just a way of looking deeply into oneself in the spirit of self-inquiry and self-understanding. (p. 12)

Another significant component of global Indigenous worldviews is how Elders are viewed. Everyone I spoke to and all that I have read describe Elders as older people who are sought by their communities for their knowledge and spiritual leadership. Each Elder has something different to offer since each has their own unique experiences, gifts, and knowledge. Through their accumulation of knowledge and experience, Elders have an ability to talk to people and help them in ways that contribute to their well-being. This knowledge and experience is acknowledged and respected by community members who go to Elders to receive teachings and assistance.

Elders can play a role in any or all of the following practices: counselling, teaching, conducting ceremonies, healing, advising, conflict resolution, group problem-solving and decision making, and role modelling. Elders also tend to be talented storytellers.

This general view of Elders is also written about by diverse Indigenous scholars such as George Dei from Ghana (Dei & Kempf, 2013), Leilani Holmes from Hawaii (2013), Njoki Nathani Wane of Kenya (2011), and Michael Hart of the Cree Nation (2014). Similar views of Elders have also been recorded around the globe by Elders themselves such as Flordemayo, Mayan Nation of Nicaragua; Rita Pitka Blumenstein, Yupik Nation of Alaska; Tsering Dolma Gyaltong of Tibet; and Bernadette Rebienot of Gabon, Africa (Schaefer, 2006). Thus, throughout the world Elders are important for their connection to the past and their knowledge of traditional teachings, stories, and ceremonies. They are often consulted to help communities with decisions regarding all areas, including, for example, community development, governmental negotiations, and land claims. Elders are also crucial to our collective endeavour to heal the earth and all that lives on Her. Indigenous Elders in the Kimberley region of Australia have a cultural practice that links "the physical movement of walking (often vast distances) with the process of maintaining spiritual, economic and familial ties to country" (Palmer et al., 2006, p. 321). During these walks, the Elders, and the youth they bring with them, conduct ceremonies, carry out land management practices such as burning areas of land, harvesting plants, and building knowledge (Palmer et al., 2006). These journeys of walking across parts of the country are one of the ways in which the Elders pass on Indigenous knowledges to youth. It is also considered that "the act of walking on country [is] also the act of looking after it" or "to fail to walk on country is to neglect it" (Palmer et al., 2006, p. 325).

Walking on country helps to clean up the earth these groups are walking on. It helps to divert youth away from social problems, reduces substance misuse, and addresses the high incidence of suicide (Palmer et al., 2006). Elders encourage youth to stand up and begin to prepare for leadership by building their strength in physical and spiritual ways. As the authors suggest, although enlisting youth participation through the typical youth forums, consultations, and committees is beneficial, they "have young people taking time away from active pursuits and adopting the rather sedentary posture of 'sitting' on committees" (Palmer et al., 2006, p. 332).

These Elders and many others around the world have been passing on knowledges to younger generations through doing, rather than sitting, since the beginning of time (Baskin, 2008; Schaefer, 2006). Much of my own education has come while doing physical labour for the Elders who have taught me, while picking and preparing medicines and preparing for ceremonies. Learning from Elders through doing seems to be a commonality amongst Indigenous Peoples globally that may also be useful to other people on the earth.

I came across another journal article from Schiff and Moore (2006) that discussed healing through the sweat lodge ceremony of Turtle Island, but also discussed how similar practices have occurred in many other places around the world:

> The process of sweating for cleansing and healing has a history that extends around the world and goes back for millennia. Both the ancient Greeks and the Romans used hot baths and sweating techniques to draw out bad humours and as a general form of relaxation and social gathering. Likewise, Finnish saunas promoted cleanliness, healing, and renewed strength. Russians used a bania, which combined steam and hot air to create a humid, healing environment, while Turkish hammans and Japanese hot tubs are widely used in their respective countries (Aaland, 1978). Sweating cleanses the body of toxic elements and boosts the immune system (Smoley, 1992).
>
> While heat and water are universal in these various manifestations of cleansing processes, only a few cultures have incorporated them into a carefully prescribed ceremony which emphasizes the spiritual element in addition to the physical healing and cleansing that are universally acknowledged. Indigenous North Americans are among those people for whom the sweating experience is a traditional ceremony that aims to purify, cleanse, and heal the body, mind, emotions, and spirit. (p. 49)

CONNECTED THROUGH COLONIZATION AND GLOBALIZATION

The other major way in which global Indigenous Peoples are connected is through a history of colonization and its present-day impacts. No Indigenous population on the planet has escaped the destruction of colonization, the genocide that murdered millions of people, raped the land, and did everything it could to wipe out the knowledges of Indigenous Peoples. The same systems that were used to colonize the Indigenous Peoples of Turtle Island were used against other Indigenous Peoples around the world, including the imposition of religion, education, and child welfare. Mazama (2002) refers to Christianity as "one of the pillars of Western supremacy" and "part and parcel of the White supremacy project" (p. 223). Given the role of Christian religions in the colonization of Indigenous Peoples worldwide, I agree with Mazama (2002) that Christianity is "responsible for more misery and suffering than any other religion" (p. 223). Throughout both Africa and Turtle Island, Christianity reduced our Indigenous spiritualities to superstitions; played a role in genocide and enslavement; and created schools that demonized our cultural practices, physically and sexually abused our children, and forbade them to speak their own languages.

Sami culture in Northern Europe, which is distinct from the Nordic culture that surrounds it, was also historically attacked through educational systems. Education was used to oppress Sami people and "outlawed Sami language, clothing and music" (Hicks & Somby, 2005, p. 280). In the twentieth century, the Sami people focused on protecting their communities and have attempted to reduce the prejudice that exists toward them and address economic hardships. According to Hicks and Somby (2005), "prior to the end of the Second World War many Sami hid their Sami identity in order to save themselves and their families from persecution" (p. 276). They faced "racist policies" in their "attempt to reduce the poverty level" for their communities (p. 277).

Child welfare in New Zealand has also implemented racist policies with regard to Indigenous children. Historically, in New Zealand, a disproportionate number of Māori children are represented in both foster and institutionalized care (Smith, 2012). Many Māori children were lost forever to their families and communities while being placed in White homes, which meant that their cultural and spiritual needs were not met (Smith, 2012). In addition, social workers within child welfare services often ignored the wishes of a child's parents in seeking family connections for the care of their children.

We, as Indigenous Peoples around the globe, have more similarities regarding the history of colonization and its current impacts than we have differences. It is this horrific history along with our worldviews that bind us together. Both our history and our worldviews will potentially help us take a stand in the future.

Today's impacts of this colonial history include extreme poverty, stolen land, and languages that have been wiped out. Colonization, however, was not completely successful. Indigenous Peoples and our knowledges have survived, which speaks to our incredible strength and spirit. And through our survival, all peoples of the world can benefit. The colonizers needed Indigenous Peoples in the past in order to survive and the descendants of the colonizers need Indigenous Peoples still today to help them to survive into the future.

Social work has functioned as an arm of colonization and this has been written about by many Indigenous scholars across the globe, from Hart (2014) in Canada, to Ling (2010) in Asia, to George and Chaze in India (forthcoming). Social work exists as a modernist Western creation that has gained influence in many parts of the world; however, despite its aims to support and assist people, social work has also historically been used to silence Indigenous Peoples in the name of helping. Notions of international social work, which seek to delineate a universal definition for the profession and create universal educational standards, can be seen as a modern form of colonization. Trends to professionalize social work in many parts of the world may be due to the profession's historical and ongoing inferiority complex. In order to address this inferiority complex, the profession has sought to gain status in the eyes of other helping professions and within society as a whole through standardization of practices and "professionalization."

Within the social work profession, there is an inherent contradiction between a desire to incorporate Indigenous ways of helping in order to be able to provide service that is in alignment with the values and needs of diverse peoples and communities, and this push to standardize social work practices according to Western values and Western models. The answer is not to try to make Indigenous ways of helping fit within Western social work models, but rather to take complete direction from Indigenous communities. Only in this way can social work avoid being part of colonialist globalization projects.

Leadership in all areas that affect Indigenous Peoples must come from Indigenous Peoples themselves, as they are the ones who know what they need. I agree with Gray, Coates, and Hetherington (2007), who write,

> Indigenous movements usually involve people collectively asserting their rights for self-determination since Indigenous people recognize that political, economic, educational, and health benefits and privileges cannot occur as long as the entire population is disenfranchised. Self-determination for Indigenous people has greater meaning in the sense that it concerns the empowerment of entire populations. The self-directing potential of individuals cannot be increased without considering historical, social, cultural, economical and political realities. (p. 56)

As Indigenous Peoples are on a natural journey of deconstructing Western hegemony, which includes the education and practice of the helping professions, they can learn from one another as they share their histories and struggles and rebuild their communities based on their worldviews. Local input is critical and must be built on the views, interests, values, and practices of local communities. Once again, however, this applies to more than Indigenous Peoples; it is also relevant to any people who live on the land, who are farmers, who have concerns about food security, or who care about the future of our earth.

MY RELATIVES IN BRAZIL

I have a story that I would like to share with you about the connections between colonization and worldviews amongst Indigenous Peoples globally.

In 2005, I was approached by Ryerson University's Centre for Studies in Food Security (CSFS) to become part of the Centre to conduct research and write about food security and Indigenous Peoples. I agreed, as food is not only a structural determinant of health, but also has cultural and spiritual meanings for Indigenous Peoples worldwide. In the spring of 2006, the Centre invited me to visit interior Brazil where the Centre's team was involved in a food security project. A small group of Indigenous Peoples, who had recently migrated to an area close to where the project was taking place, expressed an interest in what the team was doing in the area of food security. Everyone agreed that the Indigenous person involved with the Centre should be one of the members to meet with this group. My intention in meeting with the group in Brazil was to learn something about how food (e.g., traditional foods and their meanings, access and choices, past and present practices) is connected to identity. I had no idea that my visit was going to be a spiritual journey.

With the arrival of Europeans in Brazil over 500 years ago, much of the Indigenous Peoples' land was taken over by ranchers and industrial projects. Indigenous Peoples were forced onto pieces of land similar to reserve communities in Canada, and poverty levels are high (Baskin, 2008). Languages, cultures, and livelihoods have also been negatively impacted and the exploitation of Indigenous Peoples threatens traditional knowledges and practices (Baskin, 2008). All of these impacts have affected the Pankararu and Pataxo people whom I visited. These people have been dislocated at least twice and have had to start a whole new community in an arid area.

Worldviews that exist between these two tribes in Brazil had much in common with my own worldviews in Canada. As one of the community members explained,

> We have a vision about what we want our community to be like based on working with nature around us. In our vision, everything is connected and has a purpose…. We feel we are solution-focused and believe we can help heal the land that has been almost destroyed by White ranchers, miners and the government. The whole principle is to work responsibly with the earth, take care, nourish and restore what is there, and do as little harm as possible to Her. (Baskin, 2008, p. 8)

All of the people gathered to spend time with me when I visited their territory. Most of the discussions were initiated by the community's Elder and a young political leader. The Elder took on the role of escorting me around the village, explaining things and offering teachings. He stated that even though he is only middle-aged, he is the oldest one in the community. He clearly feels a huge responsibility in his role as Elder, as he humbly stated, "I have a lot to learn in order to be the people's Elder." He, like all the other people present, was welcoming, open, and generous. Their openness and generosity was expressed through their sharing of information and allowing photographs to be taken.

The Indigenous Brazilian people were interested in learning as much as they could about Indigenous Peoples in Canada. They were especially interested in learning about the different Nations, life today, commonalities between us and them, traditional foods, and representation in government. They also wanted to know about me, my family, and my community. Through a translator and drawing diagrams in the dirt with a stick, I explained as best I could. Afterwards, the Elder announced, "all Indigenous peoples are related. You are our relative."

When I first arrived in the community, the people were dressed in shorts and skirts, but later, they changed into their traditional regalia. They wanted to conduct a ceremony for me. They formed a circle and danced while singing. Then they called out, asking, "where is our relative?" They brought me into the circle to dance with them and sang an honour song. The Elder explained the meaning of the song: "Your strength comes to us and our strength goes to you. Your clan is the fish and the fish from where our original territory is will protect you and give you strength always." This was only the first time I cried because I was feeling spiritually overwhelmed. They asked me for a song and, of course, I sang a song of thanks. When it was time to leave, the families presented gifts of jewellery. The Elder gave me one of his shakers and a bow with three arrows. I cried again. We joked and laughed for a bit before my departure. Ten years have passed, but these memories remain vivid. I was fundamentally changed by this visit to the interior of Brazil in ways that are impossible to articulate (Baskin, 2008).

I remain in touch with my Pankararu and Pataxo relatives. Three of these relatives travelled to Toronto a few years ago as part of my food security research project. Besides that visit, we have continued to exchange letters and gifts from time to time. Their community has grown and prospered throughout the years due to their incredible hard work and sacrifices. New babies have arrived, the people are now able to grow some vegetables, and they have created an irrigation system. A few have become nurses and teachers to better care for their community. These relatives of mine have many positive messages for the world. One message comes from one of the young women from the community. When I mentioned how inspired I was by the people of her village who have so little materially and yet are so generous and glowing with happiness, she responded:

> We need money for certain things, so we can be comfortable, but that's all. We don't need or want many materialistic things. We don't want to accumulate a lot of things, but rather share amongst ourselves. We are a group of people who want to be together and enjoy doing things together. We love to live. We like each other. We like ourselves. We want to live free. (Baskin, 2008, p. 9)

TAKING A STAND

We are living in a time when we all need to strive for wellness and balance. In the Lakota philosophy, the phrase *mitakuye oyasin* emphasizes that we are all related. The well-being of one group of people necessarily influences the well-being of others. The Medicine Wheel of the Anishnawbe teaches us that all people from the four directions are needed in order to maintain a world that is in balance. Hopi teachings say that their people must continue their ceremonies or the world will end. They pray for the well-being of all of us. While Indigenous Peoples see themselves as members of their own communities and citizens of their own Nations, they also see themselves as members of the world community.

Taking a stand to promote Indigenous worldviews can happen in many ways and in many spaces, from the classroom to demanding the return of cultural objects to their original communities, to adopting Indigenous helping practices and learning about oneself. All helping professions, and the world at large, need a movement toward a global dialogue where all worldviews have an equal place, but this will not happen as long as we stay centred on theoretical models and analysis. Moving into action requires a revolutionary transformation in how we teach and practise helping work. Educators in the helping professions, in particular, have the power and privilege to be inclusive of all worldviews. And it is educators who change the practice of our professions in communities. This change can be seen in the social work field as a move toward anti-oppressive practice. Furthermore, it is educators who prepare learners to work in the field, so we have endless opportunities to create spaces where inclusiveness is honoured.

Learners need to be encouraged to challenge educators about what they are teaching. Learners need to be able to safely take the risk of challenging educators if they do not see the worldviews of their communities reflected in their education. If educators are open to listening, and learners know they can contribute to the education process through respectful challenges, then genuine conversations can occur, which can potentially lead to action and transformation.

I am reminded of the recent movements of professionals beyond borders, such as doctors, dentists, and social workers who "reach beyond borders to address human catastrophe around the world" (Social Workers Beyond Borders, 2015), as well as "a beyond boundaries approach ... using multiple perspectives and practices ... to work with those who walk between worlds" (Marais & Marais, 2007, p. 819). I would say that not only Indigenous Peoples, but many populations across the planet walk between worlds. Thus, how well the helping professions do in the future may well depend on the ability of service providers to walk between worlds.

Both Indigenous and non-Indigenous peoples can also take an action-oriented stand when it comes to land claims, Indigenous Peoples' rights, and the reclamation of cultural objects that do not belong in museums. It can be incredibly painful for Indigenous Peoples to see their sacred, spiritual, and cultural objects—such as eagle staffs, pipes, and scrolls—displayed in museums. What is particularly difficult about this situation is that White people and tourists have access to these objects, but Indigenous people do not. Referred to as "artifacts" by the West, Indigenous cultural objects are collected and housed in museums in order to preserve Indigenous knowledges and cultures. Although some anthropologists advocate that Indigenous Peoples should be involved in the extraction and review of their own cultural objects, others continue to insist that these objects should not be returned to Indigenous Peoples, unless the rightful owners have the proper facilities to keep them safe (West, 1995). According to one source, "returning collections to communities that have no resources or commitment to care for them, for the sake of political appeasement, is unacceptable" (Janes & Arnoldas, as cited in West, 1995, p. 284).

Such statements are not only insulting, they are illogical. How can it be that archaeologists and museologists acknowledge a need to be educated by Indigenous Peoples in the practice of their professions, but still insist that cultural objects that belong to Indigenous Peoples must remain within the formal structures of these professions? I call this exploitation and, of course, a misuse of power. Indigenous and non-Indigenous people are called upon to question this present-day form of colonization and work toward its eradication. If, for example, communities do not have the resources to safely care for their cultural objects, then the money spent on caring for these objects in museums can be transferred to those communities.

Unfortunately, there has not been much movement on this issue over the past two decades. In Canada, although a few provinces, such as Alberta and B.C., have made some gains, at the federal level, there are no specific laws focused on the repatriation of Indigenous Peoples' sacred objects from museums (Fisher, 2012). Furthermore, laws and policies regarding cultural property rights and conservation do not address the interests and rights of Indigenous groups. Thus, there are many tensions between Indigenous and Canadian laws. As outlined by Fisher (2012),

> The First Nations relationship to artefacts is not about ownership of the object, but rather about a connection to the item that cannot be broken or changed. The Common Law understanding of ownership, on the other hand, is that it is alienable or transferable to another owner. This

> ideological clash is frustrating for First Nations groups as
> they try to prove their ownership claims in terms accept-
> able to the Canadian legal system. (para. 11)

All of us can also take a stand when it comes to poisoning the earth and the
people who live on Her. I continue to appreciate Derek Rasmussen's (2001)
creative, insightful, and direct writing about the environment and land claims.
A non-Indigenous activist and meditation teacher, Rasmussen was the senior
policy advisor to Nunavut Tunnagavick Inc., a land claims organization, for
12 years. He writes, "Nunavut's and the US's communities are tied together by
the US's invisible exhalation of death. The US breathes out, Inuit die" (p. 113).
According to Rasmussen (2001), dioxin from incinerators and iron-smelting
plants rise with warm air, but fall with cold temperatures when they reach
the Far North. Since it is too cold for them to evaporate, they settle and are
absorbed by lichen, which are eaten by caribou, which are then eaten by Inuit.
    Rasmussen (2001) has a humorous yet serious suggestion on what can
be done to learn about these situations first-hand:

> Go on a field trip to Alpena, Michigan or Hartford, Il-
> linois. Figure out how to clean it up, slow it down, stop
> it. It's the Euro-American way of life that needs to be put
> under the microscope, not intriguing tribes in faraway
> lands. Instead of exotic slide shows on the Arctic, how
> about US Schools exotic field trips to the municipal incin-
> erators in Bethlehem Steel and US Steel's iron-smelting
> plants in Chesterton and Gary, Indiana. (p. 113)

The message to the U.S. is clear: learn about the self and learn about
what is happening around you, which includes learning about those of
us who are living just to the north, in Canada. Then take action in the
form of teachings, such as those offered through Buddhism, which have
existed for about 2,500 years: "First, cease to do evil; then learn to do
good" (Rasmussen, 2001, p. 113; 2013). North America uses 80 percent
of the world's resources and takes resources from many other parts of the
world with little regard for the people who are often forced to give up these
resources. Since a North American way of life is the cause of the majority
of the world's problems, what is needed is for North Americans to address
the excess of this way of life and move toward change (Rasmussen, 2001,

2013). As sociologist Robert R. Paine wrote in 1977, in what he considered his most important message to White people, drop the illusion that you are "in the Arctic to teach the Inuit" and instead focus on "learning about white behaviour" (p. xii, as cited in Rasmussen, 2001, p. 113; 2013).

Rasmussen (2001) builds on Paine's suggestion by stating that, for those who want to live harmoniously with others on the planet, it is necessary to become deeply aware of what has formed one's present culture. This author advises people living in North America to let go of their belief in cultural superiority, put an end to forcing their values and lifestyles on every civilization in the name of progress, and stop the delusion that materialism and individualism equal happiness (Rasmussen, 2001, 2013). In coming to understand themselves, North Americans "must cease to do evil. Only then, with full awareness of the assumptions and values that we carry with us as Euro-Americans, can we have the clarity, wisdom, and insight to learn to do good" (Rasmussen, 2001, p. 114; 2013). This insight is, of course, applicable to all of us in the West, including Canada.

CONCLUSION

This chapter has shown how Indigenous Peoples across the globe are connected through their worldviews, their history of colonization, and their hopes for the future. Throughout the world, Indigenous Peoples and their allies are taking political and cultural stands as well as building social movements. There are now some allies who are publishing strong messages that Indigenous worldviews and rights need to be privileged in order to begin to heal the earth. Others write about the urgent need for non-Indigenous Peoples to closely examine their values and lifestyles in order to learn how to do good in the world.

All of these messages are particularly significant for those involved in the helping professions. We are beginning to learn how not to perpetuate evil as evidenced in the rise in anti-oppression education and practice, and the rise of values of self-determination and social justice. The question still remains about how exactly we will implement these values to do good in the world. There are endless possibilities and opportunities awaiting us if we begin to listen and be informed by Indigenous knowledges.

REFERENCES

Baskin, C. (2008). Indigenous youth exploring identities through food security in Canada and Brazil. *Maori and Indigenous Peoples Review, 3*(5), 1–11. Retrieved from http://ojs.review.mai.ac.nz.

Davis, A.Y. (1974). *With my mind on freedom: An autobiography*. New York: Bantam.

Dei, G.J.S. (2000). African development: The relevance and implications of "Indigenousness." In G. Dei, B. Hall, & D. Rosenburg (Eds.), *Indigenous knowledges in global contexts: Multiple readings of our world* (pp. 70–86). Toronto: University of Toronto Press.

Dei, G.J.S., & Kempf, A. (2013). *New perspectives on African-centred education in Canada*. Toronto: Canadian Scholars' Press Inc.

Fisher, D. (2012) Repatriation issues in First Nations heritage collections. *Journal of Integrated Studies, 1*(3). Retrieved from http://jis.athabascau.ca/index.php/jis/article/view/79/75.

Garrett, M., Brubaker, M., Torres-Rivera, E., West-Olatunji, C., & Conwill, W.L. (2008). The medicine of coming to center: Use of the Native American centering technique—Ayeli—to promote wellness and healing in group work. *The Journal for Specialists in Group Work, 33*(2), 179–198. doi: 10.1080/01933920801977322

George, P., & Chaze, F. (forthcoming). Challenging state's authority and reclaiming citizenship: A case on action against eviction and deportation of pavement dwellers in Mumbai, India. In N. Yu & D. Mandell (Eds.), *Subversive social action: Extra-legal and illegal action for social justice*. Waterloo, ON: Wilfrid Laurier University Press.

Gray, M., Coates, J., & Hetherington, T. (2007). Hearing Indigenous voices in mainstream social work. *Families in Society, 88*(1), 55–66. doi: 10.1606/1044-3894.3592

Hart, M.A. (2014). Indigenous ways of helping. In P. Menzies & L. Lavallée (Eds.), *Aboriginal people with addiction and mental health issues: What health, social service and justice workers need to know* (pp. 73–86). Toronto: CAMH.

Hicks, C.J.B., & Somby, A. (2005). Sami responses to poverty in the Nordic countries. In R. Eversole, J. McNeish, & A.D. Cimadamore (Eds.), *Indigenous peoples and poverty: An international perspective* (pp. 275–289). London: Zed Books.

Holmes, L. (2013). *Ancestry of experience: A journey into Hawaiian ways of knowing*. Honolulu: University of Hawai'i Press.

hooks, b. (1984). *From margin to centre*. Boston: South End Press.

Kabat-Zinn, J. (2005). *Full catastrophe living: Using the wisdom of your body and mind to face stress, pain, and illness*. New York: Bantam Dell.

Ling, H.K. (2010). The development of culturally appropriate social work practice in Sarawak, Malaysia. In M. Gray, J. Coates, & M. Yellow Bird (Eds.), *Indigenous social work around the world: Towards culturally relevant education and practice* (pp. 97–106). Surrey, UK: Ashgate.

Marais, L., & Marais, L.C. (2007). Walking between worlds: An exploration of the interface between Indigenous and first-world industrialized culture. *International Social Work, 50*(6), 809–820. doi:_10.1177/0020872807081920

Mazama, M.A. (2002). Afrocentricity and African spirituality. *Journal of Black Studies, 33*(2), 218–234. Retrieved from http://www.jstor.org.

Odora Hoppers, C.A. (2002). Indigenous knowledge and the integration of knowledge systems: Towards a conceptual and methodological framework. In C.A. Odora Hoppers (Ed.), *Indigenous knowledge and the integration of knowledge systems: Towards a philosophy of articulation* (pp. 2–22). Claremont, South Africa: New Africa Books.

Palmer, D., Watson, J., Watson, A., Ljubic, P., Wallace-Smith, H., & Johnson, M. (2006). "Going back to country with bosses": The Yiriman project, youth participation and walking along with elders. *Children, Youth, and Environments, 16*(2), 316–337.

Porsanger, J. (2004). An essay about Indigenous methodology. *Nordlit, 15*, 105–120. Retrieved from http://septentrio.uit.no/index.php/nordlit/article/view/1910/1776.

Rasmussen, D. (2001). Qallunology: A pedagogy for the oppressor. *Canadian Journal of Native Education, 25*(2), 105–116.

Rasmussen, D. (2013, April 4). Qallunology 101: A lesson plan for the non-Indigenous. *Buddhist Peace Fellowship.* Retrieved from http://www.buddhistpeacefellowship.org/qallunology-101-a-lesson-plan-for-the-non-indigenous/.

Schaefer, C. (2006). *Grandmothers counsel the world: Women Elders offer their vision for our planet.* Boston: Trumpeter Books.

Schiff, J.W., & Moore, K. (2006). The impact of the sweat lodge ceremony on dimensions of well-being. *American Indian and Alaska Native Mental Health Research: The Journal of the National Centre, 13*(3), 48–69.

Smith, L.T. (2012). *Decolonizing methodologies: Research and Indigenous peoples* (2nd ed.). Dunedin, New Zealand: University of Otago Press.

Social Workers Beyond Borders. (2015). *Working together for global change.* Retrieved from http://www.socialworkersbeyondborders.org/.

Steinhauer, E. (2002). Thoughts on an Indigenous methodology. *Canadian Journal of Native Education, 26*(2), 69–81.

Wane, N. (2011). African Indigenous feminist thought: An anti-colonial project. In N. Wane, A. Kempf, & M. Simmons (Eds.), *The politics of cultural knowledge* (pp. 7–22). Rotterdam: Sense Publications.

West, D.A. (1995). Epistemological dependency and Native peoples: An essay on the future of Native/non-Native relations in Canada. *Canadian Journal of Native Studies, 15*, 279–291.

Chapter Seventeen

So You Wanna Be an Ally?

INTRODUCTION

I had no idea that there were so many definitions of the word "ally." Dictionary.com (n.d.) defines ally in two ways: one is "to unite formally, as by treaty, league, marriage, or the like," such as "Russia allied itself to France," and the second is "to associate or connect by some mutual relationship, as resemblance or friendship." According to Vocabulary.com (n.d.), the word ally "comes from the Latin word *alligare*, meaning 'to bind to,' like nations who are allies in wartime—they will act together, and protect one another. You can also use ally as a verb, meaning 'join forces with.' For example, you might ally yourself with influential people to advance your career."

This chapter takes up the word "ally" in terms of relationships between Indigenous and non-Indigenous peoples whereby the latter supports and stands beside the former for Indigenous rights. It takes the position that what is occurring in Canada today is not an "Indigenous problem," but rather a Canadian one. Considering the final recommendations of the Truth and Reconciliation Commission (2015), this is an important and timely discussion.

WHAT DOES AN ALLY LOOK LIKE?

A strong ally to Indigenous Peoples in Canada at the time of the residential school system was Dr. Peter Bryce, the Medical Inspector for the Department of Indian Affairs (DIA) for 17 years from 1904 to 1921 (Green, 2006). Bryce reported to DIA Assistant Superintendent Frank Pedley in 1909 that the death rate for Indigenous children in these schools was as high as 50 percent and was mostly due to healthy children deliberately being exposed to those who had tuberculosis. However, the deaths were suppressed by the government and churches and, despite findings being published in the *Ottawa Citizen* and the *Montreal Star*, Bryce's report was buried (Green, 2006). Then, in 1921, Superintendent Duncan Campbell Scott eliminated the position of Medical Inspector, so Bryce was out of a job.

In 1922, Bryce released his book, *The Story of a National Crime: Being a Record of the Health Conditions of the Indians of Canada from 1904–1921*, which he referred to as an appeal for justice for the Indigenous Peoples of Canada (Green, 2006). This document described his visits to the schools over the years in the role of reporting on the health conditions of the children. Even in 1922, he noted that the deaths of children continued to be alarmingly high in the schools. At the same time, Bryce also repeatedly charged that the government's treatment of the Indigenous population was a criminal disregard for their treaties with them (Green, 2006). Clearly, he was correct, as the government at the time silenced him.

None of Bryce's recommendations were ever taken up, but his work and the documentation of it is available for all to see. It offers substantial proof of the horrific treatment inflicted on Indigenous children for so long. Bryce knew what was right, stood up for Indigenous children, and peacefully kept on trying for them despite the criticism he endured (FNCFCSC, 2014). Today, there is a P.H. Bryce Award for children and youth who advocate for the safety, health, and well-being of Indigenous children and youth (FNCFCSC, 2014). That is what an ally looks like.

ALLYSHIP IN THE PRESENT DAY

Allyship, as a modern concept, first appeared when LGBTQ communities sought the support of non-LGBTQ communities in the fight against the systemic discrimination the former faced based on heterosexism and homophobia (Kendall, 2006). In recent years, allyship as a focus of research has expanded to include allies for people with (dis)abilities, women, and people of colour (Brown & Ostrove, 2013). Allies have been defined by many as those who work for social justice from a position of power or membership within the dominant group. Patton and Bondi (2015) elaborate:

> Allies for social justice recognize the interconnectedness of oppressive structures and work in partnership with marginalized persons toward building social justice coalitions. They aspire to move beyond individual acts and direct attention to oppressive processes and systems. Their pursuit is not merely to help oppressed persons but to create a socially just world which benefits all people. (p. 490)

The term ally carries with it a certain level of responsibility, which includes the responsibility to educate oneself, engage in self-examination, offer support, and, most importantly, challenge the dominant forces at play (Aveling, 2013; Kendall, 2006). Allyship is not as simple as aligning one's beliefs and words with a cause or population. Rather, these beliefs must be turned into action (Aveling, 2013; Patton & Bondi, 2015). Brown and Ostrove (2013) explain that allies are dominant group members who work to end prejudice in their personal and professional lives, and relinquish social privileges conferred by their group status through their support of non-dominant groups…. This broad conceptualization of allies has been extended beyond just dominant group individuals to include people who themselves may be members of a different non-dominant group (e.g., lesbians serving as allies for gay men). (p. 2211)

Although the term ally is widely used, some believe that it indicates a belief that one is fighting someone else's battle, instead of actually aligning themselves within the battle. For example, when asked about the role of allies in Black women's activism, bell hooks (as cited in Samatar, 2013) challenged the term, saying,

If someone is standing on their own beliefs and their own beliefs are anti-patriarchal and anti-sexist, they are not required to be anybody's ally. They are on their front line in the same way that I'm on my front line. (para. 5)

That being said, many scholars use the term regularly, emphasizing that it not only helps to name an issue that marginalizes and oppresses non-dominant communities, but also that it highlights the fact that they are not the ones who are most at risk or most affected by discrimination. In addition, allies must be willing to acknowledge their privileges. According to Ewuare Xola Osayande, an African-American political activist, poet, and academic (as cited in Patton & Bondi, 2015), privileges held by White allies include:

1. The ability to paraphrase and/or otherwise exploit the analysis of black liberation struggles and have it received by others as though it were their own.
2. The ability to emotionally express their views about racism without having that expression dismissed as "angry" or "too emotional."
3. Being honored for their anti-racist work as their black activist counterparts and other activists of color are denounced and derided. (p. 489)

Other activists and academics write about such privileges as well. For example, when it comes to emotions—particularly anger—within Two-Spirit activism, Cameron Greensmith, another non-Indigenous ally (2015), refers to the fact that the "historical process of service provision ... regularly requires Indigenous peoples to stifle their anger—and indeed be content with their own genocide—and assimilate themselves into white settler normativity if they are ever to receive adequate support and care" (p. 172). The rewards of recognition and praise received by non-Indigenous allies for the work they do are rarely given when the work is done by Indigenous Peoples. There is a stark contrast between the acknowledgement experienced by non-Indigenous peoples for their humanitarian efforts and the experience of many Indigenous Peoples, who are frequently faced with resistance, judgement, and labelling (Greensmith, 2015; Patton & Bondi, 2015). The element of choice on the part of non-Indigenous peoples is often highlighted, whereas a lack of choice for Indigenous Peoples regarding whether or not to act is often left unexamined, and, therefore, not addressed. After all, having a choice itself is a privilege that Indigenous Peoples may not have.

ALLIES AND INDIGENOUS PEOPLES

Historically, the relationship between Indigenous Peoples and the social services and health sectors has been one of cultural decimation (Baskin, 2011; Cowie, 2010). In order to avoid further complicity in assimilative and colonial practices, non-Indigenous helpers must develop a clear understanding of their privilege and of their professions' complicity in past and present colonial practices embedded in their practice (Baskin, 2011; Bishop, 2015; Cowie, 2010; Rossiter, 2011).

Building a knowledge base of the vast differences between Indigenous and mainstream worldviews must take precedence over the implementation of Western standards and perceptions of society within education. Indigenous helpers, academics, and leaders must be at the front of this movement (Baskin, 2011; Rossiter, 2011). The value held in Indigenous knowledges and traditions for all peoples must be appreciated by professionals in the helping fields if service users and mainstream society are to benefit from them. Key to the development of one's own position as an ally is the development of awareness of the strengths of Indigenous frameworks, methodologies, and ways of being. These strengths must be highlighted and put forward as points of focus and strong contributions to society. Framing Indigenous Peoples as solely being in need of assistance sets them up to be seen as less capable, flawed, and in need of help in comparison to dominant populations, and further solidifies existing power imbalances. Thus, allies present a counter-narrative that includes the relationship between anti-colonialism, anti-racism, Indigenous knowledges, and decolonization. The ongoing work of decolonization means to interrogate settler society, with an emphasis on the fact that equity for Indigenous Peoples is far from being achieved. The work of allies in taking this up must be constantly open to ongoing feedback.

The recent research of Kovach (Plains Cree and Saulteaux), Carrière (Métis), Montgomery (Mi'kmaq), Barrett (non-Indigenous), and Gillies (Métis, Chinese, and Norwegian) (2015) asked the question, "What is the relevance to integrating Indigenous Knowledges into instruction and core curriculum" of postsecondary education (p. 42)? Much of this work focused on what it means to be an ally who counteracts the deficit theorizing of Indigenous Peoples. One of the research participants spoke to this by stating,

> I am very aware in Social Work that for many years what we did is spend a lot of time focusing on negatives ... the stories of Indigenous peoples are always—sort of—very problem based. I try and reframe things and say—"What would it look like if we challenged the deficit thinking we have about Aboriginal Peoples and turn that around and look at the deficit thinking of the status quo." (Kovach et al., 2015, p. 44)

Examining one's own privilege and relationship to it is crucial to becoming an ally (Bishop, 2015; Kendall, 2006; Nattrass, 2015). Locating oneself within the systems of oppression one is part of, but trying to work against them, and understanding history and current contexts are pivotal. Speaking to the importance of this exploration, Ben Carniol, a White ally and Professor Emeritus and Program Coordinator for First Nations Technical Institute's Bachelor of Social Work program in partnership with Ryerson University, states,

> From a mainstream perspective, what I see as being important for an ally, is to unlearn a lot of the stuff that

we have been socialized to believe from a very young age and has been reinforced day by day with the prevailing narrative of colonialism that is still very, very strong in sometimes subtle ways and sometimes not so subtle ways. That unlearning means a recognition of the oppression of colonialism, a recognition of why people are being oppressed, and that goes back to history. So mainstream allies need to understand about the dispossession, the theft of land, the violation of treaties, the assimilative role of government policies and of mainstream, non-Indigenous people in general. (B. Carniol, personal communication, May 13, 2015)

Carniol's views also show up in Kovach and colleagues' (2015) work, which stresses the importance of examining colonialism and racism prior to introducing Indigenous knowledges. As one participant put it,

And so I'm afraid of slipping into that idea of "Oh, let's just be nice to each other." Because it's so much more difficult than that. Because the way I see it, is that Indigenous people have offered the pipe to non-Indigenous people for five hundred years. And it hasn't made a difference. They [non-Indigenous people] don't value it. They don't see us as human beings, to be acknowledged or to be seen as legitimate. So you have to unpack that first. (p. 42)

There is a caution, however, in how educators introduce learners to the contemporary impacts of colonization. On a number of occasions, students in my classes have asked me to take them to a First Nations community, so that they can directly see for themselves what these impacts are, reminding me of a kind of show-and-tell activity. There is an obvious assumption within such a request that all First Nations are noticeably struggling with extreme poverty, despair, and social ills. Of course, this stems from what they have seen on the news and read in the newspapers that typically show only communities such as Attawapiskat, which is depicted as not having any schools or drinking water. Some of the participants in Kovach and colleagues' (2015) research also expressed this experience with students who wished to go to a particular area of a large Canadian city: "Students often want to go to the Downtown Eastside which has a large population of folks that are Indigenous and homeless. It's like, 'Why?' Right? Sort of looking at that kind of saviour thing" (p. 43). Another explained this phenomena by stating, "I think for many of us—we've kind of skipped over the being part and gone right into becoming an ally, without knowing about how to be in this place" (p. 43).

I, of course, completely agree with the above statement, believing that first, an ally must identify their own privilege and location in terms of power, as well as be prepared to challenge those who share this privilege but are not ready to forfeit it in the name of equity. Individuals within the dominant group, whether allies or not, are not free from implication. Awareness of the privilege attained as a result of the oppression of Indigenous Peoples is necessary if one wishes to build a relationship with them (Kendall, 2006). The examination and deconstruction of Whiteness, with its power at a structural level, is just as important as understanding how an individual fits into it. Carniol contends,

> There's an emotional component here that's not just intellectual, not just understanding, it goes beyond those levels and in academe, there's a risk that one may feel, "Well, I understand the logic and the concepts, so I now know all about being an ally!" I would say that that's a mistake. The becoming of an ally will happen if the student moves beyond the intellectual conceptual frame into the emotional courage arena of facing questions like "Who taught me this? Why do I believe these things? How are my previously held beliefs contradicted by the facts of history or by the data about the harm done by colonization, which up till now I haven't even thought about because I've learned to deny it?" It's a journey that requires courage. (B. Carniol, personal communication, May 13, 2015)

A strong non-Indigenous ally and social worker, Wendy Martin provides an example of what Carniol is expressing in a real-life practice situation:

> In the past few years, I have been working in community health care. Some of the challenges I have experienced

> is the lack of inclusion of Aboriginal communities—not represented in staff and program delivery. Staff at the Centre are not aware that we have Aboriginal communities within the communities we serve. Additionally, a client of the health centre may not "appear" Aboriginal, but they identify as having Native background. In one such situation, a health care provider told me that a shared client of the Centre that had identified as having an Aboriginal background, was "not Native." (W. Martin, personal communication, July 24, 2015)

Why did this health-care provider believe that the service user was not Indigenous? Because, in this worker's eyes, the person did not "look" like what she was convinced an Indigenous person looks like. This thinking perpetuates the racist notion that all Indigenous people look alike and outsiders, rather than Indigenous Peoples, will decide whether or not a person is Indigenous or not regardless of how a person identifies. We have been living with this racism for over a century via the Indian Act, which is a colonialist piece of legislation that was created without any input from Indigenous Peoples. This is yet another example of how colonization is alive and well today.

There can be much reward for engaging in allyship at an individual level because there is much less risk than when engaging at the structural level. There is an undercurrent that pulls people of the dominant culture to allyship in order to avoid implication, lessen guilt, or be seen as a good person; some are engaging in allyship in hopes of being praised or to gain respect or prestige. In their study, which examined how White male faculty and administrators engaged in allyship, Patton and Bondi (2015) explain how this provided opportunities for positive feedback, acceptance, and reward. They state,

> It is important to note that participants benefitted [the reward of status] because given their societal standing, they are neither expected nor forced to engage in understanding ally work. However, because they were among very few in their institutions who at least tried, the level of respect they received was significantly higher. Being white men provided some privileges, but being white men

who could articulate and understand those privileges, when they did not have to, was further beneficial and increased their credibility. (p. 506)

Allyship requires a move beyond common decency. Merely supporting people who are used to not receiving support does not make someone an ally. To be an ally is to avoid remaining solely at the individual or micro level while building awareness of systemic, structural, and institutional levels of inequity (Nattrass, 2015). If allies focus exclusively on working at an individual level, then systems of oppression are not addressed and are allowed to continue. Remaining at the micro level can also be seen as a reflection of the power to choose what aspects of inequality to address and which to exclude (Patton & Bondi, 2015). Allyship involves a forfeiture of such choices and therefore power, and the taking of a stance that challenges the structures that enforce that power. Thus, being an ally often means having to experience internal discomfort, pain, and struggle; it is not a role to be assumed for the attainment of praise and acceptance, or avoidance of guilt.

Carniol further elaborates on this as well:

> For mainstream people, it's important to understand the dynamics [of the relationship with non-dominant people] and not to feel guilty. Some allies, in early efforts at allyship, may feel guilty because "these things have been done by whites and I'm white so I have some responsibility for that situation." It's important to get past those feelings because [otherwise] it's about you as a person and the whole idea of an ally is to be really listening, to be comfortable not saying anything, just be present. That doesn't come easy because most folks who are either in social work or other helping professions feel that they have a tool kit. They've been trained to do this and this and just listening seems like they're not doing anything. [They feel] like "I'm not carrying out my role," not doing what professionals should do. That gets a lot of people in trouble and can lead them to violate the essential principle of allyship, which is to listen, be present and take it in, while unlearning what we've been taught. (B. Carniol, personal communication, May 13, 2015)

Non-Indigenous helpers must consistently critically examine their own positioning in relation to colonization, privilege, and oppression. Andrea Cowie (2010) contends that for social workers, "understanding one's role in oppression should be examined within a structural framework where individuals are part of a collective where systemic oppression and marginalization are produced and maintained" (p. 49). Further, she explains that non-Indigenous social workers must "maintain a learner's stance and a constant position of curiosity in terms of expanding their knowledge of First Nations culture(s), traditions and ways of being" (p. 49).

There is action involved in being an ally, not only in one's own learning, but in educating others. Acting like an ally, then, means situating oneself in that position, as explained in an amusing way by another of Kovach and colleagues' (2015) respondents:

> I know some of my Indigenous colleagues call me "The White House." And so if they wanted a white person to talk to a white person about something Indigenous, they would call me and say, "I can't do this! I will hit them or something. Can you do this? Can you talk white to them?" That has happened three times, and I thought "Oh, that felt good"—because I can talk white to them about something important. (p. 43)

Such a stance truly supports Indigenous scholars as non-Indigenous ones must not fall into the trap of thinking that because their department has hired Indigenous educators, they can sit back and expect that the Indigenous educators will do all of the work regarding decolonization. This position was raised by one of Kovach and colleagues' (2015) participants, who noted that "they [non-Indigenous faculty] wouldn't challenge an Indigenous person even if they don't agree with stuff, not easily, because of not wanting to be perceived as racist" (p. 59). I have seen this in my own postsecondary institution, as evidenced by the silence that sometimes occurs when these issues arise. I understand that someone may be afraid to speak up, but my advice to non-Indigenous allies, particularly White ones, is get a backbone. If you are afraid, consider for a moment how afraid Indigenous faculty are. I will acknowledge, however, that some Indigenous faculty are not encouraging when they forcefully call out non-Indigenous ones as racist, which inevitably shuts them down. Clearly, we are all in these processes together and have a great deal to learn about our interpersonal relationships.

Fortunately, not all of Wendy Martin's experiences as an ally are negative. She describes an example of what Cowie (2010) writes about above, as well as a collaboration between various service providers to meet the needs of an Indigenous service user:

> I was working with a woman of Aboriginal heritage who was experiencing depression and anxiety, but she did not want to take medication, much to her family doctor's frustration. The client and I had discussed connecting with the Aboriginal community in Toronto through Native specific services, and she decided to do this. In terms of her treatment plan she engaged in services at an Aboriginal specific organization, attended counselling with me (social worker/therapist), a CBT [Cognitive Behavioural Therapy] therapist, and continued to be monitored by her medical doctor. It was no surprise [to me] that this woman made the most progress by connecting with her community. She developed relationships with other women of Aboriginal background and learned cultural practices that assisted with her healing. Consequently, even her family doctor was impressed with her recovery. (W. Martin, personal communication, July 24, 2015)

NOT ALL ALLIES LOOK ALIKE, HOWEVER

Thus far, I have been referring to non-Indigenous allies as White people. But there are other groups of people that are non-Indigenous, at least to Turtle Island, who are not White. People of colour do not have the same privileges as White people and have many similarities to Indigenous Peoples due to their worldviews, experiences of colonization, and forms of resistance. Proof of this lies in the fact that the genocide that took place in the Americas has been the biggest holocaust the world has ever experienced, resulting in a quarter of the earth's population being exterminated over 150 years. It has been estimated that somewhere between two and five percent of the Indigenous Peoples of Turtle Island remained (Amadahy & Lawrence, 2009). Another holocaust took place when 20 million Black people were stolen from Africa, from the

1400s to the 1800s, during the trans-Atlantic slave trade, which was used to create global imperialism for Britain and a few other European countries (Amadahy & Lawrence, 2009; Historica-Dominion Canada, 2008). The circumstances of European settlers who chose to immigrate to Canada and Black people and other people of colour who were forcibly brought here are vastly different. Thus, settler colonialism in the Americas "is premised on a 'logic of elimination,' in which settler colonialism in the Americas depended and continues to depend upon removing indigenous peoples from their land and bringing in other racialized bodies to 'work' the land" (Wolfe, as cited in Macgillivray, 2011, p. 15). The labour of Black people and other people of colour was necessary for settlement to occur; however, their involvement with settlement processes does not make them complicit with settler colonialism (Macgillivray, 2011). Rather, it demonstrates that in differing ways, both Indigenous and Black peoples experience the violence of settler colonialism.

Like the attempts at erasing the history of colonization as it relates to Indigenous Peoples in Canada, the attempted erasure of Black people and places within this settler state also occurred and continues. This has been partly accomplished by:

- the demolition of Africville near Halifax in Nova Scotia and Hogan's Alley in Vancouver, B.C.;
- threatening and carrying out Black diaspora deportation;
- the renaming of Negro Creek Road to Moggie Road in Holland Township, Ontario;
- the silence around and concealment of Canada's largest slave burial ground, Nigger Rock, in the eastern townships of Quebec;
- racist immigration policies;
- the ploughing over of the Black Durham Road Cemetery in southwestern Ontario; and
- the commonly held belief that Black Canada is only recent and only urban. (Macgillivray, 2011)

Of particular interest to me, as a Mi'kmaq person, is the relationship between my people and Black people in the Atlantic provinces. In her book *African Nova Scotian-Mi'kmaw Relations*, Jamaican-Canadian author Paula Madden (2009) writes,

> The lives of black and Mi'kmaw people in the province [Nova Scotia] ran a parallel course because, since the beginning of their contact with settlers, both groups were subjected to unequal treatment and racialized violence as a result of the settler state. Policies of settler colonialism in Canada forced both indigenous and black communities outside mainstream society, and many people within the communities lacked the means and opportunities to support themselves and their families. While the government did not identify black spaces as reserves or legislate black spaces in an equivalent way to the reserve systems, if one looks only at the material conditions of life in these communities, they are extremely similar. (p. 63)

Nevertheless, despite the commonalities and connections between Indigenous Peoples and Black people and other people of colour, there are tensions between us. One significant tension is the debate about who has been oppressed the most. Each of these two groups believe that the oppression toward them is unique and they have endured the most suffering. Referred to as "the hierarchy of oppression" or "the oppression Olympics," when conversations fall into the trap of arguing about who is more oppressed, this game of "my oppression is worse than your oppression" gets in the way of collaboration (Bishop, 2015; McDonald & Coleman, 1999). Such an emphasis is, in my opinion, useless because it keeps us all in a place of comparison, which prevents solidarity and the potential this offers.

Another tension is that Black people benefit from the theft of land and resources on Turtle Island, although they are not the ones who stole them, at the ongoing expense of the original people of Turtle Island. This area of study has begun to appear in both Indigenous and anti-racist scholarship, but more of these courageous conversations need to take place (Amadahy & Lawrence, 2009; Lawrence & Dua, 2005; Macgillivray, 2011; Simpson, James, & Mack, 2011). For instance, even though it is not their fault because they have not learned about this in school or other sources of information, people of colour tend to be ignorant of the history of colonization and how Indigenous Peoples today are living with the impacts. Even when educated, people of colour, like White people, may be reluctant to acknowledge this reality and their complicity in it. In addition, when it comes to relationships with the land, these two groups are in different places in terms of how they live on it. It is only Indigenous Peoples who can claim title to the land on Turtle Island, which is also tied into their unique relationship with the Canadian government.

Without a doubt, the relationship between Indigenous Peoples and people of colour in the Americas is complicated. Are Black people settlers when their ancestors came here under forced migration? What do we make of the coming together of Black and Indigenous peoples over the centuries? What does this mean for us today? The potential for partnerships is strong and if we could be allies to one another, focusing our attention on what we have in common today, we would have a much stronger revolution than if we embark on our separate ones. I believe this coming together is a critical task for both these groups, as it will counter the divide-and-conquer mentality of those who continue to oppress us. But each of us needs to be educated about the other, especially Black people learning about the colonization of Turtle Island since, regardless of how they came here, they are benefiting.

Despite the fact that I write and advocate for the coming together of Indigenous Peoples and racialized populations, I am not sure, after all, that we are ready to do so. Each group has ongoing challenges within their communities, such as internalized racism and colonialism, that likely need to be addressed before we are ready to join together. Most importantly, we both have a great deal of healing to do, including the monumental task of uniting our own diverse communities, which may need to be done before we are ready to come together.

Indigenous and Black peoples have different experiences of White supremacy, which needs to be taken up when we consider embarking on decolonizing relationships. This means that people of the Black diaspora and other racialized groups have a somewhat different relationship with Indigenous Peoples, which then means a different journey in becoming allies. I think, right now, what is needed is education and more education and then more education alongside the healing processes. When it comes to decolonization and supporting the interests of justice, Stephanie Irlbacher-Fox (2013), who is a White ally and adviser for Indigenous organizations in the Northwest Territories and lives in Yellowknife, also believes that education is the medicine that is so greatly needed:

> I am convinced that such a shift needs to start early: it has been said that it is easier to build strong children than repair broken men. As the mother of two boys, I am con-

vinced that they are the key to settler change: they and all the other settler children in Canada who will in future people Canadian institutions and society. A critical settler responsibility is consciously educating our kids away from the constant barrage of social, educational, and structural influences that reinforce an omniscient patriarchal heterosexual white male birthright. This task is crucial because children are open; their "normal" is created by us as parents. What this means is parenting in a consciously decolonizing way. So far some basic rules for me include supporting my boys' developing relationships with people and places that are decolonizing; fostering their respectful spiritual and physical relationship with the land; and, supporting them in developing critical thinking faculties necessary for an ethics of compassionate discernment.

The Seven Fires Prophesies, which tell about the time of Creation, European contact, colonization and its impacts, and present-day healing, come to mind as, at this particular time, a concentration on healing is greatly needed. Once that has come full circle, it is prophesized that Mother Earth's people will need to come together to heal Her and everything on Her. Perhaps it is Black people and other racialized populations that will be the first ones to join with us. Certainly, anti-colonial and anti-racist critique will be strengthened by analyses that account for the complexities of intertwined colonial and racist legacies.

SOMETIMES IT MEANS KNOWING WHEN TO SHUT UP

Along with learning comes a conscious avoidance of the notion of an expert role in working with Indigenous communities, which is essential to breaking the cycle of paternalism in engaging with Indigenous communities (Baskin, 2011; Rossiter, 2011). The helping professions are legitimized through knowledge of people and experience and the fundamental principle that professionals hold this "expert knowledge" comes with power and privilege (Cowie, 2010; Rossiter, 2011). The idea that non-Indigenous helping professionals are capable of holding such knowledge about Indigenous Peoples must be challenged in order to facilitate change in the way that they approach working as allies. Allies must remain humble and open to feedback about their actions, thoughts, and contributions (Nattrass, 2015). Amy Rossiter (2011), Professor of Social Work at York University, describes how "the violence that ensues from capturing 'the Other' in our knowledge schemas devalues and discredits the unique nature of individuals and differences between communities, while imposing preconceived notions of identity and categorization on them" (p. 986).

True allies understand the importance of recognizing when to be the voice versus when to stand beside, support, and learn from Indigenous Peoples. This means that Indigenous perspectives are to be heard through Indigenous voices. It is Indigenous Peoples who carry Indigenous knowledges. It is Indigenous Peoples who understand the nuances of their teachings. Therefore, those in the helping professions must look to Indigenous Peoples to learn about and develop approaches that are less based in Western values and more based in Indigenous ones. This stand is reflected in Rossiter's (2011) and others' (Cowie, 2010; Koptie, 2009, 2010; NAHO, 2006) discussions of non-Indigenous helpers building relationships with Indigenous Peoples and communities while deconstructing their privileges.

In his paper *Power, Practice and a Critical Pedagogy for Non-Indigenous Allies*, Rick Wallace (2011), a non-Indigenous independent researcher and international peace-building consultant, shares the perspectives of Indigenous community members who participated in his research on relationships with non-Indigenous people. The community members drew attention to problems arising from existing power dynamics at the structural level, including those within "legislature, ethnocentrism …[,] colonialism …[,] class and corporate exploitation …[,] non-Indigenous fear and guilt … [,] exclusion from local space" and issues regarding treaties (p. 158). Wallace also describes ways in which allies might engage in action that is unhelpful: "when actions limit or come into conflict with Indigenous beliefs, practices and choices, leading to reinforcement of existing inequities; when there is mistrust within the relationship; and when non-Indigenous voices are positioned in a privileged manner above Indigenous ones" (p. 160).

KNOW YOURSELF FIRST

Building relationships is crucial to the success of shifting away from oppressive practice, and in order to build relationships, allies must maintain a stance of humility and a strong awareness of self (Baskin, 2011; Cowie, 2010). Banakonda Kennedy-Kish Bell, a traditional practitioner and knowledge keeper of Anishnawbe/Irish descent, shares her perspective on this:

> I think what is needed for one to be a strong ally is a deep sense of one['s] own place and roots.... It needs to be in-itiated in you [the ally], needs to be clear in me, and then needs to be recreated mutually in this place that belongs to both of us ... [I]t's from both of those places that we create a narrative, a landscape that we travel on together. To me, that's the main ingredient of allyship.
>
> For me, as a Native person, when I'm engaging with non-Native people as allies, [I'm always] carrying who I am and where I come from. I'm carrying a family that has been deeply wounded from residential school, that's just the plain reality, it's the landscape that I navigate on. The non-Native person that I'm engaging with, that wants to be an ally, has to be willing to confront that truth and the foundations of it in their own socio-political roots. (B. Kennedy-Kish Bell, personal communication, May 13, 2015)

Indigenous approaches to helping can benefit all people who experience them, whether those people are Indigenous or non-Indigenous. The inclusion of holistic considerations, such as spirituality, are slowly growing more present in the helping professions and mainstream society as a whole while Western individualistic approaches continue to erode for many people (Baskin, 2011; Cowie, 2010). Just as Indigenous approaches have the potential to be of incredible benefit to all people, decolonization is not possible without the efforts of both Indigenous and non-Indigenous peoples. When Indigenous Peoples come forward to present knowledges and perspectives that are much needed in the helping professions, non-Indigenous allies in turn need to create space for worldviews and approaches that are not only those of mainstream society (Baskin, 2011; Cowie, 2010; Koptie, 2010; Rossiter, 2011). These methods of relationship-building are also a necessary component of decolonization. The systemic issues faced by Indigenous Peoples are not only an Indigenous problem. If we are to see lasting change, it must be as result of collaboration between Indigenous and non-Indigenous helpers and services with strong Indigenous leadership at the forefront (Baskin, 2011; Cowie, 2010). Kennedy-Kish Bell elaborates on this and on the importance of challenging feelings of guilt and shame in order to change one's approach and motivation for allyship:

It's important to never engage in minimizing who you are, your culture and where you come from. That's a ground rule and that's for everyone. It's not an easy thing, but it's essential. When a white person comes to us, they can't come full of apology and shame; they have to come there in worth and value and say "I want something different, this doesn't work, I'm reaching for something better, I'd like to work on that with you, I'd like to stand up for that with you. Can we talk, can we explore, where can we jointly put this energy forward?" (B. Kennedy-Kish Bell, personal communication, May 13, 2015)

CONCLUSION

In hearing from several scholars and activists, we have learned that being an ally is not to be taken lightly. It is not simply calling oneself an ally based on one's beliefs and principles about social justice and doing the right thing. Being an ally is putting such principles into action, regardless of the uncomfortable, and sometimes frightening, explorations of the self; discussions with those one becomes an ally to; and challenging the attitudes and behaviours of other non-Indigenous people. Being an ally involves sharing one's power with Indigenous Peoples, taking their lead on every endeavour, and sometimes giving up one's privileges, while at other times using them, to the benefit of Indigenous Peoples.

As you will see in the final chapter of this book, becoming an ally is the first step in changing the world for the better, which benefits all of us.

REFERENCES

Ally. (n.d.). In *Dictionary.com*. Retrieved from https://www.google.ca/webhp?sourceid=chrome-instant&ion=1&espv=2&ie=UTF-8#q=definition%20of%20ally.

Ally. (n.d.). In *Vocabulary.com*. Retrieved from http://www.vocabulary.com/dictionary/ally.

Amadahy, Z., & Lawrence, B. (2009). Indigenous peoples and black people in Canada: Settlers or allies? In A. Kempf (Ed.), *Breaching the colonial contract: Anti-colonialism in the US and Canada* (pp. 105–136). New York: Springer Science + Business Media.

Aveling, N. (2013). "Don't talk about what you don't know": On (not) conducting research with/in Indigenous contexts. *Critical Studies in Education, 54*(2), 203.

Baskin, C. (2011). *Strong helpers' teachings: The value of Indigenous knowledges in the helping profession*. Toronto: Canadian Scholars' Press Inc.

Bishop, A. (2015). *Becoming an ally: Breaking the cycle of oppression in people* (2nd ed.). Black Point, NS: Fernwood Publishing.

Brown, K.T., & Ostrove, J.M. (2013). What does it mean to be an ally?: The perception of allies from the perspective of people of color. *Journal of Applied Social Psychology, 43*(11), 2211–2222.

Cowie, A. (2010). Anti-oppressive social work practice in child welfare: Journeys of reconciliation. *Critical Social Work, 11*(1), 46–51.

FNCFCSC. (2014). 2014 P.H. Bryce award for children and youth—who was Peter Henderson Bryce? Retrieved from http://www.fncaringsociety.com/2014-ph-bryce-award-chilren-and-youth-who-was-peter-henderson-bryce.

Green, A.J. (2006). Telling 1922's story of a national crime: Canada's First Chief Medical Officer and the aborted fight for Aboriginal health care. *Canadian Journal of Native Studies 2*, 211–228.

Greensmith, C. (2015). Settler colonialism, volunteerism, and Indigenous mis-recognition. In C. Janzen, D. Jeffery, & K. Smith (Eds.), *Unravelling encounters ethics, knowledge, and resistance under neoliberalism* (pp. 95–126). Waterloo, ON: Wilfrid Laurier University Press.

Historica-Dominion Canada. (2008). *Black history in Canada: Education guide*. Retrieved from http://www.blackhistorycanada.ca/education/LearningTools.pdf.

Irlbacher-Fox, S. (2013, June 25). *#IdleNoMore: Settler responsibility for relationship*. Retrieved from http://idlenomore_settler_responsibility_for_relationship.htm.

Kendall, F.E. (2006). Becoming an ally and building authentic relationships across race: The challenge and necessity of making race our issue. In F.E. Kendall (Ed.), *Understanding white privilege: Creating pathways to authentic relationships across race* (p. 171–191). New York: Routledge.

Koptie, S. (2009). Irihapeti Ramsden: The public narrative on cultural safety. *First Peoples Child & Family Review, 4*(2), 30–43.

Koptie, S. (2010). Indigenous self-discovery: "Being called to witness." *First Peoples Child & Family Review, 4*(2), 114–125.

Kovach, M., Carrière, J., Montgomery H., Barrett, M.J., & Gillies, C. (2015). Indigenous presence: Experiencing and envisioning Indigenous knowledges within selected sites of education and social work. Unpublished report. Retrieved from http://www.usask.ca/education/profiles/kovach/Indigenous-Presence-2014-Kovach-M-et-al.pdf.

Lawrence, B., & Dua, E. (2005). Decolonizing anti-racism. *Social Justice, 32*(4), 120–143.

Macgillivray, E.J. (2011). *Red and black blood: Teaching the logic of the Canadian settler state*. (Master's thesis). Retrieved from https://qspace.library.queensu.ca/bitstream/1974/6651/1/Macgillivray_Emily_J_201108_MA.pdf.

Madden, P.C. (2009). *African Nova Scotian–Mi'kmaw relations*. Halifax: Fernwood Publishing.

McDonald, P., & Coleman, M. (1999). Deconstructing hierarchies of oppression and adopting a "multiple model" approach to anti-oppressive practice. *Social Work Education: The International Journal, 18*(1), 19–33. doi: 10.1080/02615479911220031

National Aboriginal Health Organization (NAHO). (2006). Fact sheet: Cultural safety. Retrieved from http://www.naho.ca/documents/naho/english/Culturalsafetyfactsheet.pdf.

Nattrass, S.H. (2015). *The white professional's journey to gaining acceptance and becoming an ally to Aboriginal communities in British Columbia*. (Master's thesis). Retrieved from ProQuest LLC (UMI 1586681).

Patton, L.D., & Bondi, S. (2015). Nice white men or social justice allies?: Using critical race theory to examine how white male faculty and administrators engage in ally work. *Race Ethnicity and Education, 18*(4), 488–514.

Rossiter, A. (2011). Unsettled social work: The challenge of Levinas's ethics. *British Journal of Social Work, 41*, 980–995.

Samatar, S. (2013, November 14). bell hooks & Melissa Harris-Perry: Thoughts on the conversation [blog post]. Retrieved from http://sofiasamatar.blogspot.ca/2013/11/bell-hooks-melissa-harris-perry.html.

Simpson, J.S., James, C.E., & Mack, J. (2011). Multiculturalism, colonialism, and racialization: Conceptual starting points. *Review of Education, Pedagogy, and Cultural Studies, 33*, 285–305. doi: 10.1080/10714413.2011.597637

Truth and Reconciliation Commission. (2015). Truth and Reconciliation Commission of Canada: Calls to Action. Retrieved from http://www.trc.ca/websites/trcinstitution/File/2015/Findings/Calls_to_Action_English2.pdf.

Wallace, R. (2011). Power, practice and a critical pedagogy for non-indigenous allies. *Canadian Journal of Native Studies, 31*(2), 155.

Chapter Eighteen

THE END OF THE WORLD AS WE KNOW IT

INTRODUCTION

As I began the final chapter of this book for the first edition in 2011, I found myself thinking that writing this book was much more like a beginning than an ending. My hope is that some readers will see the messages in these pages as a beginning, a way to begin to incorporate Indigenous worldviews into their work and lives in ways that lead to action. I've learned so much in the writing of this book thanks to all the brilliant scholars who have published their work and the gifted people who shared their stories with me. I stand firm in the knowledge that Indigenous Peoples around the globe can make our world a much better place, not only in the area of social work, but in other helping work as well. In 2015, as I write for the second edition of the book, I can say with absolute confidence that many readers in many helping professions are doing just this, whether they be educators, students, or practitioners. A big, heart-filled *we'lalin* to all of you who have been in touch.

I am truly surprised and honoured that so many schools in the helping professions across Canada and beyond see value in what I have to share. But, please, always remember that I am the messenger, rather than the creator. All I know has, after all, come from others. I will continue to pray and meditate that new readers will also see the value of Indigenous knowledges for themselves, their work, and the world. I encourage all the magnificent academic warriors who are coming up to continue the journey that has been started. I pass the teachings on to you with the wish that you make these teachings stronger and pass them on to as many of the world's people as possible. Now, I have just a few more things to say.

STAYING CURRENT

What I have written about in this book is not new knowledge, although I'm certain that some readers will receive it as such. Rather, most of what is written in this book is ancient knowledge that can be applied to our current time. Consider medicines as an example. Plenty of the early colonists benefited from and survived diseases due to the generosity of Indigenous Peoples sharing their medicines with them (Mancini, 2004, as cited in Portman & Garrett, 2006). Clearly, these healing practices were successful in treating people during this period.

Subsequently, Indigenous medicines were shunned as inferior to European ones. However, due to socio-economic necessity near the beginning of the 19th century, Indigenous medicines were taken up again.

Significant examples of this phenomenon were during the Revolutionary War and the War of 1812, between England and what became the United Sates. During these wars, it became very difficult to access European medicines and doctors, as ships were limited in their ability to transport goods and people to Turtle Island (Mancini, 2004, as cited in Portman & Garrett, 2006). Hence, attitudes toward Indigenous medicines and helpers shifted again. Mancini (2004, as cited in Portman & Garrett, 2006) reported there was a

> post revolutionary shift in American medical literature with greater attention paid to Native American medicine. This is evident in early 19th Century publications such as Indian Doctor's Dispensatory (1812), the first U.S. Pharmacopeia (1820), Medical Flora of the U.S. (1828), and The Indian Physician (1829). (p. 454)

In addition, documentation of Indigenous medicines over a 200-year period in three Indigenous communities in the United States shows that Indigenous healing practices that implemented the same medicinal plants prevailed over time, thereby "leaving a healing thread across two centuries" (Portman & Garrett, 2006, p. 454). It is no wonder, then, that Indigenous medicines have greatly influenced current medical and naturopathic medicine and that some people believe that "cures" for modern illnesses may be found within Indigenous healing practices. Thus, staying current means remembering the past, acknowledging where knowledges originate from, and listening to Indigenous Peoples as they may have the key to saving Westerners once again.

Another area in which education and practice can stay current is how we view oppression. It seems as though the anti-oppression model sees two groups of people: those who dominate (the oppressors) and those who are dominated (the oppressed or victims). But these are not the only two possible roles that people can have. There is a continuum of power and privileges that exists at one end of the spectrum, and a continuum of oppressions that exists at the other end. The majority of us live somewhere along that continuum. Power is neither good nor bad, and there are many kinds of power. Education might want to consider assisting both learners and practitioners to tap into their own personal power and use the power they have to make positive change. As much as awareness is necessary, I don't think it is either healthy or helpful to stay stuck in critiques of the system without assisting those in our classrooms to take action in initiating change and healing. It is time for us to stop merely talking about what's wrong and start doing something to make it right. As educators in particular, we need to constantly keep in mind that academic discourse on its own will do little to improve the well-being of the families and communities that we seek to assist and are supposed to be accountable to. All social work educators could learn about turning knowledge into action from Cree scholar Cora Weber-Pillwax (2001):

> If my work as an Indigenous scholar cannot or does not lead to action, it is useless to me or anyone else. I cannot be involved in research and scholarly discourse unless I know that such work will lead to some change out there in that community, in my community. (p. 169)

A POST-COLONIAL LENS

One of the ways in which education can stay current is through incorporating post-colonial theory, which was taken up in Chapter Four, into its curriculum. According to Innu social work educator Gail Baikie (2009), "post colonial thought ... raises the possibility of creatively drawing upon the knowledge from diverse cultures (including the diversity of Indigenous cultures) or creating new Indigenous knowledge applicable to contemporary social challenges" (p. 56). Although I would refer to "worldviews" rather than "cultures," I agree that post-colonial theory offers the potential for creativity with regard to putting Indigenous knowledges into practice for the benefit of all. Post-colonial theory provides a language and ideas that help to explain the common experiences of Indigenous Peoples globally (Baikie, 2009; Battiste, 2004; Tamburro, 2010, 2013).

One of the ways in which post-colonial theory is promising is that it counters what has been written about Indigenous Peoples by Western authors and examines the relationships between those who are colonized and those who are the colonizers, as documented by many great minds (Baikie, 2009; Battiste, 2004; Tamburro, 2010, 2013). A focus on relationships is critical if we are to make positive changes between the present-day descendants of the colonized and the colonizers. Positive changes equal decolonization, which, in large part, must focus on relationships. Within education, post-colonial theory is a way in which Indigenous authors can be brought from the margins into the centre of academic discourses. However, proponents of Eurocentric theories are cautioned not to co-opt a post-colonial lens in order to claim it as their own. This would simply be another form of appropriation.

An Indigenous post-colonial lens offers a way in which academia can examine its curriculum and suggests ways in which Indigenous world-views can inform current discourses in the helping professions. This lens also offers an analysis of what is not included in most curriculums. A groundbreaking thesis dissertation by Andrea Tamburro (2010), of the Piqua Shawnee Tribe, examines the Canadian Association for Social Work Education policy (CASWE) on Indigenous content in social work curriculum. Tamburro (2010) not only discusses what is included in this policy, but also shines a light on what is missing:

> A post-colonial examination of the CASWE policy on Aboriginal content shows that the policy did not include several themes that were included in the literature. These themes include history from Aboriginal perspectives, Indigenous worldviews, and current issues foregrounding the effects of colonization. This ahistorical approach to Aboriginal content is an important omission from the CASWE Accreditation Standard SB 5.10.13. Omitted from the policy was the need to decolonize social work practice with Indigenous-centric content and a post-colonial theoretical or anti-colonial approach. (p. 276)

Tamburro's work offers clear directions on how the CASWE can add to its relevancy when it comes to addressing Indigenous content in education. Tamburro also raises the important issue of decolonization, which can only be achieved by Indigenous and non-Indigenous peoples working together:

> In order to create a Canadian society that is equitable, fair, and just, the Indigenous people of this land, the colonizers and their descendents, must work together to find solutions to decolonize society and to address the inequities that were created by colonization. Post-colonial writers provide useful insights on how to create social

justice because they also struggle with these issues. They ask questions useful to Aboriginal peoples in Canada. For example, what is the importance of identity and nationhood in global awareness of our world? Post-colonial writers also explore ways that people who have been colonized remember their history and reclaim their self-determination. They also explore how decolonization happens within communities. Post-colonial writers also explore ways in which cultures recover and re-form after being colonized…. Post-colonial theory addresses the transformation of the people who have been colonized and also provides insights into ending oppression for those who were or are oppressive, calling into question those who have a privileged place in society today. (pp. 77–78)

Thus, post-colonial writers examine issues of colonization, exploitation, re-sistance, healing, and transformation, all of which are critical to the work of decolonization.

Tamburro (2010, 2013) discusses how post-colonial theory can assist non-Indigenous helpers through the teaching of values, knowledge, and skills, so that they can become allies and develop partnerships with Indigenous communities. Post-colonial writers identify strategies for decolonization, while Indigenous helpers can provide leadership and guidance in this area. Post-colonial writers emphasize the significance of Indigenous Peoples remembering and speaking about their histories and present-day situations, and the importance of non-Indigenous peoples listening to these stories. Also of importance is that post-colonial theory urges all helpers to support Indigenous Peoples' self-determination and self-governance, and that Indigenous Peoples must be able to determine their own solutions and processes of decolonization and healing. Of course, as Tamburro (2010, 2013) reminds us, solutions will vary based on the history, current issues, and specific circumstances of each individual community.

Tamburro's (2010, 2013) work also provides concrete ways in which educators can examine their curriculum for what is and is not included with regard to Indigenous content. Tamburro (2010, 2013) suggests that educators first consult with Indigenous communities, organizations, and agencies to define what topics are relevant to cover in their curriculum.

Next, educators can review their course outlines to identify how the topics are addressed and if the resources that are used are current and accurate. Program documents, such as mission statements, program descriptions, and goals, can also be reviewed based on the identified topics.

Educators can compare their program's course outlines to reveal what courses address which topics and decide where expansion and clarity is needed. Through this process, they can also identify what topics are missing and decide what courses would be best to take up those topics. Educators may need to conduct literature reviews in order to locate relevant writing by Indigenous Peoples that can be included in their courses. Educators can also look to videos and guest speakers as resources for topics. However, they must ensure that guest speakers are compensated for sharing their knowledge. As Tamburro (2010) states, "this process provides an excellent opportunity for faculty to engage in this meaningful analysis of their curriculum" (p. 322).

By incorporating curriculum that includes Indigenous content, educators can better prepare learners to join with Indigenous Peoples in co-creating effective and relevant social services for both Indigenous and non-Indigenous communities and agencies that centre decolonization and healing. From a post-colonial standpoint, this process can encourage educators to see beyond critical theory and take in a much broader picture that focuses on Indigenous Peoples' resistance and strengths (Tamburro, 2010, 2013). Hence, identifying an educational discipline's strengths and gaps, there is the potential for further inclusion of Indigenous worldviews along with local, national, and international community-based content within such curriculum (Tamburro, 2010, 2013).

OUR MOTHER IS COUNTING ON US

It would appear that some of us Indigenous scholars think alike. Anishnawbe scholar Deborah McGregor shared her wisdom in an interview for *First Nations House Magazine* (2009), called "Can Indigenous Education Save the World?" McGregor (2009) recounts that Indigenous Peoples have been making their position about the interconnectedness of all Creation known for many years. She notes, for example, that the National Indian Brotherhood (now the Assembly of First Nations) wrote in 1972 that the survival of our earth in the 20th century means that people must live in harmony with nature in order to preserve the balance between people and the environment (McGregor, 2009).

McGregor (2009) emphasizes the importance of finding appropriate ways to share Indigenous worldviews with all peoples across the globe. She asks, "Given that such sharing is already beginning to take place, what might Indigenous education mean in relation to the environmental crisis facing the planet [today]?" (p. 17).

In answering this question, McGregor (2009) reminds us that Indigenous Creation stories provide instructions about how to live harmoniously with all beings, and that such teachings were passed on for generations, from the beginning of time to the present day. McGregor (2009) also points out that the responsibilities that come through Indigenous education are necessary in order to ensure that Creation continues. Today, these teachings are referred to as "traditional knowledge (TK)" and are becoming important to what environmentalists and scientists are now calling "sustainability." According to McGregor (2009), there is an interest throughout the world to learn more about traditional knowledges in order to use these knowledges to address the environmental crisis that our planet is currently facing.

McGregor (2009) beautifully connects some of the teachings of the Anishnawbe Creation story to our current environmental challenges:

> Key principles that emerge from the Anishinawbe Re-Creation Story for example, are that: "everything is important," "all beings in Creation have a role," "cooperation and co-existence will lead to survival," "everything is connected to everything else," and "all life must be respected." Principles such as these, adhered to not only in ceremony but in everyday living, ensured that Indigenous peoples lived harmoniously and in balance with the rest of Creation. Today these principles can also be thought of as vital principles in ecological science. For example, we now know that industrial activities in one part of the world affect people and the environment in another—climate change being the currently most well-known example. One can't help but feel that today's world might have been a "greener" place had colonial societies paid heed to at least some of these Aboriginal examples of ecological thinking. Given that we are where we are, however, it seems that now more than ever the principles and values that inform traditional knowledge are needed. (p. 18)

I could not agree more.

Two questions arise out of McGregor's interview: What are appropriate ways to share traditional knowledges? And how do we ensure that such knowledges are used in the ways that they were intended? To answer such questions, I turn to the Elders and Traditional Teachers who shared their wisdom with me for this book.

Mary Lou Smoke explains how she and Dan, her partner, share their knowledge in the Department of Journalism at the University of Western Ontario:

> We teach Aboriginal and non-Aboriginal students. This provides opportunities for all students to gain an appreciation of what we have been taught. Students can believe or not, accept or not. Our approach is non-threatening, not intended to evoke guilt in students. We believe it is important for us to share Aboriginal worldviews as we see that all people can be a part of these. We believe that we are to teach the foundations of Aboriginal worldviews to all people because we know that these foundations are similar for all peoples of the world.
>
> We believe that Aboriginal ways can help others to heal. We put non-Aboriginal people in touch with Elders and Traditional Teachers who include non-Aboriginal people in their circles and ceremonies. We stress that Aboriginal people are meant to share the gifts that have been given to us by the Creator. Aboriginal people have always shared what they had which is what they did when non-Aboriginal people first came to Turtle Island. Students tell us that prior to taking classes with us, they were searching so much for instant gratification, but afterwards they feel more human, they have been changed. (M.L. Smoke, personal communication, February 20, 2009)

Dan added:

> People from all over the world and their knowledge need to come together in order for there to be the best of anything. Many people are looking for serenity and they do

not want to be negative, so they are drawn to Aboriginal worldviews. However, it is important for everyone
to understand that this place—Turtle Island—is the
Mother of the original peoples who were placed here by
the Creator. People of European and other descents have
their own Mother in their places of origin. Their journey
is to go look for their roots, beliefs and cultures. This will
help to ensure that appropriation of Aboriginal teachings
does not happen. (D. Smoke, personal communication,
February 20, 2009)

Mary Lou agrees with Dan about appropriation, stating,

We as Aboriginal peoples need to decide what to share
and what not to share based on our intuition or what spirit shows or tells us to share. I share knowledge with others
for their personal growth, but I caution them "I don't
want to see a sign on your front lawn saying 'ceremonies
for sale.'" (M.L. Smoke, personal communication, February 20, 2009)

Grafton Antone is Oneida from Oneida of the Thames First Nation. He
was the Elder in Residence at the University of Toronto's First Nations
House and taught the Oneida language in this university's Aboriginal
Studies Program for many years. Both he and his partner, Eileen, who first
appeared in Chapter Eight, are respected Elders who conduct teachings
and ceremonies.

Grafton has encouraging words about sharing Indigenous knowledges:

We as Aboriginal people are Indigenizing the country. We
need to teach and coach others. They need to listen as
we speak out. We're at the [table of the] United Nations
now, so our problems have been heard, but now we need
to state our positions, say what we value, talk to others
about worldviews. People need to stand with their hands
open to receive our teachings. They may be ready now.
(G. Antone, personal communication, July 10, 2009)

Eileen offers words of grounding and simplicity for sharing knowledges:

> All my relations means that everything and everyone is included. In an individualistic society, people don't talk about being related to other people and everything else around them, but they are. It can be difficult for Aboriginal peoples to put into language what all these relationships mean. Modern language as expressed in English makes it seem like it is new information, but none of it is. It's ancient knowledge, not new concepts or ideas. (E. Antone, personal communication, July 10, 2009)

Joanne Dallaire, who appeared earlier, also has words of encouragement that fit perfectly with what the other Elders shared with me:

> A holistic approach is for all people: how can anyone not acknowledge all aspects of a person? These are human issues as everyone knows what it is to feel pain, for example. Creator gave teachings and medicines to all people of the world—just not exactly the same ones. It is no mistake that North America is a place made up of people from everywhere. This is a continent built on survivors as all of them came from persecution of some sort. It's healthy to come together to learn from each other, educate ourselves about other peoples' experiences. Coming together is not a compromise of self, but rather about a common humanity and finding common ground. (J. Dallaire, personal communication, July 23, 2009)

Jacqui Lavalley is very direct about her understanding about the teachings she has been given in terms of the spirit which exists in all of us. She states,

> It doesn't matter to the spirits about the colour of one's skin. [When we pray or conduct ceremonies], we call out to wise old ones who sit in the four directions asking them to enter our minds, bodies and hearts. (J. Lavalley, personal communication, June 22, 2009)

Jacqui's statement relates to some of the teachings from Elders that talk about the four directions. Carol Schaefer (2006) has published a beautiful collection of female Elders' teachings about how Indigenous knowledges can heal the world. Thirteen Grandmothers from the Arctic; North, South, and Central America; Africa; Tibet; and Nepal came together to speak about "ways of bringing about sustainability, sovereignty, and a united alliance among all the Earth's people" (Schaefer, 2006, p. 8). These Grandmothers are following a Hopi prophecy that states that people from the four directions must come together before there can be peace on the earth. They are fulfilling this prophecy by coming together with their teachings and healing methods for the first time in history, in order to find ways of creating a better world (Schaefer, 2006). These Grandmothers have also met with Western women Elders as they know this connection is vital for the future of the earth. Their humility, generosity, and love for all of humanity is expressed by Schaefer (2006), who writes, "prophecy revealed to each one that they must now share even their most secret and sacred ways with the very people who have been their oppressors, as the survival of humanity, if not the entire planet, is at stake" (p. 4).

The 13 Grandmothers know that the world as we know it is coming to an end. Many Indigenous Nations of the world have had prophecies about environmental changes such as global warming, changes in the weather, disease, and the hole in the ozone layer, which the Hopi call "the hole in our lodging" (Schaefer, 2006, p. 119). These are prophecies that have all been realized. However, dire prophecies are only fulfilled when people refuse to make changes. We still have choices.

Omyene Grandmother Bernadette Rebienot of Gabon, Africa, explains why the earth is in such turmoil. She states that because male energies across the world are in control, power cannot be balanced; women's power is undermined and women's wisdom and access to feminine energy is often cut off (Schaefer, 2006). Everything in the world is connected, which includes politics and consciousness. The Grandmothers are certain that women will show us a different way of being in this world.

This group of women Elders encourage all of us to do our personal healing as this is a necessary first step to healing the world. These Elders emphasize that people need to resolve the conflicts they have within themselves in order to see how we unconsciously create damage to our world. Healing and resolving conflicts are a part of what helping professions do, so we can see how we as social work educators, learners, and practitioners can act on the teachings of these Elders.

The Grandmothers also speak about forgiveness, releasing the past, and letting go of judgements. Yupik Elder Rita Pitka Blumenstein of Alaska tells us that when we do this, "we give ourselves permission to define ourselves, rather than being defined by others or past events. We are free to become who we are" (as cited in Schaefer, 2006, p. 142). Release such as this is part of the healing process that helping professionals can be a part of.

The Grandmothers tell us that it is women's wisdom that will save the world. Women need to build alliances and share their wisdom. When women come together in circles, they can awaken the wisdom in each other's hearts and spirits. This hope is expressed by Grandmother Agnes Baker Pilgrim of the Takelma Siletz Nation in Oregon:

> It is my hope that the Grandmothers' Council will have a mushroom effect throughout the world. That women will start circling up, come together, and bond together, to help one another to be better and stand tall with their voices, to say they've had enough of oppression. It is my hope that they will form matriarchal bridges with each other and be a voice again for our Mother Earth and Her children. (Schaefer, 2006, p. 143)

For more information and updates on the Grandmothers' activities, see the video "For the Next 7 Generations" at forthenext7generations.com and visit their Website at www.grandmotherscouncil.org.

Another group of Grandmothers located in Ontario, Canada, is doing similar work as the 13 Grandmothers. In 2003, an Anishnawbe Grandmother, Josephine Mandamin from Wikwemikong First Nation on Manitoulin Island, began an annual water walk, which she named the Mother Earth Water Walk, to raise awareness about how polluted our water is becoming. She was joined by a small group of women and, to date, they have walked around each of the Great Lakes and along the St. Lawrence River. They are accompanied by volunteers who help with food, camp set-ups, and laundry, as well as public relations personnel who take care of media releases, advertising, and meetings with the women walkers (Mother Earth Water Walk, 2014).

The walk always begins in the spring, which is the time of rebirth and regrowth, and every year brings more supporters. The walk is a unique event as it requires dedicated people to pick up such a challenge. The originality of this is explained on the group's Website:

Society today is taught to rely on technological equipment and the mere thought of a walk being more than 15 minutes is a task for many.... We are doing this walk [based] on our own beliefs within our own aboriginal [Anishnawbe] culture and values of the importance of our water [which] is very precious and sacred to our being, as it is one of the basic elements needed for all life to exist. (Mother Earth Water Walk, 2014)

Josephine Mandamin of the Mother Earth Water Walk (2015) speaks of each body of water as having her own personality, such as Lake Superior who is sometimes unforgiving and treacherous, but also kind, strong, and majestic. She also shares that each water walk shows the group signs of the ancestors and provides messages. On the first walk, which was around Lake Superior, the message was that women and men must work together, so the following year in 2014, men began to join. A striking message was given to the women as they walked around Lake Ontario. They noticed that the water they were carrying from this lake was very heavy and so it was a more difficult and tiring walk where they were forced to take many breaks. Sometime later, Josephine (Mother Earth Water Walk, 2015) received an article in a magazine that referred to Lake Ontario as being "heavy water" because of the amount of pollution in it.

Talking about the Mother Earth Water Walk to others, educating them about the state of our lakes, and joining it as either those who walk or those who volunteer is a remarkable way to not only be an ally to Indigenous Peoples, but an ally for the earth, which, of course, is vital to all of us. And if further encouragement is needed, in 2015, Josephine Mandamin was 73 years old and still does the walk almost every year. As I write this, the organizers of the Water Walk are planning an event for July 2016 in Garden River First Nation on the shores of Lake Huron to discuss the serious concerns about the health of the Great Lakes, and what can be done about this.

There is even more evidence of the spiritual connections between people, water, and the earth, and the power of our prayers and thoughts to impact them. Dr. Masaru Emoto became a Doctor of Alternative Medicine at the Open International University for Alternative Medicine in India in 1992. He has become famous throughout the world in the field of alternative medicine and for his work with water. He published his first book, *The Messages of Water 1*, in 1999, followed by three other volumes in 2002, 2004, and 2008. His work, in the form of writing, photographs, and videos, has also been picked up by independent publishing companies. He has published further books, such as *Water Knows the Answer* (2001), created a movie titled *What the Bleep Do We Know!?*, and published in the *Journal of Alternative and Complementary Medicine*. His work is seen by many in his field as proven scientific research. Although Dr. Emoto passed into the spirit world in 2014, his experiments with water have been replicated by hundreds of scientists and ordinary people in their homes with the same startling results (High Existence: Daily Boosts to Your Consciousness, n.d.).

Throughout the 1990s, Dr. Emoto performed a number of experiments observing the physical effects of words, prayers, music, and environment on water. He had photographers take pictures of water after it had been exposed to these different variables (High Existence: Daily Boosts to Your Consciousness, n.d.). Some of the water samples were told things such as "you make me sick, I will kill you" and referred to as "Adolf Hitler." Other samples were spoken to with words like "love and appreciation" and "thank you." The water that received positive words, was prayed to, and played beautiful music to was more symmetrical and aesthetically pleasing than that stamped with dark, negative phrases, no prayers, and heavy metal music (sorry to those of you who like this type of music), which was discoloured, murky, and ugly (High Existence: Daily Boosts to Your Consciousness, n.d.).

Of course, Emoto's work has been criticized as some claim that his photographs were taken by biased photographers or based on his own biased photo selection. His response to these criticisms was to do further experiments, and in an interview, he explained that

> from continuing these experiments we have come to the conclusion that the water is reacting to the actual words. For example, for our trip to Europe we tried using the words "thank you" and "you fool" in German. The people on our team who took the actual photographs of the water crystals did not understand the German for "you fool," and yet we were able to obtain exactly the same kind of results in the different crystal formations based on the words used. (High Existence: Daily Boosts to Your Consciousness, n.d.)

Emoto's evidence is remarkable. The message is clear: if the words and thoughts that come out of us have this effect on water, imagine what kind of effects they have on the earth and the people who live on Her, especially when we recall that two-thirds of the planet is water and human beings are 60 percent water. People can literally change things at the molecular or cellular level, which helps to explain concepts such as "blood memory" and the power of meditation to actually change the brain and heal the earth. How is this any different from the spiritual teachings of Indigenous Peoples or the practices of Buddhism? And does it not speak directly to the work of Josephine Mandamin and the Mother Earth Water Walk? We are all connected!

WHAT IF ...

... there had been a partnership rather than colonization between Indigenous Peoples and settler societies? Let's begin with the Mi'kmaq and the treaties they made with the British. The treaties had spiritual meanings and were shared only through oral teachings. This ensured that they were told from the heart, which meant that the truth was told. There was no other way of sharing the true spirit of treaty teachings except by sharing spirit from person to person, face to face. Through the spirit of the treaties, the Mi'kmaq agreed to share their knowledge of the land with the Europeans believing "that a true human being was one who could live in peace and friendship" (Kirmayer, Dandeneau, Marshall, Phillips, & Williamson, 2012, p. 402). In signing the Treaty of 1752, the Mi'kmaq recognized the newcomers as vulnerable people and so brought them under the protection of the Treaty, thinking they could teach them how to live in reciprocal peaceful co-existence (Kirmayer et al, 2012).

To this day, the spirit of the treaties is honoured by the Mi'kmaq, as evidenced by the incredible example provided by Kirmayer and colleagues (2012):

> A group of Mi'kmaq construction workers who, upon learning of the destruction of the World Trade Center on September 11, 2001, decided they must travel to Manhattan to assist in rescue efforts because they had to honour the spirit of their treaties, which stated: "Indians shall use their best endeavours to save the lives and goods of any people shipwrecked on the coast ..." (Treaty of 1752, Article 7)

(Marshall and Kirmayer, 2009). This sense of moral agency
and power drawn from the treaties stands in marked contrast
to the usual view of the disempowering and humiliating relationship of colonizer and colonized. (p. 402)

Some of my Haudenosaunee Elders and friends tell me there was a partnership at one time between their ancestors and the settlers as well. This
partnership is represented by the Two Row Wampum, which still exists today
(Antone, 2005; J. Bomberry, personal communication, April 6, 2009; A. Jock,
personal communication, August 7, 1986). Historically, wampum belts were
used to communicate and seal agreements or treaties. Those historical wampum belts continue to represent such agreements. In addition, today these belts
are seen as teaching tools used to pass on history and traditional teachings.

The Two Row Wampum has two rows of purple shells or beads
that run along the two outer stretches of a belt. There is a white row of
shells that separates the two purple rows. One purple row represents the
Haudenosaunee while the other represents the settlers. The row in between
the two represents the river that divides them. The general idea of the Two
Row Wampum is that the two groups made an agreement that they would
both live on Turtle Island, but they would be separate from one another.
Each would retain their own worldviews, languages, and processes of
government and not interfere with each other. Needless to say, the settler
society did not live up to its part of the agreement. But what if they had?

When I envision a partnership between the Indigenous Peoples of
Turtle Island and the settler society, it is somewhat different from the one
depicted in the Two Row Wampum. I wholeheartedly support the idea of
non-interference, meaning that there should be no religious imposition or
any other interference on the part of the settlers. But it saddens me to think
that both groups are supposed to live separately forever. I picture more of
an interconnected relationship, a sharing of knowledges, a discovering of
commonalities, and a desire to reach consensus when it comes to differences. Each group could take up whatever they see as valuable from each
others' values and ways of doing things and be able blend what might be
equally beneficial for all.

I envision the newcomers as people who did not see themselves as superior to anyone or anything else, and who are ever appreciative of the
generosity of the original peoples of Turtle Island. Out of both respect and
common sense, the newcomers would have relied on the teachings of the

Indigenous Peoples, not only to survive in the harsh environmental conditions of this part of the world, but also to learn how to live in harmony with the environment.

Since the settlers left their original territories in search of a better life for themselves and their families, I picture them doing just that, leaving behind the systems and beliefs that oppressed them, listening to the teachings of the Indigenous Peoples of Turtle Island. These teachings would include values based on egalitarianism, sharing, respect for all life, and an understanding that all people are valuable and have much to offer. Now imagine what such a place might look like today.

Over the years that I have been privileged to learn about traditional knowledges and teachings from many Elders and Traditional Teachers, there have been a few times when I've been briefly told about a future prophecy. This future prophecy is an extension of the Seven Fires Prophecies, which tell about the time of Creation, European contact, colonization and its impacts, and present-day healing, which is the time of the Seventh Fire (E. Benton-Banai, personal communication, 1982; J. Dumont, personal communication, 1983; G. Kidd, personal communication, 1982; E. Manitowabi, personal communication, 1984).

According to the Elders who speak of an Eighth Fire, this Eighth Fire will occur at an unknown time in the future once the healing of Indigenous Peoples is complete. This Eighth Fire will occur at a time when the non-Indigenous peoples of the world turn to Indigenous Peoples for help and healing (E. Benton-Banai, personal communication, 1982; J. Dumont, personal communication, 1982; G. Kidd, personal communication, 1982; E. Manitowabi, personal communication, 1984). I sometimes catch glimpses of this future time in the present, as seen throughout this book. In addition, Elder Jacqui Lavalley spoke to me about her interpretations of the teachings of the prophecies of the Eighth Fire:

> Within Anishnawbe teachings, there are prophesies which are explained as fires which were brought to the people by certain grandfathers and grandmothers a long time ago. Up until 10 years ago, I was always told by my teachers that there were teachings that were to be kept to ourselves as Aboriginal people. Yet, I was raised to share everything so I always wondered about this, and so struggled with what to share and not to share. More

recently, some of the old people have told me that we are in the eighth fire and we don't need to worry about others abusing our knowledges any longer. Rather we need to share our knowledges with others. We need to give the teachings over to others. Some of our foundational principles within our worldviews tell us not to be judgemental and to understand that everyone has the right to learn about Indigenous worldviews. I believe strongly that we're in the eighth fire now and I no longer struggle with what to share and not to share. (J. Lavalley, personal communication, June, 29, 2009)

To me, this seems like the final piece of an entire journey around the circle of history. The future will be a return to the past, to the first contact with Indigenous and European peoples, when the latter required the assistance of the former to survive. At the time, my ancestors chose to help the Europeans, but will the future generation of Indigenous Peoples make the same choice?

I suspect the pleas for help will likely focus on the survival of our planet. I cannot say for sure, but I do know that our Mother is watching and counting on us. I also know for sure that another, better world is possible if we all choose to transform it together.

"A PERIOD OF CHANGE IS BEGINNING"

These words came from Justice Murray Sinclair, the Chair of the Truth and Reconciliation Commission (TRC), on December 15, 2015, regarding the findings from a six-year gathering of stories about the residential school system in Canada. The TRC's final report makes 94 recommendations, several of which focus on child welfare, education, journalism, and missing and murdered Indigenous women. The report has been published in seven languages: English, French, Mi'kmaq, Ojibwa, Inuktitut, Cree, and Dené (Mas, 2015a, para. 39).

Justice Sinclair spoke of this day as marking the beginning of a new chapter in relationships between Indigenous and non-Indigenous peoples in Canada. He stated, "I stand before you here, hopeful that we are at a threshold of a new era in this country. A period of change is beginning that, if sustained by the will of the people, will forever realign the shared history of indigenous and non-indigenous peoples in Canada" (Mas, 2015a, para. 2).

Canada's Prime Minister Justin Trudeau, also at the release of the final TRC report, added, "Our goal, as we move forward together, is clear. It is to lift this burden from your [Indigenous peoples'] shoulders, from those of your families and communities. It is to accept fully our responsibilities and our failings, as a government and as a country" (Mas, 2015a, para. 25). Trudeau has committed to implementing the 94 calls to action with the intention of renewing the federal government's relationship with Indigenous Peoples. He stated, "I give you my word that we will renew and respect that relationship" (Mas, 2015a, para. 31)

In conclusion, the prime minister emphasized who needs to do the work of renewing relationships by adding, "We will remember that reconciliation is not an Aboriginal issue, it is a Canadian issue" (Mas, 2015a, para. 32). The end of 2015 left all of us who believe in social justice and healing with hope. However, we must also take heed of Justice Sinclair's concluding remarks that, "Change, of course, will not be immediate. It will take years, perhaps generations" (Mas, 2015a, para. 12). So true, but could this monumental event be the actual beginning of the Eighth Fire? Needless to say, only time will tell.

During the same week as the TRC announcement, Prime Minister Trudeau called for a national inquiry into the 1,200 missing and murdered Indigenous women and girls, which the federal government before him refused to do. Trudeau appointed Jody Wilson-Raybould, a descendant of the Musgamagw Tsawataineuk and Laich-Kwil-Tach peoples, who are part of the Kwakwaka'wakw from the northern end of Vancouver Island and the Central Coast of B.C., and a member of the We Wai Kai Nation, as the first Indigenous person to serve as justice minister (Burritt & Laanela, 2015, paras. 18 & 19). Wilson-Raybould, along with Indigenous Affairs Minister Carolyn Bennett, announced on December 8, 2015, that the first of two phases in the creation of a national public inquiry on the missing and murdered Indigenous women was about to begin (Mas, 2015b, para. 1).

As shared by Wilson-Raybould, who worked as a regional chief for the Assembly of First Nations before being elected to Parliament, "As a first step, we will meet with the families in the National Capital Region with the goal of hearing their views on the design of the inquiry and what it needs to achieve. And over the next two months, we will hear from more families, other indigenous peoples, national aboriginal organizations and a range of front-line services workers and others" (Mas, 2015b, para. 3). Such meetings began just a few days later and I participated in the two-day event in Toronto.

Bennett assured in her part of the announcement that the inquiry will set a new tone for "a collaborative, inclusive" process of which phase one of the inquiry will determine its objectives, focus, and parameters. She added, "It will also help identify potential terms of reference for the inquiry, outline possible activities and participants, and potentially help identify the commissioners" (Mas, 2015b, para. 12). Phase two will be the actual inquiry itself, which Bennett hoped would begin in the spring of 2016. As of this writing, although commitments have been made and funding put aside, no details have been released.

However, of critical significance, Bennett stressed that the first phase of the inquiry will take as long as needed "to get it right," thereby committing to a respectful process that will be steered by the families of our stolen sisters (Mas, 2015b, para. 13). Wilson-Raybould added a further commitment that the process "requires openness and the ability to listen. We have heard this loudly and clearly, and we have heard that this cannot be just another report" (Mas, 2015b, para. 6). "Just another report" is the fear of all of us, but, for the first time, there is hope that things will be different.

CONCLUSION

As I finish writing this book, I am reminded of Elder Grafton Antone's words to me when I first told him what I was writing about. He said I was "creating a new song for the people" (G. Antone, personal communication, July 10, 2009). Writing this book has certainly been a creative endeavour. But as I think back on the experience of writing this book, it feels more like a meditation or a prayer for the world. However, singing, meditating, and praying are all connected, as each piece is a spiritual activity.

I feel both humbled and affirmed by what I was able to learn while writing this book. I was humbled by the messages that I need to put aside ego and begin to forgive. I was affirmed in that I believe that I am on the right journey in my desire to teach about helping in the ways that I do. I know that my work of bringing Indigenous and non-Indigenous learners together and sharing the knowledge that has been passed on to me is the absolute right thing to do.

The helping professions have great potential for healing the world and for being a positive force in creating change for the better. It is my hope that all of us will be able to come together to share our knowledges and experiences, and that Indigenous worldviews and teachings will no longer be left out of the world's discourses. Educators, learners, and practitioners can, like the Council of the Thirteen Grandmothers, change the world.

Msit no'kmaq—all my relations.

We'lalin—thank you for listening.

Now, connect with your inner self and go out into the world and do some good, please!

REFERENCES

Antone, E. (2005). *Reconciling Aboriginal and non-Aboriginal perspectives in Aboriginal literacy practice.* Retrieved from http://www.cst.ed.ac.uk.

Baikie, G. (2009). Indigenous-centred social work: Theorizing a social work way-of-being. In R. Sinclair, M.A. Hart, & G. Bruyere (Eds.), *Wicihitowin: Aboriginal social work in Canada* (pp. 42–61). Winnipeg: Fernwood Publishing.

Battiste, M. (2004). *Animating site of post-colonial education: Indigenous knowledge and the humanities.* Paper presented at the Canadian Society for Studies in Education, Winnipeg, Manitoba. Retrieved from http://www.usask.ca/education.

Burritt, D., & Laanela, M. (2015, November 4). B.C. MP Jody Wilson-Raybould named justice minister. *CBC News.* Retrieved from http://www.cbc.ca/news/canada/british-columbia/justice-minister-jody-wilson-raybould-1.3303609.

Emoto, M. (1999). *Messages of water 1.* Berlin: Hado Kyoiku-Sha.

Emoto, M. (2001). *Water knows the answer.* Tokyo: Sunmark Publishing.

Emoto, M. (2002). *Messages of water 2.* Berlin: Hado Kyoiku-Sha.

Emoto, M. (2004). *Messages of water 3.* Berlin: Hado Kyoiku-Sha.

Emoto, M. (2008). *Messages of water 4.* Berlin: Hado Kyoiku-Sha.

High Existence: Daily Boosts to Your Consciousness. (n.d.). *Emoto's water experiment: The power of thoughts.* Retrieved from http://www.highexistence.com/water-experiment/

Kirmayer, L.J., Dandeneau, S., Marshall, E., Phillips, M.K., & Williamson, K.J. (2012). Toward an ecology of stories: Indigenous perspectives on resilience. In M. Unger (Ed.), *The social ecology of resilience: A handbook of theory and practice* (pp. 399–414). New York: Springer Science + Business Media.

Mas, S. (2015a, December 15). Truth and Reconciliation chair says final report marks start of "new era." *CBC News.* Retrieved from http://www.cbc.ca/news/politics/truth-and-reconciliation-final-report-ottawa-event-1.3365921.

Mas, S. (2015b, December 8). Missing and murdered indigenous women: 1st phase of public inquiry outlined. *CBC News.* Retrieved from http://www.cbc.ca/news/politics/missing-murdered-inquiry-1.3355492.

McGregor, D. (2009). Can Indigenous education save the world? *First Nations*

House Magazine, 1, 17–19.

Mother Earth Water Walk. (2014). Welcome to Mother Earth Water Walk. Retrieved from www.motherearthwaterwalk.com/?p=1.

Mother Earth Water Walk. (2015). Ojibwa grandmother recounts walk around the Great Lakes #2. Retrieved from https://youtu.be/wPega7E8Lhg?t=456.

Portman, T.A.A., & Garrett, M.T. (2006). Native American healing traditions. *International Journal of Disability, Development and Education, 53*(4), 453–469. doi: 10.1080/10349120601008647

Schaefer, C. (2006). *Grandmothers counsel the world: Women elders offer their wisdom for our planet.* Boston: Trumpeter Books.

Tamburro, A. (2010). *A framework and tool for assessing Indigenous content in Canadian social work curricula.* (Ph.D. dissertation). Simon Fraser University, Surrey, British Columbia.

Tamburro, A. (2013). Including decolonization in social work education and practice. *Journal of Indigenous Social Development, 2*(1), 1–16.

Weber-Pillwax, C. (2001). What is Indigenous research? *Canadian Journal of Native Education, 25*(2), 166–174.